NATIONAL SECURITY

ISSN 1543-5407

NATIONAL SECURITY

Kim Masters Evans

INFORMATION PLUS® REFERENCE SERIES
Formerly Published by Information Plus, Wylie, Texas

GALE
CENGAGE Learning®

Detroit • New York • San Francisco • New Haven, Conn • Waterville, Maine • London

National Security

Kim Masters Evans

Kepos Media, Inc.: Paula Kepos and Janice Jorgensen, Series Editors

Project Editors: Kathleen J. Edgar, Elizabeth Manar, Kimberley McGrath

Rights Acquisition and Management: Robyn Young

Composition: Evi Abou-El-Seoud, Mary Beth Trimper

Manufacturing: Rita Wimberley

For product information and technology assistance, contact us at **Gale Customer Support, 1-800-877-4253.**
For permission to use material from this text or product, submit all requests online at **www.cengage.com/permissions.**
Further permissions questions can be e-mailed to **permissionrequest@cengage.com**

Cover photograph: © Sascha Hahn/Shutterstock.com

Gale
27500 Drake Rd.
Farmington Hills, MI 48331-3535

ISBN-13: 978-0-7876-5103-9 (set)
ISBN-13: 978-1-4144-8147-0

ISBN-10: 0-7876-5103-6 (set)
ISBN-10: 1-4144-8147-0

ISSN 1543-5407

This title is also available as an e-book.
ISBN-13: 978-1-5730-2285-9 (set)
ISBN-10: 1-5730-2285-3 (set)
Contact your Gale sales representative for ordering information.

Printed in the United States of America
1 2 3 4 5   17 16 15 14 13

TABLE OF CONTENTS

PREFACE

National Security is part of the *Information Plus Reference Series.* The purpose of each volume of the series is to present the latest facts on a topic of pressing concern in modern American life. These topics include the most controversial and studied social issues of the 21st century: abortion, capital punishment, care for the elderly, crime, energy, the environment, gambling, gun control, health care, immigration, minorities, social welfare, women, youth, and many more. Even though this series is written especially for high school and undergraduate students, it is an excellent resource for anyone in need of factual information on current affairs.

By presenting the facts, it is the intention of Gale, Cengage Learning to provide its readers with everything they need to reach an informed opinion on current issues. To that end, there is a particular emphasis in this series on the presentation of scientific studies, surveys, and statistics. These data are generally presented in the form of tables, charts, and other graphics placed within the text of each book. Every graphic is directly referred to and carefully explained in the text. The source of each graphic is presented within the graphic itself. The data used in these graphics are drawn from the most reputable and reliable sources such as from the various branches of the U.S. government and from private organizations and associations. Every effort was made to secure the most recent information available. Readers should bear in mind that many major studies take years to conduct and that additional years often pass before the data from these studies are made available to the public. Therefore, in many cases the most recent information available in 2013 is dated from 2010 or 2011. Older statistics are sometimes presented as well, if they are landmark studies or of particular interest and no more-recent information exists.

Although statistics are a major focus of the *Information Plus Reference Series*, they are by no means its only content. Each book also presents the widely held positions and important ideas that shape how the book's subject is discussed in the United States. These positions are explained in detail and, where possible, in the words of their proponents. Some of the other material to be found in these books includes historical background, descriptions of major events related to the subject, relevant laws and court cases, and examples of how these issues play out in American life. Some books also feature primary documents or have pro and con debate sections that provide the words and opinions of prominent Americans on both sides of a controversial topic. All material is presented in an evenhanded and unbiased manner; readers will never be encouraged to accept one view of an issue over another.

HOW TO USE THIS BOOK

National security has been foremost in the minds of many Americans since the September 11, 2001, terrorist attacks. The United States has taken many major steps since that time, including the formation of the U.S. Department of Homeland Security, increased security measures at airports, the enactment of the Patriot Act of 2001, and the invasions of Afghanistan and Iraq. This book covers all these topics and more by providing the history of national security in the United States, descriptions of the various conventional and nonproliferation treaties and regimes, and information on countries of concern to the United States. Nuclear, chemical, and biological weapons are discussed in detail, as are domestic and international terrorism and Americans' feelings regarding national security after the September 11, 2001, terrorist attacks.

National Security consists of 10 chapters and three appendixes. Each chapter is devoted to a particular aspect of U.S. national security. For a summary of the information that is covered in each chapter, please see the synopses that are provided in the Table of Contents. Chapters generally begin with an overview of the basic facts and background information on the chapter's topic, then proceed to examine subtopics of particular interest. For example, Chapter 6: Countries of Concern discusses the threats posed to U.S. national security by the countries of Iran, North Korea, Cuba, Sudan, and Syria. For each country the status of historical and current relations with the United States is examined. Links to terrorism and activities related to the development of weapons of mass destruction (particularly nuclear weapons) are described, when applicable. In addition, the chapter presents polls showing U.S. public opinion about the countries and how opinions have changed over time. Readers can find their way through a chapter by looking for the section and subsection headings, which are clearly set off from the text. They can also refer to the book's extensive Index, if they already know what they are looking for.

Statistical Information

The tables and figures featured throughout *National Security* will be of particular use to readers in learning about this topic. These tables and figures represent an extensive collection of the most recent and valuable statistics on national security, as well as related issues—for example, graphics cover the Geneva Conventions, U.S. casualties in the wars in Afghanistan and Iraq, organization charts for the various governmental departments and agencies that play a role in U.S. national security, and public opinion about predominantly Muslim countries. Gale, Cengage Learning believes that making this information available to readers is the most important way to fulfill the goal of this book: to help readers understand the issues and controversies surrounding national security in the United States and reach their own conclusions.

Each table or figure has a unique identifier appearing above it, for ease of identification and reference. Titles for the tables and figures explain their purpose. At the end of each table or figure, the original source of the data is provided.

To help readers understand these often complicated statistics, all tables and figures are explained in the text. References in the text direct readers to the relevant statistics. Furthermore, the contents of all tables and figures are fully indexed. Please see the opening section of the Index at the back of this volume for a description of how to find tables and figures within it.

Appendixes

Besides the main body text and images, *National Security* has three appendixes. The first is the Important Names and Addresses directory. Here, readers will find contact information for a number of government and private organizations that can provide further information on aspects of national security. The second appendix is the Resources section, which can also assist readers in conducting their own research. In this section, the author and editors of *National Security* describe some of the sources that were most useful during the compilation of this book. The final appendix is the Index. It has been greatly expanded from previous editions and should make it even easier to find specific topics in this book.

ADVISORY BOARD CONTRIBUTIONS

The staff of Information Plus would like to extend its heartfelt appreciation to the Information Plus Advisory Board. This dedicated group of media professionals provides feedback on the series on an ongoing basis. Their comments allow the editorial staff who work on the project to continually make the series better and more user-friendly. The staff's top priority is to produce the highest-quality and most useful books possible, and the Information Plus Advisory Board's contributions to this process are invaluable.

The members of the Information Plus Advisory Board are:

- Kathleen R. Bonn, Librarian, Newbury Park High School, Newbury Park, California

- Madelyn Garner, Librarian, San Jacinto College, North Campus, Houston, Texas

- Anne Oxenrider, Media Specialist, Dundee High School, Dundee, Michigan

- Charles R. Rodgers, Director of Libraries, Pasco-Hernando Community College, Dade City, Florida

- James N. Zitzelsberger, Library Media Department Chairman, Oshkosh West High School, Oshkosh, Wisconsin

In addition, Information Plus staff owe special thanks to Dr. Harold Molineu, Professor of Political Science at Ohio University, for his particular assistance as an acting adviser on *National Security*. Dr. Molineu's substantial background in the field allowed him to provide expert advice and indispensable recommendations on content and organization.

COMMENTS AND SUGGESTIONS

The editors of the *Information Plus Reference Series* welcome your feedback on *National Security*. Please direct all correspondence to:

Editors
Information Plus Reference Series
27500 Drake Rd.
Farmington Hills, MI 48331-3535

CHAPTER 1
A HISTORICAL OVERVIEW

Throughout its existence, the United States has faced several major external threats to its national security. The first and most enduring threat was the quest for land by other nations desiring to expand their empires. This threat persisted through the 1940s, culminating in World War II (1939–1945). Following the war, U.S. security was threatened by the spread of communism (an economic and political system completely in opposition to the principles of democracy and capitalism embraced by the United States). The Cold War period lasted into the early 1990s and pitted the United States against the world's only other superpower of the time: the Soviet Union. The U.S. government made many foreign policy decisions during the Cold War that affected its future national security.

Even before the Cold War ended, a new threat arose from political and ideological forces sweeping the planet. Terrorism gained prominence as a means for individuals with common grievances to challenge national governments. The United States has become a target for terrorist groups bent on destroying the military, political, economic, and social factors that have catapulted the United States to a position of dominance. At the same time, technological advances have allowed unfriendly nations to acquire new weapons that could inflict mass destruction on the United States. There is a real threat that such weapons could fall into the hands of terrorist groups that would not hesitate to use them against the United States.

Protecting U.S. national security means protecting its key assets: people, territory, infrastructure, economy, and sovereignty (supreme and independent political authority). Since its birth as a nation in 1776, the United States has developed a massive array of systems, tools, and weapons to safeguard these assets. However, national security is not just about defending the homeland and reacting to attacks. The U.S. government also takes a proactive approach, meaning that it anticipates future threats and uses its power to try to manipulate world

affairs to its own political and economic benefit. U.S. goals for self-preservation and prosperity in the 21st century revolve around maintaining military supremacy, eliminating terrorism and weapons of mass destruction, and spreading democratic principles throughout the world. To understand how the United States arrived at this juncture, it is necessary to review the historical factors that have shaped U.S. foreign policy since the nation was founded.

COLONIALISM AND EMPIRE BUILDING

The United States was born in 1776 in a world that was consumed with colonialism and empire building. For several centuries, European superpowers—primarily Britain, France, Portugal, and Spain—had colonized territories throughout the Western Hemisphere by military force or gradual settlement. Russia had expanded its own empire throughout eastern Europe. In China the Ch'ing dynasty had conquered large parts of southern Asia. The Turkish Ottoman Empire controlled a long swath of land around the Mediterranean Sea encompassing parts of the Middle East, northern Africa, and southern Europe.

When European colonists first came to the New World, they found a vast expanse of land inhabited by indigenous peoples that the new settlers called Indians. Many of the first colonies were business ventures financed by wealthy English businessmen and landowners. The king of England granted limited political rights to these colonies, but exerted heavy taxation on them. During the late 1700s the colonists' desire for self-governance and tax relief drove them to seek independence from Britain and establish a new nation: the United States of America.

REVOLUTIONARY WAR

Even before the Revolutionary War (1775–1783), the North American colonies had formed militias (groups of private citizens devoted to military missions). Some militias were relatively well trained and equipped, whereas others were not. Among the militia members were minutemen—named for their claim that they could be ready to fight in a minute. Some of the colonial militias gained valuable military experience fighting with the British against French and Native American forces during the French and Indian War (1754–1763). Among these fighters was a young officer named George Washington (1732–1799), who would be named commander in chief of the colonists' Continental army at the onset of the Revolutionary War.

The Continental army overcame enormous obstacles to defeat the professional British army, which was supplemented with thousands of Hessians (German mercenary soldiers). The colonists were aided in their struggle by a variety of European nations, particularly France, Britain's longtime enemy. In 1778 the colonists signed the Treaty of Alliance with France; it was the last bilateral (two-party) military agreement the United States would make for nearly two centuries. The military operations of the Revolutionary War ended in 1781, when the last British troops surrendered. The war was officially declared over two years later with the signing of the Treaty of Paris.

THE 1800S

During the 1800s the new United States grew tremendously in terms of territory, population, and economic might. More than two dozen states were added to the Union. Expansionism was accompanied by violent conflicts with Great Britain (the War of 1812), Mexico (the Mexican War, 1846–1848), and Spain (the Spanish-American War, 1898). In addition, the so-called Indian Wars were waged for many years against Native American tribes.

The U.S. military matured throughout the 19th century as it secured and seized territory from Europe's colonial powers and Mexico. The growth of the U.S. Navy was driven in part by threats from the Barbary pirates—bands of pirates positioned around the Mediterranean Sea, primarily in North Africa, who terrorized and captured sailing ships and demanded ransom payments from the hostages' governments for their safe return. Some nations, including the United States, paid annual fees to the pirates to ensure the safe passage of their ships through the region. However, the U.S. government tired of this arrangement in 1801 and launched military attacks against the pirates. The U.S. Navy eventually prevailed, and a treaty ended the threat to U.S. sailing ships.

Meanwhile in the United States, deep divisions developed between northern and southern states and territories on the morality of slavery and associated political and economic issues. In 1861 a devastating civil war erupted between Union (northern) and Confederate (southern) forces. When the war ended in 1865, hundreds of thousands of military personnel had died. (See Table 1.1.) Over the following decades the nation was consumed with reconstruction and internal affairs. The U.S. government vowed to stay out of territorial disputes simmering in Europe and the rest of the world.

THE WORLD WARS

In 1914 World War I began in Europe. It pitted Britain, France, Italy, and Russia (collectively known as the Allied powers) against Germany, Austria-Hungary, and the Ottoman Empire (collectively known as the Central powers). The United States was reluctant to get involved, but it eventually entered the war in April 1917 on the side of the Allies and fought until the war ended in November 1918. The Allies were victorious: Austria-Hungary and the Ottoman Empire were divided into a number of separate nations, and severe economic sanctions were imposed against Germany. Reacting to the tremendous loss of life and devastation caused by the war, the United States developed during the 1920s an isolationist stance, in that it was determined to stay out of any future European conflicts. This position was to be short lived.

During the 1930s Germany, Japan, and Italy began aggressive military campaigns against their neighbors. In 1939, after years of aggressive expansion, Germany invaded Poland. In response, Britain, France, and Canada declared war on Germany, thereby marking the beginning of World War II. The German blitzkrieg (bombing raids that resembled a so-called lightning war) was incredibly successful. By 1941 German forces had defeated and occupied France and invaded the Soviet Union. War had spread throughout Europe, North Africa, parts of China, and the North Atlantic and South Pacific oceans. In the United States President Franklin D. Roosevelt (1882–1945) publicly adhered to the isolationist sentiment of the American public; however, as early as 1939 he began quietly expanding the nation's military capabilities.

On December 7, 1941, Japanese forces staged a surprise attack on the U.S. naval base at Pearl Harbor, Hawaii. Within days, the United States was at war with Japan, Germany, and Italy. A flood of U.S. goods and military might turned the tide of the war. By early 1945 Germany and Italy had been defeated. In August of that year Japan surrendered after two of its cities were devastated by U.S. atomic bombs. World War II was over, and a new world order had been established. The United States abandoned its isolationist stance and assumed an active role in international affairs.

THE UNITED NATIONS

Only months after World War II ended, the representatives of dozens of nations met in the United States and drafted a constitution for a new world organization called the United Nations (UN). The UN's purpose was twofold. First, it was to provide a medium through which international disagreements could be settled peacefully. Second,

TABLE 1.1

U.S. military personnel and casualties in major wars, 1775–1991

War/conflict	Branch of service	Number serving	Total deaths	Battle deaths	Other deaths	Wounds not mortal[a]
			Casualties			
Revolutionary War 1775–1783	Total	—[b]	4,435	4,435	—	6,188
War of 1812 1812–1815	Total	286,730[c]	2,260	2,260	—	4,505
Mexican War 1846–1848	Total	78,718[c]	13,283	1,733	11,550	4,152
Civil War (Union Forces only)[d] 1861–1865	Total	2,213,363	364,511	140,414	224,097	281,881
Spanish-American War	Total	306,760	2,446	385	2,061	1,662
World War I 1917–1918	Total	4,734,991	116,516	53,402	63,114	204,002
World War II 1941–1946[e]	Total	16,112,566	405,399	291,557	113,842	670,846
Korean War 1950–1953[f]	Total	5,720,000	36,574	33,739	2,835	103,284
Vietnam conflict 1964–1973[g]	Total	8,744,000	58,220	47,434	10,786	Hosp. care reqd. 153,303 No hospital care 150,341
Persian Gulf War 1990–1991[h]	Total	2,225,000	383	148	235	467

Notes: Data prior to World War I are based on incomplete records in many cases. Casualty data are confined to dead and wounded and, therefore, exclude personnel captured or missing in action who were subsequently returned to military control.

[a]Marine Corps data for World War II, the Spanish-American War, and prior wars represent the number of individuals wounded, whereas all other data in this column represent the total number (incidence) of wounds.

[b]Not known, but estimates range from 184,000 to 250,000.

[c]As reported by the Commissioner of Pensions in the annual report for fiscal year 1903.

[d]Authoritative statistics for the Confederate forces are not available. Estimates of the number who served range from 600,000 to 1,500,000. The final report of the Provost Marshal General, 1863–1866, indicated 133,821 Confederate deaths (74,524 battle and 59,297 other) based upon incomplete returns. In addition, an estimated 26,000 to 31,000 Confederate personnel died in Union prisons.

[e]Data are for the period December 1, 1941, through December 31, 1946, when hostilities were officially terminated by Presidential Proclamation, but a few battle deaths or wounds not mortal were incurred after the Japanese acceptance of the Allied peace terms on August 14, 1945. Number serving from December 1, 1941, through August 31, 1945, were: Total–14,903,213.

[f]Worldwide military deaths during the Korean War totaled 54,246. In-theater casualty records are updated annually.

[g]Number serving covers the period August 5, 1964 ("Vietnam era" begins) through January 27, 1973 (date of cease-fire). Deaths include the period November 1, 1955 (commencement date for the Military Assistance Advisory Group) through May 15, 1975 (date last American servicemember left Southeast Asia). Casualty records are updated annually, including current deaths that are directly attributed to combat in the Vietnam Conflict. Additional detail now on table shows number of WIA (Wounded in Action) servicemembers not requiring hospital care.

[h]Report does not include one POW (Prisoner of War)(Speicher). Casualty records are updated annually.

SOURCE: Adapted from "Principal Wars in Which the United States Participated—U.S. Military Personnel Serving and Casualties (1775–1991)," in *Defense Casualty Analysis System*, U.S. Department of Defense, Defense Manpower Data Center, 2012, https://www.dmdc.osd.mil/dcas/pages/report_principal_wars .xhtml (accessed July 2, 2012)

the UN would tackle vexing humanitarian issues, such as world hunger and disease. A similar organization, called the League of Nations, had sprung up after World War I, but fell apart soon afterward for a variety of reasons, including the United States' refusal to join the organization. However, the ravages of World War II had convinced Americans that such a body was needed. In late 1945 Congress overwhelmingly ratified the UN Charter. The UN Security Council would play a major role in determining the course of future conflicts around the world. The Security Council was set up so that five nations (the so-called permanent members) have special veto powers over UN resolutions. The permanent members are China, France, Russia (formerly the Soviet Union), the United Kingdom, and the United States.

UN programs are funded through assessed and voluntary contributions by member countries. Assessments are based on each country's financial assets. In *United Nations System Funding: Congressional Issues* (January 14, 2011, https:// opencrs.com/document/RL33611/2011-01-14/download/ 1005/), Marjorie Ann Browne of the Congressional Research Service notes that the United States has been the single largest financial contributor since the UN was founded. Table 1.2 shows the top 10 contributors to the UN regular budget (excluding special programs) between 2009 and 2011. The U.S. assessment for 2011 was $582.7 million, or 22% of the total.

COMMUNISM AND THE COLD WAR

The Soviet Union had been a wartime ally of the United States, but relations became strained after World War II ended. During the war the Soviet army "liberated" a large part of eastern Europe from Nazi occupation. Through various means, the Union of Soviet Socialist Republics (USSR) took political control over these nations. The USSR assumed a major role in international affairs, placing it in direct conflict with the only other superpower of the time: the United States. A cold war began between two rich and powerful nations with completely different political, economic, and social goals for the world. The war was called "cold" because it was fought mostly by politicians and diplomats. A direct and large-scale military conflict (or hot war) between U.S. and Soviet forces never occurred.

Even though a massive military conflict between U.S. and Soviet forces never took place, an expensive arms race began in which both sides produced and stockpiled large amounts of weapons as a show of force and to deter a first strike by the enemy. In addition, both sides

TABLE 1.2

Top 10 contributors to the United Nations (UN) regular budget, by member state, 2009–11

Member state	Percentage of budget 2009	Assessments for 2009 in U.S. $	Percentage of budget 2010 and 2011	Assessments for 2010 in U.S. $ // 2011 in U.S. $
United States*	22.00	598,292,101	22.00	517,133,507 // 582,678,514
Japan	16.624	452,091,268	12.530	294,531,038 // 331,861,899
Germany	8.577	233,252,334	8.018	188,471,657 // 212,359,833
United Kingdom*	6.642	180,629,824	6.604	155,234,070 // 174,909,496
France*	6.301	171,356,297	6.123	143,927,658 // 162,170,025
Italy	5.079	138,123,890	4.999	117,506,837 // 132,400,450
Canada	2.977	80,959,799	3.207	75,383,962 // 84,938,636
Spain	2.968	80,715,043	3.177	74,678,780 // 84,144,075
China*	2.667	72,529,320	3.189	74,960,853 // 84,461,899
Mexico	2.257	61,379,331	2.356	55,380,297 // 62,399,572

*Permanent members of the U.N. Security Council.

SOURCE: Marjorie Ann Browne, "Table 3. Top 10 U.N. Regular Budget Contributors for 2009, 2010, and 2011," in *United Nations System Funding: Congressional Issues*, Congressional Research Service, January 14, 2011, https://opencrs.com/document/RL33611/2011-01-14/download/1005/ (accessed July 2, 2012)

provided financial and military support to countries around the world in an attempt to influence the political leanings of those populations. Communist China joined the Cold War during the 1950s and often partnered with the Soviet Union against U.S. interests.

Containment

U.S. political and military reaction to the threat posed by the Soviet Union was a policy called containment. The gist of containment was explained by President Harry S. Truman (1884–1972; August 29, 2001, http://www.nato.int/docu/speech/1947/s470312a_e.htm) in a speech to Congress on March 12, 1947, and came to be known as the Truman Doctrine: "It must be the policy of the United States to support free peoples who are resisting attempted subjugation by armed minorities or by outside pressures." The Truman Doctrine marked an important change in U.S. foreign policy, which up to that time had mostly taken a hands-off approach to the internal affairs of other nations.

At the end of World War II, the United States was in sound economic shape. All other major nations had suffered great losses during the war in their infrastructure, financial stability, and populations. Hoping to instill an atmosphere that was conducive to peace and the spread of capitalism, the United States invested heavily in the postwar economies of Western Europe and Japan. U.S. barriers to foreign trade were relaxed to build new markets for U.S. exports and to allow some war-ravaged

nations to make money by selling goods to U.S. consumers. Meanwhile, the United States enacted the Marshall Plan (1948–1952), which was designed to rebuild the allied nations of Europe and combat communism. Hundreds of millions of dollars in U.S. aid were transmitted to the governments of Greece and Turkey to help them stave off communist-led insurgencies (rebellions). Billions more went to the war-torn nations of Western Europe.

Nervousness in Western Europe about the closeness of Soviet military forces led to the creation in 1949 of the North Atlantic Treaty Organization (NATO)—a military coalition between the United States and 11 other nations. The NATO alliance provided added security for all the nations involved, because an attack against one was considered to be an attack against all. In 1958 the United States and Canada formed the North American Aerospace Defense Command to provide a warning and defense system against aircraft, missiles, and space vehicles entering North American air space.

In 1962 the United States and the Soviet Union came to the brink of nuclear war when U.S. intelligence agencies discovered that the Soviets had installed nuclear missile facilities in Cuba. In response, President John F. Kennedy (1917–1963) imposed a blockade to prevent Soviet ships from bringing new supplies to Cuba. He demanded that the nuclear facilities be removed and publicly warned the Soviets that any attack from Cuba on the United States would spur retaliation against the Soviet Union. After a suspenseful 12-day standoff, the

Soviets backed down and removed the missiles. The Cuban missile crisis was a turning point in the Cold War. Negotiations began between the two superpowers on treaties to limit the testing and proliferation (growth or multiplication) of nuclear weapons. These talks would proceed sporadically for decades.

Korea and Vietnam

In 1950 North Korean forces backed by the Soviet military invaded South Korea, setting off the Korean War. Caught off guard by the invasion, the United States rushed to defend South Korea from a communist take-over. Over the next three years U.S. and allied forces under the UN fought against North Korean and Chinese troops that were supported by the Soviet Union. The war ended in a stalemate, with both sides back where they had started: on either side of the 38th parallel (a line of latitude). In 1953 a cease-fire agreement ended the armed conflict in Korea. North Korea remained under communist control, whereas South Korea became a democracy protected by UN troops (primarily U.S. forces).

Also during the 1950s the U.S. military became involved in a conflict between communist North Vietnam and noncommunist South Vietnam. In an effort to bolster the defenses of the country, the United States sent thousands of military advisers to South Vietnam during the late 1950s and early 1960s. In 1964 the conflict escalated into full-scale civil war. Once again, the United States found itself in a remote Asian country trying to prevent the spread of communism.

The fight in Vietnam turned out to be a long and difficult one in which U.S. forces, assisted by a handful of other countries, were pitted against highly motivated forces equipped and backed by the Soviet Union and China. During the 1960s the United States was preoccupied with explosive social problems. Furthermore, there were widespread protests against the Vietnam War. By 1968 there were half a million U.S. troops in Vietnam. Nightly television coverage provided a bleak picture of the war's progress and helped turn public opinion against the war and President Lyndon B. Johnson (1908–1973). The United States was engaged in the war for more than a decade before withdrawing the last of its troops in 1975 and leaving South Vietnam to a communist takeover.

In both the Korean and Vietnam Wars the United States chose to fight in a limited manner without using its arsenal of nuclear weapons or engaging Chinese and Soviet troops directly for fear of sparking another world war.

Fighting for Influence

The Cold War firmly divided dozens of nations into two military coalitions or blocs. The western bloc included the United States and its NATO allies. The eastern or Soviet bloc included the Soviet Union and numerous central and east European countries. In addition, the Soviet Union enjoyed relatively good political relations with other nations around the world that embraced or leaned toward communist or socialist rule, such as Afghanistan, Cambodia, and Cuba.

Throughout the Cold War the United States and the Soviet Union sought to wield political influence in nations that were not strongly aligned with either side. Both countries used diplomacy, commercial trade, foreign aid, and the sales of military hardware as tools to promote political alliances. During the 1970s these efforts were focused on countries in and around the Middle East (i.e., northern Africa and southwestern Asia). The importance of the region in terms of oil production and strategic location (e.g., sea access) became abundantly clear to both sides. The Soviet Union watched uneasily as the United States forged relations with the Middle Eastern countries Saudi Arabia and Egypt (a former Soviet ally) and began playing a larger political role in the region's affairs.

The Afghanistan Invasion

In 1979 the Soviet Union invaded Afghanistan because the Soviets feared the communist Afghan government would fall due to widespread revolt within the country. The United States strongly condemned the invasion and worried that the Soviets were trying to extend their territory into the Middle East to control the flow of oil from that region.

President Jimmy Carter (1924–) implemented economic sanctions, including a grain embargo, against the Soviet Union. He and his successor, President Ronald Reagan (1911–2004), funneled large amounts of money to Afghanistan's neighbor Pakistan, because it was helping to arm and train Afghan rebel factions known collectively as the mujahideen. Meanwhile, the Soviets became mired down in Afghanistan as they fought against the mujahideen. Unable to achieve military victory, the Soviet Union withdrew the last of its troops from Afghanistan in 1989.

The End of the Cold War

Throughout the 1980s the Soviet Union was suffering from numerous domestic problems. These problems were exacerbated by the long war in Afghanistan. Meanwhile, the United States was conducting a massive and expensive buildup in military strength, forcing the Soviet Union to do likewise. In addition, Reagan began a new space-based military defense program that was intended to protect the United States from any incoming Soviet missiles.

In 1985 the newly elected Soviet premier Mikhail Gorbachev (1931–) began implementing political reforms that he hoped would quell growing discontent among his people. Gorbachev's new policy, called *glasnost* (which is Russian for "openness") marked a historic change for the communist government. However, the reforms appeared to be too little and too late, as dissent (political opposition) and unrest continued to spread across many Soviet territories. The unrelenting weight of economic and sociopolitical problems precipitated a breakup of the Soviet Union during the late 1980s and early 1990s into individually governed republics. The Cold War was over, but its effects on U.S. national security and world politics would be long lasting.

U.S. POST-VIETNAM MILITARY

The Vietnam War severely dampened the United States' willingness to commit U.S. troops to foreign conflicts. The long war had not saved South Vietnam from a communist takeover and had been costly in terms of money and human suffering. Over 8.7 million U.S. military personnel served during the Vietnam conflict. (See Table 1.1.) U.S. casualties included 58,220 killed and 303,644 wounded. In addition, the war brought death and misery to millions of Vietnamese civilians. As a result, the American public and U.S. politicians were not eager to commit U.S. forces to future foreign conflicts.

During the 1980s the U.S. military had additional setbacks. An attempt to rescue hostages from the U.S. embassy in Iran in 1980 had to be aborted after a helicopter crash killed eight U.S. military personnel. (See Table 1.3.) U.S. Marines sent to Lebanon as part of a UN peacekeeping effort suffered a calamitous terrorist attack in 1983. More than 250 of them were killed. U.S.

TABLE 1.3

U.S. military deaths worldwide in selected military operations, selected years 1980–96

Military operation/incident	Casualty type	Total
Iranian Hostage Rescue Mission		
April 25, 1980	Nonhostile	8
Lebanon peacekeeping, August 25,		
1982–February 26, 1984*	Hostile	256
	Nonhostile	9
	Total	265
Urgent Fury, Grenada, 1983	Hostile	18
	Nonhostile	1
	Total	19
Just Cause, Panama, 1989	Hostile	23
Persian Gulf War, 1990–1991		
Desert Shield	Nonhostile	84
Desert Storm	Hostile	148
	Nonhostile	151
	Total	299
Desert Shield/Storm	Total	383
Restore Hope/UNOSOM, Somalia,		
1992–1994	Hostile	29
	Nonhostile	14
	Total	43
Uphold Democracy, Haiti, 1994–1996	Nonhostile	4

*Place of casualty, Lebanon   Note: UNOSOM = United Nations Operations in Somalia

SOURCE: Adapted from "Worldwide U.S. Active Duty Military Deaths—Selected Military Operations (1980–1996)," in *Defense Casualty Analysis System*, U.S. Department of Defense, Defense Manpower Data Center, 2012, https://www.dmdc.osd.mil/dcas/pages/report_operations.xhtml (accessed July 2, 2012)

troops did conduct successful operations in Grenada and Panama during the decade, but these were small and limited in scope. These incidents did not indicate to the American public or the world at large the full capabilities of the maturing U.S. military.

An influx of money during the 1970s and 1980s from the Carter and Reagan administrations financed the development of sophisticated weapons and computer technology. Training was also a priority, as was the reorganization of the military hierarchy at the top levels. As a result, U.S. forces performed extremely well in 1991, when a UN coalition was formed to drive Iraqi troops from Kuwait during Operation Desert Storm. It was the first of several major conflicts that would take place in a new theater for the U.S. military: the Middle East.

THE MIDDLE EAST

Geographically, the Middle East is a region at the intersection of Asia, Africa, and Europe. There is no official designation of the countries that make up the Middle East. The term is largely a sociopolitical one used by those in the Western world to collectively describe a group of countries in and around the Arabian Peninsula. This group is often thought to extend from Iran in the east to the northwest coast of Africa. Some observers include other nearby countries, such as Turkey, Afghanistan, and Pakistan. (See Figure 1.1.) In a historical context, most of the region now known as the Middle East was once the core of the Ottoman Empire, which was splintered into individual nations following World War I.

Peoples and Religions

In *The Modern Middle East: A Political History since the First World War* (2005), Mehran Kamrava of California State University, Northridge, notes that "there are vast differences between and within the histories, cultures, traditions, and politics" of the Middle Eastern countries. However, there are also powerful unifying characteristics within the region, primarily religion and historic ethnic commonalities.

Westerners tend to describe all Middle Eastern people as Arabs. The term *Arab* is actually an ethnic designation applied to certain tribes descended from Shem (or Sem), the oldest son of Noah in biblical history. The descendants of Shem are called Semites; they include the Babylonians and Phoenicians and the Hebrew tribes of ancient times. The Hebrews embraced the religion of Judaism and settled the kingdom of Israel. Arab tribes were scattered throughout the region and were governed by various kings and tribal rulers. During the seventh century a new Arab leader emerged named Muhammad (c. 570–632), who would change the world by introducing a new religion called Islam.

FIGURE 1.1

Map including the Middle East, Northeast Africa, and Southwest Asia

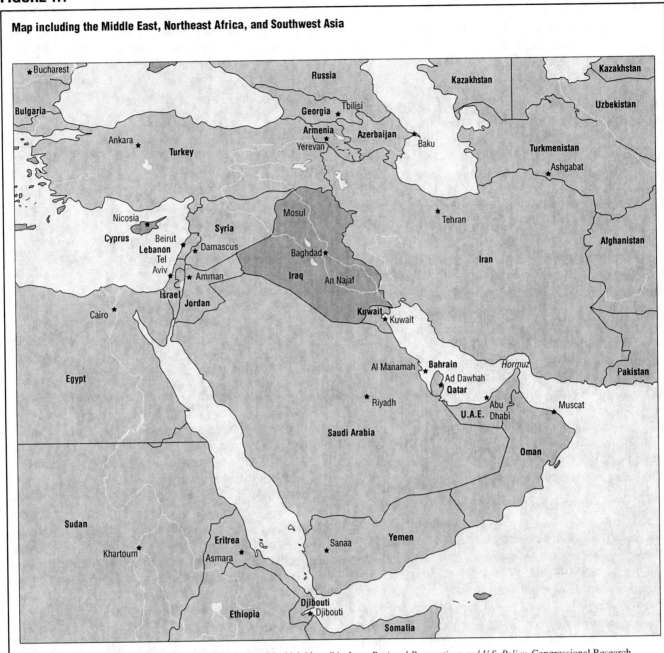

SOURCE: Christopher M. Blanchard et al., "Figure 1. Iraq and Its Neighbors," in *Iraq: Regional Perspectives and U.S. Policy*, Congressional Research Service, October 6, 2009, http://assets.opencrs.com/rpts/RL33793_20091006.pdf (accessed July 2, 2012)

The followers of Islam are called Muslims. They worship one God (whom they call Allah) and believe that Allah's messages were passed by the angel Gabriel to the prophet Muhammad in what is now modern-day Saudi Arabia. God's messages are called the Koran. This term is also used to refer to the messages in written form, which make up Islam's holy book. Most Muslims consider Islam much more than a religious practice; they believe it encompasses all areas of life, including social, economic, and political aspects.

By far, Islam is the most predominant religion in the Middle East. However, as with most religions, there are diverse sects within Islam. The two largest sects are called Sunni and Shia; their respective followers have historical disagreements about issues related to governance and theological interpretations. These disagreements sometimes lead to violent confrontations between fellow Muslims. Many other religions are practiced throughout the region but by small populations in most countries. The notable exception is Judaism, which is the predominant religion of Israel.

Ethnically, the modern Middle East is dominated by Arab peoples who reside mostly in Saudi Arabia, Jordan, Lebanon, Syria, Iraq, Egypt, and parts of northern Africa.

There are, however, substantial pockets of non-Arabs; for example, Persians descended from tribes in southwest Asia predominate in Iran, Turks in Turkey, Kurds in northern Iraq, and Jewish descendants of the ancient Hebrew tribes in Israel.

Thus, the Middle East is a complicated mosaic of societies in which some widely shared characteristics provide grounds for unity among much of the population. However, cultural, political, and religious differences within the region are a source of often violent confrontations between peoples. One such confrontation has grown to dominate the sociopolitical affairs of the Middle East and has become a source of great concern to U.S. national security interests: the Israeli-Palestinian conflict.

Israel and Palestine

Following World War I the League of Nations placed some territories of the former Ottoman Empire under the administration of Great Britain and France. Iraq and Palestine were administered by Great Britain, and Syria and Lebanon by France. This arrangement was called the Mandates System and was designed to be temporary, lasting only until the territories could mature into independent nations ruled by their own governments. The populations of the administered countries greatly resented foreign intervention in their affairs and viewed the arrangement as colonialism. As a result, there was much political and social unrest in these countries. Eventually, Iraq, Syria, and Lebanon did gain their independence.

Palestine was supposed to become a nation called the Palestinian Arab State. A variety of factors prevented this from happening as described by the UN in *The Question of Palestine and the United Nations* (2008, http://unispal .un.org/pdfs/DPI2499.pdf). The UN indicates that the Palestinian Mandate was in effect from 1922 to 1947. However, the British government had already promised Jewish leaders a "national home" for the Jewish people in Palestine. That promise had been made in a November 1917 letter from the British foreign secretary Arthur James Balfour (1848–1930) to Lord Lionel Walter Rothschild (1868–1937). The Balfour Declaration (2012, http:// avalon.law.yale.edu/20th_century/balfour.asp) stated in part: "'His Majesty's Government view with favour the establishment in Palestine of a national home for the Jewish people, and will use their best endeavours to facilitate the achievement of this object, it being clearly understood that nothing shall be done which may prejudice the civil and religious rights of existing non-Jewish communities in Palestine, or the rights and political status enjoyed by Jews in any other country.'"

The Balfour Declaration pleased Zionists—Jews around the world seeking an independent Jewish state on the land inhabited in ancient times by the Hebrew tribes, that is, the Land of Israel. Most Jews had been driven from

Palestine by the end of the second century. The land was subsequently ruled by the Byzantine Empire, the Persians, a series of Muslim rulers, and the Ottoman Empire. The many non-Jewish people (primarily Arab Muslims) inhabiting Palestine during the early 20th century did not want to lose their own chance at statehood and give up land their ancestors had inhabited for centuries.

STATE OF ISRAEL. The Balfour Declaration spurred mass migrations of Jews from around the world to Palestine. The UN explains in *The Question of Palestine and the United Nations* that migrations were particularly heavy during the 1930s from Nazi Germany and eastern Europe—areas where Jews were subject to harsh persecution and even extermination. Violence grew between the Arab Palestinians and the incoming Jewish peoples— both of whom claimed the land as their own. In 1947 the British government turned the problem over to the UN, which proposed splitting Palestine into two approximately even-sized states, one Jewish and one Arab. Jerusalem, a city considered sacred to both Jews and Muslims, was to be ruled under a Special International Regime. The partition plan did not please Arab rulers, and the violence in Palestine escalated.

In 1948 the Jewish population of Palestine declared itself a nation—the State of Israel—and found itself immediately at war with the armies of Palestine's neighbors and Arab supporters: Egypt, Transjordan (later Jordan), Iraq, Syria, and Lebanon. During the war Israeli forces captured more than three-fourths of the original territory of Palestine and most of Jerusalem. The remainder of the territory was held by the governments of Egypt and Jordan. These areas are called the Gaza Strip and the West Bank, respectively. (See Figure 1.2.) In the Six-Day War of 1967, Israel captured both of these areas and all of Jerusalem. In response, the UN issued Resolution 242, which called on Israel to withdraw from the areas it had just captured and for all states in the region to cease their "belligerency" and live in peaceful coexistence. This did not occur.

PALESTINIAN TERRITORIES. In 1964 the Palestine Liberation Organization (PLO) was appointed by a group of Arab nations to represent the political aspirations of Palestine. The PLO was an umbrella organization for a variety of Palestinian groups with varying views on the use of politics and violence to achieve their goals. The main group was al Fatah, which was led by Yasir Arafat (1929–2004). During its early years the PLO was often associated with acts of violence against Israeli civilians and soldiers. PLO splinter groups have been linked to many acts of terrorism around the world, including the killing of Israeli athletes at the 1972 Olympic Games in Munich, Germany. Meanwhile, Palestinian refugees fleeing wars and other violence spread throughout the Middle East and parts of Europe. They have played a substantial role in raising money and eliciting sympathy and support for the Palestinian cause around the world.

FIGURE 1.2

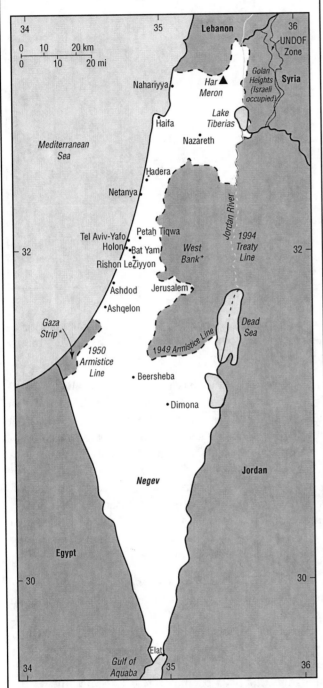

Map of Israel, the West Bank, the Gaza Strip, and the Golan Heights, 2012

*Israeli-occupied with current status subject to the Israeli-Palestinian interim Agreement—permanent status to be determined through further negotiation.

SOURCE: "Map of Israel," in "Middle East: Israel," *The World Factbook*, Central Intelligence Agency, June 26, 2012, https://www.cia.gov/library/publications/the-world-factbook/geos/is.html (accessed July 2, 2012)

During the 1990s the PLO achieved a measure of legitimacy as the United States worked to obtain a peace agreement in the decades-old dispute over Palestine. In 1993 Arafat officially recognized the State of Israel as a legitimate government. In return, the Israeli government extended official recognition to the PLO as the legitimate representative of the Arab Palestinians. That same year the two sides reached an agreement called the Oslo Accords that laid out a plan for limited Palestinian control over some of its territories by a new government called the Palestinian National Authority (PNA). Full implementation of the plan was thwarted by continued violence between the Palestinians and the Israelis. However, in 2005 Israel did withdraw its troops from the Gaza Strip.

Arafat died in 2004 and was replaced by a close associate, Mahmoud Abbas (1935–), who was elected president of the PNA in 2005. In 2006 Palestinian voters gave members of the organization Hamas majority control of the PNA, relegating al Fatah to a minority position. The United States considers Hamas a foreign terrorist organization under U.S. law. The United States and al Fatah refused to recognize Hamas as the legitimate leading party in Palestine. Furthermore, the U.S. government forbade direct economic aid to Palestine following the Hamas elections. Abbas began an internal political battle with the elected Prime Minister Ismail Haniyeh (1962–), a member of Hamas. A near civil war erupted between Palestinian peoples allied with either side. In June 2007 Abbas declared a state of emergency and officially dissolved Haniyeh's government after Hamas forces routed al Fatah forces and seized military and political control of the Gaza Strip. Abbas appointed a new prime minister, Salam Fayyad (1952–), but the appointment was largely ignored by Hamas leaders and supporters. The United States lifted its earlier sanctions to encourage development of the Abbas government.

Egypt controls one land crossing on the border between its territory and the Gaza Strip. Following the Hamas takeover in 2006, Israel requested that Egypt begin blocking most of the people and cargo that cross at that border. Israel conducted its own much wider blockade to prevent the transport of certain goods into the Gaza Strip, because the latter was the source of frequent missile attacks on settlements in southern Israel. Despite the blockades, Hamas continued to launch missiles into Israel. In June 2008 Egypt brokered a shaky truce between Hamas and Israel, but it proved to be short lived. In early January 2009 Israeli ground forces invaded the Gaza Strip in retaliation for continued missile attacks. After three weeks of fighting, Israel declared a cease-fire, withdrew its troops, and imposed a near-total blockade on ground and sea transports of materials and supplies to the Gaza Strip. In May 2010 a flotilla of ships manned by foreign activists determined to defy the blockade was boarded by Israeli forces, resulting in the deaths of nine of the activists. The Israeli action drew international condemnation, even from the United States.

FIGURE 1.3

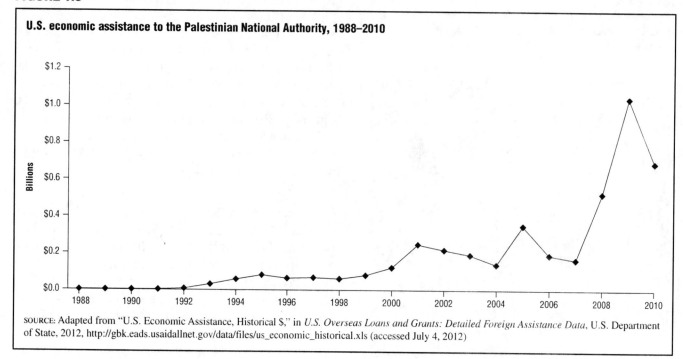

U.S. economic assistance to the Palestinian National Authority, 1988–2010

SOURCE: Adapted from "U.S. Economic Assistance, Historical $," in *U.S. Overseas Loans and Grants: Detailed Foreign Assistance Data*, U.S. Department of State, 2012, http://gbk.eads.usaidallnet.gov/data/files/us_economic_historical.xls (accessed July 4, 2012)

In June 2010 Israel and Egypt began relaxing their blockades to allow more shipments into the Gaza Strip; however, as of October 2012, both countries continued to limit the flow of people and goods into the area.

The PNA is hugely dependent on financial assistance from Western nations, including the United States. According to the U.S. Department of State, in "U.S. Overseas Loans and Grants: Detailed Foreign Assistance Data" (2012, http://gbk.eads.usaidallnet.gov/data/files/us_economic_historical.xls), the United States committed over $4.3 billion in aid to the PNA between 1988 and 2010, including just over $1 billion in 2009 alone. (See Figure 1.3.) Nevertheless, the PNA has struggled financially. The article "Citing Crisis, Palestinians Can't Pay Salaries" (Associated Press, July 3, 2012) reports that in July 2012 the PNA was unable to pay the salaries of its government workers "because of a financial crisis in the West Bank." The article notes that many donor countries reduced their contributions to the PNA due to the worldwide financial downturn that lasted from 2008 to about mid-2009. Even though that downturn was officially over by 2012, its effects were still being felt worldwide, and as a result the PNA expected a $1.1 billion budget deficit for 2012.

U.S. Connection to the Middle East

Since World War I, U.S. political, economic, and military affairs have become greatly entangled with circumstances in the Middle East. During the first decade of the 21st century U.S. military forces occupied two nations in the region: Afghanistan and Iraq. (See Figure 1.1.) Both invasions were driven by perceived threats to U.S. national security. In addition, there were ongoing issues related to the United States' alliance with Israel and U.S. dependence on petroleum from oil-rich nations of the Middle East.

The United States has been a staunch ally of Israel since that nation was founded. Support for Zionism within the United States was not strong before World War II but grew tremendously when the horrors of the Jewish holocaust in Europe came to light. President Truman was a strong advocate for a Jewish state in Palestine. In *Outline of U.S. History* (2005, http://www.america.gov/media/pdf/books/historytln.pdf#popup), the Department of State's Bureau of International Information Programs notes that Truman officially recognized the new nation of Israel only 15 minutes after it was formed.

U.S. political and financial support for Israel—one of the few true democracies in the region—has continued for decades and is a source of deep resentment among the predominantly Muslim peoples of the Middle East. Israel is considered to be a close ally of the United States and is a major trading partner. Israel also enjoys popular support among the American people. Figure 1.4 shows the results of polling that was conducted by the Gallup Organization between 1988 and 2012 regarding American sympathies in the Israeli-Palestinian conflict. In 2012, 61% of Americans expressed sympathy for Israel in the conflict. Only 19% of Americans expressed sympathy for the Palestinians. The historical results indicate that strong support for Israel has persisted in the United States for more than two decades.

Oil is another important connection between the United States and the Middle East. The United States and other

FIGURE 1.4

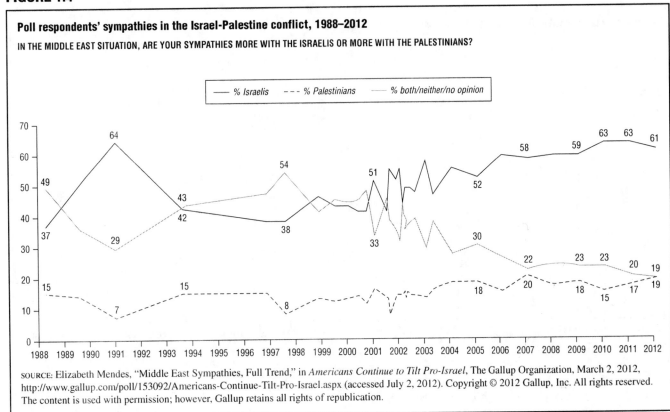

Poll respondents' sympathies in the Israel-Palestine conflict, 1988–2012

IN THE MIDDLE EAST SITUATION, ARE YOUR SYMPATHIES MORE WITH THE ISRAELIS OR MORE WITH THE PALESTINIANS?

— % Israelis   - - - % Palestinians   ⋯⋯ % both/neither/no opinion

industrialized nations consume much more oil than they produce and need a steady supply at low prices for their economies to function. Saudi Arabia, Iran, Iraq, Kuwait, and other nations along the Persian Gulf are all rich in oil, and significant deposits are found elsewhere in the Middle East as well. In fact, in the late 20th and early 21st centuries the Middle East was by far the world's top oil-producing region. This means that Middle Eastern oil producers can influence the United States and other nations by manipulating, or threatening to manipulate, the supply of oil. Furthermore, anything that endangers the flow of oil from the Middle East, such as war or political instability in the region, threatens U.S. national security and may motivate a response.

The United States faces a challenging problem in trying to maintain both its alliance with Israel and good relations with the oil-rich Middle Eastern countries, where anti-Israel sentiment festers and threatens to boil over into full-fledged war.

COST OF NATIONAL SECURITY

The United States spends a great deal of money to protect its national security. Tasks within this area fall to a number of federal agencies, primarily the U.S. Department of Defense, the U.S. Department of Homeland Security, and the Central Intelligence Agency (CIA). Certain components and resources of other agencies, such as the Department of State and the Federal Bureau of Investiga-

tion, are also devoted to national security interests. From a cost standpoint, the largest expense is for national defense.

National Defense

Spending on national defense by the United States, particularly during wartime, has historically been extremely high. It spiked during World War II, reaching nearly 90% of the nation's total outlays. (See Figure 1.5.) It dropped dramatically following the war and then rebounded during the early years of the Cold War. Spending steadily decreased between 1954 and 2001 before it began to rise slowly again beginning in 2002.

In 2011 the United States spent 20% of its outlays on national defense. (See Figure 1.5.) The Office of Management and Budget indicates in *Historical Tables, Budget of the United States Government, Fiscal Year 2013* (January 2012, http://www.whitehouse.gov/sites/default/files/omb/budget/fy2013/assets/hist.pdf) that the United States was expected to spend $701.8 billion on national defense in 2013, down from $716.3 billion in 2012. (See Table 1.4.) Defense spending increased dramatically between 2001 and 2012 due to the wars in Afghanistan and Iraq. However, spending after 2012 was expected to decrease significantly.

A Gallup poll conducted in February 2012 found that 54% of Americans felt the nation's national defense is "about right." (See Figure 1.6.) Another 32% said it is "not strong enough." Only 13% believed national defense

FIGURE 1.5

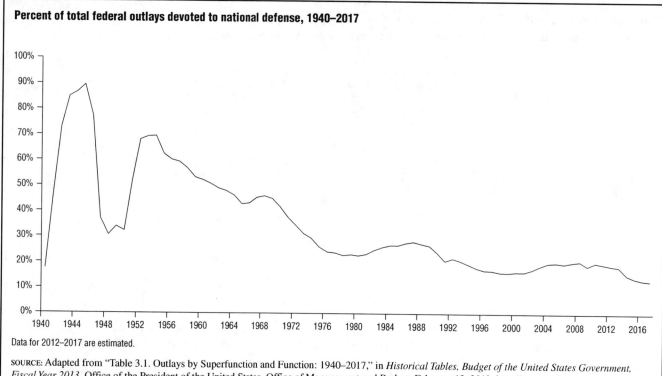

Percent of total federal outlays devoted to national defense, 1940–2017

Data for 2012–2017 are estimated.

SOURCE: Adapted from "Table 3.1. Outlays by Superfunction and Function: 1940–2017," in *Historical Tables, Budget of the United States Government, Fiscal Year 2013*, Office of the President of the United States, Office of Management and Budget, February 13, 2012, http://www.whitehouse.gov/sites/default/files/omb/budget/fy2013/assets/hist.pdf (accessed July 2, 2012)

TABLE 1.4

Federal spending on national defense, 2010–13

[In millions of dollars]

Function and subfunction	2010	2011	2012 estimate	2013 estimate
National defense:				
Department of Defense—military:				
Military personnel	155,690	161,608	156,185	155,862
Operation and maintenance	275,988	291,038	294,513	294,153
Procurement	133,603	128,003	139,869	124,559
Research, development, test, and evaluation	76,990	74,871	75,904	71,820
Military construction	21,169	19,917	18,067	19,403
Family housing	3,173	3,432	2,110	2,103
Other	90	−805	1,607	4,975
Subtotal, Department of Defense—military	666,703	678,064	688,255	672,875
Atomic energy defense activities	19,315	20,410	19,765	20,722
Defense-related activities	7,568	7,151	8,280	8,170
Total, national defense	**693,586**	**705,625**	**716,300**	**701,767**

N/A = Not available.
On-budget unless otherwise stated.

SOURCE: Adapted from "Table 3.2. Outlays by Function and Subfunction: 1962–2017," in *Historical Tables, Budget of the United States Government, Fiscal Year 2013*, Office of the President of the United States, Office of Management and Budget, February 13, 2012, http://www.whitehouse.gov/sites/default/files/omb/budget/fy2013/assets/hist.pdf (accessed July 2, 2012)

is "stronger than needs to be." In the same poll, Gallup asked about national defense and military spending. Less than a quarter (24%) of respondents said the United States spends "too little" on national defense and the military. (See Figure 1.7.) Thirty-two percent thought spending is "about right," and 41% thought it is "too much."

Gallup pollsters have also periodically questioned Americans about the strength of the U.S. military. As shown in Figure 1.8, more than half (54%) of the respondents in 2012 said the United States is "no. 1 in the world militarily." Forty-five percent thought the U.S. military is "only one of several leading military powers." Since the

FIGURE 1.6

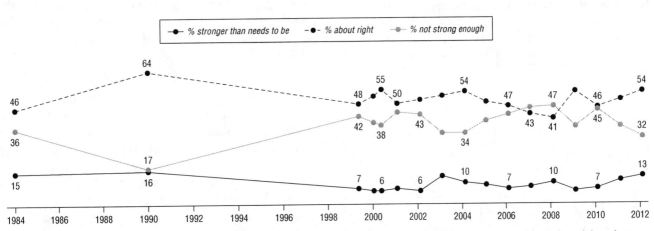

Public opinion on the strength of U.S. national defense, 1984–2012

DO YOU, YOURSELF, FEEL THAT OUR NATIONAL DEFENSE IS STRONGER NOW THAN IT NEEDS TO BE, NOT STRONG ENOUGH, OR ABOUT RIGHT AT THE PRESENT TIME?

SOURCE: Jeffrey M. Jones, "Do you, yourself, feel that our national defense is stronger now than it needs to be, not strong enough, or about right at the present time?" in *Fewer Americans Say U.S. Is No. 1 Military Power*, The Gallup Organization, March 12, 2012, http://www.gallup.com/poll/153185/Fewer-Americans-Say-No-Military-Power.aspx (accessed July 2, 2012). Copyright © 2012 Gallup, Inc. All rights reserved. The content is used with permission; however, Gallup retains all rights of republication.

FIGURE 1.7

Public opinion on U.S. national defense and military spending, 1970–2012

THERE IS MUCH DISCUSSION AS TO THE AMOUNT OF MONEY THE GOVERNMENT IN WASHINGTON SHOULD SPEND FOR NATIONAL DEFENSE AND MILITARY PURPOSES. HOW DO YOU FEEL ABOUT THIS? DO YOU THINK WE ARE SPENDING TOO LITTLE, ABOUT THE RIGHT AMOUNT, OR TOO MUCH?

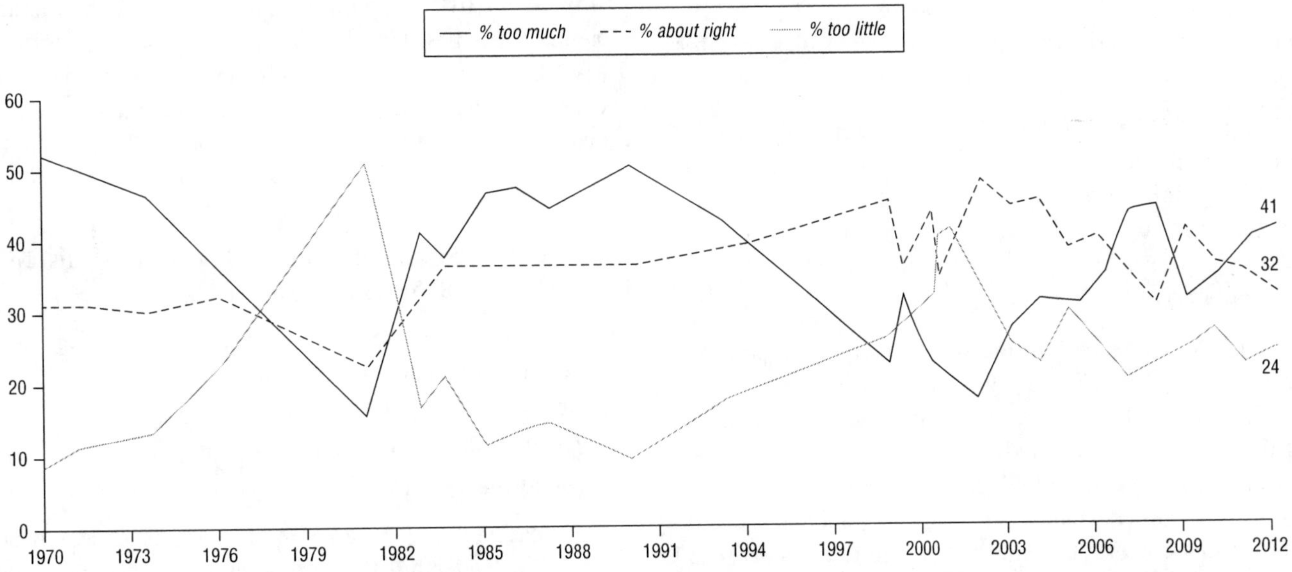

SOURCE: Jeffrey M. Jones, "Americans' Views of U.S. Spending on National Defense and the Military," in *Fewer Americans Say U.S. Is No. 1 Military Power*, The Gallup Organization, March 12, 2012, http://www.gallup.com/poll/153185/Fewer-Americans-Say-No-Military-Power.aspx (accessed July 2, 2012). Copyright © 2012 Gallup, Inc. All rights reserved. The content is used with permission; however, Gallup retains all rights of republication.

question was first asked in 1993 greater percentages of Americans have ranked the U.S. military as the world's best than have said it is one of several leading military powers.

Other Spending

National security encompasses more than military operations. The United States spends substantial amounts on foreign aid and homeland security. Most foreign aid is

FIGURE 1.8

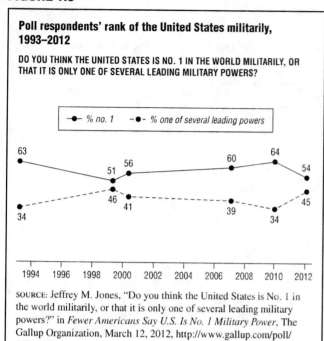

Poll respondents' rank of the United States militarily, 1993–2012

DO YOU THINK THE UNITED STATES IS NO. 1 IN THE WORLD MILITARILY, OR THAT IT IS ONLY ONE OF SEVERAL LEADING MILITARY POWERS?

- % no. 1   - % one of several leading powers

SOURCE: Jeffrey M. Jones, "Do you think the United States is No. 1 in the world militarily, or that it is only one of several leading military powers?" in *Fewer Americans Say U.S. Is No. 1 Military Power*, The Gallup Organization, March 12, 2012, http://www.gallup.com/poll/153185/Fewer-Americans-Say-No-Military-Power.aspx (accessed July 2, 2012). Copyright © 2012 Gallup, Inc. All rights reserved. The content is used with permission; however, Gallup retains all rights of republication.

distributed by the U.S. Agency for International Development, an independent federal agency. Additional major donors include the U.S. Departments of State and Agriculture. In fiscal year (FY) 2010 the United States distributed $37.7 billion in foreign economic assistance. (See Table 1.5.) Another $15.1 billion was spent on military assistance for foreign countries.

Figure 1.9 lists the top 10 countries that received the most U.S. economic and military assistance during FY 2010. Afghanistan received, by far, the most money during this period: $11.4 billion. Other major recipients included Pakistan and Israel. Afghanistan and Pakistan are predominantly Muslim.

The Department of Homeland Security is responsible for preventing terrorists from striking inside the United States, fortifying U.S. defenses against an attack, and preparing the American people and emergency responders in case an attack does occur. Its budget is discussed in Chapter 2. The CIA is also devoted exclusively to national security pursuits. However, as explained further in Chapter 2, the CIA's budget and spending are classified.

THE UNITED STATES' ROLE IN THE WORLD

In February 2012 the Gallup Organization asked Americans what kind of role they thought the United States should play in trying to solve international problems. Only 19% of those asked said the nation should play a "leading role" in world affairs. (See Table 1.6.) Just over half (52%)

believed the United States should play a "major role," whereas 24% preferred a "minor role." Another 3% said the nation should play "no role" in world affairs, and 1% had no opinion on the matter. As shown in Tabel 1.6, the percentage of respondents expressing a desire for the United States to take the "leading role" in world affairs has varied from 16% to 26% since Gallup first posed the question in 2001.

The United States is often described as "the world's policeman" because of its history of intervening in foreign conflicts in an effort to shape the outcome. The nation has a vested interest in seeing a world free of tyranny and filled with democratically governed nations that are friendly to the United States. Regardless, there is debate over the extent to which the United States should interfere in the internal matters of foreign countries. Even though the American people strongly support national defense and certain aspects of the policeman role, they are less certain about the United States' early 21st-century ventures into so-called nation building. The United States waged successful military campaigns against Afghanistan and Iraq that routed tyrannical leaders. However, the resulting power vacuums left it struggling to rebuild these war-torn and politically and ethnically diverse countries. The unprecedented role the United States has played in the day-to-day operations of these countries is described in Chapter 4.

NATIONAL SECURITY STRATEGY

In May 2010 the administration of President Barack Obama (1961–) issued *National Security Strategy* (http://www.whitehouse.gov/sites/default/files/rss_viewer/national_security_strategy.pdf). The 52-page document outlines broad strategic measures and specific priorities for achieving what President Obama calls "four enduring national interests." They are as follows:

- Security—the security of the United States, its citizens, and U.S. allies and partners.

- Prosperity—a strong, innovative, and growing U.S. economy in an open international economic system that promotes opportunity and prosperity.

- Values—respect for universal values at home and around the world.

- International order—an international order advanced by U.S. leadership that promotes peace, security, and opportunity through stronger cooperation to meet global challenges.

The national security strategy encompasses many concerns; however, this book focuses on the priorities that are listed for the security interest, as shown in Table 1.7. The measures that the United States has taken, is taking, and plans to take to achieve these priorities will be discussed in detail in the remaining chapters.

TABLE 1.5

Foreign economic and military assistance, 1946–2010

[In millions of dollars]

	Post-war relief period 1946–48	Marshall Plan period 1949–52	Mutual Scty Act period 1953–61	Foreign Assistance Act (FAA) period 1962–2006	2007	2008	2009	2010	Total FAA period 1962–2010	Total loans & grants 1946–2010	Of which loans 1946–2010	Outstanding amount as of 09/30/2010
I. Total economic assistance	12,482.0	18,634.3	24,050.0	434,778.9	27,303.0	32,502.1	33,619.6	37,670.6	565,874.2	621,040.5	66,666.4	11,508.2
II. Total military assistance	481.2	10,064.2	19,302.2	195,911.9	13,753.9	16,478.7	14,898.1	15,057.6	256,100.2	285,947.8	42,589.2	2,605.9
III. Total economic & military assistance	12,963.2	28,698.5	43,352.2	630,690.7	41,056.9	48,980.8	48,517.7	52,728.2	821,974.4	906,988.3	109,255.6	14,114.1

SOURCE: Adapted from "Summary of All Countries: Fiscal Year 2010 U.S. Overseas Loans and Grants—Obligations and Loan Authorizations, in $US Millions," in *U.S. Overseas Loans and Grants: Obligations and Loan Authorizations, July 1, 1945–September 30, 2010,* U.S. Agency for International Development, 2012, http://pdf.usaid.gov/pdf_docs/PNADX500.pdf (accessed July 3, 2012)

FIGURE 1.9

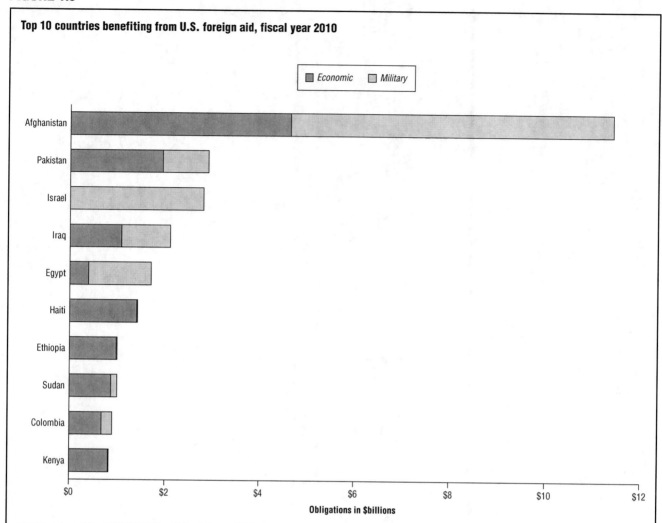

Top 10 countries benefiting from U.S. foreign aid, fiscal year 2010

Legend: ☐ *Economic* ☐ *Military*

SOURCE: Adapted from "FY2010 Top 10 Recipients of U.S. Economic and Military Assistance," in *U.S. Overseas Loans and Grants: Foreign Assistance Fast Facts: FY2010*, U.S. Agency for International Development, 2012, http://gbk.eads.usaidallnet.gov/data/fast-facts.html (accessed July 3, 2012)

TABLE 1.6

Public opinion on the role the U.S. should play in trying to solve international problems, selected dates, 2001–12

NEXT WE WOULD LIKE YOU TO THINK ABOUT THE ROLE THE U.S. SHOULD PLAY IN TRYING TO SOLVE INTERNATIONAL PROBLEMS. DO YOU THINK THE U.S. SHOULD—[ROTATED: TAKE THE LEADING ROLE IN WORLD AFFAIRS, TAKE A MAJOR ROLE, BUT NOT THE LEADING ROLE, TAKE A MINOR ROLE, (OR) TAKE NO ROLE AT ALL IN WORLD AFFAIRS]?

	Leading role	Major role	Minor role	No role	No opinion
	%	%	%	%	%
2012 Feb 2–5	19	52	24	3	1
2011 Feb 2–5	16	50	25	7	1
2010 Feb 1–3	19	52	22	6	*
2009 Feb 9–12	23	52	17	6	2
2008 Feb 11–14	19	56	19	5	1
2007 Feb 1–4	15	58	21	4	2
2006 Feb 6–9	19	55	20	4	1
2005 Feb 7–10	19	53	21	5	2
2004 Feb 9–12	21	53	21	4	1
2003 Feb 3–6	26	53	16	3	2
2002 Feb 4–6	26	52	16	4	2
2001 Feb 1–4	16	57	21	4	2

SOURCE: "Next we would like you to think about the role the U.S. should play in trying to solve international problems. Do you think the U.S. should—[ROTATED: take the leading role in world affairs, take a major role, but not the leading role, take a minor role, (or) take no role at all in world affairs]?" in *U.S. Position in the World*, The Gallup Organization, 2012, http://www.gallup.com/poll/116350/Position-World.aspx (accessed July 3, 2012). Copyright © 2012 Gallup, Inc. All rights reserved. The content is used with permission; however, Gallup retains all rights of republication.

TABLE 1.7

U.S. national security strategic goals, 2010

Strengthen security and resilience at home

Enhance security at home
Effectively manage emergencies
Empowering communities to counter radicalization
Improve resilience through increased public-private partnerships
Engage with communities and citizens

Disrupt, dismantle and defeat Al-Qa'ida and its violent extremist affiliates in Afghanistan, Pakistan, and around the world

Prevent attacks on and in the homeland
Strengthen aviation security
Deny terrorists weapons of mass destruction
Deny Al-Qa'ida the ability to threaten the American people, our allies, our partners and our interests overseas
Deny safe havens and strengthen at-risk states
Deliver swift and sure justice
Resist fear and overreaction
Contrast Al-Qa'ida's intent to destroy with our constructive vision

Reverse the spread of nuclear and biological weapons and secure nuclear materials

Pursue the goal of a world without nuclear weapons
Strengthen the nuclear non-proliferation treaty
Present a clear choice to Iran and North Korea
Secure vulnerable nuclear weapons and material
Support peaceful nuclear energy
Counter biological threats

Advance peace, security, and opportunity in the greater Middle East

Complete a responsible transition as we end the war in Iraq
Pursue Arab-Israeli peace
Promote a responsible Iran

Invest in the capacity of strong and capable partners

Foster security and reconstruction in the aftermath of conflict
Pursue sustainable and responsible security systems in at-risk states
Prevent the emergence of conflict

Secure cyberspace

Investing in people and technology
Strengthening partnerships

SOURCE: Adapted from *National Security Strategy*, Office of the President of the United States, May 27, 2010, http://www.whitehouse.gov/sites/default/files/rss_viewer/national_security_strategy.pdf (accessed July 23, 2012)

CHAPTER 2

THE ORGANIZATION OF NATIONAL SECURITY

The U.S. national security framework consists of government agencies and offices with responsibilities in various disciplines: policy making, military activities, intelligence gathering and analysis, diplomacy, criminal investigation, immigration control, and law enforcement. Interaction and cooperation between separate government entities and disciplines is crucial to ensure that U.S. goals are met for foreign policy and homeland security. Coordination of all functions is ultimately the responsibility of the president of the United States, who is the commander in chief of the nation's military forces and the chief decision maker for matters related to national security.

NATIONAL SECURITY COUNCIL

The National Security Council (NSC) is the top entity in the U.S. national security structure. It lies within the executive office of the president and includes decision makers at the highest levels of government. Table 2.1 lists the regular members and occasional attendees who are associated with the NSC. It was created following World War II (1939–1945) by the National Security Act of 1947, which was amended in 1949.

The NSC provides a forum for the president to discuss national security issues with his top advisers. The decisions and policies resulting from these meetings are implemented by the department heads within the government, chiefly the secretaries of the U.S. Departments of State (foreign affairs), Defense (military affairs), and the Treasury (economic affairs). The chair of the Joint Chiefs of Staff is the highest ranking officer within the U.S. military and advises the president on military issues. The director of national intelligence heads a collection of agencies that are devoted to intelligence gathering and analysis. The assistant to the president for national security affairs is more commonly called the national security adviser. This person is not a member of a particular department or branch within the government but is chosen by the president to offer an independent viewpoint on national security matters.

U.S. DEPARTMENT OF DEFENSE

The U.S. Department of Defense (DOD) traces its history back to 1789, when it was created as the Department of War under the administration of President George Washington (1732–1799). Some branches of the nation's armed forces (U.S. Army, Navy, and Marine Corps) were already in operation, having been established in 1775 for the Revolutionary War (1775–1783). Following World War II Congress created a civilian (nonmilitary) agency within the government, led by a secretary of defense who had direct control over the armed forces including the newly created U.S. Air Force. This agency was eventually called the Department of Defense.

Figure 2.1 lists the main entities that are organized under the DOD. The Department of the Army evolved from the former Department of War. The Department of the Navy (which oversees the U.S. Marine Corps) was created in 1798. The Department of the Air Force was created following enactment of the National Security Act of 1947. The Office of the Inspector General is responsible for auditing the operations and finances of the DOD to ensure they are carried out in accordance with U.S. law and government policy.

The combatant commands are the operational arms of the U.S. combat forces. Some combatant commands have global responsibilities, whereas others are assigned specific geographic regions; for example, the European Command covers most of Europe, parts of the Middle East, and most of Africa. Each combatant command includes forces from two or more branches of the military (army, navy, marines, or air force).

The Joint Chiefs of Staff are planners and advisers on issues of national security. This office includes a chair,

TABLE 2.1

Membership of the National Security Council, 2012

Chair	President
Regular attendees	Vice President
	Secretary of State
	Secretary of the Treasury
	Secretary of Defense
	Assistant to the President for National Security Affairs
Military advisor	Chairman of the Joint Chiefs of Staff
Intelligence advisor	Director of National Intelligence
Invited to any meeting	The Chief of Staff to the President
	Counsel to the President
	Assistant to the President for Economic Policy
Attend meetings pertaining to their responsibilities	The Attorney General
	Director of the Office of Management and Budget
Attend meetings when appropriate	The heads of other executive departments and agencies, as well as other senior officials.

SOURCE: Adapted from "National Security Council," in *National Security Council*, Office of the President of the United States, 2012, http://www.whitehouse.gov/administration/eop/nsc/ (accessed July 3, 2012)

vice chair, and four chiefs of the military services: the chief of staff of the army, the chief of naval operations, the chief of staff of the air force, and the commandant of the marine corps. The Joint Chiefs advise the president, the secretary of defense, and the NSC.

Reserve Components

Besides the regular forces of the U.S. military, there is an additional contingency force that makes up the reserve components. These include the Army, Navy, Air Force, and Marine Forces Reserves and two National Guard components: the Army National Guard and Air National Guard. The personnel in the reserve components are part time, meaning that they are technically civilians but can be called to service when needed. The Army, Navy, Air Force, and Marine Forces Reserves provide a backup source of trained personnel to their respective services. Many reservists are former members of the regular armed forces.

The National Guard evolved from the militias of early colonial America, which used trained civilian fighters who were under state control. It became a backup source for troops for the regular military services. The modern National Guard plays a dual federal-state role. State governments use the troops to provide security and protection services during natural disasters or other public emergencies. At the federal level the troops are trained, equipped, and deployed worldwide to support national security concerns. While deployed, these troops are integrated into the forces under the combatant commands.

Military Personnel

The DOD states in "About the Department of Defense" (2012, http://www.defense.gov/about/) that in 2012 it had 718,000 civilian employees.

Table 2.2 indicates that the active military duty forces were expected to number more than 1.4 million men and women at the end of fiscal year (FY) 2012. (A federal fiscal year extends from October through September; thus, FY 2012 covered October 2011 through September 2012.) The U.S. Army contained the largest number—562,000 members—followed by the U.S. Air Force with 332,800 members, the U.S. Navy with 325,700 members, and the U.S. Marine Corps with 202,100 members. Table 2.3 shows that the reserve component end strength was expected to be 847,100 in FY 2012 and decline to 837,400 by FY 2013 and to 825,600 by FY 2017.

As shown in Table 2.2, the number of active duty military forces is also projected to decline through FY 2017. This is due in part to the expected diminished role of the U.S. military in the war in Afghanistan. In addition, the DOD, like other federal agencies, expects to have budget cuts throughout the remainder of the second decade of the 21st century. In *Overview: United States Department of Defense Fiscal Year 2013 Budget Request* (February 2012, http://comptroller.defense.gov/defbudget/fy2013/FY2013 _Budget_Request_Overview_Book.pdf), the DOD notes that its future military forces "will be smaller and leaner."

Budget

Table 2.4 shows the DOD budgets for FYs 2001 to 2013. Note that the budget amount for FY 2013 is the requested amount. The DOD request for FY 2013 was $613.9 billion. This included $525.4 billion for the base budget and $88.5 billion for the United States' Overseas Contingency Operations (OCO)—the wars in Afghanistan and Iraq. The DOD budget doubled between FY 2001 (the year OCO began) and FY 2012. Table 2.5 provides a breakdown of the budgets for FYs 2012 (enacted) and 2013 (requested) by appropriation title. For both years the largest single budgeted item is operation and maintenance ($284 billion in FY 2012 and $272.7 billion in FY 2013). In *United States Department of Defense Fiscal Year 2011 Budget Request* (February 2010, http://www.defense.gov/news/d2010rolloutbrief1.pdf), the DOD describes the major components of each appropriation title as follows:

- Military personnel—salaries, wages, and allowances for subsistence and housing

- Operation and maintenance—training, base operating support, equipment maintenance, and communication and information technology systems

- Procurement—attainment of new ships, aircraft, missiles, and so on

- Research, development, testing, and evaluation (RDT&E)—research and development of new weapons and equipment

- Military construction—construction of military facilities and infrastructure

FIGURE 2.1

Department of Defense (DOD) organization chart, March 2012

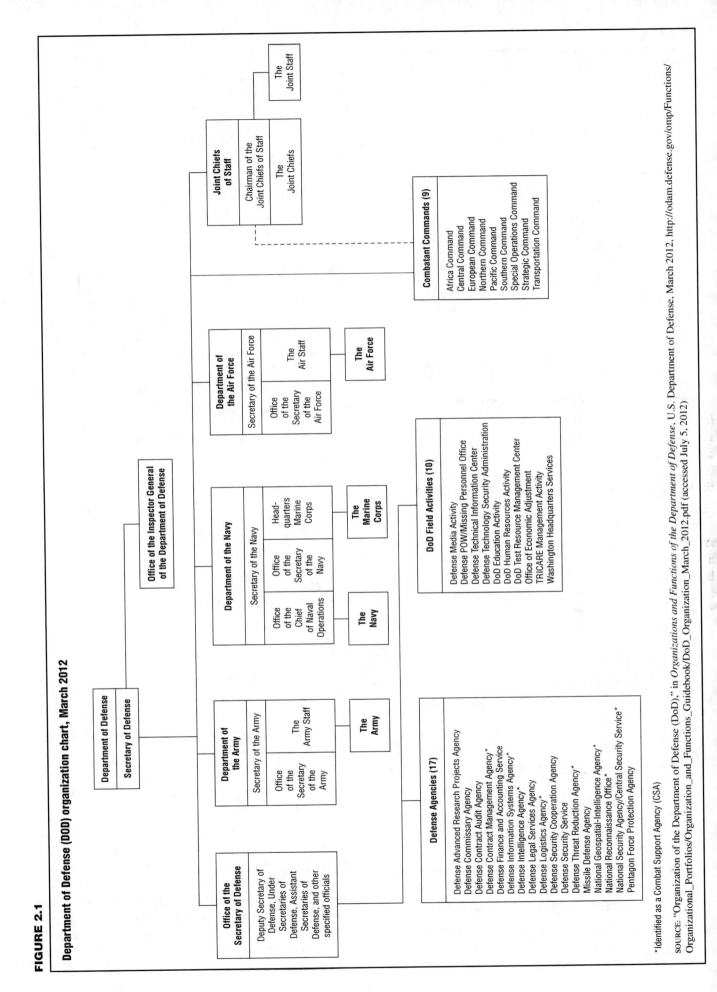

*Identified as a Combat Support Agency (CSA)

SOURCE: "Organization of the Department of Defense (DoD)," in *Organizations and Functions of the Department of Defense*, U.S. Department of Defense, March 2012, http://odam.defense.gov/omp/Functions/Organizational_Portfolios/Organization_and_Functions_Guidebook/DoD_Organization_March_2012.pdf (accessed July 5, 2012)

TABLE 2.2

Active duty military personnel, fiscal years 2001, 2012, 2013, and 2017

End strength	Fiscal year 2001	Fiscal year 2012ᵃ	Fiscal year 2013ᵇ	Fiscal year 2017 plan
Army	480,801	562,000	552,100	490,000
Navy	377,810	325,700	322,700	319,500
Marine Corps	172,934	202,100	197,300	182,100
Air Force	353,571	332,800	328,900	328,600
Total	**1,385,116**	**1,422,600**	**1,401,000**	**1,320,200**

Notes: Data for 2012–2017 are estimated.
OCO = Overseas Contingency Operations.
ᵃIncludes end strength funded in OCO appropriations. The OCO component of the fiscal year 2012 budget includes funding for 14,600 additional active Army soldiers—a temporary wartime allowance—to help the Army meet its commitments in Iraq and Afghanistan.
ᵇThe fiscal year 2013 Army base budget funds enduring end strength of 490,000 plus 12,400 Temporary End Strength Army Medical (TEAM) associated with non-deployable soldiers in the Integrated Disability System. Includes end strength funded in fiscal year 2013 OCO—49,700 Army and 15,200 Marine Corps.

SOURCE: "Figure 4-2. Active Military End Strength," in *Overview: United States Department of Defense Fiscal Year 2013 Budget Request*, U.S. Department of Defense, February 2012, http://comptroller.defense.gov/defbudget/fy2013/FY2013_Budget_Request_Overview_Book.pdf (accessed July 5, 2012)

TABLE 2.3

Military reserve personnel, fiscal years 2012, 2013, and 2017

[End strength in thousands]

Selected reserve	Fiscal year 2012 authorized	Fiscal year 2013 request	Fiscal year 2017 plan
Army reserve	205.0	205.0	205.0
Navy reserve	66.2	62.5	57.1
Marine Corps reserve	39.6	39.6	39.6
Air Force reserve	71.4	70.5	69.5
Army National Guard	358.2	358.2	353.2
Air National Guard	106.7	101.6	101.2
Total	**847.1**	**837.4**	**825.6**

Note: Data for 2012–2017 are estimated.
Numbers may not add due to rounding.

SOURCE: "Figure 4-4. Reserve Component End Strength," in *Overview: United States Department of Defense Fiscal Year 2013 Budget Request*, U.S. Department of Defense, February 2012, http://comptroller.defense.gov/defbudget/fy2013/FY2013_Budget_Request_Overview_Book.pdf (accessed July 5, 2012)

- Family housing—housing for families of active-duty military personnel

- Revolving and management funds—miscellaneous expenses such as fuel, commissaries (discount stores for active-duty and retired military personnel and their families), and renovations to the Pentagon

The DOD's budgets for fiscal years beyond 2013 were difficult to predict as of October 2012, because of uncertainties about future federal government spending.

Political wrangling over the nation's high debt and its spending priorities led to passage of the Budget Control Act of 2011. This act, which raised the U.S. national debt ceiling, included steep across-the-board cuts to spending by federal agencies, including the DOD, that are to go into effect in January 2013 unless Congress takes action. In "Defense Firms Fear U.S. Budget Cuts" (*Wall Street Journal*, July 9, 2012), Nathan Hodge reports that the Budget Control Act will cut over $1.2 trillion from the federal budget between 2013 and 2022; more than half of this amount is slated to come from the DOD budget.

SECTION 1206 FUNDS. DOD funds are not devoted solely to U.S. military forces. Section 1206 of the Fiscal Year 2006 National Defense Authorization Act authorized the DOD to use some of its allocated funds to train and equip the military forces of what are called "partner nations" to conduct counterterrorism activities or related military operations. According to Nina M. Serafino of the Congressional Research Service, in *Security Assistance Reform: "Section 1206" Background and Issues for Congress* (January 13, 2012, http://www.fas.org/sgp/crs/natsec/RS22855.pdf), as of February 2011 nearly $1.6 billion of DOD funds had been allotted or promised to other countries. The 10 largest recipients were:

- Yemen—$252.6 million

- Pakistan—$203.4 million

- Lebanon—$128.5 million

- Philippines—$82.8 million

- Indonesia—$80 million

- Bahrain—$50.3 million

- Malaysia—$43.8 million

- Georgia—$38.5 million

- Kenya—$34.3 million

- Kazakhstan—$31.8 million

The Section 1206 authorization was set to expire at the end of FY 2012; however, Congress included a one-year extension in its proposed National Defense Authorization Act for FY 2013. As of October 2012, that bill had not yet been passed.

THE INTELLIGENCE COMMUNITY

Intelligence is information, specifically information with strategic importance. Intelligence gathering means collecting information about individuals, groups, or nations that may pose a threat to U.S. national security. Reliable intelligence helps policy makers make sound decisions, plan effective strategies, and set reasonable priorities for the nation. Thus, intelligence is useful across many areas of national security, including military activities, foreign affairs, and law enforcement.

TABLE 2.4

Department of Defense (DOD) budget, fiscal years 2001–13

$ in billions	FY 01	FY 02	FY 03	FY 04	FY 05	FY 06	FY 07	FY 08	FY 09	FY 10	FY 11	FY 12	FY 13[a]
Base	296.9	328.1	364.9	376.5	400.0	410.5	431.4	479.0	513.2	527.9	528.2	530.6	525.4
OCO/Supplementals	13.4	16.8	72.5	90.7	75.6	115.7	166.2	186.9	145.6	162.3	158.8	115.1	88.5
Other[b]	5.8	—	—	0.3	3.2	8.1	3.1	—	7.4	0.7	—	—	—
Total	**316.2**	**345.0**	**437.4**	**467.6**	**478.9**	**534.4**	**600.9**	**665.9**	**666.3**	**690.9**	**687.0**	**645.7**	**613.9**

Notes: Numbers may not add due to rounding.
OCO = Overseas Contingency Operations.
Data is discretionary budget authority. Fiscal year 2001 through fiscal year 2011 are actual levels. The fiscal year 2012 is the appropriated or enacted amount.
[a]Budget request.
[b]Non-war supplemental appropriations, e.g. funding needed in base budget for fuel costs, hurricane relief, and other disaster relief.

SOURCE: "Figure 1–2. Department of Defense Topline since September 11th Attacks," in *Overview: United States Department of Defense Fiscal Year 2013 Budget Request*, U.S. Department of Defense, February 2012, http://comptroller.defense.gov/defbudget/fy2013/FY2013_Budget_Request_Overview_Book.pdf (accessed July 5, 2012)

TABLE 2.5

U.S. Department of Defense (DOD) budget by appropriation title, fiscal year 2012 and requested for fiscal year 2013

[Dollars in thousands]

Total budget	Fiscal year 2012 enacted	Fiscal year 2013 request	Delta '12–'13
Military personnel	153,111,873	149,171,893	−3,939,980
Operation and maintenance	283,989,327	272,745,422	−11,243,905
Procurement	120,579,571	108,510,595	−12,068,976
RD T&E	71,902,070	69,653,283	−2,248,787
Military construction	11,366,701	9,571,929	−1,794,772
Family housing	1,682,946	1,650,781	−32,165
Revolving and management funds	3,075,098	2,627,684	−447,414
Total	**645,707,586**	**613,931,587**	**−31,775,999**

RDT&E = research, development, testing, and evaluation.
Notes: Reflects disc retionary budget authority. Numbers may not add due to rounding

SOURCE: "Table 8-5. Total DoD Budget by Appropriation Title," in *Overview: United States Department of Defense Fiscal Year 2013 Budget Request*, U.S. Department of Defense, February 2012, http://comptroller.defense.gov/defbudget/fy2013/FY2013_Budget_Request_Overview_Book.pdf (accessed July 5, 2012)

TABLE 2.6

Components of the U.S. intelligence community

Central Intelligence Agency (CIA)
Bureau of Intelligence and Research, Department of State (INR)
Defense Intelligence Agency (DIA)
National Security Agency (NSA)
National Reconnaissance Office (NRO)
National Geospatial-Intelligence Agency (NGA)
Federal Bureau of Investigation (FBI)
Army intelligence
Navy intelligence
Air Force intelligence
Marine Corps intelligence
Department of Homeland Security (DHS)
Coast Guard (CG)
Treasury department
Energy department
Drug Enforcement Agency (DEA)

Note: As defined at 50 U.S.C. 401a(4).

SOURCE: Adapted from Richard A. Best, Jr., "Intelligence Community," in *Intelligence Issues for Congress*, Congressional Research Service, March 3, 2011, https://opencrs.com/document/RL33539/2011-03-03/download/1005/ (accessed July 5, 2012)

Counterintelligence is a related field in which the goal is to thwart the intelligence gathering and hostile acts of one's enemies. The National Security Act of 1947 defines counterintelligence as "information gathered, and activities conducted, to protect against espionage, other intelligence activities, sabotage, or assassinations conducted by or on behalf of foreign governments or elements thereof, foreign organizations, or foreign persons, or international terrorist activities." For example, counterintelligence operations might include passing false information to known enemy spies. Both intelligence and counterintelligence are areas in which secrecy and espionage (spying) play important roles.

The U.S. intelligence community (IC) consists of 16 federal agencies and departments that are engaged in intelligence activities. (See Table 2.6.) The Central Intelligence Agency (CIA) is the primary agency concerned with U.S.

intelligence and is self-contained. All other agencies are part of larger organizations devoted to other tasks within the government. For example, eight of the agencies are part of the DOD. Their mission is primarily to support military operations. Cooperation and sharing of information between IC components is considered critical to protecting national security.

The Office of the Director of National Intelligence

The IC is overseen by the director of national intelligence. In "About the ODNI" (2012, http://www.dni.gov/who.htm), the Office of the Director of National Intelligence (ODNI) notes that it began operating in 2005 following passage of the Intelligence Reform and Terrorism Prevention Act of 2004. The ODNI's goal is "to effectively integrate foreign, military and domestic intelligence in defense of the homeland and of United States

TABLE 2.7

Office of the Director of National Intelligence organization chart, 2012

Leadership
Director (DNI)
Principal Deputy Director (PDDNI)
Chief Management Officer (CMO)

Core Mission
Intelligence Integration (DDNI/II)
Assistant Deputy DNI Intelligence Integration (ADDNI/II)

Integration Management Council (IMC)
• National Intelligence Managers (NIMs)
National Intelligence Council (NIC)
Mission Integration Division (MID)

National Counterterrorism Center (NCTC)*
National Counterproliferation Center (NCPC)*
National Counterintelligence Executive (NCIX)*
*Leaders of these organizations also serve as National Intelligence Managers.

Enablers

Policy & Strategy (P&S)

Partner Engagement (PE)

Acquisition, Technology, & Facilities (AT&F)

Systems & Resource Analyses (SRA)

Chief Human Capital Officer (CHCO)

Chief Financial Officer (CFO)

Chief Information Officer (CIO)

Information Sharing Environment (ISE)

Oversight

General Counsel (GC)

Civil Liberties and Privacy Office (CLPO)

Public Affairs (PAO)

Inspector General (IG)

IC Equal Employment Opportunity & Diversity (EEOD)

Legislative Affairs (OLA)

SOURCE: "Office of the Director of National Intelligence: Organizational Chart," in *Office of the Director of National Intelligence Organization Chart*, Office of the Director of National Intelligence, 2012, http://www.dni.gov/index.php/about/organization (accessed July 9, 2012)

interests abroad." Table 2.7 shows the organizational structure of the ODNI. The ODNI lists in *ODNI Fact Sheet* (July 2010, http://www.fas.org/irp/news/2010/07/odni071610.pdf) the following duties for the director of national intelligence:

- Acts as "the principal intelligence advisor" to the president

- Sets IC priorities with "clear and measurable goals and objectives"

- Forms policies and budgets

- Leads the IC and ensures its "personnel, expertise, and capabilities" are integrated across agencies

- Monitors the performance of the IC agencies and their leaders

- Oversees the National Intelligence Program (NIP) budget

In "National Intelligence Program: The Budget for Fiscal Year 2013" (February 2012, http://www.gpo.gov/fdsys/pkg/BUDGET-2013-BUD/pdf/BUDGET-2013-BUD-8.pdf), the ODNI notes that the NIP funds IC activities for the ODNI, the CIA, and "six Federal departments." According to the Federal Bureau of Investigation (2012, http://www.fbi.gov/about-us/nsb/faqs), its National Security Branch is funded by the NIP. Intelligence agency budgets have historically been considered confidential by the federal government. The ODNI indicates that the NIP budget request for FY 2013 was $52.6 billion; however, it does not provide any details as to how this money was divided among the respective IC members.

The National Intelligence Strategy

In August 2009 President Barack Obama (1961–) released the most recent version of *The National Intelligence Strategy of the United States of America* (http://www.hsdl.org/?view&did=33833). This document is updated every four years. The NIS, as it is called, describes the strategic national security challenges that the United States faces, lists goals and objectives for the IC to meet, and outlines the role of the director of national intelligence in leading the IC. The NIS divides national security challenges into three categories:

- Nation-states—Iran, North Korea, China, and Russia

- Nonstate and substate actors—violent extremist groups, insurgents, and transnational criminal organizations (e.g., organizations that traffic drugs, weapons, and cash)

- Transnational forces and trends—global economic crises, failed states and ungoverned spaces, climate change and energy competition, rapid technological change and dissemination of information, and the risk of pandemic disease

In addition, the NIS lists four "strategic goals" for the IC:

- Enable wise national security policies by continuously monitoring and assessing the international security environment to warn policymakers of threats and inform them of opportunities

- Support effective national security action

TABLE 2.8

Mission and enterprise objectives of the intelligence community

Mission objectives

MO1: Combat violent extremism
MO2: Counter WMD proliferation
MO3: Provide strategic intelligence and warning
MO4: Integrate counterintelligence
MO5: Enhance cybersecurity
MO6: Support current operations

Enterprise objectives

EO1: Enhance community mission management
EO2: Strengthen partnerships
EO3: Streamline business processes
EO4: Improve information integration and sharing
EO5: Advance S&T/R&D
EO6: Develop the workforce
EO7: Improve acquisition

WMD = Weapons of mass destruction.
S&T/R&D = Science and technology/research and development

SOURCE: "Goals and Objectives," in *The National Intelligence Strategy of the United States of America*, Director of National Intelligence, August 2009, http://www.hsdl.org/?view&did=33833 (accessed July 5, 2012)

- Deliver balanced and improving capabilities that leverage the diversity of the IC's unique competencies and evolve to support new missions and operating concepts

- Operate as a single integrated team

The first two goals are supported by six mission objectives. (See Table 2.8.) The last two goals are supported by seven enterprise objectives.

The National Counterintelligence Strategy

According to the National Counterintelligence Policy Board, in *The National Counterintelligence Strategy of the United States of America* (2009, http://www.ncix.gov/publications/strategy/docs/NatlCIStrategy2009.pdf), the IC conducts counterintelligence activities in both a defensive and offensive manner. The board lists four specific areas of focus for the nation's counterintelligence (CI) efforts:

- Detect insider threats—detect insiders who seek to exploit their authorized access in order to harm U.S. interests.

- Penetrate foreign services—penetrate hostile foreign intelligence services to determine their intentions, capabilities, and activities.

- Integrate CI with cyber—employ CI across the cyber domain to protect critical infrastructure.

- Assure the supply chain—assure the national security community's supply chain from foreign intelligence exploitation.

CENTRAL INTELLIGENCE AGENCY

The CIA is the leading provider of U.S. intelligence and the primary support provider for the other IC agencies. It is a civilian agency charged with collecting and analyzing intelligence and taking action to protect U.S.

national security. The CIA headquarters are located in Langley, Virginia, at the George Bush Center for Intelligence. The CIA's analytical capabilities are supposed to be all-encompassing, and its reach is intended to be worldwide (outside the borders of the United States). In "CIA Vision, Mission & Values" (December 30, 2011, https://www.cia.gov/about-cia/cia-vision-mission-values/index.html), the CIA describes itself as follows:

We are the nation's first line of defense. We accomplish what others cannot accomplish and go where others cannot go. We carry out our mission by:

- Collecting information that reveals the plans, intentions and capabilities of our adversaries and provides the basis for decision and action.

- Producing timely analysis that provides insight, warning and opportunity to the President and decisionmakers charged with protecting and advancing America's interests.

- Conducting covert action at the direction of the President to preempt threats or achieve US policy objectives.

Figure 2.2 shows the organization chart for the major components of the CIA as of 2011.

History of the CIA

The CIA's roots lie in the Office of the Coordinator of Information, which was created by President Franklin D. Roosevelt (1882–1945) in July 1941. The surprise Japanese attack on the U.S. naval base at Pearl Harbor, Hawaii, later that year was viewed as an immense intelligence failure and spurred the creation of a much more sophisticated and powerful agency called the Office of Strategic Services (OSS). The OSS began operating in June 1942. After World War II ended in 1945, the OSS was officially abolished, and its functions were transferred to the U.S. Department of State (DOS) and the Department of War (later part of the DOD).

In 1946 President Harry S. Truman (1884–1972) created a new civilian intelligence agency called the Central Intelligence Group. It was tasked with detecting strategic threats to the United States via the operation of clandestine (secret) activities around the world. The National Security Act of 1947 created a new intelligence structure in which a Central Intelligence Agency operated under the direction of a National Security Council and the president. However, the scope of the CIA was limited to matters outside of law enforcement and outside U.S. borders.

The passage of the Central Intelligence Agency Act in 1949 granted the CIA unprecedented financial freedom. In *The Work of a Nation* (August 2009, https://www.cia.gov/library/publications/additional-publications/the-work-of-a-nation/86402%20Factbook-low.pdf), the CIA notes that the act "exempted CIA from many of the usual limitations on the expenditure of federal funds. It provided that CIA funds

FIGURE 2.2

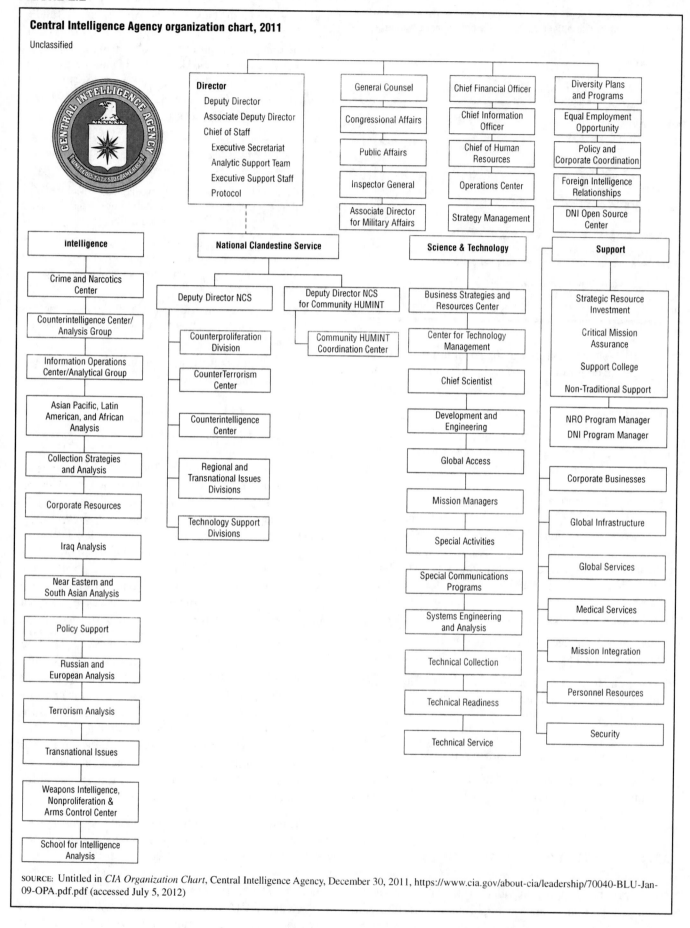

Central Intelligence Agency organization chart, 2011

Unclassified

SOURCE: Untitled in *CIA Organization Chart*, Central Intelligence Agency, December 30, 2011, https://www.cia.gov/about-cia/leadership/70040-BLU-Jan-09-OPA.pdf.pdf (accessed July 5, 2012)

could be included in the budgets of other departments and then transferred to the Agency without regard to the restrictions placed on the initial appropriation." The act also allowed the agency to use "confidential fiscal and administrative procedures." In other words, the CIA's budget and spending became state secrets.

DOD INTELLIGENCE AGENCIES

Four IC members are defense agencies under the DOD: the Defense Intelligence Agency, the National Geospatial-Intelligence Agency, the National Reconnaissance Office, and the National Security Agency/Central Security Service. (See Figure 2.1.) In addition, the four military branches—the army, navy, marine corps, and air force—each have an intelligence agency that is a member of the IC. A summary of the activities of the eight DOD intelligence agencies is included in Table 2.9.

Military intelligence is information that is important to military decisions and activities. The agencies and activities related to military intelligence are collectively known as the military intelligence program (MIP).

TABLE 2.9

Intelligence agencies within the Department of Defense (DOD)

Defense Intelligence Agency

Produces and manages foreign military intelligence to provide assessments of foreign military intentions and capabilities to U.S. military commanders and civilian policymakers.

National Geospatial-Intelligence Agency

Collects and generates information about the Earth, which is used for navigation, national security, U.S. military operations, and humanitarian aid efforts.

National Reconnaissance Office

Staffed by detailees from CIA, the Air Force and other IC agencies and elements. The NRO is our nation's eyes and ears in space. They design, build, and operate the nation's signals and imagery reconnaissance satellites. Information from these satellites is used to warn of potential foreign military aggression, monitor weapons programs, enforce arms control and environmental treaties, and assess the impact of natural and manmade disasters.

National Security Agency

Our nation's cryptologic organization charged with protecting the government's information systems and producing foreign signals intelligence information. Their work includes cryptanalysis, cryptography, mathematics, computer science, and foreign language analysis.

U.S. Air Force, Intelligence, Surveillance and Reconnaissance

Conducts surveillance and reconnaissance to provide a tactical advantage to our troops.

U.S. Army, Army Military Intelligence

Supplies relevant and timely information, pertaining to ground troops and movements, to Army and other military personnel at all levels.

U.S. Marine Corps, Marine Corps Intelligence Activity

Responsible for intelligence, counterintelligence, terrorism, classified information, security review, and cryptologic activities.

U.S. Navy, Office of Naval Intelligence

Support maritime operations worldwide and defend U.S. naval borders. Naval intelligence professionals are deployed throughout the Navy as well as the Department of Defense.

SOURCE: Adapted from *Our Strength Lies in Who We Are*, U.S. Intelligence Community and Office of the Director of National Intelligence, 2012, http://www.intelligence.gov/about-the-intelligence-community/member-agencies/ (accessed July 9, 2012)

Defense Intelligence Agency

The Defense Intelligence Agency (DIA) coordinates the overall performance of military intelligence for the MIP. The agency (May 18, 2012, http://www.dia.mil/about/faq) states that its mission is to "prevent strategic surprise and deliver a decision advantage to warfighters, defense planners, and policymakers." In 2012 the DIA had over 16,500 military and civilian employees worldwide. Figure 2.3 shows the organization chart for the DIA. The agency is headquartered at the Pentagon, which is located in Arlington, Virginia, but it has a Washington, D.C., address. Other major DIA facilities include the Defense Intelligence Analysis Center at Bolling Air Force Base in Washington, D.C.; the National Center for Medical Intelligence at Fort Detrick in Frederick, Maryland; and the Missile and Space Intelligence Center at Redstone Arsenal in Huntsville, Alabama.

Like the ODNI, the DOD publishes only its total budget request for intelligence each year. No details or specifics are provided by the government. In the press release "DOD Releases Military Intelligence Program Requested Top Line Budget for Fiscal 2013" (February 13, 2012, http://www.defense.gov/releases/release.aspx?releaseid=15058), the DOD notes that it requested $19.2 billion for the MIP for FY 2013.

DOD AND CIA INTELLIGENCE REFORM

During the 1970s DOD and CIA intelligence operations came under fire when stories were published in the media about surveillance that was conducted against U.S. civilians. In 1970 Christopher H. Pyle, a former army intelligence officer, alleged that his agency had collected massive amounts of intelligence on Americans who were engaged in protest activities, primarily against the Vietnam War (1954–1975). Pyle also claimed that plainclothes undercover army agents had been spying on protest groups since the 1960s. The allegations resulted in federal investigations led by Senators Sam J. Ervin (1896–1985; D-NC) and Frank Forrester Church III (1924–1984; D-ID).

In 1974 Seymour M. Hersh stunned the nation when he alleged in "Huge C.I.A. Operation Reported in U.S. against Antiwar Forces, Other Dissidents in Nixon Years" (*New York Times*, December 22, 1974) that the CIA had engaged in a "massive, illegal domestic intelligence operation" against antiwar protesters and other groups. Hersh claimed that the CIA had intelligence files on at least 10,000 U.S. citizens and had engaged in illegal surveillance activities, such as wiretapping and mail interdiction (secretly opening and reading mail sent to other people) since the 1950s. Spying on Americans was a direct violation of the CIA charter.

The U.S. Senate and the U.S. House of Representatives conducted investigations that uncovered more questionable activities by the CIA, including attempts to assassinate

FIGURE 2.3

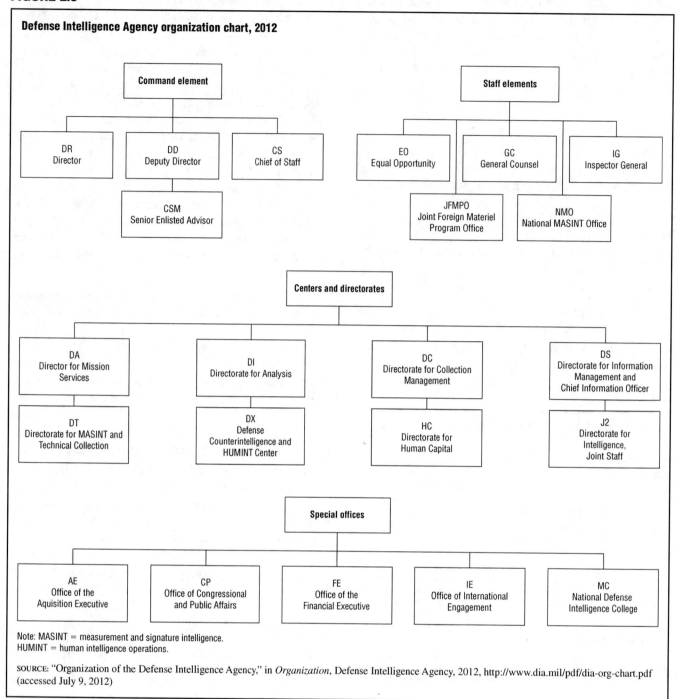

Defense Intelligence Agency organization chart, 2012

Note: MASINT = measurement and signature intelligence.
HUMINT = human intelligence operations.

SOURCE: "Organization of the Defense Intelligence Agency," in *Organization*, Defense Intelligence Agency, 2012, http://www.dia.mil/pdf/dia-org-chart.pdf (accessed July 9, 2012)

foreign leaders in Chile, the Congo, Cuba, the Dominican Republic, and Vietnam. In response, President Gerald R. Ford (1913–2006) issued an executive order banning the assassination of foreign officials. The Foreign Intelligence Surveillance Act (FISA) of 1978 established the Foreign Intelligence Surveillance Court (FISC) from which authorization must be obtained for the conduct of electronic surveillance or physical searches of people alleged to be acting on behalf of a foreign power to threaten U.S. national security. More detailed information about FISA and the FISC is provided in Chapter 8.

THE FEDERAL BUREAU OF INVESTIGATION'S NATIONAL SECURITY BRANCH

The Federal Bureau of Investigation (FBI) is the nation's premier agency devoted to law enforcement and operates under the U.S. Department of Justice. John F. Fox explains in "The Birth of the Federal Bureau of Investigation" (July 2003, http://www.fbi.gov/about-us/history/highlights-of-history/articles/birth) that the FBI was created in 1908. Its primary focus was the investigation of a handful of federal crimes, such as land fraud. During World War I (1914–1918) the FBI acquired new responsibilities in counterintelligence, in particular the prevention of espionage and sabotage.

During the 1920s and 1930s the agency was preoccupied with gangsters and bank robbers. At the onset of World War II, the FBI once again took a key role in combating foreign spies. It was also granted power to investigate subversives (people who attempt to undermine or overthrow the government). Throughout the Cold War the FBI considered Communist Party members and sympathizers within the United States to be a serious threat to national security. During the late 1960s a new element arose within American society that concerned the FBI. It was called the "new left," and it included violent anti–Vietnam War, antiestablishment protesters and activists. J. Edgar Hoover (1895–1972), the head of the FBI, established the Counter Intelligence Program, a massive surveillance program, that would later arouse claims that the agency had violated the civil liberties of law-abiding Americans engaged in peaceful antiwar protests. During the 1970s new limits were placed on the FBI's abilities to conduct counterintelligence and domestic security investigations.

Terrorism became a priority for the nation as the Cold War fizzled out. In 1986 Congress gave the FBI jurisdiction over terrorist acts that were committed against American citizens outside U.S. borders. The agency played a crucial role in investigating the bombings at the Khobar Towers (a housing facility for U.S. military personnel) in Saudi Arabia in 1996, the bombings at two U.S. embassies in East Africa in 1998, and a terrorist attack against the USS *Cole* in Yemen in 2000. The FBI also played a crucial role in investigating the terrorist bombing of the World Trade Center in 1993 and the terrorist attacks of September 11, 2001.

The Uniting and Strengthening America by Providing Appropriate Tools Required to Intercept and Obstruct Terrorism (USA PATRIOT) Act of 2001 (which is known simply as the Patriot Act) greatly expanded the FBI's role in counterterrorism by allowing broader use of surveillance techniques by intelligence agents. In 2005 President George W. Bush (1946–) directed the FBI to combine all of its intelligence and counterterrorism elements into one organization under the direction of a high-ranking FBI official. The result was the FBI's National Security Branch (NSB). According to the NSB (2012, http://www.fbi.gov/about-us/nsb/mission), its mission is "to lead and coordinate intelligence efforts that drive actions to protect the United States."

The organizational structure of the NSB is shown in Figure 2.4. Its major components (August 2011, http://www.fbi.gov/about-us/nsb/national-security-branch-brochure-2011) are as follows:

- Counterintelligence Division—prevents and investigates foreign intelligence activities conducted within the United States

- Counterterrorism Division—uses an "intelligence-driven approach" to investigate domestic and international terrorism

- Directorate of Intelligence—provides a workforce that is devoted to collecting intelligence; its agents work at the FBI headquarters and are embedded in Field Intelligence Groups spread throughout the country

- Terrorist Screening Center—maintains a comprehensive watch list of known or suspected terrorists that is made available to federal, state, and local authorities

- Weapons of Mass Destruction Directorate—leads U.S. efforts to prevent countries and subnational entities (i.e., groups and individuals) from obtaining materials and technologies related to weapons of mass destruction, such as nuclear bombs and chemical and biological weapons

As noted earlier in this chapter, the NSB's budget is part of the NIP budget.

OTHER INTELLIGENCE AGENCIES

Besides the CIA, the eight DOD intelligence agencies, and the NSB, the IC includes six other members whose roles are described by the IC and the ODNI in "Our Strength Lies in Who We Are" (2012, http://www.intelligence.gov/about-the-intelligence-community/member-agencies/). The following is a brief summary of the six agencies:

- U.S. Department of Energy, Office of Intelligence and Counterintelligence—provides technical intelligence regarding energy issues and foreign nuclear weapons and materials.

- U.S. Department of Homeland Security (DHS), Intelligence and Analysis—collects intelligence related to terrorist threats within the United States. The overall DHS activities are described in detail in Chapter 5.

- U.S. Coast Guard Intelligence—an agency of the DHS that collects intelligence related to maritime security and homeland defense.

- DOS, Intelligence and Research—conducts intelligence activities to support diplomatic goals. According to the DOS, in *Congressional Budget Justification, Volume 1: Department of State Operations, Fiscal Year 2012* (February 2012, http://www.state.gov/documents/organization/181061.pdf), the budget request for its intelligence operations totaled $68.7 million for FY 2013.

- U.S. Department of the Treasury, Office of Intelligence and Analysis—collects intelligence related to domestic and international financial matters. It lies within the Treasury's Office of Terrorism and Financial Intelligence, which is described later in this chapter.

FIGURE 2.4

Federal Bureau of Investigation's National Security Branch organization chart, 2012

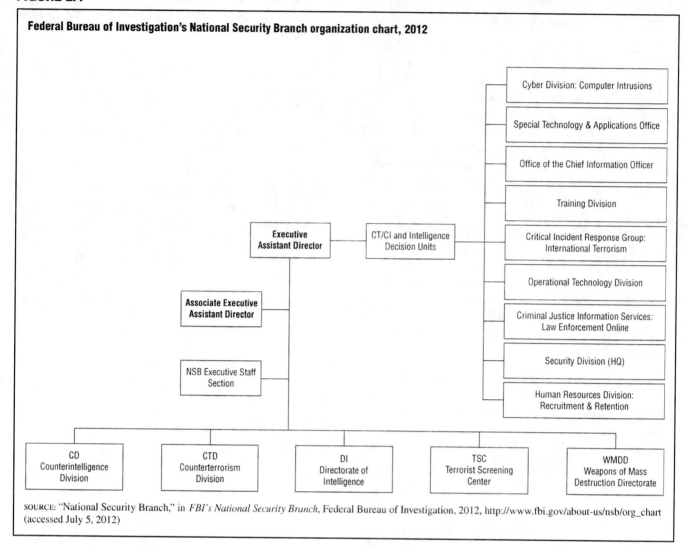

SOURCE: "National Security Branch," in *FBI's National Security Branch*, Federal Bureau of Investigation, 2012, http://www.fbi.gov/about-us/nsb/org_chart (accessed July 5, 2012)

- Drug Enforcement Administration—conducts drug enforcement activities. Any intelligence relevant to national security that is obtained during these activities is shared with the IC.

Intelligence Disciplines

According to the IC, in "Data Gathering" (2012, http://www.intelligence.gov/about-the-intelligence-community/how-intelligence-works/data-gathering.html), there are six major intelligence collection disciplines:

1. Human-Source Intelligence (HUMINT)—the collection of intelligence from human sources. This includes both overt (open) activities by diplomats and military attachés and covert (secret) actions conducted by spies. HUMINT sources include documents, photographs, and people who live or work in foreign countries or travel to them. This intelligence discipline is widely used by the CIA, the DOD, the DOS, and the NSB. The National Clandestine Service, a unit formed by the CIA and ODNI, is considered to be "the national authority" on HUMINT operations.

2. Signals Intelligence (SIGINT)—the interception of electronic communications or other transmitted signals. The National Security Agency oversees SIGINT operations for the IC and is considered to be the nation's premier cryptologic organization.

3. Imagery Intelligence (IMINT)—the analysis of images obtained via photography, radar imaging, and other optical and electronic methods. The National Geospatial-Intelligence Agency manages all IMINT activities for the IC.

4. Measurement and Signature Intelligence (MASINT)—the IC describes MASINT as "scientific and technical intelligence information used to locate, identify, or describe distinctive characteristics of specific targets." This discipline relies on techniques in a variety of scientific fields, including acoustics, optics, chemistry, materials, and nuclear science. The DIA operates the central MASINT organization for the IC.

5. Geospatial Intelligence (GEOINT)—the analysis and production of imagery and mapping data. Sources

include government and commercial satellites, reconnaissance aircraft, maps, commercial databases, and other data. GEOINT is conducted primarily by the National Geospatial-Intelligence Agency.

6. Open-Source Intelligence (OSINT)—the collection and translation of publicly available information from non-U.S. media sources that are accessed through the Internet, television, newspapers, radio, and commercially produced databases. The major collectors of OSINT are the Foreign Broadcast Information Service and the DOD's National Air and Space Intelligence Center.

U.S. DEPARTMENT OF STATE

As noted earlier, the DOS Bureau of Intelligence and Research is part of the IC; however, that bureau represents just a small part of the role that the DOS plays in national security. The DOS is the primary agency tasked with representing U.S. interests abroad through the use of diplomacy. Diplomacy is defined by *Merriam Webster's Collegiate Dictionary* (2003) as "the art and practice of conducting negotiations between nations" and "skill in handling affairs without arousing hostility." In a modern political sense, diplomacy can be defined as any foreign policy action short of armed aggression, such as a trade embargo imposed on another nation to punish it for some transgression.

History

The DOS was created in 1789 from a previous agency known as the Department of Foreign Affairs. Historians consider Benjamin Franklin (1706–1790) to be the nation's first diplomat. In 1778 he was pivotal in securing two treaties with France: the Treaty of Amity and Commerce (which promoted trade) and the Treaty of Alliance (which formed a military alliance between the two nations). Franklin was called a plenipotentiary, a word derived from a Latin phrase meaning "full power." In other words, he had been granted full power to represent the U.S. government abroad.

The Treaty of Amity and Commerce was the first of many treaties the United States would forge with other nations regarding peaceful relations, commerce, travel, navigation, extradition of criminals, and other nonmilitary affairs. The Treaty of Alliance would be the only bilateral military agreement assumed by the United States for nearly two centuries.

Organization and Personnel

At the highest level, DOS officials craft U.S. foreign policy in concert with the president and negotiate with the leaders and foreign ministers of other nations. The DOS is headed by the secretary of state, who is a member of both the president's cabinet and the NSC. Figure 2.5 shows the organization chart for the main components of the DOS as of 2012. The two positions located underneath and to the left of the secretary of state are the administrators of the U.S. Agency for International Development (USAID) and the U.S. Mission to the United Nations. The latter is more widely known as the U.S. ambassador to the United Nations. This person is appointed by the president and confirmed by the U.S. Senate to represent the United States at the United Nations. USAID is the principal agency through which the federal government provides financial assistance to foreign nations and peoples.

In *United States Department of State Fiscal Year 2011 Agency Financial Report* (November 2011, http://www.state.gov/documents/organization/177397.pdf), the DOS notes that it employed 29,832 full-time employees in FY 2011—13,518 Americans worked in the Foreign Service (i.e., stationed in foreign countries), 10,645 Americans worked primarily in DOS offices in Washington, D.C., and 5,669 foreign nationals (i.e., citizens of foreign countries) worked at locations around the world.

Mission, Goals, and Budget

Figure 2.6 lists the mission statement and goals of the DOS and USAID for FYs 2012 and 2013. Even though all the goals relate in some way to U.S. national security, the first goal is the most direct, in that it calls for the agencies to "counter threats to the United States." Note that the mention of "frontline states" in the second goal refers to Afghanistan, Iraq, and Pakistan.

The DOS indicates in *Executive Budget Summary: Function 150 & Other International Programs, Fiscal Year 2013* (February 2012, http://www.state.gov/documents/organization/183755.pdf) that its budget request for FY 2013 was $51.6 billion. This amount includes $8.2 billion devoted to OCO.

U.S. Diplomatic Relations

According to the DOS, in the fact sheet "Independent States in the World" (January 3, 2012, http://www.state.gov/s/inr/rls/4250.htm), the United States recognized 195 independent states around the world in 2012. An independent state is defined by the DOS as "people politically organized into a sovereign state with a definite territory recognized as independent by the US." The DOS indicates that as of January 2012 the United States had official diplomatic relations with all but four of the 195 recognized independent states. Those four nations were:

- Bhutan
- Cuba
- Iran
- North Korea

Bhutan is a tiny mountainous country located between India and Tibet. For decades, Bhutan has chosen to remain isolated from the outside world to protect its

FIGURE 2.5

U.S. Department of State (DOS) organization chart, 2012

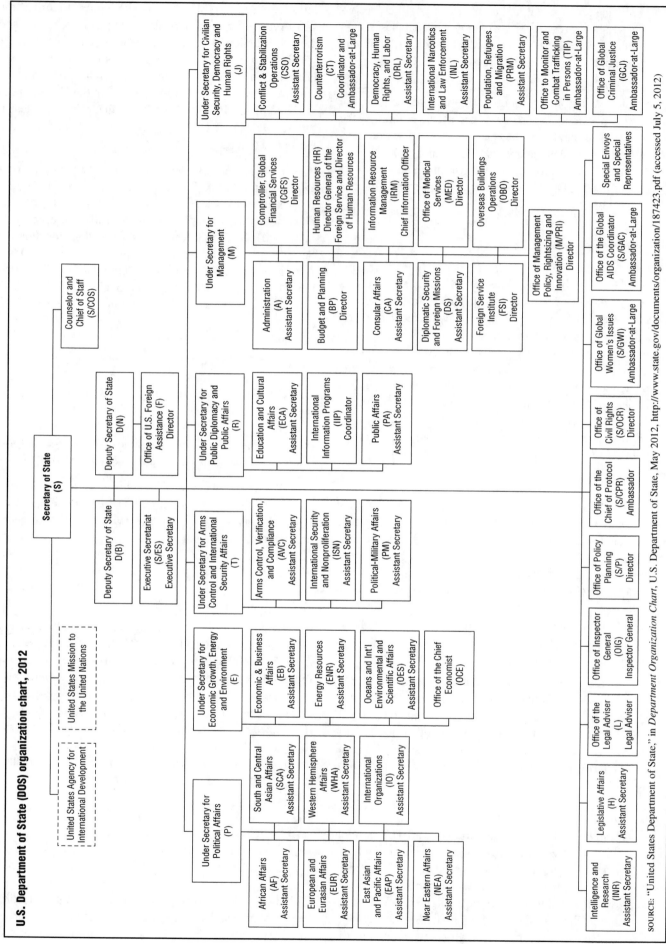

SOURCE: "United States Department of State," in *Department Organization Chart*, U.S. Department of State, May 2012, http://www.state.gov/documents/organization/187423.pdf (accessed July 5, 2012)

FIGURE 2.6

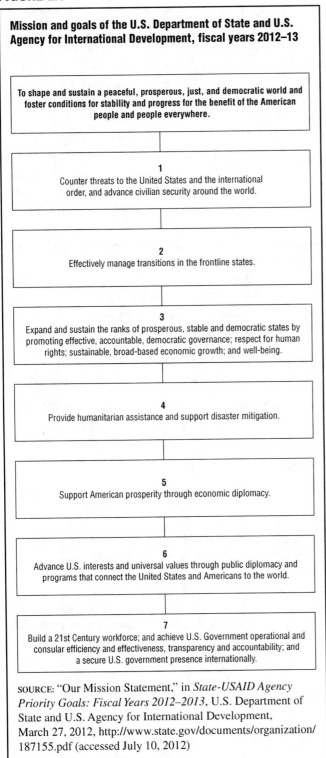

Mission and goals of the U.S. Department of State and U.S. Agency for International Development, fiscal years 2012–13

To shape and sustain a peaceful, prosperous, just, and democratic world and foster conditions for stability and progress for the benefit of the American people and people everywhere.

1
Counter threats to the United States and the international order, and advance civilian security around the world.

2
Effectively manage transitions in the frontline states.

3
Expand and sustain the ranks of prosperous, stable and democratic states by promoting effective, accountable, democratic governance; respect for human rights; sustainable, broad-based economic growth; and well-being.

4
Provide humanitarian assistance and support disaster mitigation.

5
Support American prosperity through economic diplomacy.

6
Advance U.S. interests and universal values through public diplomacy and programs that connect the United States and Americans to the world.

7
Build a 21st Century workforce; and achieve U.S. Government operational and consular efficiency and effectiveness, transparency and accountability; and a secure U.S. government presence internationally.

SOURCE: "Our Mission Statement," in *State-USAID Agency Priority Goals: Fiscal Years 2012–2013*, U.S. Department of State and U.S. Agency for International Development, March 27, 2012, http://www.state.gov/documents/organization/187155.pdf (accessed July 10, 2012)

deeply religious Buddhist society. The United States conducts informal relations with Bhutan through the U.S. embassy in India.

In January 1961 the United States broke diplomatic ties with Cuba after it became obvious that Fidel Castro (1926–), the new Cuban leader, intended to form a communist government. In 1977 the United States opened an Interests Section office in Havana, Cuba. Even though it

is staffed by U.S. Foreign Service personnel, the office is officially a part of the Swiss embassy. The U.S. Interests Section handles requests for visas and performs other diplomatic functions. Cuba maintains a similar office at the Swiss embassy in Washington, D.C.

In April 1980 the United States broke diplomatic relations with Iran after the Iranian government refused to intervene on behalf of the U.S. diplomats who were taken hostage by Iranian militants at the U.S. embassy. A U.S. Interests Section office was later opened at the Swiss embassy in Tehran, Iran. Likewise, Iran maintains an Interests Section office at the Pakistani embassy in Washington, D.C.

Following World War II the Korea Peninsula was split into two occupied territories: the north under Soviet control and the south under U.S. control. This was intended to be a temporary arrangement until the two halves could be reunited as one nation. In 1948 South Korea adopted a constitution and became a sovereign nation. However, Cold War politics and the Korean War (1950–1953) prevented reunification from occurring. The United States did not form diplomatic relations with the communist government that assumed power in North Korea.

Travel Documents: Passports and Visas

One of the functions performed by the DOS is the issuance of international travel documents: passports for U.S. citizens and visas for foreign citizens.

A passport is an official travel document that verifies a person's identity and nationality. The DOS issues passports to U.S. citizens. Most foreign governments require U.S. visitors to possess a passport and show it when entering and leaving their countries. Likewise, a passport is typically required for U.S. citizens to reenter the United States after traveling abroad.

A visa is a document that indicates permission has been given by a government for a person of foreign nationality to travel to that country. DOS offices at U.S. embassies and consulates can grant visas to foreign nationals to travel to the United States. A U.S.-granted visa indicates a person is eligible to enter the United States for a specific purpose. However, the determination of whether or not to grant entry is made by immigration officers at U.S. ports of entry (airports and land border crossings).

FOREIGN ECONOMIC ASSISTANCE

One of the historic diplomatic policies of the United States has been foreign aid. As noted in Chapter 1, there are two major types of foreign aid: economic assistance and military assistance. Foreign economic assistance includes humanitarian aid that is designed to generate goodwill for the United States. Since the terrorist attacks of September 11, 2001, foreign economic assistance has been increasingly viewed as a tool of national security.

As shown in Table 2.10, USAID distributed nearly $14.1 billion in foreign economic assistance in FY 2010, while the DOS distributed $12.2 billion. Combined, the two agencies provided $387.9 billion in total foreign economic assistance between FYs 1946 and 2010.

PUBLIC DIPLOMACY

Public diplomacy is diplomacy directed toward the foreign public at large, rather than just toward foreign governments. Public diplomacy projects are conducted by various entities within the U.S. government, including the DOS, the DOD, USAID, and the Broadcasting Board of Governors. The projects are designed in accordance with guidance that is provided by the White House and the NSC (specifically the deputy national security adviser for strategic communications and global outreach).

Broadcasting Board of Governors

The Broadcasting Board of Governors (BBG) oversees government and government-sponsored international broadcasting services, including both radio and television. Even though these services have a variety of different audiences, they have the common goal of delivering information about U.S. actions, goals, culture, and opinions to people who might otherwise not have access to such data. According to the BBG, in *2011 Annual Report, U.S. International Broadcasting: Impact through Innovation and Integration* (June 2012, http://www.bbg.gov/wp-content/media/2012/06/BBGAnnualReport_LoRes_Part1.pdf), its broadcasting services reach "televisions, radios, laptops and mobile devices in more than 100 countries, bringing news and information to scattered populations in 59 languages." The BBG estimates that its broadcasts had a weekly audience of 187 million people in 2011. The International Broadcasting Bureau (2012, http://www.bbg.gov/about-the-agency/organizational-chart/) performs the administrative and marketing activities of the BBG and provides transmission services for the broadcasters. In 2012 there were five broadcasters:

- Voice of America (http://www.bbg.gov/broadcasters/voa/)—this service includes programs in 43 languages via radio, television, and the Internet. It airs approximately 1,500 hours of news, information, and educational and cultural shows per week. Its worldwide weekly audience was estimated at 141 million people in 2012.

- Radio Free Europe/Radio Liberty (http://www.bbg.gov/broadcasters/rferl/)—this service can be heard across eastern Europe and central and southwestern Asia. The broadcasts are in 28 languages and are available over the radio, television, and Internet. Key outlets include Radio Azadi in Afghanistan, Radio Mashaal in Pakistan, and Radio Farda in Iran.

- Radio and TV Martí (http://www.bbg.gov/broadcasters/ocb/)—these two services are operated by the Office of Cuba Broadcasting from its headquarters in Miami, Florida. According to the BBG, "Radio and TV Martí serve as consistently reliable and authoritative sources of accurate, objective, and comprehensive news for people in Cuba, where media are controlled and highly censored by the authorities."

- Radio Free Asia (http://www.bbg.gov/broadcasters/rfa/)—this service is operated out of Washington, D.C., and is funded by a grant from the BBG. Radio Free Asia broadcasts in nine languages via radio and the Internet to Burma (Myanmar), Cambodia, China, Laos, North Korea, Tibet, and Vietnam.

- Middle East Broadcasting Networks Inc. (http://www.bbg.gov/broadcasters/mbn/)—this nonprofit organization operates Alhurra Television and Radio Sawa under a grant from the BBG. Alhurra Television broadcasts in Arabic to 22 countries throughout the Middle East and North Africa. A second channel—Alhurra-Iraq—broadcasts specifically to Iraq. Radio Sawa focuses on reaching young Middle Eastern populations (i.e., people under the age of 35 years) by featuring popular music, news, and other information.

The BBG had a budget of $746.9 million in FY 2011. The allocation of this funding is shown in Figure 2.7.

U.S. DEPARTMENT OF ENERGY

As will be explained in Chapter 7, one of the greatest threats to U.S. national security is the proliferation (growth or multiplication) of weapons, particularly weapons of mass destruction, such as nuclear bombs. The U.S. Department of Energy (DOE) has long held responsibility for nuclear weapons development and production within the United States. In 2000 Congress established within the DOE the National Nuclear Security Administration (NNSA). The organizational structure of the NNSA is shown in Figure 2.8. According to the NNSA (2012, http://www.nnsa.energy.gov/aboutus/ourhistory), its responsibilities are as follows:

Managing and ensuring the security of the nation's nuclear weapons stockpile

Nuclear nonproliferation, that is, stemming the growth or multiplication of nuclear weapons around the world

Supporting work on naval reactors, for example, nuclear-powered submarines and aircraft carriers

Responding to nuclear and radiological emergencies within the United States and around the world

Providing "safe and secure" transportation of nuclear weapons, components, and materials

As shown in Table 2.11, the NNSA's budget request for FY 2013 was $11.5 billion, up 4.9% from its enacted budget for FY 2012.

TABLE 2.10

Foreign economic and military assistance, by agency, fiscal years 1946–2010

[In U.S. dollars millions]

	Post-war relief period 1946–48	Marshall Plan period 1949–52	Mutual Scty Act period 1953–61	Foreign Assistance Act (FAA) period					Total FAA period 1962–2010	Total loans & grants 1946–2010	Of which loans 1946–2010	Outstanding amount as of 09/30/2010
				1962–2006	2007	2008	2009	2010				
I. Total economic assistance	**12,482.0**	**18,634.3**	**24,050.0**	**434,778.9**	**27,303.0**	**32,502.1**	**33,619.6**	**37,670.6**	**565,874.2**	**621,040.5**	**66,666.4**	**11,508.2**
A. USAID and predecessor	—	14,505.9	16,883.2	234,875.2	11,416.0	9,427.7	11,793.4	14,068.6	281,580.9	312,970.0	30,106.1	4,895.5
Economic Support Fund/security support assistance	—	348.2	8,853.1	101,838.0	5,412.6	5,165.6	7,033.7	7,190.0	126,639.9	135,841.2	—	—
Development assistance	—	—	—	12,672.5	1,508.9	1,602.5	1,842.4	2,345.3	19,971.7	19,971.7	—	—
Child survival & health	—	—	—	10,623.5	2,107.9	161.8	15.5	5.3	12,914.1	12,914.1	—	—
Other USAID assistance	—	14,157.7	8,030.1	109,741.1	2,386.6	2,497.7	2,901.7	4,527.9	122,055.2	144,243.0	30,106.1	4,895.5
B. Department of Agriculture	—	83.2	6,415.0	71,952.4	1,835.4	2,883.1	2,700.7	2,637.9	82,009.6	88,507.8	28,496.1	6,407.2
Food aid total	—	83.2	6,415.0	71,862.0	1,809.8	2,869.1	2,687.0	2,335.3	81,563.4	88,061.6	28,496.1	6,407.2
Title I	—	—	3,866.4	29,628.7	72.5	13.0	154.8	91.2	29,960.2	33,826.6	28,496.1	6,407.2
Title II (USAID implemented)	—	83.2	2,548.6	33,954.2	1,599.5	2,693.8	2,467.7	2,146.4	42,861.5	45,493.3	—	—
Food for Education	—	—	—	491.9	66.5	0.1	59.8	74.0	692.3	692.3	—	—
Other food aid programs	—	—	—	7,787.3	71.3	162.2	4.7	23.8	8,049.4	8,049.4	—	—
Other USDA assistance	—	—	—	90.4	25.6	14.0	13.7	302.6	446.2	446.2	—	—
C. State Department	—	—	—	35,715.9	5,746.2	9,872.2	11,328.1	12,224.3	74,886.7	74,886.7	—	—
Global health and child survival	—	—	—	—	—	5,238.1	6,135.4	6,436.1	17,809.6	17,809.6	—	—
Global HIV/AIDS initiative	—	—	—	3,481.7	2,642.3	416.6	142.5	54.9	6,738.0	6,738.0	—	—
Narcotics control	—	—	—	11,512.2	1,249.7	1,850.4	2,679.8	2,887.7	20,179.7	20,179.7	—	—
Migration and refugee assistance	—	—	—	16,419.8	1,021.1	1,373.3	1,729.8	1,830.8	22,374.8	22,374.8	—	—
Nonproliferation, anti-terrorism, demining and related	—	—	—	1,549.7	360.4	418.1	332.5	705.7	3,366.3	3,366.3	—	—
Other State Department assistance	—	—	—	2,752.5	472.7	575.7	308.1	309.2	4,418.2	4,418.2	—	—
D. Other economic assistance	11,847.0	4,045.2	562.9	45,108.5	6,571.9	8,434.4	5,469.5	5,836.2	71,420.4	87,875.5	8,064.2	205.5
Millennium Challenge Corporation	—	—	—	1,149.8	1,546.5	3,266.0	1,686.9	1,617.3	9,266.5	9,266.5	—	—
Peace Corps	—	—	0.3	6,926.2	315.7	326.5	336.1	353.7	8,258.2	8,258.5	—	—
Department of Defense Security assistance	—	—	—	22,493.5	1,787.0	2,003.1	1,313.1	1,277.7	28,874.3	28,874.3	—	—
Other active grant programs	11,847.0	4,045.2	562.6	12,083.2	2,922.7	2,838.8	2,133.5	2,587.5	22,565.7	22,565.7	—	—
Inactive programs	—	—	—	2,455.8	—	—	—	—	2,455.8	18,910.6	8,064.2	205.5
E. Voluntary contributions to multilateral organizations	635.0	—	188.9	47,126.9	1,733.4	1,884.8	2,327.9	2,903.7	55,976.6	56,800.5	—	—
II. Total military assistance	**481.2**	**10,064.2**	**19,302.2**	**195,911.9**	**13,753.9**	**16,478.7**	**14,898.1**	**15,057.6**	**256,100.2**	**285,947.8**	**42,589.2**	**2,605.9**
III. Total economic & military assistance	**12,963.2**	**28,698.5**	**43,352.2**	**630,690.7**	**41,056.9**	**48,980.8**	**48,517.7**	**52,728.2**	**821,974.4**	**906,988.3**	**109,255.6**	**14,114.1**
Non-concessional U.S. loans	2,091.4	899.8	3,652.6	71,888.4	1,401.2	1,326.5	6,316.0	6,085.9	87,017.9	93,661.7	93,661.7	8,684.5
Export-import bank loans	2,091.4	899.8	3,652.6	61,760.3	-0.0	356.0	3,657.4	4,260.6	70,034.3	76,678.1	76,678.1	7,448.7
OPIC & other non-concessional U.S. loans	—	—	—	10,128.1	1,401.2	970.5	2,658.6	1,825.3	16,983.6	16,983.6	16,983.6	1,235.8
Annual obligations to international organizations (assessed)	—	—	—	16,220.1	2,731.5	3,289.1	3,925.7	3,780.5	29,946.8	29,946.8	—	—

SOURCE: "Summary of All Countries: Fiscal Year 2010 U.S. Overseas Loans and Grants—Obligations and Loan Authorizations, in $US Millions," in *U.S. Overseas Loans and Grants: Obligations and Loan Authorizations, July 1, 1945–September 30, 2010,* U.S. Agency for International Development, 2012, http://pdf.usaid.gov/pdf_docs/PNADX500.pdf (accessed July 3, 2012)

U.S. LAW ENFORCEMENT AGENCIES

U.S. law enforcement agencies play an important part in defending national security through counterintelligence operations, which have already been described, and through counterterrorism activities. Law enforcement agencies attempt to detect potential terrorists or other foreign agents and prevent them from carrying out harmful actions. If spying or a terrorist attack does occur, they investigate the incident and help capture those responsible.

After the September 11, 2001, terrorist attacks on the United States, lawmakers quickly put together the Patriot Act, which was designed to help the United States fight the terrorist threat. (The act is described in detail in Chapter 8.) One of the purposes of the act is to facilitate better cooperation and information sharing between government agencies, particularly between the IC and law enforcement agencies.

The law enforcement agencies engaged in counterterrorism activities include the U.S. Departments of the Treasury, Justice, and Homeland Security.

U.S. Department of the Treasury

As noted earlier in this chapter, the U.S. Department of the Treasury operates the Office of Intelligence and Analysis within its Office of Terrorism and Financial Intelligence. The latter office combines intelligence and enforcement functions to protect the U.S. financial system against foreign threats, including rogue nations, narcotics traffickers, and terrorist financiers and money launderers. The organization chart for the Office of Terrorism and Financial Intelligence is shown in Figure 2.9.

According to the Department of the Treasury, in *Departmental Offices—S&E FY 2013 President's Budget Submission* (February 2012, http://www.treasury.gov/about/budget-performance/Documents/2%20-%20FY%202013%20DO%20SE%20CJ.pdf), the FY 2013 budget request for the Office of Terrorism and Financial Intelligence was $100 million. The office expected to obtain an additional $18.9 million in funds from other sources.

U.S. Department of Justice

The primary agency of the U.S. Department of Justice (DOJ) that is devoted to counterterrorism and counterintelligence is the FBI, which was described earlier in this chapter.

U.S. Department of Homeland Security

The U.S. Department of Homeland Security (DHS) was established in 2002 following passage of the Homeland

FIGURE 2.7

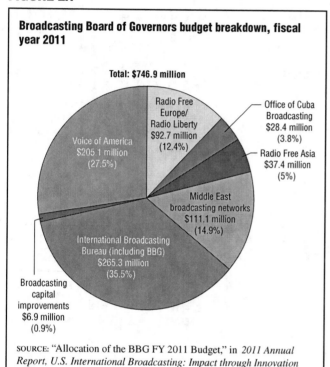

Broadcasting Board of Governors budget breakdown, fiscal year 2011

Total: $746.9 million

Voice of America $205.1 million (27.5%)

Radio Free Europe/Radio Liberty $92.7 million (12.4%)

Office of Cuba Broadcasting $28.4 million (3.8%)

Radio Free Asia $37.4 million (5%)

Middle East broadcasting networks $111.1 million (14.9%)

International Broadcasting Bureau (including BBG) $265.3 million (35.5%)

Broadcasting capital improvements $6.9 million (0.9%)

SOURCE: "Allocation of the BBG FY 2011 Budget," in *2011 Annual Report, U.S. International Broadcasting: Impact through Innovation and Integration*, Broadcasting Board of Governors, undated, http://www.bbg.gov/wp-content/media/2012/06/BBGAnnualReport_LoRes_Part2.pdf (accessed July 10, 2012)

FIGURE 2.8

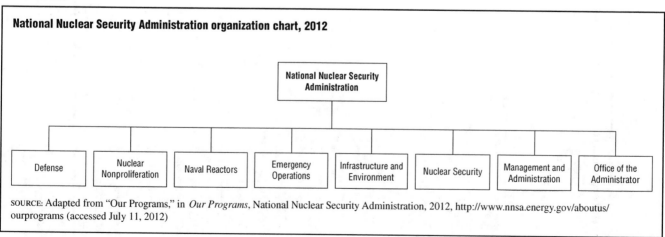

National Nuclear Security Administration organization chart, 2012

National Nuclear Security Administration

Defense | Nuclear Nonproliferation | Naval Reactors | Emergency Operations | Infrastructure and Environment | Nuclear Security | Management and Administration | Office of the Administrator

SOURCE: Adapted from "Our Programs," in *Our Programs*, National Nuclear Security Administration, 2012, http://www.nnsa.energy.gov/aboutus/ourprograms (accessed July 11, 2012)

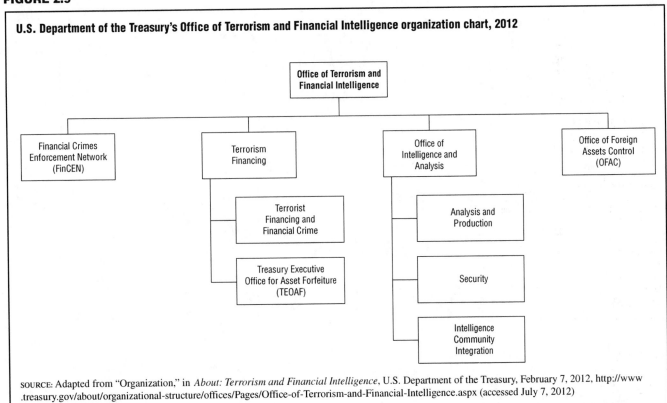

TABLE 2.11

National Nuclear Security Administration budget, fiscal years 2011–13

[Dollars in thousands. Office of Management and Budget scoring.]

	Fiscal year 2011 current	Fiscal year 2012 enacted*	Fiscal year 2013 request	Fiscal year 2013 vs.	Fiscal year 2012
				$	%
National Nuclear Security Administration:					
Weapons activities	6,865,775	7,214,120	7,577,341	363,221	+5.0%
Defense nuclear nonproliferation	2,281,371	2,295,880	2,458,631	162,751	+7.1%
Naval reactors	985,526	1,080,000	1,088,635	8,635	+0.8%
Office of the administrator	393,293	410,000	411,279	1,279	+0.3%
Total, National Nuclear Security Administration	**10,525,965**	**11,000,000**	**11,535,886**	**+535,886**	**+4.9%**

*The "Fiscal year 2012 enacted" reflects a rescission of $73,300 associated with savings from the contractor pay freeze; $600M ($500M Strategic Petroleum Reserve, $100M Northeast Home Heating Oil) was rebased as mandatory after enactment.

SOURCE: Adapted from "Department of Energy Appropriation Account Summary," in *Department of Energy FY 2013 Congressional Budget Request: National Nuclear Security Administration*, U.S. Department of Energy, February 2012, http://www.cfo.doe.gov/budget/13budget/content/volume1.pdf (accessed July 5, 2012)

FIGURE 2.9

U.S. Department of the Treasury's Office of Terrorism and Financial Intelligence organization chart, 2012

SOURCE: Adapted from "Organization," in *About: Terrorism and Financial Intelligence*, U.S. Department of the Treasury, February 7, 2012, http://www.treasury.gov/about/organizational-structure/offices/Pages/Office-of-Terrorism-and-Financial-Intelligence.aspx (accessed July 7, 2012)

Security Act. Prior to the act homeland security was not overseen by one high-level agency, but by a variety of departments and bureaus that were scattered throughout several government agencies. According to the DHS, in "Creation of the Department of Homeland Security" (2012, http://www.dhs.gov/creation-department-homeland-security), it was created to be "a stand-alone, cabinet-level department to further coordinate and unify national homeland security efforts." As explained by the White House (2012, http://www.whitehouse.gov/administration/

cabinet), the cabinet is a collection of agencies whose leaders "advise the President on any subject he may require."

The DHS began operations in 2003. Major counter-terrorist and counterintelligence agencies within the DHS are the Transportation Security Agency, the U.S. Coast Guard, the U.S. Customs and Border Protection, the U.S. Immigration and Customs Enforcement, and the U.S. Secret Service. The roles of these agencies are discussed at length in Chapter 5.

CHAPTER 3
TERRORISM

During the late 20th century terrorism replaced the Cold War as the United States' greatest national security concern. Terrorism is not new. It has plagued the world for centuries. What is different is the scope and reach of terrorist acts. In the past the vast majority of terrorist acts were committed by people with domestic or regional grievances. The terrorists had narrow agendas and limited resources for achieving them. This is no longer true. The goals and means of some terrorist groups have broadened considerably. The technological advancements that have made international travel and communication possible have made it easier for terrorists to extend their reach to all parts of the world. Likewise, their weapons and methods are much more sophisticated and deadly. The combination of all these factors has made the U.S. homeland a viable and attractive target for terrorism.

As will be explained in this chapter, many of the terrorist groups that threaten U.S. national security are based in the Middle East, North Africa, and Southwest Asia. (See Figure 3.1.) Many of the terrorists and groups from this region have names in Arabic, which uses an alphabet that is completely different from that of English. Transliteration is a means for rendering words in one alphabet into another alphabet. However, it is not an exact or universally agreed on process. Information sources, such as U.S. government agencies, news organizations, and so on have differing transliteration practices. For example, the Arabic name of the terrorist group al Qaeda is also transliterated as "al Qa'ida," "al-Qaida," "al-Qaeda," and "Al Qaeda"—to name just a few variations. Note that throughout this book transliterated Arabic words may appear in different forms between the graphics and the text, depending on the sources from which the information was obtained. However, the text will consistently maintain the same transliteration for the name of each group or individual mentioned.

WHAT IS TERRORISM?

Terrorism is not easily defined. Within U.S. law and government agencies there are differing definitions of terrorism; however, for the purposes of this chapter, only one of these definitions will be used. In the U.S. Code, Title 22 (2012, http://www4.law.cornell.edu/uscode/html/uscode22/usc_sup_01_22.html) focuses on foreign relations. Chapter 38, section 2656f(d) of that code defines terrorism as "premeditated, politically motivated violence perpetrated against noncombatant targets by subnational groups or clandestine agents."

One of the key components defining terrorism is its political nature. This excludes violence committed solely for financial gain, personal reasons, or other nonpolitical purposes. A second major component of terrorism is that noncombatants (civilians) are targeted. This distinguishes terrorism from traditional war making, in which official military forces are pitted against one another. Subnational means less than (or lower than) national. Clandestine means secret. By this definition, terrorism is not perpetrated openly (as war would be) by the governments of nations. Instead, it is associated with lesser groups or with secret national agents.

COMBATING TERRORISM

The subnational nature of terrorism makes it difficult, if not impossible, to thwart using U.S. military might alone. In essence, terrorists are criminals. They do not openly act on behalf of foreign governments. Nevertheless, it is well known that some terrorist groups receive direct or indirect support from foreign governments, particularly nations that are not politically allied with the United States. In addition, terrorist groups find safe harbor in countries with governments that lack the means (or the will) to police activities within their own borders. These factors make combating terrorism a difficult international challenge. The U.S. government uses a combination of diplomatic, military, financial, and intelligence

FIGURE 3.1

Map of the Middle East and North Africa, 2012

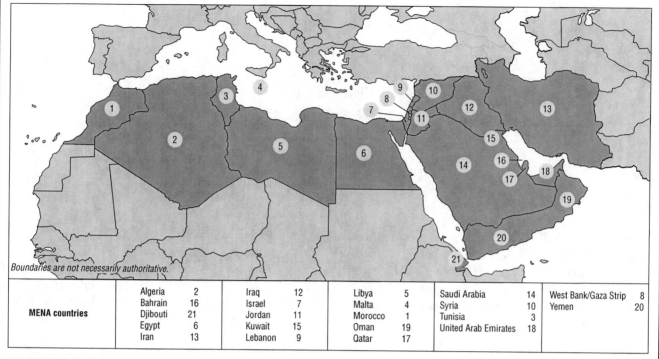

Boundaries are not necessarily authoritative.

MENA countries										
	Algeria	2	Iraq	12	Libya	5	Saudi Arabia	14	West Bank/Gaza Strip	8
	Bahrain	16	Israel	7	Malta	4	Syria	10	Yemen	20
	Djibouti	21	Jordan	11	Morocco	1	Tunisia	3		
	Egypt	6	Kuwait	15	Oman	19	United Arab Emirates	18		
	Iran	13	Lebanon	9	Qatar	17				

Note: MENA = Middle East and North Africa.

SOURCE: Rebecca M. Nelson, Mary Jane Bolle, and Shayerah Ilias, "Figure 1. Map of Middle East and North Africa," in *U.S. Trade and Investment in the Middle East and North Africa: Overview and Issues for Congress*, Congressional Research Service, January 20, 2012, http://fpc.state.gov/documents/organization/183739.pdf (accessed July 24, 2012)

(information) gathering measures to thwart terrorists. These efforts are collectively known as counterterrorism.

The overall organization of the U.S. national security framework was described in Chapter 2. Some of the federal agencies that play a key role in counterterrorism are:

- The Bureau of Counterterrorism within the U.S. Department of State (DOS). Formerly called the Office of the Coordinator for Counterterrorism, the Bureau of Counterterrorism (2012, http://www.state.gov/j/ct/) oversees diplomatic counterterrorism efforts and helps forge national policies, strategies, and programs devoted to counterterrorism.

- The National Counterterrorism Center (NCTC) within the Office of the Director of National Intelligence (ODNI). The ODNI is the head of the U.S. intelligence community, which was described in Chapter 2.

- The Office of Terrorism and Financial Intelligence (TFI) within the U.S. Department of the Treasury. The TFI gathers financial-based intelligence and seeks to halt the illicit financing of terrorist organizations by enforcing economic sanctions against them.

- The National Security Branch (NSB) within the Federal Bureau of Investigation (FBI). The NSB is a member of the intelligence community and focuses on law enforcement within the United States. It also has investigative jurisdiction over terrorist acts that are committed against U.S. citizens in foreign countries.

FOREIGN TERRORIST ORGANIZATIONS

Throughout history various violent groups have been called terrorist organizations. During the late 20th century the U.S. government established a process by which a foreign organization is officially deemed to be a terrorist group. In 1996 Congress passed the Antiterrorism and Effective Death Penalty Act, which amended Section 219 of the Immigration and Nationality Act to authorize the U.S. secretary of state to officially designate groups as foreign terrorist organizations (FTOs). This is a legal process, so any group that is deemed to be an FTO can challenge the designation in court. To be designated as an FTO, an organization must meet the following criteria:

- Be a foreign organization

- Engage in terrorist activity or terrorism as defined by federal law or retain the capability and intent to engage in terrorist activity or terrorism

- Threaten the security of Americans or the national defense, foreign relations, or economic interests of the United States through terrorist activity

As of October 2012, the most recent list of FTOs (compiled in September 2012) contained 51 organizations. (See Table 3.1.) It is illegal for any person who is in the United States or subject to U.S. jurisdiction to knowingly provide "material support or resources" to a designated FTO. U.S. financial institutions are required to take control over any funds in their possession that were deposited by an FTO or one of its agents and report the funds to the Department of the Treasury. Finally, alien members or representatives of an FTO are not allowed to enter the United States and, in some cases, can be deported.

MOTIVATIONS OF TERRORISM

As defined under U.S. law, terrorism is "politically motivated violence." One common political motivation is a desire for political autonomy (i.e., self-governance). For example, during the 20th century the Irish Republican Army waged a violent campaign to gain independence for Ireland from the United Kingdom. In the Middle East the Palestinian cause has long been a rallying point for many militant radicals. Some disillusioned Palestinians and their supporters have used terrorism against Israel and the world at large to push their agenda for statehood. Palestinians are largely of the Muslim faith, while Israelis are predominantly of the Jewish faith. Even though religion is not the driving factor in the conflict, it is an element in which the two sides differ. In reality, religious and/or ethnic identity often intertwine with the political motivations for terrorism. This is particularly true in the Middle East, where the vast majority of the population is Muslim. As will be explained in Chapter 10, many followers of Islam believe their religion provides a method for governing nations and maintaining law and order. In other words, there is not a separation between "church and state" as is common in the West.

Islamic Connection

A majority of the FTOs listed in Table 3.1 (71%, or 36 out of the 51 listed FTOs) support causes or people that are associated with the Islamic faith, particularly the most conservative and fundamentalist elements of the religion. As such, these terrorists are typically labeled as Islamic extremists or Islamic fundamentalists. Many of these FTOs seek the creation of an Islamic state or a caliphate. A caliphate is a geopolitical area spanning the territory of many countries, all under the rule of an Islamic leader called a caliph. Thus, FTOs devoted to achieving an Islamic state or caliphate are motivated by both political and religious ideology.

Within the Sunni branch of Islam there is a belief system called Salafism that has been closely associated with some of

TABLE 3.1

Listing status of Foreign Terrorist Organizations (FTOs) designated by the U.S. government, as of September 28, 2012

Designated Foreign Terrorist Organizations	
Date designated	Name
10/8/1997	Abu Nidal Organization (ANO)
10/8/1997	Abu Sayyaf Group (ASG)
10/8/1997	Aum Shinrikyo (AUM)
10/8/1997	Basque Fatherland and Liberty (ETA)
10/8/1997	Gama'a al-Islamiyya (Islamic Group) (IG)
10/8/1997	HAMAS
10/8/1997	Harakat ul-Mujahidin (HUM)
10/8/1997	Hizballah
10/8/1997	Kahane Chai (Kach)
10/8/1997	Kurdistan Workers Party (PKK) (Kongra-Gel)
10/8/1997	Liberation Tigers of Tamil Eelam (LTTE)
10/8/1997	National Liberation Army (ELN)
10/8/1997	Palestine Liberation Front (PLF)
10/8/1997	Palestinian Islamic Jihad (PIJ)
10/8/1997	Popular Front for the Liberation of Palestine (PFLF)
10/8/1997	PFLP-General Command (PFLP-GC)
10/8/1997	Revolutionary Armed Forces of Colombia (FARC)
10/8/1997	Revolutionary Organization 17 November (17N)
10/8/1997	Revolutionary People's Liberation Party/Front (DHKP/C)
10/8/1997	Shining Path (SL)
10/8/1999	al-Qa'ida (AQ)
9/25/2000	Islamic Movement of Uzbekistan (IMU)
5/16/2001	Real Irish Republican Army (RIRA)
9/10/2001	United Self Defense Forces of Colombia (AUC)
12/26/2001	Jaish-e-Mohammed (JEM)
12/26/2001	Lashkar-e Tayyiba (LeT)
3/27/2002	Al-Aqsa Martyrs Brigade (AAMB)
3/27/2002	Asbat al-Ansar (AAA)
3/27/2002	al-Qaida in the Islamic Maghreb (AQIM)
8/9/2002	Communist Party of the Philippines/New People's Army (CPP/NPA)
10/23/2002	Jemaah Islamiya (JI)
1/30/2003	Lashkar i Jhangvi (LJ)
3/22/2004	Ansar al-Islam (AAI)
7/13/2004	Continuity Irish Republican Army (CIRA)
12/17/2004	Libyan Islamic Fighting Group (LIFG)
12/17/2004	al-Qaida in Iraq (AQI)
6/17/2005	Islamic Jihad Union (IJU)
10/11/2005	Moroccan Islamic Combatant Group (GICM)
3/5/2008	Harakat ul-Jihad-i-Islami/Bangladesh (HUJI-B)
3/18/2008	al-Shabaab
5/18/2009	Revolutionary Struggle (RS)
7/2/2009	Kata'ib Hizballah (KH)
1/19/2010	al-Qa'ida in the Arabian Peninsula (AQAP)
8/6/2010	Harakat ul-Jihad-i-Islami (HUJI)
9/1/2010	Tehrik-e Taliban Pakistan (TTP)
11/4/2010	Jundallah
5/23/2011	Army of Islam (AOI)
9/19/2011	Indian Mujahedeen (IM)
3/13/2012	Jemaah Anshorut Tauhid (JAT)
5/30/2012	Abdallah Azzam Brigades (AAB)
9/19/2012	Haqqani Network (HQN)

Delisted Foreign Terrorist Organizations		
Date removed	Name	Date originally designated
10/8/1999	Democratic Front for the Liberation of Palestine-Hawatmeh Faction	10/8/1997
10/8/1999	Khmer Rouge	10/8/1997
10/8/1999	Manuel Modriguez Patriotic Front Dissidents	10/8/1997
10/8/2001	Japanese Red Army	10/8/1997
10/8/2001	Tupac Amaru Revolution Movement	10/8/1997
5/18/2009	Revolutionary Nuclei	10/8/1997
10/15/2010	Armed Islamic Group (GIA)	10/8/1997
9/28/2012	Mujahedin-e Khalq Organization (MEK)	10/8/1997

SOURCE: "Designated Foreign Terrorist Organizations," in *Foreign Terrorist Organizations*, U.S. Department of State, Bureau of Counterterrorism, September 28, 2012, http://www.state.gov/j/ct/rls/other/des/123085.htm (accessed October 2, 2012)

the most violent terrorist organizations. For example, as will be described later in this chapter, a 2012 terrorist attack on the U.S. consulate in Benghazi, Libya, was linked to Salafist extremists. Salafism is variously described as a fundamentalist, traditionalist, or orthodox approach to Islam. The growth of this religious movement during the 20th century is detailed in the Canadian Broadcasting Company documentary *War without Borders* (December 1, 2004, http://www.cbc.ca/fifth/warwithoutborders/salafist.html). It should be noted that the media often use the term *wahhabi* to refer to the Salafist branch of Islam. This word is derived from the name of an 18th-century Arab named Muhammad ibn Abd al-Wahhab (c. 1703–c. 1792), who was a well-known Salafist scholar.

According to *War without Borders*, the Salafist movement seeks to practice Islam as it was practiced by its earliest followers during the eighth century. Salafists believe that Islam has been misinterpreted and misapplied since that time. There is a minority within this faction that champions a revolutionary style of Salafism in which violence is considered justifiable to re-create the Islamic caliphates of ages past.

Revolutionary Salafism has its roots in an organization called the Muslim Brotherhood that began in Egypt in 1928. Originally dedicated to education and social reform, it evolved into a political organization that embraced terrorism during the 1940s. Over the following decades the Muslim Brotherhood adopted as its spiritual leader the Egyptian intellectual Sayyid Qutb (1906–1966). Qutb became a major proponent of Islamism (a belief that governments should operate in strict accordance with Islamic law). He briefly attended college in the United States during the 1940s and was highly critical of the "debauchery" of American society. Qutb advocated the use of violence, particularly against non-Muslims, in the quest for an Islamist society (the belief that governments should operate in strict accordance with Islamic law). This violence has been called a jihad (holy war) by the Western media. FTOs such as al Qaeda have embraced the concept of revolutionary Salafism and the use of violent jihad, even against fellow Muslims deemed to be less than true believers. Al Qaeda and other FTOs that strike at targets outside their regional base, such as at targets in the West, are said to be global jihadists. However, it should be noted that the Arabic term *jihad* translates more accurately as "struggle" and has a variety of meanings within Islamic tradition.

THE ARAB SPRING

Nearly all the nations in the Middle East have autocratic governments in which one person, family, or entity (such as the military) has wielded near-total power for decades. In 2010 the status quo began to crumble as restless peoples started demanding democratic reforms. Civil unrest and antigovernment demonstrations began in Tunisia in December 2010 and by the spring of 2011 had spread to Egypt, Libya, and Yemen. Long-ruling autocrats in these countries were ousted from power. Zine el Abidine Ben Ali (1936–) was chased from Tunisia, Hosni Mubarak (1928–) was arrested in Egypt, Muammar al-Qadhafi (1942–2011) was killed in Libya, and Ali Abdullah Saleh (1942–) was forced from the presidency in Yemen. This series of revolutions was dubbed "the Arab Spring" by the media, because many of the events occurred during the spring of 2011. However, as will be described in Chapter 6, revolutionary fever continued to thrive in some Middle Eastern countries as of October 2012. Thus, the generic term *Arab Spring* does not describe a defined period.

The Arab Spring has been remarkable in that it has not been driven by the terrorist groups that claim to represent the interests of the oppressed populations in the affected countries. Instead, the revolutions have been spurred by the shared discontent of the populace at large. It is difficult to determine the effects of the Arab Spring on the terrorist groups in the Middle East. Some analysts believe the popular uprisings caught the terrorist groups off guard and proved wrong their oft-stated claim that only violent coups led by them can topple the autocrats. In addition, the Arab Spring protesters have sought greater freedom and choices and more say in their governments, but these democratic ideals are incompatible with an Islamic caliphate. Thus, the protesters and the terrorist groups seem to be at cross-purposes with one another.

In April 2012 the ODNI held the media briefing "Media Conference Call: Background Briefing on the State of Al-Qaida" (http://www.dni.gov/), in which intelligence analysts spoke about the Arab Spring and its effects on terrorist groups, such as al Qaeda, that are devoted to global jihadism. Robert Cardillo noted that the Arab Spring "strikes at the very core of [the terrorists'] jihadist narrative." However, Cardillo warned that if the new governments spurred by the Arab Spring fail to implement promised reforms, terrorist groups will likely seize the opportunity to expand their operations.

MAJOR TERRORIST ORGANIZATIONS

Some terrorist organizations that were active during the 20th century have ceased to be major participants in terrorist attacks in the 21st century. In some cases this is because of cease-fires or other political agreements that have lessened violent opposition. For example, terrorist groups operating in Ireland have been relatively inactive since the late 1990s because of peace agreements accepted by most parties involved in the conflict. In other cases extremely hierarchal terrorist organizations have diminished in power following the deaths of their leaders.

The DOS issues an annual report to Congress on international terrorism. In *Country Reports on Terrorism*

2010 (August 2011, http://www.state.gov/documents/organization/170479.pdf) and *Country Reports on Terrorism 2011* (July 2012, http://www.state.gov/documents/organization/195768.pdf), the DOS singles out several terrorist groups for their influence on political events in the Middle East and for threatening U.S. interests. These groups are al Qaeda (including its affiliates); Harakat al-Shabaab al-Mujahidin; the Pakistan-based groups Lashkar-e Tayyiba, Tehrik-e Taliban Pakistan, and the Haqqani Network; and Hamas and Hezbollah. As of October 2012, all of these groups were officially designated as FTOs. (See Table 3.1.)

Al Qaeda and Affiliates

The FTO called al Qaeda, meaning "the foundation" or "the base," gained prominence during the 1990s as a sophisticated and well-funded organization that was capable of conducting terrorist attacks around the world, including on U.S. soil. Its members are predominantly Sunni and include some devoted adherents of Salafism.

Al Qaeda was founded in 1988 by Osama bin Laden (1957?–2011), a wealthy man from a prominent Saudi family. He followed the precepts of the Muslim Brotherhood and believed that violence was a necessary tool for ridding Muslim lands of unbelievers. During the 1980s he fought against the Soviet forces that occupied Afghanistan. Following the Soviet withdrawal, he united and trained his fighters to wage war against regional regimes he considered non-Islamist and against Israel and the United States. Bin Laden and al Qaeda's rise to power are described at length by the National Commission on Terrorist Attacks upon the United States in *The 9/11 Commission Report* (July 2004, http://www.9-11commission.gov/report/911Report.pdf).

In 1991 bin Laden left Saudi Arabia to set up his organization in Sudan in northern Africa. From there he moved to Afghanistan in 1996. Throughout the 1990s bin Laden issued statements urging Muslims around the world to kill Americans and their allies. In 1998 he and his cohorts published a fatwa in an Arabic-language newspaper in London. (A fatwa is an interpretation of Islamic law usually written by a scholar or religious authority.) Al Qaeda's fatwa declared war on the United States.

By 1998 bin Laden and al Qaeda had raised sufficient funds to launch carefully planned and directed attacks against U.S. interests. The organization was not strictly hierarchal in structure but featured a network of semi-independent cells of followers. Between 1998 and 2001 al Qaeda conducted a series of stunning terrorist attacks: in 1998 bombings at two U.S. embassies in Africa killed more than 200 people and injured another 5,000; in 2000 the bombing of the USS *Cole* in Yemen killed 17 Americans and wounded 39 others; and in 2001 over 2,700 people were killed when hijackers crashed two airplanes into both towers of the World Trade Center in New York City and a

third airplane into the Pentagon in Arlington, Virginia, just outside Washington, D.C. A fourth airplane was brought down in Pennsylvania.

Following the September 11, 2001 (9/11), terrorist attacks, the U.S. military invaded Afghanistan and killed, captured, or chased into hiding many of al Qaeda's leaders, with the exception of bin Laden. The invasion initially disrupted al Qaeda's organization and capabilities; however, the FTO regained some of its strength with help from friendly tribal leaders across the border in western Pakistan. The effects of these events on the war in Afghanistan are described in detail in Chapter 4.

Bin Laden eluded detection for 10 years, but was finally killed by U.S. special forces in May 2011 in Pakistan. Following bin Laden's death, al Qaeda's leadership was taken over by Ayman al-Zawahiri (1951–), a former physician from Egypt. In "Media Conference Call," an unidentified ODNI analyst noted that there are really two factions of al Qaeda: the so-called core faction that was founded and led by bin Laden, and a second faction consisting of affiliated terrorist groups that are motivated by al Qaeda's ideology of global jihad. According to the analyst, the core faction has been decimated by the United States' aggressive counterterrorism actions against it, including the war in Afghanistan and the assassination of bin Laden. The analyst stated, "In fact some could argue...that the organization that brought us 9/11 is essentially gone." In addition, the ODNI does not believe that al-Zawahiri has the charisma and power to rebuild the organization. Cardillo stated, "Most al-Qaida members find Zawahiri's leadership style less compelling than bin Laden's images of holy man and warrior and will not offer and have not offered the deference that they provided bin Laden, nor does Zawahiri have the centralizing, unifying effect as did [Osama bin Laden]."

AL QAEDA IN IRAQ. The ODNI assesses the terrorist groups that have affiliated themselves with al Qaeda since the September 11, 2001, attacks. One such group formed in 2004 and is called al Qaeda in Iraq (AQI). Figure 3.2 shows a map of Iraq where the AQI was active as of October 2011. The group was founded by Abu Musab al-Zarqawi (1966–2006), a Jordanian and a Sunni extremist. As will be explained in Chapter 4, during the war in Iraq the AQI waged a massive campaign of violence against allied troops, foreign workers and journalists, and Iraqi civilians. The AQI conducted many kidnappings, beheadings, and suicide bombings as part of the insurgency (resistance) movement and succeeded in fomenting near civil war between the Sunnis and Shiites in Iraq.

However, the killing of al-Zarqawi in a U.S. bombing raid in 2006 helped dampen the power and capabilities of the AQI. It was further weakened in 2007 and 2008 by U.S. military operations that were conducted in Iraq with

FIGURE 3.2

Map of area in which U.S. officials believed that al-Qa'ida in Iraq was most active, as of October 2011

SOURCE: "Al-Qa'ida in Iraq (AQI)," in *Counterterrorism 2012 Calendar*, National Counterterrorism Center, October 21, 2011, http://www.nctc .gov/site/pdfs/2012_nctc_ct_calendar.pdf (accessed July 5, 2012)

FIGURE 3.3

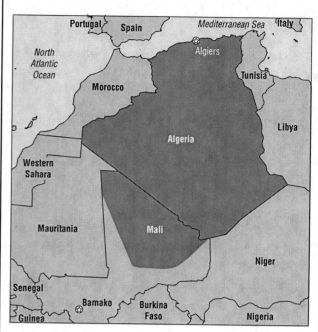

Map of area in which U.S. officials believed that al-Qa'ida in the Islamic Maghreb was most active, as of October 2011

SOURCE: "Al-Qa'ida in the Lands of the Islamic Maghreb (AQIM)," in *Counterterrorism 2012 Calendar*, National Counterterrorism Center, October 21, 2011, http://www.nctc.gov/site/pdfs/2012_nctc_ct_ calendar.pdf (accessed July 5, 2012)

help from Iraqi military forces, tribal leaders, and civilians. Nevertheless, the AQI remains a troublesome presence in Iraq and is blamed for numerous terrorist attacks that were carried out in early 2012 against Shiites and Iraqi government and police forces.

AL QAEDA IN THE ISLAMIC MAGHREB. In 2006 an Algerian Sunni jihadist group called the Salafist Group for Preaching and Combat (GSPC) aligned with al Qaeda and renamed itself Al Qaeda in the Islamic Maghreb (AQIM). *Maghreb* is a term used to collectively describe the Arab-majority countries of northern Africa, chiefly Algeria, Libya, Mauritania, Morocco, and Tunisia. Figure 3.3 shows the geographical area in which the AQIM was most active as of October 2011. According to the NCTC, in *Counterterrorism 2012 Calendar* (October 21, 2011, http://www.nctc .gov/site/pdfs/2012_nctc_ct_calendar.pdf), the AQIM seeks to overthrow the Algerian government and to establish an Islamic caliphate.

The NCTC notes that the GSPC had nearly 30,000 members at one time, but its successor is believed to have less than 1,000 members due to aggressive counterterrorism activities by the Algerian government. In "Media Conference Call," an unidentified ODNI analyst noted that the AQIM has "largely become a criminal gang" that has collected millions of dollars in ransom money by kidnapping European hostages. Even though the AQIM's leadership

adheres to al Qaeda's ideology of global jihad, the ODNI analyst believed the AQIM is preoccupied with local goals, such as seizing power in highly unstable Mali. In March 2012 Mali's democratic government was dissolved following a military coup.

In September 2012 the AQIM came under suspicion for a possible role in a violent attack on the U.S. consulate in Benghazi, Libya. On September 11, 2012, J. Christopher Stevens (1960–2012), the U.S. ambassador to Libya, and three of his staffers were killed after armed militants stormed the U.S. compound. At first media reports linked the attack to ongoing protests in the Middle East over an anti-Muslim video that originated in the United States and that sparked outrage after being posted on the Internet. However, attention soon turned to a Salafist militia in Libya with ties to al Qaeda. In "Attack on U.S. Consulate in Libya Determined to Be Terrorism Tied to al-Qaeda" (*Washington Post*, September 27, 2012), Greg Miller notes that U.S. intelligence officials suspect that the Islamist group Ansar al-Sharia planned and conducted the attack with help from the AQIM. As of October 2012, the identities and affiliations of the attackers had not been determined with certainty, but remained under investigation.

AL QAEDA IN THE ARABIAN PENINSULA. In 2009 Sunni terrorist groups based in Yemen and Saudi Arabia united to

FIGURE 3.4

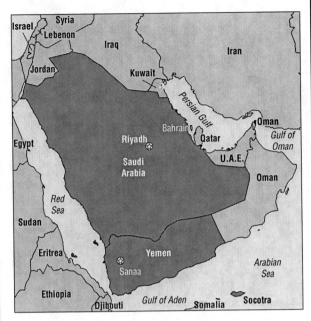

Map of area in which U.S. officials believed that al-Qa'ida in the Arabian Peninsula was most active, as of October 2011

SOURCE: "Al-Qa'ida in the Arabian Peninsula (AQAP)," in *Counterterrorism 2012 Calendar*, National Counterterrorism Center, October 21, 2011, http://www.nctc.gov/site/pdfs/2012_nctc_ct_calendar.pdf (accessed July 5, 2012).

form Al Qaeda in the Arabian Peninsula (AQAP). Figure 3.4 shows a map of the Arabian Peninsula including the two countries in which the AQAP was believed to be most active as of October 2011. In "Media Conference Call," an unidentified ODNI analyst called the AQAP "the affiliate we're most worried about." The deep concern is based on the violent history of the AQAP's predecessor group Al Qaeda in Yemen, the extremely unsecure status of Yemen's government, and the terrorism attempts that AQAP operatives have made on U.S. targets since 2009.

The AQAP is blamed for the so-called underwear bomber, who failed to detonate explosives on a commercial airliner that landed in Detroit, Michigan, in December 2009. In October 2010 AQAP-planted explosives hidden aboard cargo airplanes traveling to the United States were intercepted and disabled following tips from Saudi intelligence. In May 2012 the Saudi government announced that it had thwarted another AQAP attempt to blow up a U.S.-bound airliner. That same month an AQAP suicide bomber killed more than 90 Yemeni soldiers in Sanaa, the capital of Yemen. Ibrahim al-Asiri (1982–), a Saudi citizen, is believed to be the mastermind behind the AQAP's sophisticated bombing operations. Nasser al-Wuhayshi, a Yemeni citizen and former aide to bin Laden, is frequently mentioned as the overall leader of the AQAP.

The ODNI analyst noted that the AQAP is highly popular and dangerous, stating, "We are convinced that they continue to plot against us and their rhetoric, their propaganda is both widespread and effective." The latter effort includes an online English-language magazine called *Inspire* that the AQAP launched in 2010. The magazine was spearheaded by the AQAP recruiters Anwar al-Awlaki (1971–2011) and Samir Khan (1986–2011), young web-savvy men who were U.S. citizens and grew up in the United States. They specialized in recruiting Westerners, particularly Americans, to join the AQAP. In September 2011 al-Awlaki and Khan were killed by a U.S. missile attack in Yemen. However, the AQAP continued to publish the magazine. Randy Kreider reports in "Al Qaeda Magazine Calls for Firebomb Campaign in US" (ABCNews.com, May 2, 2012) that the May 2012 issue of *Inspire* contained articles on how to build remote-controlled explosives and urged jihadists to set massive forest fires in the western United States.

Harakat al-Shabaab al-Mujahidin

The terrorist group Harakat al-Shabaab al-Mujahidin (commonly called al-Shabaab) operates in Somalia along the northeastern coast of Africa. (See Figure 3.5.) In *Counterterrorism 2012 Calendar*, the NCTC notes that al-Shabaab began as "the militant wing" of the Somali Council of Islamic Courts, an organization that took control in 2006 over

FIGURE 3.5

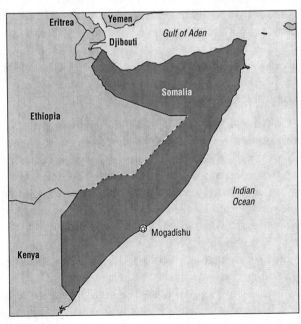

Map of area in which U.S. officials believed that al-Shabaab was most active, as of October 2011

SOURCE: "Al-Shabaab," in *Counterterrorism 2012 Calendar*, National Counterterrorism Center, October 21, 2011, http://www.nctc.gov/site/pdfs/2012_nctc_ct_calendar.pdf (accessed July 5, 2012).

much of southern Somalia. The country as a whole has been wracked by years of civil war and famine. It has not had a functioning central government since the early 1990s. Thus, Somalia provides an excellent place of refuge for terrorist organizations. According to the NCTC, al-Shabaab has focused most of its attacks against government figures, peace-keepers from the African Union, and aid workers. The FTO was particularly active during 2010, when it conducted ter-rorist attacks against multiple targets within and outside Somalia. The most notable was a pair of suicide bombings in Kampala, Uganda, that killed more than 70 people.

The group has drawn the U.S. government's attention because it has successfully recruited Westerners, including Americans, to its ranks and because some of its top commanders have expressed allegiance to al Qaeda's goals for global jihad. However, the NCTC notes that al-Shabaab's members "come from disparate clans, and the group is susceptible to clan politics, internal divisions, and shifting alliances." In "Media Conference Call," an unidentified ODNI analyst noted that al-Shabaab has "lost a great deal of their momentum and their popularity" since 2010. The FTO has been weakened by counterterrorism efforts led by African nations, chiefly Ethiopia and Kenya. In addition, the analyst believed that al-Shabaab "lost most of its local sup-port" in 2011 when it refused to allow United Nations (UN) food aid to be delivered to millions of Somalians facing starvation due to famine.

Pakistan-Based Terrorist Groups

In both *Country Reports on Terrorism 2010* and *Country Reports on Terrorism 2011*, the DOS singles out three Pakistan-based terrorist groups for special notice: Lashkar-e Tayyiba, Tehrik-e Taliban Pakistan, and the Haqqani Network. (Figure 3.6 shows a map of Pakistan.) The three groups are worrisome because they have forged ties with terrorist groups, such as al Qaeda, and with insurgents that are fighting against U.S. and UN military forces in Afghanistan. The war in Afghanistan is described in detail in Chapter 4.

LASHKAR-E TAYYIBA. Lashkar-e Tayyiba translates as "Army of the Good" or "Army of the Righteous." Accord-ing to the DOS, in *Country Reports on Terrorism 2010*, the group formed during the late 1980s in the Pakistani part of Kashmir, a disputed territory that spans northern Pakistan, northern India, and southern China. The FTO is blamed for a series of terrorist attacks in Mumbai, India, in 2008 that killed 174 people, including six Americans. U.S. authorities charged David Headley (1960–), a U.S. citizen, with aiding and abetting the FTO in the Mumbai attacks. The DOS notes that since 2008 Lashkar-e Tayyiba has largely con-ducted its terrorist operations within the Kashmir region and Afghanistan.

TEHRIK-E TALIBAN PAKISTAN. Tehrik-e Taliban Paki-stan is described by the NCTC in *Counterterrorism 2012*

FIGURE 3.6

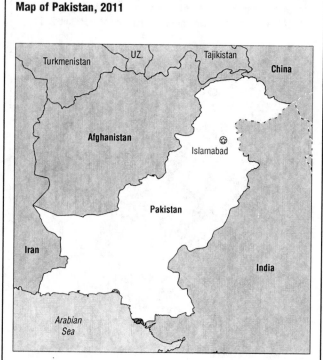

Map of Pakistan, 2011

SOURCE: "Jaish-e-Mohammed (JEM)," in *Counterterrorism 2012 Calendar*, National Counterterrorism Center, October 21, 2011, http://www.nctc.gov/site/pdfs/2012_nctc_ct_calendar.pdf (accessed July 5, 2012)

Calendar as "an alliance of militant groups" that formed in 2007. The FTO actively fights against Pakistani troops in the largely lawless area of western Pakistan along the border with Afghanistan. According to the NCTC, the group "has repeatedly threatened to attack the US homeland." A failed car bombing attempt in 2010 in New York City's Times Square was blamed on a Tehrik-e Taliban Pakistan opera-tive. In addition, the group claimed responsibility for numer-ous retaliatory terrorist attacks that occurred in Pakistan following the U.S. killing of bin Laden in May 2011.

THE HAQQANI NETWORK. The Haqqani Network is a Sunni Islamist militant group based in Pakistan. In *Counter-terrorism 2012 Calendar*, the NCTC states that the group formed during the 1980s in the lawless mountains of north-western Pakistan and is named after its founder Jalaluddin Haqqani (c. 1950–). His son, Sirajuddin Haqqani (c. 1973–), is the current leader of the group, which seeks to reinstate the Taliban to power in Afghanistan. The NCTC notes that the Haqqani Network is "considered the most lethal insurgent group targeting Coalition and Afghan forces in Afghani-stan." The terrorist group is blamed for several high-profile attacks in Afghanistan, including an assault in June 2011 at a hotel in Kabul, the capital of Afghanistan. In September 2011 Haqqani operatives staged a day-long attack on the U.S. embassy and the North Atlantic Treaty Organization's headquarters in Kabul. Even though the attackers were repelled, their success at gaining close access to these heavily secured buildings indicated sophisticated planning and coordination.

In "Brutal Haqqani Crime Clan Bedevils U.S. in Afghanistan" (*New York Times*, September 24, 2011), Mark Mazzetti, Scott Shane, and Alissa J. Rubin call the network "a ruthless crime family that built an empire out of kidnapping, extortion, smuggling, even trucking. They have trafficked in precious gems, stolen lumber and demanded protection money from businesses building roads and schools with American reconstruction funds." Media reports describe the group as a network of mercenaries that work at the behest of elements within the Pakistani government, particularly the Inter-Services Intelligence (ISI) Agency. Mazzetti, Shane, and Rubin note that the group "is an organized militia using high-profile terrorist attacks on hotels, embassies and other targets to advance its agenda to become a power broker in a future political settlement. And, sometimes, the agenda of its patrons from Pakistan's spy service, the ISI."

The United States has had a shaky political alliance with Pakistan since 2001, when the war in Afghanistan began. As will be explained in Chapter 4, that alliance has been weakened considerably by U.S drone attacks inside Pakistani territory and by the U.S. incursion into Pakistan to kill bin Laden. Although active for years, the Haqqani Network was not designated as an FTO by U.S. officials until September 2012. (See Table 3.1.) Many observers believe the U.S. government was reluctant to do so for fear of further alienating the Pakistani government. The latter has its own regional agenda that overwhelmingly focuses on India, its arch enemy. Observers allege that the Pakistani government uses heavily armed terrorist groups, such as the Haqqani Network, as proxies (i.e., agents acting on someone else's behalf). Thus, it is unlikely that the Pakistani government will cut its ties to the Haqqani Network even though the latter has been designated an FTO. Mazzetti, Shane, and Rubin state, "American officials who were once optimistic they could change Pakistani behavior through cajoling and large cash payments now accept a sober reality: as long as Pakistan sees its security under threat by India's far larger army, it will rely on militant groups like the Haqqanis, the Taliban and Lashkar-e-Taiba as occasional proxy forces."

Hamas

Hamas is an acronym for Harakat al-Muqawama al-Islamiya, meaning "Islamic Resistance Movement." Its primary area of operation is in the Palestinian territories of Israel, where it seeks to install an Islamic state. (See Figure 1.2 in Chapter 1.) Hamas evolved from the Muslim Brotherhood and uses both political and terrorist methods to pursue its goals. These two functions are carried out by different divisions within the organization.

Terrorist activities are associated with paramilitary fighters (civilians organized to function like a military unit) in the Izz al-Din al-Qassam Brigades. According to the DOS, in *Country Reports on Terrorism 2010*, the Hamas brigades have conducted many terrorist attacks, including suicide bombings, against civilian and military targets in Israel but have not directly attacked U.S. interests.

Hamas is believed to have tens of thousands of supporters and sympathizers. Its activities are chiefly funded through donations collected from Palestinians living around the world and from wealthy private individuals in Saudi Arabia and other Arab countries. The FTO's popularity in Palestine is attributed in large part to its social and charitable works, including schools, medical clinics, and youth camps. As mentioned in Chapter 1, Hamas members were elected in sufficient numbers during the January 2006 elections to take over majority control of the Palestinian National Authority (PNA)—the existing governing body of the Palestinian territories.

Hamas attacks against Israel decreased dramatically following the election, until June 2006, when Hamas forces attacked a group of Israeli soldiers, killing two and kidnapping another. In response, Israel imposed strict travel and economic sanctions against Palestinians in the Gaza Strip. Israel controls the airspace above the Gaza Strip, its ports, and all of its land border crossings, except those along the Egyptian border. The latter are controlled by Egypt. In 2007 a military-type coup by Hamas forces routed the PNA from the Gaza Strip. Hamas unofficially seized control of the area and continued to wage bomb and rocket attacks against Israeli targets. Israel and Egypt responded by implementing a strict blockade on the passage of many goods into the Gaza Strip. Cross-border skirmishes broke out between Israel and Gaza, and rocket fire was exchanged.

In early January 2009 Israeli ground forces invaded Gaza, and after three weeks of fighting Israel announced a unilateral cease-fire. Unilateral means "one-sided." In other words, Israel declared a cease-fire without negotiating it with Hamas. According to the Central Intelligence Agency (CIA), in *The World Factbook: Gaza Strip* (September 11, 2012, https://www.cia.gov/library/publications/the-world-factbook/geos/gz.html), the violence in Gaza left between 1,100 and 1,400 Palestinians dead and tens of thousands homeless. The CIA notes that $4.5 billion was pledged by international donors to rebuild the war-torn Gaza Strip, but that no major reconstruction had begun as of year-end 2011.

In May 2011 Egyptian-brokered negotiations led to an agreement between Hamas and the PNA to reunite the Palestinian territories under one government. However, the CIA notes that "the factions have struggled to finalize details on governing and security structures." Thus, as of October 2012, the PNA governed the West Bank and Hamas governed the Gaza Strip.

FIGURE 3.7

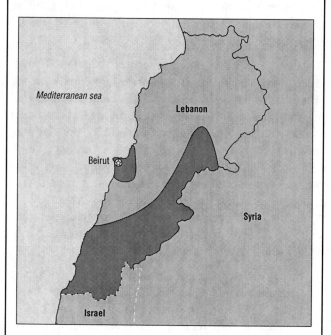

Map of area in which U.S. officials believed that Hizballah was most active, as of October 2011

SOURCE: "Hizballah," in *Counterterrorism 2012 Calendar*, National Counterterrorism Center, October 21, 2011, http://www.nctc.gov/site/pdfs/2012_nctc_ct_calendar.pdf (accessed July 5, 2012)

Hezbollah

Hezbollah is an FTO based in Lebanon. Figure 3.7 shows the areas of Lebanon in which the DOS believes that Hezbollah was most active as of October 2011. The FTO is unique in that unlike nearly all of its Middle Eastern counterparts, Hezbollah consists of Shiites (adherents to Shia Islam), rather than Sunnis. As will be explained in Chapter 10, Shia make up only about 10% to 15% of the world's Muslim population. They are mostly concentrated in India, Iran, Iraq, and Pakistan; relatively large numbers are also found in Azerbaijan, Lebanon, Turkey, Saudi Arabia, and Syria.

In English *Hezbollah* means "Party of God." The group also calls itself Islamic Jihad or Islamic Jihad for the Liberation of Palestine. It emerged in Lebanon following Israel's invasion of that nation in 1982. The FTO has ties to Iran and Syria. In *Country Reports on Terrorism 2010*, the DOS states that "Hizballah receives training, weapons, and explosives, as well as political diplomatic, monetary, and organizational aid from Iran." The FTO's relationship with Syria has deteriorated since 2005, when Syrian agents were implicated in the assassination of the former Lebanese prime minister Rafic Hariri (1944–2005).

Hezbollah is blamed for a number of terrorist attacks against Israeli and U.S. interests, including some of the most notorious incidents of the 1980s and 1990s. Specif-

ically, U.S. officials believe Hezbollah agents bombed the U.S. embassy and marine barracks in Lebanon in 1983 and 1984, killing over 300 Americans; hijacked TWA Flight 847 in 1985 and killed a U.S. Navy diver aboard the plane; and participated in the 1996 bombing of the Khobar Towers (a housing facility for U.S. military personnel) in Saudi Arabia, during which 19 Americans were killed and 515 injured.

Lebanon bounds Israel to the north. In about 2005 the Lebanese government allowed Hezbollah militants essentially to take control of southern Lebanon, ostensibly to guard against an Israeli attack. There were many skirmishes between Hezbollah militants and Israeli military forces. In July 2006 Hezbollah agents crossed the border and kidnapped two Israeli soldiers. In response, Israel conducted air strikes and fired missiles against a variety of targets in Lebanon, before launching a ground invasion. Likewise, Hezbollah fired hundreds of rockets into Israel. Following approximately a month of fighting, a cease-fire was brokered by the UN. In August 2006 the UN Security Council passed Resolution 1701, which called for the withdrawal of Israeli troops from Lebanon and the disarming of Hezbollah fighters. The DOS indicates in *Country Reports on Terrorism 2008* (April 2009, http://www.state.gov/documents/organization/122599.pdf) that after 2006 Hezbollah began reducing its overt (open) military presence in southern Lebanon; however, the group is believed to have maintained several weapons caches there.

In May 2008 Hezbollah militants seized control of West Beirut after a violent skirmish with Lebanese government supporters. In an effort to avoid civil war, an agreement was negotiated in which the Lebanese government provided Hezbollah-affiliated leaders with seats in the cabinet. This agreement gave Hezbollah substantially more power over government decisions and policies. In fact, the DOS notes in *Country Reports on Terrorism 2010* that "the Lebanese government and the majority of the Arab world still recognize Hizballah as a legitimate 'resistance group' and political party."

Hezbollah is a focal point of diplomatic tension between Israel and Iran. As will be explained in Chapter 6, that relationship became even more strained in 2011 and 2012 over Iran's alleged program to develop nuclear weapons. In July 2012 six Israelis and one Bulgarian were killed by a suicide bomber who boarded a tourist bus in Bulgaria. The Israeli government blamed the attack on Hezbollah and Iran and threatened to retaliate.

MAJOR TERRORIST ACTS AND ATTEMPTS

Palestinian resistance groups have been responsible for many acts of terrorism since the founding of Israel in 1948. Until the 1960s these acts were largely restricted to areas within Israel and the Palestinian territories. The emergence of the Palestine Liberation Organization and various splinter groups changed the dynamics of terrorism, giving it a more international reach. Airline hijackings became a vexing problem throughout the region. Palestinian militants also ventured frequently into Western Europe to carry out terrorist acts.

Except for diplomatic personnel, Americans were not usually the target of terrorist attacks before the 1980s. This changed dramatically after the 1982 invasion of Lebanon by Israel. Israeli forces withdrew in 1983 and were replaced by international forces that included U.S. troops. This precipitated a number of deadly attacks against Americans in Lebanon and other nations. Kidnappings of U.S. citizens in Lebanon also became common; however, most victims were eventually released unharmed. By the end of the decade airline hijackings around the world had largely been eliminated because of heightened airport security.

During the early 1990s terrorists began striking on U.S. soil. In 1993 there were two such attacks: an ambush at CIA headquarters in Virginia by a lone gunman and a bombing at the World Trade Center in New York City. Within the next few years the al Qaeda terrorist network under bin Laden became a major force in terrorism and began targeting U.S. interests worldwide. On September 11, 2001, members of this network hijacked and commandeered four American airliners. Three of the airplanes were purposely flown into buildings: the Pentagon in Arlington, Virginia, and both towers of the World Trade Center in New York City. The fourth plane crashed in Pennsylvania, after a struggle between the hijackers and the passengers. In total, over 2,700 people were killed in the one-day attacks. As of October 2012, the so-called 9/11 attack was the most recent terrorist attack by an FTO on U.S. soil.

The Most Serious Terrorist Incidents

Various media sources, private organizations, and government agencies maintain lists of some of the thousands of terrorist acts that have occurred around the world over the past few decades. The DOS features a listing in "Significant Terrorist Incidents, 1961–2003: A Brief Chronology" (March 2004, http://www.fas.org/irp/threat/terror_chron.html). The following are only a few of the events mentioned by the DOS that have had major effects in terms of U.S. casualties or influence on U.S. foreign policy and public opinion:

- Olympic Games, Munich, Germany (1972)—Palestinian terrorists seized 11 Israeli athletes, nine of whom were subsequently killed. West German authorities launched a bungled rescue attempt as the terrorists tried to leave the country with their hostages. The Black September group was blamed for this terrorist incident.

- Air France Airliner, Entebbe, Uganda (1976)—terrorists hijacked a plane containing 258 passengers and forced it to land in Entebbe. Israeli commandos infiltrated Uganda and rescued the hostages. The terrorists were members of the German left-wing organization Baader-Meinhof and the Popular Front for the Liberation of Palestine.

- U.S. embassy, Tehran, Iran (1979–81)—66 American diplomatic personnel were held hostage in the embassy by militant Iranian students, who were supported by the conservative Islamic government of Ruhollah Khomeini (1902?–1989). All hostages were eventually released unharmed.

- U.S. embassy, Beirut, Lebanon (1983)—Hezbollah claimed responsibility for bombing the embassy. The attack killed 63 people and injured 120.

- U.S. Marine Barracks, Beirut, Lebanon (1983)—Hezbollah claimed responsibility for a bombing that killed 242 Americans. Fifty-eight French troops were killed the same day in a similar attack on a French military compound.

- Restaurant, Torrejon, Spain (1984)—Hezbollah claimed responsibility for a bomb that killed 18 U.S. servicemen and injured 83.

- TWA Airliner (1985)—Hezbollah terrorists hijacked the flight and held it for 17 days, forcing it to fly to and from various airports around the Middle East. The terrorists killed an American hostage, a U.S. Navy sailor.

- *Achille Lauro* Cruise Liner (1985)—Palestine Liberation Front terrorists seized the cruise liner on the Mediterranean Sea with more than 700 hostages aboard. An American passenger in a wheelchair was thrown overboard.

- Pan Am Flight 103 (1988)—Libyan terrorists placed a bomb on the plane that exploded in flight over Lockerbie, Scotland. All 259 passengers and 11 people on the ground were killed.

- World Trade Center (1993)—a car bomb explosion in the underground garage killed six people and injured approximately 1,000. U.S. authorities blamed the followers of an Egyptian cleric living in the United States: Omar Abdel Rahman (1938–).

- Khobar Towers, Dhahran, Saudi Arabia (1996)—several terrorist groups claimed responsibility for bombing a housing facility for U.S. troops. Nineteen U.S. military personnel were killed and 515 were wounded.

- U.S. embassies, Nairobi, Kenya, and Dar es Salaam, Tanzania (1998)—bombs exploded nearly simultaneously at the embassies, killing 301 people and injuring thousands. Al Qaeda and bin Laden were blamed for the attacks.

- USS *Cole*, Aden, Yemen (2000)—a small explosives-laden boat rammed the U.S. destroyer and killed 17 American personnel and wounded 39. Al Qaeda was blamed for the incident.

- World Trade Center, New York City, and Pentagon, Arlington, Virginia (2001)—three hijacked planes piloted by terrorists were flown into these buildings. A fourth plane crashed before reaching its target, and all aboard were killed. In total, over 2,700 people, primarily Americans, were killed. Al Qaeda was blamed for the attacks.

- Nightclubs in Bali, Indonesia (2002)—an FTO linked to al Qaeda conducted bombings that killed 202 people, mostly foreign tourists.

More recent terrorist events include the following:

- Trains in Madrid, Spain (2004)—the Moroccan Islamic Combatant Group, an FTO linked to al Qaeda, bombed several commuter trains during morning rush hour. Nearly 200 people were killed and hundreds more were injured.

- Subway and bus in London, England (2005)—suicide bombers struck the mass transit system in different locations during morning rush hour. Over 50 people were killed and hundreds more were injured. According to the British government, in *Report of the Official Account of the Bombings in London on 7th July 2005* (May 11, 2006, http://www.official-documents .co.uk/document/hc0506/hc10/1087/1087.pdf), the bombings were carried out by four young Muslim men with extremist views.

- Multiple targets in Mumbai, India (2008)—10 heavily armed men stormed numerous facilities, including hotels, a hospital, a railway station, a Jewish center, and a café, leaving 174 dead and hundreds more wounded. Six Americans were among the dead. The attack was blamed on Lashkar-e Tayyiba, a terrorist group based in Pakistan.

- The U.S. consulate in Benghazi, Libya (2012)—four Americans, including the U.S. ambassador to Libya, died after armed militants stormed the consulate on the 11th anniversary of the September 11, 2001, terrorist attacks. As noted earlier in this chapter, the attackers are believed to have been members of a Libyan Salafist militia, Ansar al-Sharia, with ties to al Qaeda.

THWARTED ATTEMPTS. Besides the completed terrorist acts described in this chapter, there have been several major unsuccessful attempts since the 1990s in which the terrorists were thwarted by law enforcement or otherwise failed to complete their missions. The following are a few of the unsuccessful attacks:

- In 1994 a terrorist cell in the Philippines led by the Pakistani Ramzi Ahmed Yousef (1969–) was preparing to bomb nearly a dozen airliners bound from Asia to the United States and to assassinate Pope John Paul II (1920–2005). Yousef was the mastermind behind the 1993 bombing of the World Trade Center and the nephew of Khalid Sheikh Mohammed (1964–)—a top

al Qaeda figure believed to have overseen the 9/11 terrorist attacks. Both men were eventually captured by law enforcement.

- In December 1999 Ahmed Ressam (1967–) was caught trying to enter Port Angeles, Washington, near a Canadian border crossing, with a car full of explosives. Authorities believe the man was acting under al Qaeda orders to bomb targets during New Year's Eve celebrations.

- In December 2001 a Briton named Richard Colvin Reid (1973–) was on a commercial airliner flying from Paris to Miami, Florida, when he tried to set off explosives hidden in his shoes. He was thwarted and overpowered by people aboard the plane and turned over to authorities. Reid was dubbed by the media as the "shoe bomber."

- In August 2006 British police captured two dozen suspects in England who were accused of planning to blow up as many as 10 planes bound from Europe to the United States. The plot centered on the use of liquid explosives hidden in carry-on items, such as sports drinks.

- In December 2009 Umar Farouk Abdulmutallab (1986–) was on a commercial airliner flying from Amsterdam, Netherlands, to Detroit, Michigan, when he tried to ignite explosives hidden in his underwear as the plane came in for a landing. The explosives did not detonate, and he was subdued by passengers and crew members. The Nigerian-born conspirator allegedly had ties to al Qaeda operatives in Yemen. Abdulmutallab's father had warned U.S. officials in Nigeria only a month before that his son had radical Islamic beliefs.

- In May 2010 street vendors alerted police to a smoking sport-utility vehicle that was parked in the busy Times Square area of New York City. The vehicle was packed with explosives, which failed to detonate. Officials arrested Faisal Shahzad (1979–) as he tried to flee the country and charged him with the attempted attack. Born in Pakistan, Shahzad had become an American citizen in 2009 and reportedly had been trained by terrorist operatives in Pakistan.

9/11 Terrorist Attacks

For many Americans and people around the globe, the events of September 11, 2001, were the most stunning terrorist attacks. In one day 19 individuals managed to kill more than 2,700 people and completely destroy the World Trade Center—a center of international commerce and a symbol of U.S. economic power. In July 2004 the National Commission on Terrorist Attacks upon the United States published its findings on the attack in the *9/11 Commission Report.*

The report uses data and information collected from a variety of sources to re-create the events leading up to and

FIGURE 3.8

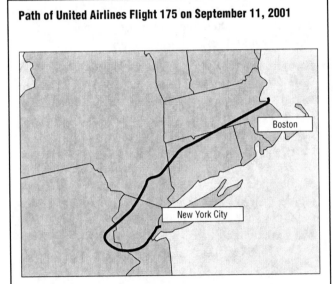

Path of American Airlines Flight 11 on September 11, 2001

SOURCE: Adapted from "American Airlines Flight 11," in *The 9/11 Commission Report*, National Commission on Terrorist Attacks upon the United States, July 22, 2004, http://www.9-11commission.gov/report/911Report.pdf (accessed July 12, 2012)

FIGURE 3.9

Path of United Airlines Flight 175 on September 11, 2001

SOURCE: Adapted from "United Airlines Flight 175," in *The 9/11 Commission Report*, National Commission on Terrorist Attacks upon the United States, July 22, 2004, http://www.9-11commission.gov/report/911Report.pdf (accessed July 12, 2012)

FIGURE 3.10

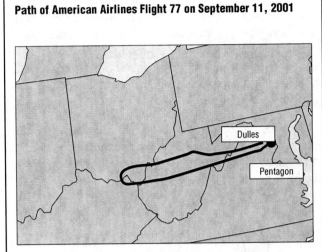

Path of American Airlines Flight 77 on September 11, 2001

SOURCE: Adapted from "American Airlines Flight 77," in *The 9/11 Commission Report*, National Commission on Terrorist Attacks upon the United States, July 22, 2004, http://www.9-11commission.gov/report/911Report.pdf (accessed July 12, 2012)

FIGURE 3.11

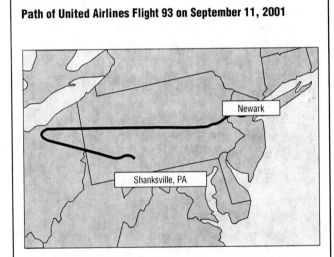

Path of United Airlines Flight 93 on September 11, 2001

SOURCE: Adapted from "United Airlines Flight 93," in *The 9/11 Commission Report*, National Commission on Terrorist Attacks upon the United States, July 22, 2004, http://www.9-11commission.gov/report/911Report.pdf (accessed July 12, 2012)

occurring on and after 9/11. On the morning of the attacks the 19 terrorists boarded four separate commercial airliners bound from the East Coast to the West Coast. Less than an hour after takeoff of each plane, the hijackers overpowered the cockpit crews and assumed piloting control. Figure 3.8, Figure 3.9, Figure 3.10, and Figure 3.11 show the flight paths of each commandeered plane. American Airlines Flight 11 and United Airlines Flight 175 crashed into the twin towers of the World Trade Center in New York City. American Airlines Flight 77 was flown into the Pentagon in Arlington, Virginia. United Airlines Flight 93 crashed into a field near Shanksville, Pennsylvania, after passengers stormed the cockpit. The hijackers' target for that plane is believed to have been the U.S. Capitol in Washington, D.C.

All the hijackers were from the Middle East; 16 of them were Saudi nationals. According to the report, six of the men were "lead operatives" who represented the most intelligent and best trained of the team. Four of these men piloted the hijacked planes after having studied for months at American flight schools. The lead operatives lived in the United States for up to a year before the day of the attacks. Thirteen of the men were so-called muscle hijackers, who were selected to assist in overpowering the flight crew and passengers. They arrived in the United States only months before the attacks after undergoing extensive training at al Qaeda terrorist camps in Afghanistan.

All the terrorists were selected for the operation because of their willingness to martyr themselves for the Islamist cause espoused by bin Laden. However, the commission found that only a handful of people within al Qaeda knew the details and scope of the hijack plan before it was carried out.

Domestic Counterterrorism Cases

Domestic counterterrorism cases involve terrorist crimes that were attempted or committed against targets and/or people within the United States. The following are a few of the major cases:

- 1993 World Trade Center Bombers—the FBI investigation of the 1993 bombing of the World Trade Center resulted in the convictions of six terrorists, including the ringleader, Ramzi Ahmed Yousef. In 1998 Yousef was sentenced to life in prison plus 240 years for his role in the bombing. Yousef had also put a bomb aboard a Filipino airliner in 1994 and masterminded a foiled plot that same year to blow up nearly a dozen airliners bound from Asia to the United States.

- Zacarias Moussaoui (1968–)—in August 2001 the FBI arrested Moussaoui for an immigration violation. He had been attending flight school in Minnesota and had aroused suspicions by his odd behavior. After 9/11 the FBI held Moussaoui as a material witness, believing that he was supposed to be the so-called 20th hijacker. He was charged with conspiring to commit terrorist acts. In May 2006 he was sentenced to life in prison.

- Lackawanna Six—this group of American citizens of Yemeni descent was accused of going to Afghanistan in early 2001 to support the Taliban and receive terrorist training at al Qaeda camps. In 2002 they were arrested by the FBI in Lackawanna, New York, and subsequently tried and convicted of supporting an FTO. Each received a sentence of between seven and 10 years in prison. A seventh conspirator was eventually arrested in Yemen and sentenced to prison.

- Portland Seven—this cell operated out of Portland, Oregon, and included six men and one woman accused of conspiring against U.S. troops in Afghanistan. All the men had tried to enter Afghanistan in 2001, but only one was successful. He was subsequently killed by Pakistani troops at an al Qaeda training camp. The remaining six were arrested in the United States in 2002 and received

varying sentences. Most of the cell members were American citizens.

- Iyman Faris (1969–)—Faris was a naturalized American citizen born in Kashmir. In 2003 he was arrested and charged with conspiring with al Qaeda to commit terrorism in the United States. He worked as a truck driver in Ohio and is believed to have been scoping out potential targets for terrorist attacks. Faris pleaded guilty and was sentenced to 20 years in prison.

- Northern Virginia Jihad—this network included 11 men of varying nationalities who were accused of operating a terrorist network in northern Virginia that supported the Taliban and Lashkar-e Tayyiba and conspired to wage war against the United States. A series of trials in 2004 resulted in convictions and sentences of various lengths for nine of the men. Two of the accused were acquitted.

- Lodi network—soon after 9/11 the FBI began investigating a mosque in Lodi, California, for alleged links between two Pakistani imams (spiritual leaders) and their followers with al Qaeda. The two imams were detained on immigration violations and ultimately left the country under threat of deportation. In early 2006 two members of the Lodi community, a father and son, were tried for terrorism charges. The father pleaded guilty to a lesser immigration charge. The son was convicted for attending a terrorist training camp in Pakistan and lying about it to the FBI.

- Fort Dix Conspirators—in May 2007 six Muslim men from New Jersey and Pennsylvania were arrested and charged with planning a terrorist attack against Fort Dix, a U.S. Army base in New Jersey. The men had collected an arsenal of weapons and hoped to kill as many soldiers as possible during the attack. In December 2008 five of the men were convicted of conspiracy to commit terrorism, but were acquitted of attempted murder charges. Four of the five received life sentences; the fifth man received a sentence of 33 years in prison. The sixth man pleaded guilty in early 2008 to firearms charges and was sentenced to 20 months. He was released from prison in March 2009.

- JFK Terror Plot—in June 2007 four men were arrested for conspiring to blow fuel supply lines and tanks at the John F. Kennedy International Airport in New York City. One of the men, an American citizen from Guyana, formerly worked at the airport. His conspirators were from Guyana and Trinidad. All four were allegedly part of a Muslim extremist network. In June 2010 one of the conspirators pleaded guilty to lesser charges in exchange for a prison sentence of no more than 15 years. In 2011 and early 2012 the other three men were convicted and given life sentences.

- New York City Subway Plot—in September 2009 authorities arrested three Afghanistan natives and charged them with plotting suicide bombings on the New York City subway. The men allegedly planned to set off backpack bombs on crowded trains during the morning rush hour. The plot was reportedly ordered by senior al Qaeda leaders in Pakistan who were later killed by U.S. drones. In early 2010 two of the accused pleaded guilty to the charges; the third man pleaded not guilty, but was convicted in May 2012 based on the testimony of his coconspirators.

- Fort Hood Shooting—in November 2009 Nidal Malik Hasan (1970?–), a U.S. Army psychiatrist, was arrested for allegedly shooting over 40 people during a rampage at the Fort Hood Army Base in Killeen, Texas. Thirteen of the victims died. Hasan was shot by military police officers. He survived but was paralyzed from the chest down. Hasan made his first court appearance in June 2010. He was charged with 13 counts of premeditated murder and 32 counts of attempted premeditated murder. Hasan allegedly had ties to the radical Islamic cleric Anwar al-Awlaki (1971–2011), who was linked to some of the 9/11 hijackers and other known and suspected terrorists. As of October 2012, Hasan's court martial was scheduled to begin later in the year.

HOMEGROWN TERRORISTS. Before 2009 very few U.S. citizens were accused or convicted of terrorist attacks against American people or targets. A notable exception was Timothy McVeigh (1968–2001), a New York native and antigovernment zealot who was executed in 2001 for the 1995 bombing of a federal building in Oklahoma that killed more than 160 people and wounded hundreds more. Beginning in 2009 a number of people who were either born in the United States or had become U.S. citizens were charged and arrested for plotting or committing terrorist attacks within the United States. These suspects are often collectively referred to as "homegrown" suspects. Figure 3.12 and Figure 3.13 list dozens of individuals, groups, and terrorist plots and attacks linked to homegrown suspects as of October 2011. Figure 3.12 gives information about the suspects themselves and their training, while Figure 3.13 summarizes the types of plots and attacks with which they have been linked and the investigative tools that helped authorities discover them. Some of these suspects converted to Islam from other religions and became radicalized—meaning that they embraced a very radical Islamic view that condones violence.

Other than Hasan, one of the most famous accused homegrown terrorists is Colleen LaRose (1963–). In October 2009 LaRose was arrested for allegedly providing material aid to terrorists and for recruiting people to murder a Swedish cartoonist who had drawn the head of Muhammad on a dog. LaRose and alleged coconspirator Jamie Paulin-Ramirez (1979–) were American-born citizens and Muslim converts. In 2011 both women pleaded guilty; as of October 2012 they had not been sentenced.

Perhaps the most wanted homegrown terrorist is Adam Gadahn (1978–), who is not listed in Figure 3.12 and Figure 3.13. Gadahn grew up in California in a Catholic and Jewish family. During the mid-1990s he converted to Islam and moved to Pakistan, where he became affiliated with al Qaeda. He appeared in numerous al Qaeda videos calling on Muslims to wage violent jihad against Jews and their supporters. In 2006 Gadahn was indicted in the United States for treason and for providing material support to al Qaeda. A charge of treason is very serious and very rare. Prior to 2006 it had been more than 50 years since anyone has been charged with treason. As of October 2012, Gadahn remained at large. There was a $1 million reward for information leading to his capture.

Worldwide Incidents Tracking System

The NCTC maintains the Worldwide Incidents Tracking System (WITS; http://www.nctc.gov/wits/wits nextgen.html). The WITS database includes statistics gathered by U.S. agencies on the number, location, and type of terrorist incidents committed around the world each year and the number of people killed, injured, or kidnapped during these incidents. The NCTC summarizes these data in annual reports. As of October 2012, the most recent publication was *The National Counterterrorism Center Report on Terrorism, 2011* (March 12, 2012, http://www.nctc.gov/docs/2011_NCTC_Annual_Report _Final.pdf). According to the NCTC, more than 10,000 terrorist attacks occurred in 2011 that affected nearly 45,000 victims in 70 countries; more than 12,500 of the victims died. Figure 3.14 shows the 15 countries that experienced the most attacks in 2011, while Figure 3.15 shows the 15 countries that experienced the most deaths due to terrorist attacks. Afghanistan, Iraq, and Pakistan had, by far, the most attacks of any of the countries. In 2011, 6,573 terrorist incidents in these three countries left 8,449 people dead. Long-running wars and civil conflicts in Iraq and Afghanistan and conflicts in Pakistan, which neighbors Afghanistan, will be described in detail in Chapter 4.

U.S. PUBLIC OPINION ON TERRORISM

Since 9/11 the possibility of new terrorist attacks on U.S. soil has been a source of concern for many Americans. However, polling shows that this concern has decreased over time as no new attack has been successfully completed. The Gallup Organization conducts polls on a variety of topics related to national security. Several Gallup polls have been performed since 2001 that asked Americans how they feel about "the nation's security from terrorism." As shown in Table 3.2, 51% (10% were "very satisfied" and 41% were "somewhat satisfied") of those asked in January 2002 were satisfied that the United States was secure from terrorism. By January 2012 that number had risen to 72%

FIGURE 3.12

Jihadist terrorist plots and attacks by U.S. citizens or legal permanent residents, by profile and training, September 2001–October 2011

Legend: ○ No   ◐ Unclear   ● Yes

Plots and attacks*	Lone wolf	Muslim convert(s)	Suicidal or sought martyrdom	Radicalized in prison	Intended or actual plotting or training abroad
May 2009–October 2011					
Rezwan Ferdaus	No	No	Unclear	No	Unclear
Agron Hasbajrami	No	No	Yes	No	Yes
Naser Abdo	Yes	No	Unclear	No	No
Emerson Begolly	No	Yes	Unclear	No	No
Abdul-Latif and Mujahidh	No	Yes	Unclear	No	No
Yonathan Melaku	Yes	No	No	No	No
Ferhani and Mamdouh	No	No	No	No	No
Khalid Ali-M Aldawsari	Yes	No	Unclear	No	No
Antonio Martinez	No	No	Unclear	No	No
Mohamed Mohamud	No	No	Unclear	No	Yes
Farooque Ahmed	No	No	Unclear	No	Yes
Abdel Shehadeh	No	No	Unclear	No	Yes
Omar Hammami	No	Yes	Unclear	No	Yes
Jehad Mostafa	No	Unclear	Unclear	No	Yes
Shaker Masri	No	Unclear	Yes	No	Yes
Zachary Chesser	No	Yes	Unclear	No	Yes
The Rockwoods	No	Yes	Unclear	No	No
Alessa and Almonte	No	Unclear	Unclear	No	Unclear
Faisal Shahzad	No	Yes	Yes	No	Yes
Collen LaRose	No	Yes	Unclear	No	Yes
Northern Virginia Five	No	No	Unclear	No	Yes
al-Shabaab Recruiting	No	No	Yes	No	Yes
Ft. Hood (Nidal Hasan)	Yes	No	Yes	No	No
David Headley	No	No	Unclear	No	Yes
Tarek Mehanna	Unclear	No	Unclear	No	Yes
Hosam Smadi	No	No	Unclear	No	No
Michael Finton	No	Unclear	Unclear	No	No
Najibullah Zazi	No	No	Unclear	No	Yes
Betim Kaziu	No	No	Unclear	No	Yes
Daniel Boyd, et al	No	Yes	Unclear	No	Yes
Abdulhakim Muhammad	Yes	Yes	No	No	No
Newburgh Four	No	Yes	No	No	No
September 11, 2001–April 2009					
Bryant Neal Vinas	No	Yes	Unclear	No	Yes
JFK Airport Pipeline Plot	No	Unclear	Unclear	No	No
Fort Dix Six	No	Yes	Unclear	No	No
Daniel Maldonado	No	Yes	Yes	No	Yes
Derrick Shareef	No	Yes	Unclear	No	Yes
Houston Taliban Plot	No	Yes	Unclear	No	Yes
Liberty City Seven	No	Yes	Unclear	No	No
Mohammed Taheri-Azar	Yes	No	Unclear	No	No
Sadequee and Ahmed	No	No	Unclear	No	Yes
Toledo, Ohio Plotters	No	Unclear	Unclear	No	Yes
JIS Plotting in So. California	No	Yes	Unclear	Unclear	No
Lodi Case (the Hayats)	No	No	Unclear	No	Unclear
Albany Plot	No	Unclear	Unclear	No	No
New York City Subway Plot	No	Yes	Unclear	No	No
Iyman Faris	No	Unclear	Unclear	No	Yes
Ahmed Omar Abu Ali	No	Unclear	Unclear	No	Yes
Virginia Jihad Network	No	Yes	Unclear	No	Yes
Hasan Akbar	Yes	No	Unclear	No	No
Lackawanna Six	No	No	Unclear	No	Yes
Jose Padilla	No	Yes	Unclear	No	Yes
Portland Seven	No	Yes	Unclear	No	Yes

*Listed in chronological order.
Notes: The four attacks are highlighted in bold and italics.

SOURCE: Jerome P. Bjelopera, "Figure B-1. Homegrown Jihadist Terrorist Plots and Attacks since 9/11: Terrorist Profile and Training," in *American Jihadist Terrorism: Combating a Complex Threat*, Congressional Research Service, November 15, 2011, http://fpc.state.gov/documents/organization/178218.pdf (accessed July 26, 2012).

FIGURE 3.13

Jihadist terrorist plots and attacks by U.S. citizens or legal permanent residents, by target, endgame, and investigation tool, September 2001–October 2011

Legend: ○ No   ◑ Unclear   ● Yes

Plots and attacks[a]	Target U.S.	Target Foreign	Endgame Firearm(s)	Endgame Explosive(s)	Foreign fighter	Investigation tools[b] Informant/undercover agent	Internet/email monitoring
May 2009–October 2001							
Rezwan Ferdaus	Yes	Yes	Unclear	Yes	Yes	Yes	Yes
Agron Hasbajrami	No	Yes	No	Unclear	Yes	No	No
Naser Abdo	Yes	No	Yes	Yes	No	Unclear	No
Emerson Begolly	Yes	No	Yes	Yes	No	Yes	Yes
Abdul-Latif and Mujahidh	Yes	No	Yes	No	No	Yes	No
Yonathan Melaku	Yes	No	Yes	Yes	Unclear	No	No
Ferhani and Mamdouh	Yes	No	Yes	Yes	No	Yes	No
Khalid Ali-M Aldawsari	Yes	No	No	Yes	No	Yes	Yes
Antonio Martinez	Yes	No	No	Yes	No	Yes	Yes
Mohamed Mohamud	Yes	No	No	Yes	No	Yes	Yes
Farooque Ahmed	Yes	No	No	Yes	Unclear	Yes	Yes
Abdel Shehadeh	No	Yes	No	No	Yes	Yes	Unclear
Omar Hammami	No	Yes	No	No	Yes	No	No
Jehad Mostafa	No	Yes	No	No	Yes	No	No
Shaker Masri	No	Yes	No	No	Yes	Yes	No
Zachary Chesser	No	Yes	No	No	Yes	No	Yes
The Rockwoods	Unclear	No	Yes	Unclear	No	No	Yes
Alessa and Almonte	Unclear	Yes	No	No	Yes	Yes	Yes
Faisal Shahzad	Yes	No	No	Yes	Yes	No	Unclear
Collen LaRose	No	Yes	No	Unclear	Yes	No	Yes
Northern Virginia Five	No	Yes	No	No	Yes	No	Unclear
al-Shabaab Recruiting	No	Yes	No	No	Yes	No	No
Ft. Hood (Nidal Hasan)	Yes	No	Yes	No	No	Unclear	Unclear
David Headley	Unclear	Yes	Unclear	Yes	Yes	Unclear	Unclear
Tarek Mehanna	Yes	Yes	Yes	No	Yes	Yes	Yes
Hosam Smadi	Yes	No	No	Yes	No	Yes	No
Michael Finton	Yes	No	No	Yes	No	Yes	Unclear
Najibullah Zazi	Yes	No	No	Yes	Unclear	Unclear	Yes
Betim Kaziu	No	Yes	Yes	No	Yes	No	Yes
Daniel Boyd, et al	Yes	Yes	Yes	No	Yes	Yes	Unclear
Abdulhakim Muhammad	Yes	No	Yes	No	Unclear	No	No
Newburgh Four	Yes	No	No	Yes	No	Yes	No
September 11, 2001–April 2009							
Bryant Neal Vinas	Yes	Yes	No	Yes	Yes	No	No
JFK Airport Pipeline Plot	Yes	Yes	No	Yes	Unclear	Yes	No
Fort Dix Six	Yes	No	Yes	Unclear	Yes	Yes	No
Daniel Maldonado	No	Yes	No	No	Yes	No	Yes
Derrick Shareef	Yes	No	No	Yes	No	Yes	Yes
Houston Taliban Plot	Unclear	Yes	No	No	Yes	No	No
Liberty City Seven	Yes	No	No	Yes	No	Yes	No
Mohammed Taheri-Azar	Yes	No	No	*Drove SUV into crowd*	No	No	Yes
Sadequee and Ahmed	Yes	No	No	No	Unclear	Yes	No
Toledo, Ohio Plotters	No	Yes	No	No	Unclear	No	No
JIS Plotting in So. California	Yes	No	Yes	Unclear	No	Yes	No
Lodi Case (the Hayats)	Yes	No	No	No	Unclear	Yes	Unclear
Albany Plot	Yes	No	No	Unclear	No	Yes	No
New York City Subway Plot	Yes	No	No	No	No	Yes	No
Iyman Faris	Yes	No	No	*Plot to blow torch bridge cables*	No	Yes	No
Ahmed Omar Abu Ali	Yes	No	No	Yes	Unclear	Yes	No
Virginia Jihad Network	No	Yes	Yes	No	Yes	No	No
Hasan Akbar	Yes	No	Yes	Yes	No	No	No
Lackawanna Six	No	Yes	No	No	Yes	No	No
Jose Padilla	Yes	No	No	Yes	Yes	No	No
Portland Seven	No	Yes	No	No	Yes	Yes	Yes

[a]Listed in chronological order. The four attacks are highlighted in bold and Italics.
[b]As indicated in open source reporting. It is possible that the use of these tools in some cases remains classified information and thus is not reflected in this figure.

SOURCE: Jerome P. Bjelopera, "Figure B-2. Homegrown Jihadist Terrorist Plots and Attacks since 9/11: Targets, Endgames, and Investigative Tools," in *American Jihadist Terrorism: Combating a Complex Threat*, Congressional Research Service, November 15, 2011, http://fpc.state.gov/documents/organization/178218.pdf (accessed July 26, 2012)

FIGURE 3.14

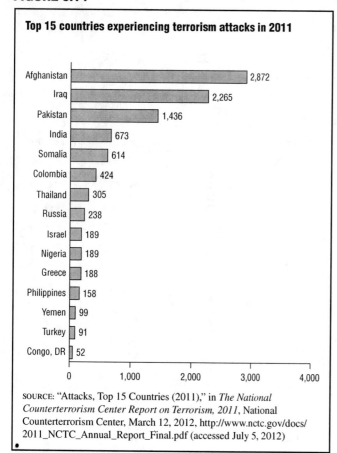

Top 15 countries experiencing terrorism attacks in 2011

SOURCE: "Attacks, Top 15 Countries (2011)," in *The National Counterterrorism Center Report on Terrorism, 2011*, National Counterterrorism Center, March 12, 2012, http://www.nctc.gov/docs/2011_NCTC_Annual_Report_Final.pdf (accessed July 5, 2012)

FIGURE 3.15

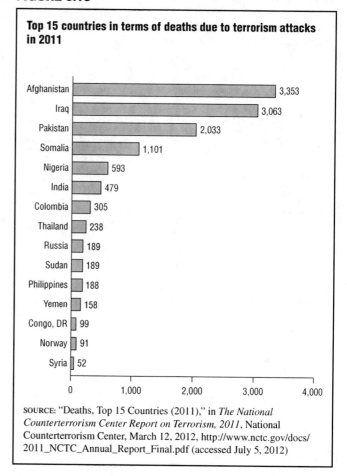

Top 15 countries in terms of deaths due to terrorism attacks in 2011

SOURCE: "Deaths, Top 15 Countries (2011)," in *The National Counterterrorism Center Report on Terrorism, 2011*, National Counterterrorism Center, March 12, 2012, http://www.nctc.gov/docs/2011_NCTC_Annual_Report_Final.pdf (accessed July 5, 2012)

(23% were "very satisfied" and 49% were "somewhat satisfied"). Likewise, fear of a terrorist act within the United States has also dissipated. Figure 3.16 shows the results of a Gallup poll in which respondents were asked "how likely is it that there will be acts of terrorism in the United States over the next several weeks." In late 2001, 85% of those asked felt that such attacks were very or somewhat likely to occur. By September 2011 that number had dropped to 38%.

However, Gallup polls reveal that respondents increasingly believe that the United States is not "winning the war against terrorism." Figure 3.17 shows public opinion on this subject recorded between late 2001 and late 2011. In September 2011 less than half (46%) of those asked said neither side was winning the war. Another 42% said the United States and its allies were winning, whereas 9% believed the terrorists were winning.

TABLE 3.2

Public satisfaction with the nation's security from terrorism, selected years 2002–12

	Very satisfied	Somewhat satisfied	Somewhat dissatisfied	Very dissatisfied	No opinion	Total satisfied	Total dissatisfied
2012 Jan 5–8	23	49	14	10	5	72	24
2008 Jan 4–6	14	44	20	17	4	58	37
2007 Jan 15–18	13	40	26	18	3	53	44
2006 Jan 9–12	16	42	23	16	3	58	39
2005 Jan 3–5	14	44	22	17	3	58	39
2004 Jan 12–15	19	51	16	13	1	70	29
2003 Jan 13–16	11	43	26	17	3	54	43
2002 Jan 7–9	10	41	27	20	2	51	47

SOURCE: Jeff Jones and Lydia Saad, "Q.10Q. Next, we'd like to know how you feel about the state of the nation in each of the following areas. For each one, please say whether you are—very satisfied, somewhat satisfied, somewhat dissatisfied, or very dissatisfied. If you don't have enough information about a particular subject to rate it, just say so. How about—The nation's security from terrorism?" in *Gallup Poll Social Series: Mood of the Nation*, The Gallup Organization, January 2012, http://www.gallup.com/file/poll/152132/Long_satisfaction_list_120123%20%20.pdf (accessed July 3, 2012). Copyright © 2012 Gallup, Inc. All rights reserved. The content is used with permission; however, Gallup retains all rights of republication.

FIGURE 3.16

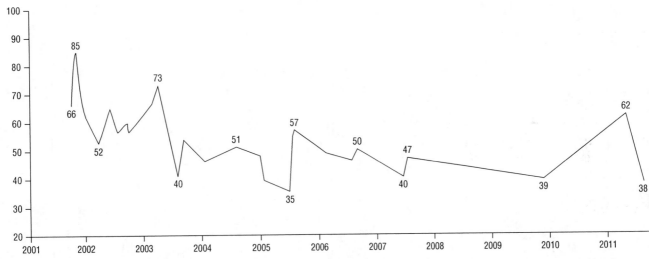

Public perceptions about the likelihood of terrorism in the United States, 2001–11

HOW LIKELY IS IT THAT THERE WILL BE ACTS OF TERRORISM IN THE UNITED STATES OVER THE NEXT SEVERAL WEEKS—VERY LIKELY, SOMEWHAT LIKELY, NOT TOO LIKELY, OR NOT AT ALL LIKELY?

[% very/somewhat likely]

SOURCE: Lydia Saad, "Perceived Likelihood of Terrorism in the U.S.—% Very/Somewhat Likely," in *Americans' Fear of Terrorism in U.S. Is Near Low Point*, The Gallup Organization, September 2, 2011, http://www.gallup.com/poll/149315/Americans-Fear-Terrorism-Near-Low-Point.aspx (accessed July 12, 2012). Copyright © 2011 Gallup, Inc. All rights reserved. The content is used with permission; however, Gallup retains all rights of republication.

FIGURE 3.17

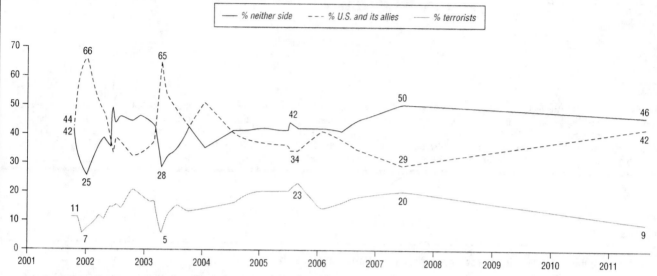

Public perceptions about who is winning the war against terror, 2001–11

WHO DO YOU THINK IS CURRENTLY WINNING THE WAR AGAINST TERRORISM—[ROTATED: THE U.S. AND ITS ALLIES, NEITHER SIDE, OR THE TERRORISTS]?

SOURCE: Frank Newport, "American's Perceptions of Who Is Winning War against Terrorism," in *Ten Years in, Many Doubt U.S. Is Winning War on Terrorism*, The Gallup Organization, September 9, 2011, http://www.gallup.com/poll/149381/Ten-Years-Later-Doubts-War-Terrorism.aspx (accessed July 12, 2012). Copyright © 2011 Gallup, Inc. All rights reserved. The content is used with permission; however, Gallup retains all rights of republication.

CHAPTER 4
THE WARS IN AFGHANISTAN AND IRAQ

The United States' immediate response to the terrorist attacks of September 11, 2001 (9/11), was to invade Afghanistan. The goal was twofold: capture or kill Osama bin Laden (1957?–2011; the mastermind of the attacks) and the other members of the al Qaeda terrorist organization and overthrow the Taliban government, which was harboring and supporting al Qaeda. The invasion was a resounding military success. The repressive Taliban government was defeated and replaced by a more liberal, U.S.-friendly regime. Major terrorist training camps were destroyed and many members of al Qaeda were captured or forced to flee. The victory was not complete, however, because bin Laden was neither captured nor killed right away. Furthermore, the Taliban and its supporters remained in Afghanistan and continued to wage a surprisingly strong insurgency (resistance) against the occupying forces. As of October 2012, U.S. troops continued to serve as part of an international military force intended to help bring stability to the war-torn country.

In 2003 the United States invaded Iraq. One of the drivers was assessments from the U.S. intelligence community that Iraq had collaborated with al Qaeda and was amassing weapons of mass destruction (WMDs). These claims were later proved to be inaccurate. The U.S. military operation in Iraq was at first successful. The longtime Iraqi dictator Saddam Hussein (1937–2006) was ousted from power, and a new, more democratic government was slowly installed. However, a fierce insurgency erupted, driven by Hussein supporters and militant elements opposed to the occupation. The violence soon widened into a bitter and deadly civil struggle between Iraqi factions divided by religious and political differences. By 2008 the worst of the insurgency was over, and the United States withdrew all of its combat troops from Iraq by the end of 2011. However, as of October 2012, the future stability of Iraq remained in question as the country was plagued by political infighting and terrorist activities.

AFGHANISTAN

Afghanistan is a landlocked country in south-central Asia. Its largest neighbors are Pakistan to the east and south and Iran to the west. (See Figure 4.1.) Turkmenistan, Uzbekistan, and Tajikistan border Afghanistan to the north. Its capital is Kabul. The Central Intelligence Agency (CIA) indicates in *The World Factbook: Afghanistan* (September 17, 2012, https://www.cia.gov/library/publications/the-world-factbook/geos/af.html) that Afghanistan covers 251,830 square miles (652,230 square km) and is slightly smaller than the state of Texas. In July 2012 the population was estimated at 30.4 million. According to the CIA, the largest ethnic groups are the Pashtun (42%) and Tajik (27%). The primary languages in Afghanistan are Afghan, Persian, and Dari, which approximately half of the population speaks, and Pashto, which is spoken by just over one-third (35%) of Afghans. Approximately 80% of Afghans are Sunni Muslims, 19% are Shia Muslims, and the remaining 1% practice other religions. The official name of the country is the Islamic Republic of Afghanistan.

A Legacy of War

The history of Afghanistan revolves around an ancient group of people called the Pashtun. As described by the article "Peoples: Pashtun" (*National Geographic*, July 2005), the Pashtun have lived in this region for centuries and have survived conquest by many invaders, including the Persians, Macedonians, Turks, and Mongols. They have earned a reputation as being fierce fighters. However, the Pashtun are also known for in-fighting and waging blood feuds among themselves. They are a group of tribes that together make up the largest surviving tribal society in the world. They adhere to an ancient strict code of conduct called *pakhtunwalimale* that specifies rules for all areas of society and everyday life. The Pashtun were known by the Persian term *Afghan* long before their land was called Afghanistan.

FIGURE 4.1

Map of Afghanistan, 2012

SOURCE: "Map of Afghanistan," in "South Asia: Afghanistan," *The World Factbook*, Central Intelligence Agency, 2012, https://www.cia.gov/library/publications/the-world-factbook/maps/maptemplate_af.html (accessed July 21, 2012).

Afghanistan's Islamic history dates back to the seventh century and is described by the Library of Congress (LOC) in *A Country Study: Afghanistan* (March 22, 2011, http://lcweb2.loc.gov/frd/cs/aftoc.html). In 637 Muslims from the Arab empire invaded the region and maintained power for several centuries. The LOC notes that "from the seventh through the ninth centuries, most inhabitants of what is present-day Afghanistan, Pakistan, southern parts of the former Soviet Union, and areas of northern India were converted to Sunni Islam."

In *World Factbook: Afghanistan*, the CIA reports that the founding of modern Afghanistan occurred in 1747, when warring Pashtun tribes were united under one leader. At that time the British Empire ruled the land to the east (India and modern-day Pakistan) and the Russians controlled Turkmenistan, Uzbekistan, and Tajikistan to the north. British and Afghan rulers warred over control of Afghanistan until 1919, when the country won its independence. What followed was a series of monarchies that culminated in a coup in 1978, which led to the installation of a highly unpopular communist government. In 1979 the Soviet Union invaded Afghanistan to prevent a brewing revolution and preserve communist rule. The Soviets waged a decade-long war but were driven out by well-armed rebels who called themselves the mujahideen (holy warriors).

Mujahideen and bin Laden

The mujahideen were young Muslims who came from around the world to fight against the Soviet forces as part of a jihad (holy war). In 1980 a wealthy young man named Osama bin Laden traveled from his homeland in Saudi Arabia to help the mujahideen. His role is described at length by the National Commission on Terrorist Attacks upon the United States in *The 9/11 Commission Report* (July 2004, http://www.9-11commission.gov/report/911Report.pdf). Bin Laden's specialty was raising money and recruiting volunteers, who came to be known as the Arab Afghans. He excelled at organizing fund-raising networks that included charities and wealthy donors throughout the world. These funds were used to buy arms and provide training for the Arab Afghans.

The United States, anxious to see its communist enemy defeated in Afghanistan, supported the mujahideen in its efforts. The *9/11 Commission Report* notes that the United States and Saudi Arabia secretly supplied billions of dollars' worth of weapons and equipment to the mujahideen through Pakistani military intelligence. However, there is no record of U.S. involvement with bin Laden or the Arab Afghans, who had their own funding sources. In 1988 the Soviets decided to withdraw from Afghanistan in the face of unrelenting resistance from the mujahideen. Bin Laden and his compatriots were reluctant to dismantle their well-funded and highly trained organization, so they decided to maintain it for future jihads. They began calling it al Qaeda, which means "the base" or "the foundation." In 1991 they set up operations in Sudan at the invitation of that country's leader and maintained camps in Afghanistan and Pakistan to train young militant Muslims as jihadists.

The Taliban and bin Laden

The demise of the communist government in Afghanistan left a power vacuum. Rival mujahideen factions began fighting for control. In *A Country Study: Afghanistan*, the LOC describes these events and notes that during the Soviet occupation the mujahideen were often described in the Western press as "'freedom fighters'—as if their goal were to establish a representative democracy in Afghanistan—in reality these groups each had agendas of their own that were often far from democratic." Civil war wracked the country until the mid-1990s, when a new political-military force—the Taliban—achieved power. The LOC points out that most members of the Taliban were Pashtun who attended or had recently graduated from religious schools called madrassas in southern Afghanistan and Pakistan.

According to the *9/11 Commission Report*, madrassas are privately funded religious schools that teach strict fundamentalist forms of Islam. Beginning in the 1970s the schools started appearing in southern Pakistan because the government could not afford to educate the many Afghan refugees who had fled there to escape the violence in their own country. The report notes that "these schools produced large numbers of half-educated young men with no marketable skills but with deeply held Islamic views." Eventually, Pakistan became concerned about the presence of so many militant young men within its borders, so it encouraged them to return to Afghanistan and restore order there.

By 1996 the Taliban had seized control over most of Afghanistan. In May of that year bin Laden moved the bulk of his al Qaeda organization from Sudan back to Afghanistan. By this time he had enlarged his focus from regional Islamic causes to what the *9/11 Commission Report* calls "hatred of the United States." This development could be traced back to the 1990 Iraqi invasion of Kuwait. At that time bin Laden reportedly approached Saudi rulers and offered to organize a mujahideen force to drive out the Iraqis, but he was turned down. Saudi Arabia allied with the United States during the subsequent Persian Gulf War (1990–1991) and allowed U.S. troops to deploy from Saudi soil. This decision infuriated Islamic fundamentalists because they opposed the presence of nonbelievers in Saudi Arabia, the birthplace of Muhammad (c. 570–632). After criticizing Saudi leaders, bin Laden had his passport taken away. However, he managed to leave the country in 1991 and eventually turned up in Afghanistan, where he enjoyed the protection of the Taliban leader Mohammed Omar (1959?–). The two men had long-standing ties, as both had fought against the Soviet occupation of Afghanistan during the late 1970s.

Throughout the 1990s bin Laden expanded his al Qaeda network with the blessing of the Afghan Taliban regime. In 1998 he publicly announced his intention to wage a jihad against the United States by issuing a fatwa (an interpretation of Islamic law usually written by a scholar or religious authority) that was published in an Arabic-language newspaper in London. As described in Chapter 3, al Qaeda operatives then carried out a series of attacks against U.S. interests, including the 1998 bombings at two U.S. embassies in Africa, the 2000 bombing of the USS *Cole* in Yemen, and 9/11.

THE INVASION OF AFGHANISTAN

According to the *9/11 Commission Report*, on the evening of the 9/11 attacks President George W. Bush (1946–) addressed the nation about the tragedy and warned, "We will make no distinction between the terrorists who committed these acts and those who harbor them." The United States quickly identified the 9/11 hijackers as al Qaeda operatives under the control of bin Laden and determined that Afghanistan was harboring them.

U.S. View of the Taliban

Peter L. Bergen claims in *Holy War, Inc.: Inside the Secret World of Osama bin Laden* (2001) that the U.S. government was optimistic about the Taliban when it first seized power in Afghanistan. Bergen writes, "The State Department, which relied heavily on the Pakistanis for information on Afghanistan, was willing to embrace any group that looked as if it might bring some degree of stability to the country." Besides security concerns, the U.S. government had other priorities in Afghanistan, including a planned oil pipeline by a U.S. energy company and curbing Afghanistan's enormous illegal drug trade. There was hope that the new Afghan regime could help in these areas. However, U.S. leaders quickly became disillusioned with the Taliban.

Bergen notes that the Taliban imposed laws that blended "ultrapurist" Islam with traditional Pashtun customs. The result was a society in which men were forbidden to shave or trim their beards. All forms of entertainment, such as listening to the radio or flying a kite, were outlawed. Women were forced to cover themselves with thick head-to-toe cloaks called burkas and were not allowed in public unless accompanied by a male relative. Most women were forbidden to work or obtain an education. Taliban laws were enforced by religious police who roamed the streets and beat violators with sticks. By this time the Afghan people had suffered from decades of war that had destroyed most of the country's infrastructure; their economy was in shambles and food was in short supply.

As 2001 began, the United States was well aware that the Taliban was harboring terrorists. In 1999 and 2000 the United Nations (UN) Security Council imposed economic sanctions against Afghanistan for a variety of infractions, including providing sanctuary to and training international terrorists, particularly bin Laden and his associates. In December 2000 the UN demanded that bin Laden be surrendered and that all terrorist training camps be closed within a month. The Taliban angrily refused to comply, insisting that there was no evidence against bin Laden and that the sanctions were motivated by anti-Islamic sentiment.

Operation Enduring Freedom Begins

Within days after 9/11, the United States had decided to target Afghanistan. In an address to Congress on September 20, 2001, President Bush publicly blamed al Qaeda and bin Laden for the attacks and demanded that the Taliban hand over bin Laden and his top lieutenants or the United States would strike. According to the *9/11 Commission Report*, the demands had already been privately passed to the Taliban through the Pakistani government, which the United States had warned "would be at risk" unless it helped the United States against Afghanistan. As expected, Afghanistan refused to comply with U.S. demands.

By October 2001 a U.S. war plan had been compiled that was originally called Infinite Justice. However, fears about offending religious sensibilities prompted a quick name change to Operation Enduring Freedom (OEF) when U.S. officials learned that Muslims associate the term *infinite justice* with God's power. The *9/11 Commission Report* indicates that OEF had four phases:

- Phase one—deploy U.S. forces to Afghanistan's neighbors in readiness for an invasion. This step was begun almost immediately and entailed the cooperation of Pakistan and Uzbekistan.

- Phase two—conduct air strikes on Afghan targets and pair Special Operations teams with Taliban opposition groups to conduct damaging raids on al Qaeda strongholds. Even before this time, the CIA had been collaborating with opposition groups in northern Afghanistan known collectively as the Northern Alliance. Phase two began on October 7, 2001, and proceeded quickly with the help of United Kingdom (UK) military forces. By the end of the month most of the objectives of this phase had been achieved.

- Phase three—launch a ground invasion of Afghanistan to "topple the Taliban regime and eliminate al Qaeda's sanctuary." By early December 2001 the coalition of U.S. and Northern Alliance forces, with the assistance of UK military forces, had captured all major Afghan cities. However, bin Laden and Omar escaped.

- Phase four—the United States called this phase "security and stability operations." It began on December 22, 2001, when Hamid Karzai (1957–; an Afghani Pashtun) was installed as the head of the nation's interim government.

Afghanistan's System of Government

Following the U.S. invasion, Afghanistan began a series of democratic reforms. In 2004 the first national presidential election put Karzai in power for a five-year term. Even though the election itself was relatively violence-free, the country continued to struggle with internal problems. In 2009 Karzai was reelected amid widespread allegations of voter fraud and intimidation. Nick Schifrin reports in "With All Polling Stations Counted, Karzai Has 54% of Afghan Vote" (ABCNews.com, September 16, 2009) that Western observers suggested that 1 million to 1.5 million votes were fraudulent, representing one quarter of all the votes cast. In addition, Schifrin notes that much of Afghanistan was under Taliban control at the time of the election. Taliban leaders reportedly threatened attacks against voters and prevented people from voting as much as possible.

Afghanistan has a governing body called the National Assembly. According to the CIA, in *World Factbook: Afghanistan*, the National Assembly includes the 102-seat

Meshrano Jirga (House of Elders) and the Wolesi Jirga (House of People), which includes no more than 250 members. Most members of the Meshrano Jirga and all members of Wolesi Jirga are elected by voters. The last national elections were in 2010, and the next elections are expected to be held in 2015. The Afghan constitution (http://www.afghan-web.com/politics/current_constitution.html) was ratified in 2005.

MILITARY FORCES IN AFGHANISTAN
The International Security Assistance Force

In December 2001 Afghan opposition leaders met with UN officials at the so-called Bonn Conference to work out a plan for establishing a new permanent government for Afghanistan. The Bonn Agreement established three priorities: security, reconstruction, and political stability. The UN called for a multinational military force to secure the area in and around Kabul, the capital of Afghanistan. The result was the International Security Assistance Force (ISAF). The countries contributing troops to the ISAF are required to fund its operations.

In 2003 the North Atlantic Treaty Organization (NATO) assumed control of the ISAF under UN mandate and at the request of the Afghan government. In 2006 the ISAF relieved many U.S. and allied troops and expanded its command to include the entire country. According to the ISAF (2012, http://www.isaf.nato.int/mission.html), its mission in Afghanistan is: "In support of the Government of the Islamic Republic of Afghanistan, ISAF conducts operations in Afghanistan to reduce the capability and will of the insurgency, support the growth in capacity and capability of the Afghan National Security Forces (ANSF), and facilitate improvements in governance and socio-economic development in order to provide a secure environment for sustainable stability that is observable to the population."

In "ISAF's Mission in Afghanistan" (2012, http://www.nato.int/cps/en/natolive/topics_69366.htm), NATO lists the ISAF's mission priorities as protecting the Afghan people, neutralizing insurgents, building the ANSF (military and police forces), and "promoting effective governance."

According to NATO, in "International Security Assistance Force (ISAF): Key Facts and Figures" (http://www.nato.int/isaf/docu/epub/pdf/placemat.pdf), as of September 10, 2012, 112,579 troops from 50 nations were in the ISAF. The largest contingents were:

- United States—74,400 troops (66% of the total)

- United Kingdom—9,500 troops (8%)

- Germany—4,645 troops (4%)

- Italy—4,000 troops (4%)

- France—2,453 troops (2%)

- Poland—2,432 troops (2%)

FIGURE 4.2

Map of Afghanistan's provinces, 2012

SOURCE: Kenneth Katzman, "Figure A-1. Map of Afghanistan," in *Afghanistan: Post-Taliban Governance, Security, and U.S. Policy*, Congressional Research Service, May 3, 2012, http://www.hsdl.org/?view&did=708508 (accessed July 20, 2012)

As shown in Figure 4.2, Afghanistan consists of 34 provinces. As of October 2012, NATO (http://www.isaf .nato.int/) had divided Afghanistan into six regional commands (RCs) for ISAF purposes:

- North—Badakhshan, Baghlan, Balkh, Faryab, Jowzjan, Kunduz, Samangan, Sar-e Pul, and Takhar Provinces

- East—Bamyan, Ghazni, Kapisa, Khost, Kunar, Laghman, Logar, Nangarhar, Nuristan, Paktika, Paktiya, Panjshayr, Parwan, and Wardak Provinces

- Capital—Kabul Province

- South—Kandahar, Daykundi, Uruzgan, and Zabul Provinces

- Southwest—Helmand and Nimroz Provinces

- West—Badghis, Farah, Ghor, and Herat Provinces

The East, South, and Southwest RCs were commanded by the United States, while Germany had lead command over the North RC, Italy over the West RC, and Turkey over the Capital RC. As of October 2012, the U.S. general John R. Allen (1953–) had overall command of the ISAF in Afghanistan.

The ISAF mission includes the formation of provincial reconstruction teams (PRTs). These are small teams of civilians and military personnel that are stationed around the country to protect and support international aid agencies and reconstruction workers. According to NATO (http://www.isaf.nato.int/), there were more than 20 PRTs operating throughout Afghanistan as of October 2012. They assist the Afghan people through infrastructure, education, and economic development projects, such as building schools, digging irrigation ditches, installing wells and reservoirs, and supplying agricultural and medical supplies and aid. Each PRT is led and supported by various nations.

OEF Troops

As noted earlier, over 74,000 U.S. troops were part of the ISAF as of September 2012. However, several thousand more U.S. troops were deployed in Afghanistan under direct U.S. command as part of OEF. For example, in *Report on Progress toward Security and Stability in Afghanistan: United States Plan for Sustaining the Afghanistan National Security Forces* (April 2012, http://www.defense.gov/pubs/pdfs/Report_Final_SecDef_04_27_12.pdf), the U.S. Department of Defense (DOD) notes that its Combined Joint Interagency Task Force 435 was responsible for detainee operations supporting OEF activities in Afghanistan.

According to the UK Ministry of Defence, in "Operations in Afghanistan: British Forces" (2012, http://mod.uk/DefenceInternet/FactSheets/OperationsFactsheets/OperationsInAfghanistanBritishForces.htm), an unnamed number of UK troops were also supporting the U.S.-led

OEF operations in 2012. OEF forces, like ISAF forces, are under the overall command of General Allen.

THE INSURGENCY RISES AND FALLS

In 2006 there was an upswing in militant violence in Afghanistan, particularly in the southern part of the country. Pam O'Toole reports in "Who Are the Militants in Afghanistan?" (BBCNews.com, August 18, 2006) that the insurgents represented a multitude of factions, including former Taliban leaders, warlords, people engaged in the lucrative drug trade, new graduates of Pakistani madrassas, and an assortment of radical Islamic militants. O'Toole states that the situation was complicated by a "complex web of shifting allegiances, tribal, ethnic and local rivalries and feuds within Afghan society." Insurgent attacks on ISAF, OEF, and ANSF forces and on civilians began increasing dramatically in 2006. Figure 4.3 shows the number of average daily attacks between March 2004 and March 2010. By August 2009 (the month in which Afghanistan held elections for the president and provincial councils) the attacks had reached a war-time high.

FIGURE 4.3

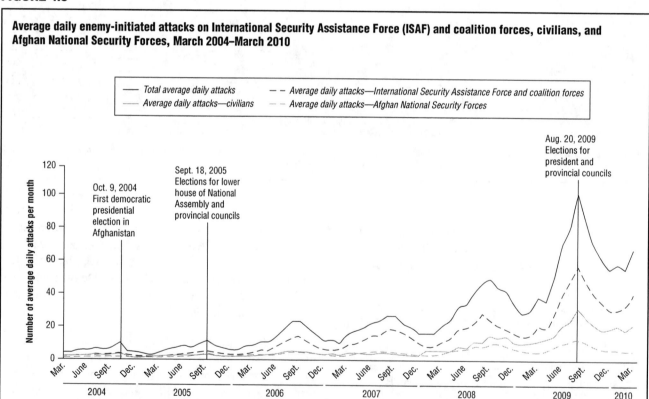

Average daily enemy-initiated attacks on International Security Assistance Force (ISAF) and coalition forces, civilians, and Afghan National Security Forces, March 2004–March 2010

Notes: Data on attacks against civilians include attacks against Afghan nationals and other civilians, U.S. and non-U.S. contractors, nongovernmental organizations, and Afghan government personnel. Data on attacks against the International Security Assistance Force and coalition forces include attacks against U.S. and International Security Assistance Force military personnel.

Defense Intelligence Agency officials, in October 2009, transitioned to using a more comprehensive source database of security incidents from which to identify enemy-initiated attacks. As such, some of the specific attack levels shown in this figure may be slightly higher than the attack levels noted for the same months in a November 2009 report because these numbers have been updated. However, the general trend of attacks remains the same as previously reported.

SOURCE: "Figure 1. Average Daily Enemy-Initiated Attacks Reported by Type in Afghanistan, March 2004 to March 2010," in *Afghanistan's Security Environment*, U.S. Government Accountability Office, May 5, 2010, http://www.gao.gov/new.items/d10613r.pdf (accessed July 31, 2012)

According to the LOC, in *Country Profile: Afghanistan* (August 2008, http://lcweb2.loc.gov/frd/cs/profiles/Afghanistan.pdf), Taliban fighters involved in the insurgency were crossing in and out of neighboring Pakistan to elude ISAF and OEF forces. The U.S. Government Accountability Office (GAO) explains in *Afghanistan's Security Environment* (May 5, 2010, http://www.gao.gov/new.items/d10613r.pdf) that "the insurgency [was] facilitated by several factors, including the porous nature of the Afghanistan-Pakistan border region, the ineffective nature of governance and services in various parts of Afghanistan, assistance from militant groups outside of Pakistan and Afghanistan, and continued financial support in the form of narcotics trafficking revenue and funds from outside of the region."

As the insurgency grew in strength, the United States responded by sending more troops to Afghanistan. In February and March 2009 President Barack Obama (1961–) ordered over 20,000 additional troops to Afghanistan. According to the article "Obama Unveils Afghanistan Plan" (Associated Press, March 27, 2009), Obama vowed to "'disrupt, dismantle and defeat' the terrorist al-Qaida network in Afghanistan and neighboring Pakistan." ISAF and OEF forces also engaged in more air strikes and raids against suspected insurgent camps and hideouts. However, this aggressive approach resulted in highly publicized deaths of Afghan civilians. For example, the article "NATO Strike Kills 27 Afghanistan Civilians" (BBCNews.com, February 22, 2010) lists a series of "botched" air raids that occurred between July 2008 and September 2009 and reportedly killed nearly 350 civilians. Even though U.S. and NATO leaders claimed the number of civilian deaths in these strikes were lower than the numbers reported by the media, Afghan officials insisted that the numbers were even higher.

McChrystal's Bleak Report: Commander's Initial Assessment

In August 2009 General Stanley A. McChrystal (1954–), the commander of the ISAF and the OEF, released the assessment report *Commander's Initial Assessment* (http://media.washingtonpost.com/wp-srv/politics/documents/Assessment_Redacted_092109.pdf?hpid=topnews). McChrystal presented a bleak outlook regarding operations in Afghanistan, noting, "Although considerable effort and sacrifice have resulted in some progress, many indicators suggest the overall effort is deteriorating." The general cited numerous problems including the growing insurgency, corruption in the Afghan government, poor performance by the ISAF, and lack of confidence of the general population in the national government. He also complained that military forces in Afghanistan were so "pre-occupied with protection of our own forces, we have operated in a manner that distances us—physically and psychologically—from the people we seek to protect."

He pointed out that civilian casualties from successful military campaigns damaged the chances for real stability in Afghanistan. In addition, he noted that the population can be a source of intelligence and resistance against the insurgents, but that "they can often change sides" and support the insurgents. He stated, "Communities make deliberate choices to resist, support, or allow insurgent influence. The reasons for these choices must be better understood."

McChrystal called for a new strategy to be employed in Afghanistan and for more troops to be sent to the battlefield. President Obama was under pressure from his liberal supporters to end U.S. involvement in the war and from conservatives to escalate the war. In December 2009 he attempted to appease both sides by announcing that 30,000 additional U.S. troops would be deployed to Afghanistan by the summer of 2010. However, he also said that the United States would begin withdrawing its forces in July 2011.

Violence and Transition

According to the GAO, in *Afghanistan's Security Environment*, by May 2010 more than half of the 30,000 troops had been deployed. Also, an additional 200 U.S. government civilians had arrived in Afghanistan to assist with security measures. Large-scale military operations were carried out in partnership with Afghan forces during the spring and early summer of 2010 in southern Afghanistan. The fighting was fierce. Figure 4.4 shows the number of enemy-initiated attacks in Afghanistan on a monthly basis between January 2008 and March 2012. It should be noted that the attacks peak each summer, which is the primary fighting season in Afghanistan. The violence reached a new high during the summer of 2010, when 4,000 or more attacks occurred each month.

On June 7, 2010, the 104-month war in Afghanistan became the longest-running war in U.S. history. There was more bad news that month. A national peace conference held in Kabul was marred by Taliban gunfire and rocket attacks. That year would prove to be the worst of the war in terms of U.S. military casualties: 437 personnel were killed in action or died from combat wounds. (See Figure 4.5.) However, by the end of the year the first official arrangements had been made for transferring security responsibility for Afghanistan from the United States and NATO to the Afghan government. In *Report on Progress toward Security and Stability in Afghanistan* (November 2010, http://www.defense.gov/pubs/November_1230_Report_FINAL.pdf), the DOD indicates that in September 2010 the Joint Afghan-NATO Inteqal Board met for the first time to discuss the transition process. NATO explains in "Transition: *Inteqal*" (October 2010, http://www.isaf.nato.int/images/stories/File/factsheets/1667-10_Inteqal_LR_en.pdf) that the term *Inteqal* means "transition" in the Afghan languages of Dari and Pashto.

FIGURE 4.4

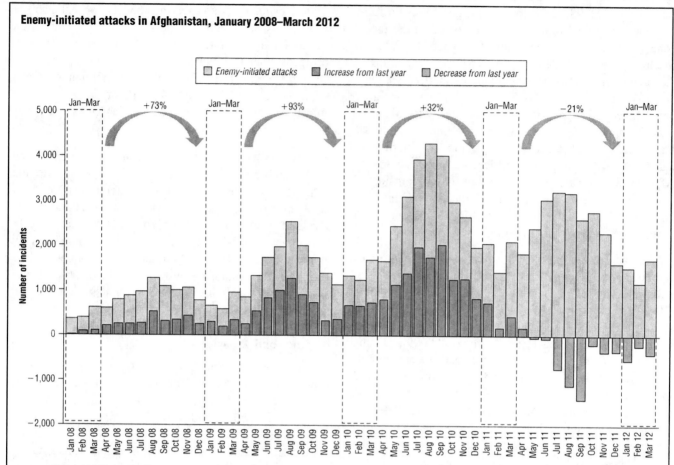

Enemy-initiated attacks in Afghanistan, January 2008–March 2012

SOURCE: "Figure 26. Enemy-Initiated Attacks Nationwide Year-over-Year Change," in *Report on Progress toward Security and Stability in Afghanistan: United States Plan for Sustaining the Afghanistan National Security Forces*, U.S. Department of Defense, April 2012, http://www.defense.gov/pubs/pdfs/Report_Final_SecDef_04_27_12.pdf (accessed July 20, 2012)

On November 20, 2010, NATO issued the "Lisbon Summit Declaration" (http://www.nato.int/cps/en/natolive/official_texts_68828.htm?mode=press release), which made the following pronouncements about the transition:

- It was to begin in early 2011

- It was to be "conditions-based, not calendar-driven"

- It would be completed before the end of 2014 at which time Afghan forces would assume "full responsibility for security across the whole of Afghanistan"

Catherine Dale of the Congressional Research Service (CRS) notes in *In Brief: Next Steps in the War in Afghanistan? Issues for Congress* (June 15, 2012, http://fpc.state.gov/documents/organization/193693.pdf) that the Inteqal plan was accelerated in May 2012 at the NATO Chicago Summit. In "Chicago Summit Declaration" (May 21, 2012, http://www.nato.int/cps/en/natolive/official_texts_87595.htm), NATO calls for the Afghan government to take lead responsibility for its national security by mid-2013. International forces will shift to a supporting role at that time. Lastly, the ISAF mission will be com-

pleted by the end of 2014. Then a 10-year transformation period will begin, during which international participants will continue to support Afghanistan.

In June 2011 President Obama announced plans to significantly drawdown U.S. troop levels in Afghanistan. According to Dale, the 2010–11 troop surge boosted the U.S. military presence in Afghanistan to 100,000 troops. Approximately 10,000 troops were scheduled to leave by year-end 2011 and another 23,000 by the end of September 2012, leaving an estimated 68,000 troops who would remain in Afghanistan. The article "Withdrawal of US Troops from Afghanistan Halfway Done, Top Commander Says" (Associated Press, July 23, 2012) reports that 10,000 U.S. troops left Afghanistan in 2011. In "Commander Nominated to Lead War in Afghanistan" (*New York Times*, October 10, 2012), Elisabeth Bumiller indicates that as of September 2012 an additional 23,000 troops had departed Afghanistan. As will be described later in this chapter, in May 2012 the United States and Afghanistan signed a partnership agreement that grants U.S. forces access to Afghan facilities only

FIGURE 4.5

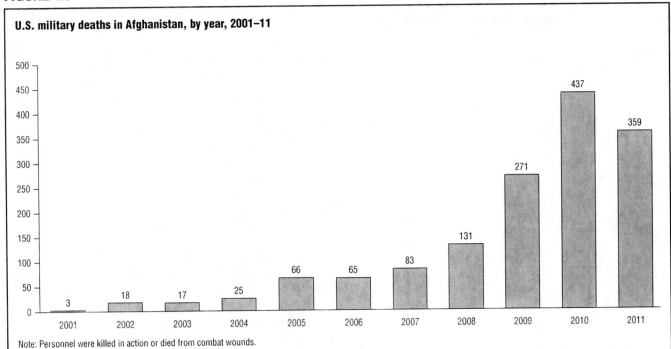

U.S. military deaths in Afghanistan, by year, 2001–11

Note: Personnel were killed in action or died from combat wounds.

SOURCE: Adapted from "U.S. Military Casualties—Operation Enduring Freedom (OEF) Casualty Summary by Month (as of July 30, 2012)," in *Defense Casualty Analysis System*, U.S. Department of Defense, July 30, 2012, https://www.dmdc.osd.mil/dcas/pages/report_oef_month.xhtml# (accessed July 31, 2012)

through 2014. However, the agreement does call for the negotiation of a bilateral security agreement that leaves open the possibility that some U.S. forces could be deployed in Afghanistan after 2014.

Casualties in Afghanistan

MILITARY CASUALTIES. NATO (2012, http://www .isaf.nato.int/article/casualty-report/index.php) publishes a brief notification statement following the death of any ISAF member in Afghanistan. However, the organization does not provide statistics regarding overall ISAF casualties. Some media sources and private organizations do track such statistics. For example, the *Wall Street Journal* estimates in "The Military Toll in Afghanistan" (http:// online.wsj.com/public/resources/documents/IRAQ-CASUALTY-COUNT.html) that as of September 2012 there had been 2,848 ISAF and OEF deaths in Afghanistan. The majority (2,091) of the deaths were reportedly U.S. personnel. The most deadly year was 2010, when 648 deaths were reported. It should be noted that the *Wall Street Journal* does not distinguish between deaths caused by combat and deaths due to other causes, for example, accidents.

Table 4.1 is a DOD record of U.S. military deaths in Afghanistan. As of July 30, 2012, 2,058 personnel had died. Of these deaths, 1,626 deaths were attributed to hostile action. The table also provides demographic details about the soldiers who were killed. Most of the deaths were among white male soldiers on active duty.

Figure 4.5 shows the number of U.S. military deaths (killed in action or died of wounds) in Afghanistan between 2001 and 2011. As noted earlier, 2010 was the deadliest year with 437 deaths. Total deaths for 2011 dropped to 359. According to the DOD (October 1, 2012, https://www .dmdc.osd.mil/dcas/pages/report_oef_month.xhtml), 269 U.S. military personnel were killed in action or died from combat wounds between January and October 2012. The DOD also notes that between October 2001 and October 2012, 446 U.S. military personnel in Afghanistan had died of accidents or other causes, while 17,684 had been wounded in action, but survived.

One of the most disturbing trends in Afghanistan has been the killing of U.S. troops by their ANSF colleagues. The military calls these attacks "green on blue attacks." Matthew Rosenberg states in "A Battle for Trust after Afghan Troops Kill GIs" (*International Herald Tribune*, June 28, 2012) that 35 U.S. service members were killed by "men in Afghan uniform" in 2011. With 359 total U.S. military deaths that year (see Figure 4.5), this means roughly 10% of the deaths were due to green on blue attacks. According to Rosenberg, another 22 U.S. service members had been killed by their Afghan colleagues as of June 2012.

Green on blue attacks make media headlines, dampen U.S. troop morale, and raise troubling questions about the alliance between the United States and Afghanistan. Rosenberg notes that U.S. military officials play down

TABLE 4.1

U.S. military deaths in Afghanistan, by category, October 7, 2001–July 30, 2012

Casualty type	Total
Hostile	1,626
Pending	4
Non-hostile	428
Total	**2,058**
Gender	
Female	36
Male	2,022
Total	**2,058**
Grade	
E1–E4	1,020
E5–E9	794
Officer	244
Total	**2,058**
Age	
<22	466
22–24	481
25–30	617
31–35	230
>35	264
Total	**2,058**
Component	
Active duty	1,771
Reserve	90
National Guard	197
Total	**2,058**
Race	
American Indian/Alaska Native	25
Asian	54
Black or African American	159
Native Hawaiian or other Pacific Islander	6
White	1,762
Multiple Races	24
Unknown	28
Total	**2,058**

SOURCE: Adapted from "U.S. Military Casualties—Operation Enduring Freedom (OEF) Military Deaths (as of July 30, 2012)," in *Defense Casualty Analysis System*, U.S. Department of Defense, July 30, 2012, https://www.dmdc.osd.mil/dcas/pages/report_oef_deaths.xhtml# (accessed July 31, 2012)

the significance of the attacks by explaining that they are typically due to "personal grievances." In *Report on Progress toward Security and Stability in Afghanistan: United States Plan for Sustaining the Afghanistan National Security Forces*, the DOD acknowledges that green on blue attacks "have a significant negative operational and strategic impact," but insists that the incidents are "rare" and have resulted in few casualties—86 dead and 115 wounded between May 2007 and March 2012. It should be noted that this total includes both military and civilian coalition personnel. The DOD explains, "Investigations have determined that a large majority of Green-on-Blue attacks are not attributable to insurgent infiltration of the ANSF, but are due to isolated personal grievances against coalition personnel. There is no indication that these recent attacks are part of a deliberate effort by insurgents, nor were they coordinated with each other."

CIVILIAN CASUALTIES. It is difficult to determine the total number civilians that have been killed or wounded during the long-running war in Afghanistan. The UN, NATO, and the DOD all publish statistics on civilian casualties; however, the Afghan government and human rights groups generally insist that these estimates are too low. Nevertheless, the statistics provide at least a partial glimpse of the war's toll on the Afghan people. Figure 4.6 shows the DOD's estimates of monthly civilian casualties between January 2009 and March 2012. Approximately 13,600 civilians were killed or wounded during this period. The most civilian casualties occurred in August 2009, when elections were held for the Afghan president and the provincial councils. During that month nearly 700 civilians were killed or wounded.

The DOD distinguishes between civilian casualties caused by insurgents and those caused by ISAF activities. One of the greatest dangers to civilians (and troops) in Afghanistan is improvised explosive devices (IEDs), which are basically "homemade" bombs planted by insurgents. Like traditional landmines, IEDs are triggered by movement and are typically placed beneath or beside roads. Figure 4.7 shows DOD statistics on the number of IED and mine explosions that occurred in Afghanistan between October 2009 and March 2012. Hundreds of the explosions took place each month; most occurred during the summer fighting season. IED and mine explosions showed a slight downward trend in early 2012, compared with early 2011. In *ISAF Monthly Data: Trends through June 2012* (July 25, 2012, http://www.isaf.nato.int/images/media/PDFs/20120725_niu_isaf_monthly_data-release_final.pdf), NATO presents data indicating that the number of IEDs and mine explosions increased to around 400 in April 2012, 570 in May, and 700 in June. NATO notes that nearly half of the civilian casualties in Afghanistan are believed to be caused by "indiscriminate IED explosions."

THE PAKISTAN PROBLEM

When the war in Afghanistan began in 2001, the U.S. goal was to rout the Taliban from power and to prevent terrorists from having safe harbor there. As of October 2012, the United States and NATO were partially successful in achieving this goal because the Taliban had been removed from power. As described in Chapter 3, bin Laden's death in 2011 and more than 10 years of military and counterterrorism activities have weakened the strength of al Qaeda. However, the Taliban and al Qaeda have survived. They continue to pose a threat to the future stability of Afghanistan and the national security interests of the United States. This is due in part to the actions (or inactions) of Pakistan. Dale points out that to completely defeat an insurgency, it needs to be "smother[ed]" within a closed environment." This has proven impossible in Afghanistan. Dale states, "Pakistan—Afghanistan's permanent neighbor—has long posed a

FIGURE 4.6

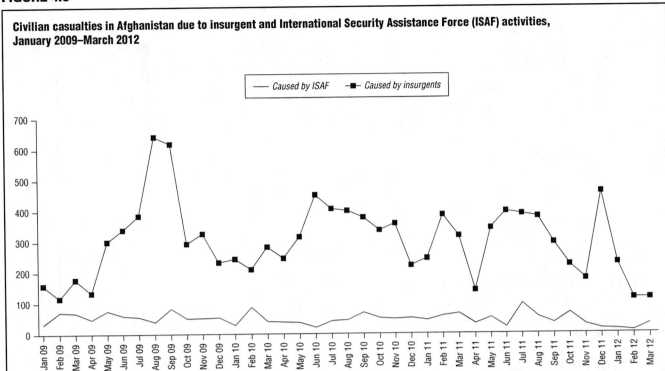

Civilian casualties in Afghanistan due to insurgent and International Security Assistance Force (ISAF) activities, January 2009–March 2012

SOURCE: Adapted from "Figure 23. Monthly Civilian Wounded or Killed by Insurgents and ISAF (October 2009–March 2012)," in *Report on Progress toward Security and Stability in Afghanistan: United States Plan for Sustaining the Afghanistan National Security Forces*, U.S. Department of Defense, April 2012, http://www.defense.gov/pubs/pdfs/Report_Final_SecDef_04_27_12.pdf (accessed July 20, 2012), and "Figure 15. Weekly CIVCAS versus Security Incidents (July 2008–September 2010)," in *Report on Progress toward Security and Stability in Afghanistan*, U.S. Department of Defense, November 2010, http://www.defense.gov/pubs/November_1230_Report_FINAL.pdf (accessed July 31, 2012)

FIGURE 4.7

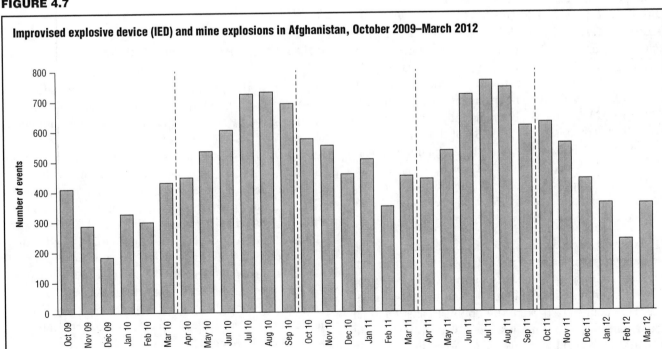

Improvised explosive device (IED) and mine explosions in Afghanistan, October 2009–March 2012

SOURCE: "Figure 35. Monthly IED and Mine Explosions (October 2009–March 2012)," in *Report on Progress toward Security and Stability in Afghanistan: United States Plan for Sustaining the Afghanistan National Security Forces*, U.S. Department of Defense, April 2012, http://www.defense.gov/pubs/pdfs/Report_Final_SecDef_04_27_12.pdf (accessed July 20, 2012)

conundrum for the campaign in Afghanistan by offering safe havens to Afghan insurgent leaders and fighters. The access those havens provide to recruiting, financing, training, and leadership direction grossly complicates the campaign in Afghanistan."

Figure 4.8 shows the areas within Pakistan and Afghanistan in which the U.S. government believes the Taliban still had influence and presence as of 2011. The region labeled "FATA" (Federally Administered Tribal Areas) lies within Pakistan along its western border with Afghanistan. The FATA is one of the poorest and most rugged regions of the country and has a separate legal structure that makes it difficult to control by the central Pakistani government. As a result, the FATA has long been accused of providing safe haven for Afghan Taliban and al Qaeda fighters.

The United States has had an inconstant relationship with Pakistan since the beginning of the war in Afghanistan. One technique widely employed by the U.S. military against al Qaeda in Pakistan has been drone attacks. Drones are small, reusable, robotic aircraft that are capable of firing short-range missiles with great precision. According to media reports, hundreds of U.S. drone attacks have occurred in Pakistan, mostly targeting senior al Qaeda leaders. Even though the attacks are praised by military leaders, they are criticized by social activists for allegedly killing innocent civilians. In September 2012 researchers at the Stanford Law School's International Human Rights and Conflict Resolution Clinic and the New York University School of Law's Global Justice Clinic published data they had collected on civilian casualties in *Living under Drones: Death, Injury, and Trauma to Civilians from US Drone Practices in Pakistan* (September 2012, http://livingunderdrones.org/wp-content/uploads/2012/09/Stanford_NYU_LIVING_UNDER_DRONES.pdf). According to the researchers, between June 2004 and mid-September 2012 an estimated 2,562 to 3,325 people had been killed by drone strikes in Pakistan. Approximately 474 to 881 of those killed were believed to be civilians, including 176 children. Another 1,228 to 1,362 people were estimated to have been wounded by drone strikes. The continued use of drones within Pakistani territory has been a source of controversy between the U.S. and Pakistani governments.

However, according to Dale the alliance between the two nations began improving in 2009 as U.S., Afghan, and Pakistani military commanders jointly developed initiatives and coordinated operations against insurgents. At that time, U.S. commanders were still optimistic that Pakistan would take action against insurgent safe havens within its borders. In 2011 two events occurred that severely weakened the alliance. In May 2011 U.S. special forces secretly entered Pakistan to kill bin Laden at his compound in Abbottabad, a city about 30 miles (48 km) north of

Islamabad, the capital of Pakistan. (See Figure 4.8.) Pakistan was angry that the United States had entered its territory to conduct the raid; the United States was angry that bin Laden had been living with impunity in Pakistan. Dale notes this action also "left many in the U.S. with the view that bin Laden could not have found sanctuary for so long without some official Pakistani knowledge or support."

In November 2011 tensions spiked again when more than 20 Pakistani troops were killed at a border checkpoint after being fired on by ISAF helicopters. The incident occurred in the northern part of the FATA at a checkpoint called Salala. NATO insisted the helicopters were responding to gunfire that came from the area; Pakistan contended the attack was unprovoked. Widespread outrage spurred the Pakistani government to close down NATO supply lines that ran through the country. Because Afghanistan is a landlocked country, U.S. and NATO forces use Pakistani land routes to truck in supplies. The Pakistani government demanded an unconditional apology from the United States for the Salala attack as a condition for reopening the supply lines. Months of tense negotiations ensued. In July 2012 the U.S. secretary of state Hillary Rodham Clinton (1947–) issued an apology for the Salala incident, and shortly thereafter the Pakistani supply lines were reopened. Eric Schmitt reports in "Clinton's 'Sorry' to Pakistan Ends Barrier to NATO" (*New York Times*, July 3, 2012) that the closure cost the United States an extra $100 million per month in transportation expenses because supplies had to be shipped into Afghanistan through the country's northern neighbors.

WHAT LIES AHEAD FOR AFGHANISTAN?

In May 2012 the United States and Afghanistan signed a historic agreement. The Enduring Strategic Partnership Agreement between the United States of America and the Islamic Republic of Afghanistan (http://iipdigital.usembassy.gov/st/english/texttrans/2012/05/201205024930.html#axzz2899weRlg) notes that the two countries share "a common desire for peace and to strengthen collective efforts to achieve a region that is economically integrated, and no longer a safe haven for al-Qaeda and its affiliates." Afghanistan agreed to provide U.S. forces with access to Afghan facilities through 2014 and stated that access after that date would be granted through a bilateral security agreement. The continued access would be "for the purposes of combating al-Qaeda and its affiliates, training the Afghan National Security Forces, and other mutually determined missions to advance shared security interests."

In July 2012 the U.S. government designated Afghanistan a "major non-NATO ally." According to the U.S. Department of State (DOS), in "Major Non-NATO

FIGURE 4.8

Map of areas of Taliban influence and presence in Afghanistan and Pakistan, 2011

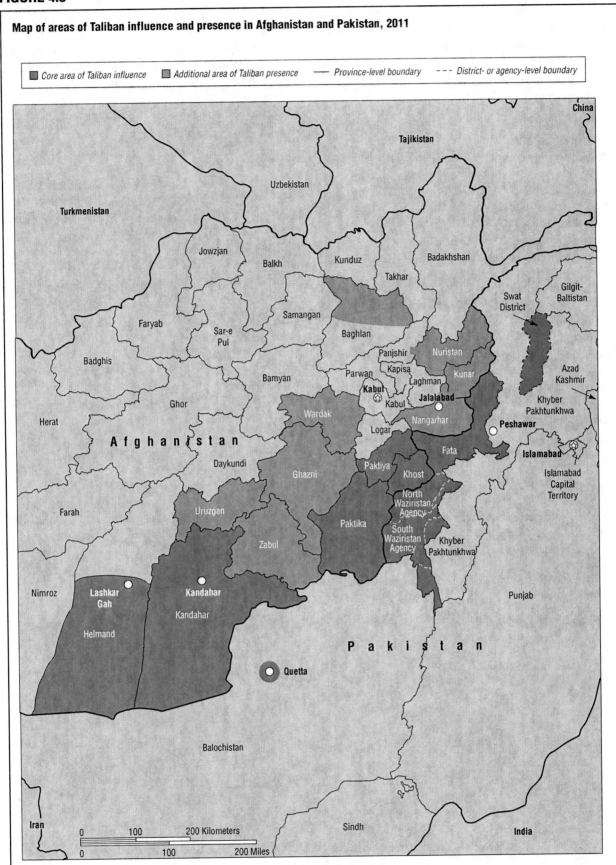

SOURCE: "Taliban Strength," in *Counterterrorism 2012 Calendar*, National Counterterrorism Center, October 21, 2011, http://www.nctc.gov/site/pdfs/2012_nctc_ct_calendar.pdf (accessed July 5, 2012)

Ally Status for Afghanistan" (July 7, 2012, http://www.state.gov/r/pa/prs/ps/2012/07/194662.htm), the designation "provides a long-term framework for our security and defense cooperation." Afghanistan will be eligible for "training, loans of equipment for cooperative research and development, and ultimately Foreign Military Financing for commercial leasing of certain defense articles."

In "Chicago Summit Declaration," NATO calls for the ANSF to maintain a force of 228,500 personnel following the withdrawal of the ISAF in 2014. The estimated cost of operating the ANSF at this level will be $4.1 billion per year. The international community will bear the entire expense until 2015, when Afghanistan will begin paying a percentage of the cost. By 2024 Afghanistan will assume the full cost.

THE WAR IN AFGHANISTAN: PUBLIC OPINION

Since the start of the war in 2001, the Gallup Organization has asked Americans whether sending military forces to Afghanistan has been "a mistake." Figure 4.9 shows the poll results on this issue. In late 2001 and in early 2002 the vast majority of respondents (89% and 93%, respectively) said the United States had not made a mistake in sending military forces to Afghanistan. Over time, the percentage supporting this viewpoint shrank considerably. By 2011 only 58% of respondents said the United States had not made a mistake in sending military forces to Afghanistan.

As noted earlier, ISAF operations will end in Afghanistan by late 2014. In March 2012 Gallup asked Americans whether they favored withdrawing U.S. troops on that timetable, speeding up the withdrawal, or keeping U.S. troops in Afghanistan "as long as it takes to accomplish its goals." In *Afghanistan* (2012, http://www.gallup.com/poll/116233/Afghanistan.aspx), Gallup indicates that 50% of the respondents said they would like to speed up the withdrawal. Nearly a quarter (24%) preferred the 2014 timetable, and 21% said the troops should stay until the United States' goals are accomplished. Another 4% had no opinion on the matter.

IRAQ

Iraq is bordered on the east by Iran, on the north by Turkey, on the west by Syria and Jordan, and on the south by Saudi Arabia. (See Figure 4.10.) The tiny nation of Kuwait also lies to the south and abuts Iraq's small stretch of coastline on the Persian Gulf. The capital of Iraq is Baghdad. According to the CIA, in *The World Factbook: Iraq* (September 12, 2012, https://www.cia.gov/library/publications/the-world-factbook/geos/iz.html), Iraq covers 169,235 square miles (438,317 square km) and is slightly larger than the state of Idaho doubled. Iraq is crossed by two large rivers—the Tigris and Euphrates—whose waters provide a broad fertile plain in the center of the country. The remainder of the landscape is primarily desert. In July 2012 the population was estimated at nearly 31.1 million. Most of the population is Arab (75% to 80%) but includes a Kurdish sector (15% to 20%) and other ethnic minorities. The Kurds are an ethnic group found mostly in the mountainous regions of northern Iraq. They see themselves as a distinct group and have long pursued their own independent nation. Nearly all Iraqis are Muslim (97%), with 60% to 65% Shiite and 32% to 37% Sunni.

FIGURE 4.9

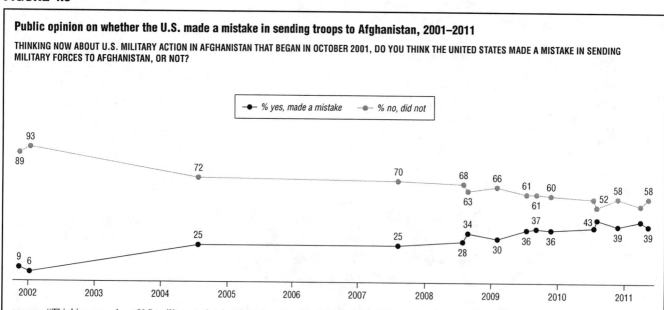

Public opinion on whether the U.S. made a mistake in sending troops to Afghanistan, 2001–2011

THINKING NOW ABOUT U.S. MILITARY ACTION IN AFGHANISTAN THAT BEGAN IN OCTOBER 2001, DO YOU THINK THE UNITED STATES MADE A MISTAKE IN SENDING MILITARY FORCES TO AFGHANISTAN, OR NOT?

SOURCE: "Thinking now about U.S. military action in Afghanistan that began in October 2011, do you think the United States made a mistake in sending military forces to Afghanistan, or not?" in *Afghanistan*, The Gallup Organization, 2012, http://www.gallup.com/poll/116233/Afghanistan.aspx (accessed July 21, 2012). Copyright © 2012 Gallup, Inc. All rights reserved. The content is used with permission; however, Gallup retains all rights of republication.

FIGURE 4.10

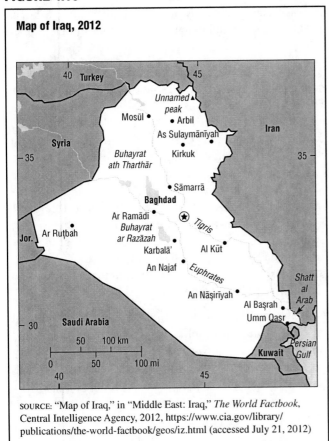

Map of Iraq, 2012

SOURCE: "Map of Iraq," in "Middle East: Iraq," *The World Factbook*, Central Intelligence Agency, 2012, https://www.cia.gov/library/publications/the-world-factbook/geos/iz.html (accessed July 21, 2012)

The United States has fought two wars with Iraq. The first war, which is commonly called the Persian Gulf War, spanned several months between 1990 and 1991. The second war began in 2003, but its roots lie within the earlier war.

The Persian Gulf War

Iraq was ruled by Saddam Hussein, a brutal dictator who had been in power since the early 1970s. In 1990 Iraqi military forces invaded Kuwait. The article "On This Day: 1990—Iraq invades Kuwait" (BBC News, 2010) notes that Hussein accused the Kuwaitis of taking oil from an oil field near the border between the two countries. The international community almost universally condemned Iraq's actions. The UN imposed strict economic sanctions that would remain in place for many years. President George H. W. Bush (1924–) put together a U.S.-led coalition of international military forces for Operation Desert Storm, which began in January 1991 with the bombing of strategic targets within Iraq. By the end of February the coalition had liberated Kuwait and seriously damaged Iraq's infrastructure and military capabilities. As shown in Table 1.1 in Chapter 1, the United States lost 383 troops during the Persian Gulf War. Over 2.2 million U.S. military personnel served during the war.

THE KURDS. The struggle of the Iraqi Kurds against Hussein and the Iraqi government is reviewed by Frank Viviano in "The Kurds in Control" (*National Geographic*, January 2006). During the 1980s and early 1990s Hussein's government killed an estimated 100,000 to 180,000 Kurds and destroyed thousands of their villages. Much of the killing occurred near the end of the Iran-Iraq War (1980–1988) as punishment for Kurdish support of Iran. The genocide included the use of chemical weapons against the Kurds during the so-called Anfal Campaign. (For more information about this campaign, see the Human Rights Watch report *Genocide in Iraq: The Anfal Campaign against the Kurds* [July 1993, http://www.hrw.org/reports/1993/iraqanfal/].)

According to Viviano, the United States chose at first to ignore the genocide so as not to antagonize Hussein, a would-be American ally during the late 1980s. This attitude changed following Iraq's invasion of Kuwait in 1990. Immediately after the Persian Gulf War, U.S., British, and French military forces began enforcing a no-fly zone over the Kurdish territories in northern Iraq to prevent Hussein from attacking the Kurds with aircraft or bombs. In addition, a no-fly zone was established over southern Iraq to protect the largely Shiite population, which was repressed by Hussein's predominantly Sunni Muslim government.

In April 1991 the UN Security Council passed Resolution 687 (http://www.iaea.org/OurWork/SV/Invo/resolutions/res687.pdf), which set forth the terms of the cease-fire between Iraq and Kuwait. It also called on Iraq to "agree not to acquire or develop nuclear weapons" or any related technology and to declare the "locations, amounts, and types" of all existing nuclear weapons and usable materials within Iraq and turn them over to the International Atomic Energy Agency (IAEA) for destruction. For the remainder of the decade Iraq followed a pattern of denial and deception with IAEA inspectors and refused to abide by Resolution 687 and subsequent Resolutions 707, 715, 1051, 1284, and 1441. In 1998 a defiant Hussein had the IAEA inspectors kicked out of the country. (For a timeline of events, see the IAEA's "In Focus: IAEA and Iraq" [2012, http://www.iaea.org/NewsCenter/Focus/IaeaIraq/index.shtml].)

The 2003 War in Iraq

By the time of 9/11, the United States had experienced an entire decade of problems with Iraq. Iraq denounced the no-fly zones within its borders as illegal and often fired at U.S. and British warplanes that enforced them. Hussein's continuing defiance of UN resolutions was worrying to U.S. officials, who feared that Iraq was hiding a program to build WMDs.

According to the *9/11 Commission Report*, President George W. Bush "wondered immediately after the [9/11] attack whether Saddam Hussein's regime might have had a hand in it." The U.S. intelligence community investigated possible connections and found no compelling case of Iraqi involvement. Nevertheless, some members of the Bush administration, particularly the U.S. deputy secretary of defense Paul D. Wolfowitz (1943–), thought the United States should strike Iraq as part of the ensuing War on Terror. On January 29, 2002, during his annual State of the Union speech (http://georgewbush-whitehouse.archives .gov/stateoftheunion/2002/), President Bush described Iraq as a member of an "axis of evil" in the world.

Throughout the remainder of the year the Bush administration worked to garner UN approval for a military strike against Iraq. These efforts were driven by reports from the U.S. intelligence community that Iraq was amassing WMDs. In October 2002 intelligence officials presented Bush with "National Intelligence Estimate: Iraq's Continuing Programs for Weapons of Mass Destruction" (http://homepage.ntlworld.com/jksonc/docs/nie-iraq-wmd.html). This document declared that Iraq had restarted its nuclear weapons program and would likely have a nuclear weapon within a decade. Iraq was also thought to have new chemical and biological weapons. The evolution of this report was later examined in *Report to the President of the United States* (March 31, 2005, http://govinfo .library.unt.edu/wmd/report/wmd_report.pdf) by the Commission on the Intelligence Capabilities of the United States Regarding Weapons of Mass Destruction.

In February 2003 the U.S. secretary of state Colin Powell (1937–) addressed the UN and presented the U.S. case for military action against Iraq. The UN had already passed Resolution 1441 in late 2002, which condemned Iraq for its continuing defiance of previous UN resolutions and for refusing to allow IAEA inspectors back into the country. However, the United States was unable to convince the UN that a military response was necessary. Only the United Kingdom pledged to fully support the U.S. plan for war.

The coalition gathered by the United States for the impending war was smaller than the one garnered against Iraq in 1991. In 2003 only Great Britain pledged troops; many other nations, though, contributed small military forces, money, or equipment (most notably Spain, Australia, and Israel). France, Russia, and China, in particular, were opposed to military action against Iraq.

WAR BEGINS IN IRAQ

Operation Iraqi Freedom (OIF) began on March 20, 2003, with a massive bombardment of Iraqi targets. By the end of April, the invasion was complete. According to the DOS, in *Patterns of Global Terrorism 2003* (April 2004, http://www.state.gov/documents/organization/31912.pdf), by the end of 2003 coalition forces had killed or captured 42 of the 55 most-wanted members of Iraq's former regime, including Hussein, who was captured in December 2003. In October 2005 Hussein stood trial in Iraq for war crimes committed against his people during his rule. He was found guilty by a five-member Iraqi tribunal (group of judges) and hanged for his crimes in December 2006.

Even though the military goals of the war were accomplished easily, the U.S.-led coalition forces were unable to achieve stability in Iraq. Following the invasion, mass looting and lawlessness broke out and many buildings were burned. U.S. troops were unsuccessful at restoring civil order. Looting and mayhem continued to be a problem in other occupied areas as well. Over the ensuing years a massive insurgency erupted that took the lives of many Iraqis, Americans, and other foreigners within Iraq. These attacks were carried out by a wide variety of individuals and groups with various grievances and agendas. During 2006 bloody sectarian violence escalated between Iraq's minority Sunni population and the majority Shiite population.

By early 2007 Iraq was in a state of near-total civil war. The American public was increasingly displeased with the course of the war. More than 3,000 U.S. military personnel had been killed during OIF, and there was no end in sight to the hostilities. In an attempt to quell the violence in Iraq, the Bush administration responded with a troop surge.

According to the GAO, in *Securing, Stabilizing, and Rebuilding Iraq: Progress Report: Some Gains Made, Updated Strategy Needed* (June 2008, http://gao.gov/new .items/d08837.pdf), the number of U.S. forces increased by approximately 32,000 troops during the troop surge, peaking at around 169,000 troops in August 2007. Fierce fighting resulted in high U.S. military casualties—764 deaths in 2007, the highest since the start of the war. (See Table 4.2.) However, in 2008 the casualty rate dropped dramatically as insurgent attacks decreased. Likewise, the GAO reports there was a substantial decline in the number of deaths among Iraqi civilians and security forces.

U.S. INTELLIGENCE: "DEAD WRONG"

During and after the invasion of Iraq, U.S. forces searched the country for WMDs, but they found none. An outcry in the American media spurred President Bush to establish an investigatory commission to find out why U.S. prewar intelligence about Iraq had been wrong.

In March 2005 the Commission on the Intelligence Capabilities of the United States Regarding Weapons of Mass Destruction issued *Report to the President of the United States*. The commission's assessment was extremely critical, noting, "We conclude that the Intelligence Community was dead wrong in almost all of its pre-war judgments about Iraq's weapons of mass destruction." The commission found that U.S. intelligence agents had been shocked following the Persian Gulf War

TABLE 4.2

U.S. military deaths as a result of Operation Iraqi Freedom (OIF), by year, as of July 20, 2012

Month/year	Killed in action/ died of wounds Total	Accidents/ other deaths Total	Total deaths Total	Wounded in action Total
2003	311	175	486	2,420
2004	712	134	846	8,001
2005	673	171	844	5,943
2006	704	116	820	6,412
2007	764	139	903	6,109
2008	218	95	313	2,045
2009	74	74	148	678
2010	15	33	48	318
2011	0	0	0	0
February 2012	0	1	1	0
Totals	**3,471**	**938**	**4,409**	**31,926**

SOURCE: Adapted from "U.S. Military Casualties—Operation Iraqi Freedom (OIF) Casualty Summary by Month (as of July 20, 2012)," in *Defense Casualty Analysis System*, U.S. Department of Defense, July 20, 2012, https://www.dmdc.osd.mil/dcas/pages/report_oif_month.xhtml# (accessed July 21, 2012)

to learn that Iraq's nuclear weapons program had advanced much more than they suspected and that Hussein had previously unknown stockpiles of chemical weapons. Their suspicions had deepened throughout the 1990s because of Hussein's dogged defiance of IAEA inspections. The commission acknowledged that "Saddam acted to the very end like a man with much to hide. And the dangers of underestimating our enemies were deeply underscored by the attacks of September 11, 2001."

The commission learned that U.S. intelligence agents had obtained much false information from unreliable informants and poor data sources. For example, the evidence that Iraq had purchased yellowcake from Niger turned out to be based on documents that were forgeries. Intelligence officials had ignored information that did not support their preconceived notion about Iraq's guilt. Some analysts had reported that there were no conclusive links between Iraq and al Qaeda and believed that Hussein (a secular leader) and bin Laden (a religious fundamentalist) did not trust or like each other, making cooperation extremely unlikely.

The commission found that Iraq did have an active and productive nuclear weapons program through 1991. However, much of the infrastructure had been destroyed by coalition bombing during the Persian Gulf War, and the Iraqi scientists involved in the program had been reassigned to other tasks. Thus, there had been no active program within Iraq to develop or acquire WMDs for quite some time. The commission noted, "The harm done to American credibility by our all too public intelligence failings in Iraq will take years to undo." The commission's findings were embarrassing to the Bush administration, which had pressed the international community for the invasion.

THE BEGINNING OF THE END

Even though the casualty rate declined significantly in 2008, widespread American public support for the war in Iraq had faded. When the war began in 2003, Americans were torn, but generally favorable, about invading Iraq. This support waned as the insurgency raged and the death toll rose. In 2003 the Gallup Organization began conducting polls on American attitudes regarding the war in Iraq. Gallup reports in *Iraq* (2012, http://www.gallup.com/poll/1633/Iraq.aspx) that in one of those polls Americans were asked whether the United States "made a mistake in sending troops to Iraq." In early 2003, 75% of respondents said it had not been a mistake to send U.S. troops to Iraq. However, over the following six years support for the war dropped dramatically. By early 2008 only 36% of respondents thought the United States had not erred by sending troops to Iraq. By contrast, the percentage of respondents who thought the war had been a mistake increased from 23% in early 2003 to 63% in early 2008, its highest point.

Between 2007 and 2008 the Bush administration and the Iraqi government conducted negotiations that resulted in two important agreements: the Status of Forces Agreement (SOFA), which focused on security and military matters, and the Strategic Framework, which addressed the future cooperation between the two countries in areas not specifically covered by the SOFA, chiefly diplomacy. In the SOFA the United States agreed to withdraw all of its combat forces from Iraqi "urban areas" by June 30, 2009, and withdraw all American troops by the end of 2011. However, the U.S. and Iraqi governments began negotiating the possibility of establishing permanent U.S. military bases in Iraq.

On June 30, 2009, Iraq celebrated a new holiday— National Sovereignty Day—as U.S. troops completed withdrawing from the nation's urban areas. Tim Cocks and Muhanad Mohammed report in "Iraqis Rejoice as U.S. Troops Leave Baghdad" (Reuters, June 29, 2009) that the Iraqi population was pleased about the withdrawal, but extremely frustrated that its quality of life had not improved after six years of U.S. occupation.

On August 31, 2010, OIF officially ended in Iraq, marking a formal end to U.S. military combat actions. As of July 20, 2012, 4,409 U.S. military personnel had died as a result of OIF. (See Table 4.3.) Most of the deaths (3,479) were due to hostile actions. The remainder were due to accidents or other causes. The largest number of deaths was among white male troops on active duty. Table 4.2 shows that 31,926 U.S. military personnel had been wounded in action during OIF but survived their wounds.

Between September 1, 2010, and December 15, 2011, the U.S. military conducted Operation New Dawn (OND) in Iraq. The DOD explains in "U.S. Forces Transition to Operation New Dawn" (September 1, 2010,

TABLE 4.3

U.S. military deaths as a result of Operation Iraqi Freedom (OIF), by category, as of July 20, 2012

Casualty type	Total
Hostile	3,479
Pending	1
Non-hostile	929
Total	**4,409**
Gender	
Female	110
Male	4,299
Total	**4,409**
Grade	
E1–E4	2,540
E5–E9	1,442
Officer	427
Total	**4,409**
Age	
<22	1,283
22–24	1,073
25–30	1,125
31–35	426
>35	502
Total	**4,409**
Component	
Active duty	3,498
Reserve	414
National Guard	497
Total	**4,409**
Race	
American Indian/Alaska Native	43
Asian	77
Black or African American	439
Native Hawaiian or other Pacific Islander	17
White	3,638
Multiple Races	62
Unknown	133
Total	**4,409**

SOURCE: Adapted from "U.S. Military Casualties—Operation Iraqi Freedom (OIF) Military Deaths—All (as of July 20, 2012)," in *Defense Casualty Analysis System*, U.S. Department of Defense, July 20, 2012, https://www.dmdc.osd.mil/dcas/pages/report_oif_all.xhtml# (accessed July 21, 2012)

TABLE 4.4

U.S. military deaths as a result of Operation New Dawn (OND), by category, as of July 20, 2012

Casualty type	Total
Hostile	38
Non-hostile	28
Total	**66**
Gender	
Male	66
Total	**66**
Grade	
E1–E4	38
E5–E9	20
Officer	8
Total	**66**
Age	
<22	11
22–24	15
25–30	25
31–35	5
>35	10
Total	**66**
Component	
Active duty	54
Reserve	6
National Guard	6
Total	**66**
Race	
Asian	1
Black or African American	5
Native Hawaiian or other Pacific Islander	1
White	58
Multiple races	1
Total	**66**

SOURCE: Adapted from "U.S. Military Casualties—Operation New Dawn (OND) Military Deaths (as of July 20, 2012)," in *Defense Casualty Analysis System*, U .S. Department of Defense, July 20, 2012, https://www.dmdc.osd.mil/dcas/pages/report_ond_deaths.xhtml# (accessed July 21, 2012)

http://www.af.mil/news/story.asp?id=123220049) that OND was dedicated to "advising, assisting, and training the Iraqi Security forces; conducting partnered counterterrorism operations; and providing support to provincial reconstruction teams and civilian partners as they help build Iraq's civil capacity." As of July 20, 2012, 66 U.S. military personnel had died as a result of OND. (See Table 4.4.) Thirty-eight of the deaths were due to hostile actions.

In late December 2011 the U.S. military completed its troop withdrawals, leaving behind only a few hundred personnel as guards and training specialists at U.S. embassies and related facilities in Iraq.

The Special Inspector General for Iraq Reconstruction (SIGIR) is an office within the U.S. government. According to SIGIR (2012, http://www.sigir.mil/about/index.html), it oversees "all obligations, expenditures, and revenues associated with reconstruction and rehabilitation activities in Iraq." In *The Human Toll Of Reconstruction Or Stabilization Operations during Operation Iraqi Freedom* (July 27, 2012, http://www.sigir.mil/files/lessonslearned/SpecialReport2.pdf#view=fit), SIGIR provides statistics on the number of casualties that occurred between May 1, 2003, and August 31, 2010, during U.S.-led reconstruction and stabilization efforts in Iraq. These activities included building or rebuilding physical infrastructure (e.g., roads, buildings, and bridges), establishing or reestablishing political and social institutions, and providing products or services to the Iraqi people. SIGIR estimates that 719 people died during this period:

- 271—Iraqis

- 264—U.S. military

- 111—third-country nationals (i.e., citizens of countries other than the United States or Iraq)

- 54—U.S. civilians

- 19—unknown

Various media outlets have estimated that tens of thousands of Iraqis died during the course of the war and its aftermath.

WHAT LIES AHEAD FOR IRAQ?

In October 2011 President Obama announced that his administration and the Iraqi government had failed to reach a consensus on the establishment of permanent U.S. military bases in Iraq. One of the major sticking points was the United States' insistence that its personnel would not be subject to prosecution by the Iraqi justice system for any off-base criminal activities. The rejection of the bases was a major disappointment to the DOD and some politicians who had hoped to station tens of thousands of U.S. troops in Iraq as a deterrent to neighboring Iran.

U.S. interests were further eroded when the Iraqi government rejected U.S. plans for a huge diplomatic presence in Iraq. In *Mission Iraq: State and DOD Face Challenges in Finalizing Support and Security Capabilities* (June 28, 2012, http://www.gao.gov/assets/600/591997.pdf), the GAO notes that the DOD and the DOS had originally planned for a "civilian-led presence" in Iraq of more than 16,000 personnel at 14 sites around Iraq. The vast majority of the personnel were to be contractors devoted to security and other services. Mission Iraq was also to include a massive Police Development Program (PDP) to train Iraqi police forces. According to the GAO, it would have been the largest program of its kind in the world. However, the Iraqi government balked at such a huge U.S. presence within its borders. The GAO states that "the Iraqi Foreign Minister questioned the size, location, and security requirements of U.S. sites."

SIGIR presents quarterly and semiannual reports to Congress on the status of Iraq and U.S. interests there. As of October 2012, the most recent report was *Special Inspector General for Iraq Reconstruction: Quarterly Report and Semiannual Report to the United States Congress* (July 30, 2012, http://www.sigir.mil/files/quarterly reports/July2012/Report_-_July_2012.pdf#view=fit). SIGIR notes that in mid-2012 Mission Iraq and the PDP were undergoing "downsizing" at the request of the Iraqi government. According to SIGIR, the number of U.S. personnel to be devoted to the PDP was reduced from a planned high of 350 to only 36. In "US Downsizing Operations in Iraq" (Voice of America, August 6, 2012), Mark Snowiss indicates that senior U.S. officials are concerned that Iraq is rejecting U.S. influence in favor of closer ties with Iran. However, he notes that some analysts believe the Iraqis will "keep the Americans in reserve because they [the Iraqis] don't want to be completely beholden to Iran."

The United States' hope for stability in Iraq following the war has proven elusive because the nation has been plagued by violence and political turmoil. As noted in Chapter 3, the terrorist group al Qaeda in Iraq (AQI) continues to wreak havoc among the populace. For example, the AQI is believe to be responsible for coordinating attacks in July 2012 that killed over 120 people and injured dozens more. The inability of the U.S.-led coalition and Afghan Security Forces to maintain order has frustrated the Iraqi people.

Meanwhile, the Iraqi government has been wracked with infighting. The elections that were held in 2006 and 2010 produced a Shiite-led government, but deep political divisions between Shiite factions have impeded government action on the country's pressing domestic problems. One Shiite politician has become particularly worrisome to U.S. authorities: Moktada al-Sadr (1973–). Al-Sadr led a fierce insurgency against U.S. forces during the war before fleeing to Iran in 2007. In 2011 he returned to Iraq and became a major player in high-level politics.

Another troubling development was the decision in early 2012 by the Iraqi prime minister Nuri Kamal al-Maliki (1950–), a Shiite, to welcome the group Asaib Ahl al-Haq (League of the Righteous) into his political bloc. The Shiite militia was a violent insurgency group during the war and, like al-Sadr, is vehemently anti-American. U.S. authorities believe the militia has been funded by Iran and received training from the latter's elite military unit, the Qods Force. Iran denies this claim, and Asaib Ahl al-Haq insists that it has given up violence in favor of political activism. Nevertheless, Jack Healy and Michael S. Schmidt lament in "Political Role for Militants Worsens Fault Lines in Iraq" (*New York Times*, January 5, 2012) al-Maliki's embrace of Asaib Ahl al-Haq, noting, "By doing so, Iraq's government could embolden a militia with an almost nonexistent track record of peace while potentially handing Tehran [Iran] greater influence in a country where the United States spent billions of dollars and lost nearly 4,500 American soldiers in nearly nine years of war."

A similarly pessimistic view is expressed by Snowiss, who states that "as U.S. power in Iraq has steadily declined since the 2003 invasion, Maliki's embattled government has increasingly aligned itself with the region's dominant Shi'ite state, Iran, which is at odds with the U.S. on several fronts." The troubled relations between the United States and Iran are discussed in Chapter 6.

One bright spot for the United States is that Iraq, unlike Afghanistan, has deep financial resources, chiefly substantial reserves of petroleum. As shown in Table 4.5, Iraq was the 11th-largest producer of oil in 2011. In addition, the U.S. Energy Information Administration (2012, http://www.eia.gov/countries/country-data.cfm?fips=IZ&trk=p1) notes that "Iraq may be one of the few places left where vast oil

TABLE 4.5

Top 15 oil producers, 2011

[Thousand barrels per day]

1	Saudi Arabia	11,153
2	Russia	10,229
3	United States	10,088
4	China	4,303
5	Iran	4,234
6	Canada	3,665
7	United Arab Emirates	3,096
8	Mexico	2,959
9	Kuwait	2,682
10	Brazil	2,641
11	Iraq	2,635
12	Nigeria	2,528
13	Venezuela	2,470
14	Norway	2,007
15	Algeria	1,884

SOURCE: Top World Oil Producers, 2011, in *Countries*, U.S. Department of Energy, U.S. Energy Information Administration, 2012, http://www.eia.gov/countries/index.cfm (accessed August 3, 2012)

reserves have barely been exploited." As a result, the nation has become financially self-sufficient, which means the United States will not have to continue to spend large sums to fund the training of Iraq's security forces and rebuild the nation's infrastructure.

In late 2011 the Iraqi government ordered three dozen U.S. F-16 fighter jets for its air force. According to the article "Iraq Seeks to Speed up F-16 Deliveries" (United Press International, July 16, 2012), Iraq expects to spend more than $10 billion on U.S. defense goods during the second decade of the 21st century. The article notes that this development is welcome news for U.S. defense contractors who face declining revenues following the war's end and, as explained in Chapter 2, expected cutbacks in U.S. defense spending. However, the article also indicates that al-Maliki's political rivals (i.e., Iraqi Sunnis and Kurds) are "alarmed" about the purchases, because his political moves are "widely per-

ceived as his drive to establish a dictatorship." In addition, the article states that the United States is wary about selling certain advanced weapons systems to al-Maliki, "in part because of concerns about who the Iraqi leader might use them against."

WAR COSTS AND BUDGETS

As noted in Chapter 1, the United States' War on Terror was renamed Overseas Contingency Operations (OCO) in 2009 by the Obama administration. The major and most costly components of the OCO have been the wars in Afghanistan and Iraq. Table 4.6 shows CRS estimates of the yearly and cumulative OCO costs from fiscal year (FY) 2001 (when the war in Afghanistan began) through FY 2012. The total OCO costs were estimated at $1.4 trillion during this period, with $823.2 billion devoted to the war in Iraq, $557.1 billion spent on the war in Afghanistan, $28.7 billion spent on enhanced security at DOD bases, and $5.5 billion in unallocated funds (i.e., the CRS could not determine to which operation the money was devoted). Table 4.7 provides a breakdown of OCO funding by funding source and operation. The DOD accounted for more than $1.3 trillion in OCO funds. The remainder was allocated to the DOS and U.S. Agency for International Development ($77.4 billion) and to the U.S. Department of Veterans Affairs' (VA) medical fund ($11.4 billion). The VA provides medical treatment and numerous other services and benefits to veterans.

In February 2012 President Obama presented to Congress his federal budget request for FY 2013. The details about funding for DOD operations are provided in Chapter 2. Figure 4.11 shows the trends in OCO funding and troop levels for FYs 2008 to 2012 and for the FY 2013 budget request. The OCO funding request for FY 2013 was $89 billion to support an annual average of 68,000 troops. All of those troops would be deployed to Afghanistan.

TABLE 4.6

Estimated war funding, by operation, fiscal years 2001–11 and requested for fiscal year 2012

[CRS estimates in billions of dollars of budget authority]

Operation and source of funds	Fiscal year 2001 & 2002	Fiscal year 2003	Fiscal year 2004	Fiscal year 2005	Fiscal year 2006	Fiscal year 2007	Fiscal year 2008	Fiscal year 2009	Fiscal year 2010	Fiscal 2011 CRA P.L. 112-6*	Fiscal year 2012 request	Cumulative enacted, fiscal years 2001–2011 as of 3-18-11	Cum. total w/ fiscal year CRA & fiscal year 2012 request
Iraq	0.0	53.0	75.9	85.5	101.6	131.2	142.1	95.5	71.3	49.3	17.7	805.5	823.2
Afghanistan	20.8	14.7	14.5	20.0	19.0	39.2	43.5	59.5	93.8	118.6	113.7	443.0	557.1
Enhanced Security	13.0	8.0	3.7	2.1	0.8	0.5	0.1	0.1	0.1	0.1	0.1	28.6	28.7
Unallocated	0	5.5	0	0	0	0	0.1	0	0	0			5.5
Total	**33.8**	**81.2**	**94.1**	**107.6**	**121.4**	**170.9**	**185.7**	**155.1**	**165.3**	**168.1**	**131.7**	**1,283.3**	**1,414.8**
Annual change	NA	140%	16%	13%	13%	41%	9%	−16%	7%	2%	−22%	NA	NA
Change since fiscal year 2003	NA	NA	16%	33%	50%	111%	129%	91%	104%	107%	62%	NA	NA

CRS = Congressional Research Service.
CRA = Continuing Resolution Amendment.
P.L. = Public Law.
DOD = U.S. Department of Defense.
USAID = U.S. Agency for International Development.
Notes: NA = not applicable. Totals may not add due to rounding. Total includes $5.5 billion in fiscal year 2003 of DOD funds that cannot be allocated between Iraq and Afghanistan because DOD records are incomplete.
*The sixth fiscal year 2011 Continuing Resolution was signed by the president on March 18, 2011, and extended funding for all agencies till April 8, 2011 generally at the fiscal year 2010 enacted level. In the case of DOD and the Department of Veterans' Affairs, war funding was close to the administration's request, but for the State Department and USAID, fiscal year 2011 funding levels could be $1 billion lower than requested.

SOURCE: Amy Belasco, "Table 1. Estimated War Funding by Operation: FY2001–FY2012 War Request," in *The Cost of Iraq, Afghanistan, and Other Global War on Terror Operations since 9/11,* Congressional Research Service, March 29, 2011, http://www.fas.org/sgp/crs/natsec/RL33110.pdf (accessed July 20, 2012)

TABLE 4.7

Estimated war funding, by operation and agency, fiscal years 2001–11 and requested for fiscal year 2012

[CRS estimates in billions of dollars of budget authority]

Operation and funding source	Fiscal year 2001 & 2002	Fiscal year 2003	Fiscal year 2004	Fiscal year 2005	Fiscal year 2006	Fiscal year 2007	Fiscal year 2008	Fiscal year 2009	Fiscal year 2010	Fiscal year 2011 CRA P.L. 112-6	Fiscal year 2012 request	Cumulative enacted, fiscal years 2001–2011	Cum. total w/ fiscal year CRA & fiscal year 2012 request
Iraq													
DOD	0	50.0	56.4	83.4	98.1	127.2	138.5	92.0	66.5	45.7	10.6	757.8	768.8
State/USAID	0	3.0	19.5	2.0	3.2	3.2	2.7	2.2	3.3	2.3	6.2	41.4	47.6
VA Medical	0	0	0	0.2	0.4	0.9	0.9	1.2	1.5	1.3	0.9	6.3	7.2
Total: Iraq	**0**	**53.0**	**75.9**	**85.6**	**101.7**	**131.3**	**142.1**	**95.5**	**71.3**	**49.3**	**17.7**	**805.5**	**823.2**
Afghanistan													
DOD	20.0	14.0	12.4	17.2	17.9	37.2	40.6	56.1	87.7	113.3	107.3	416.2	523.5
State/USAID	0.8	0.7	2.2	2.8	1.1	1.9	2.7	3.1	5.7	4.1	4.3	25.1	29.4
VA Medical	0	0	0	0	0	0.1	0.1	0.2	0.5	1.1	2.1	2.1	4.2
Total: Afghanistan	**20.8**	**14.7**	**14.6**	**20.0**	**19.0**	**39.2**	**43.4**	**59.5**	**93.8**	**118.6**	**113.7**	**443.5**	**557.1**
Enhanced security													
DOD	13.0	8.0	3.7	2.1	.8	0.5	0.1	0.1	0.1	0.1	0.1	28.6	28.7
Total: Enhanced security	**13.0**	**8.0**	**3.7**	**2.1**	**.8**	**0.5**	**0.1**	**0.1**	**0.1**	**0.1**	**0.1**	**28.6**	**28.7**
Unallocated													
Unallocated DOD	0	5.5	0	0	0	0	0	0	0	0	0	5.5	5.5
All missions													
DOD	33.0	77.4	72.4	102.6	116.8	164.9	179.2	148.3	154.3	159.1	118.0	1,208.1	1,326.3
State/USAID	0.8	3.7	21.7	4.8	4.3	5.0	5.4	5.4	9.1	6.5	10.6	66.7	77.4
VA Medical	0	0	0	0.2	0.4	1.0	1.0	1.5	1.9	2.4	3.0	8.4	11.4
Total: All missions	**33.8**	**81.1**	**94.1**	**107.6**	**121.5**	**170.9**	**185.6**	**155.1**	**165.3**	**168.1**	**131.6**	**1,283.3**	**1,414.8**

CRS = Congressional Research Service.
CRA = Continuing Resolution Amendment.
P.L. = Public Law.
DOD = U.S. Department of Defense.
USAID = U.S. Agency for International Development.
Notes: NA = not applicable. Totals may not add due to rounding. Updated to reflect enactment of the fiscal year 2011 Continuing Resolution (H. Res. 44/P.L. 112-4) on March 2, 2011.

SOURCE: Amy Belasco, "Table 3. Estimated War Funding by Operation, Agency and Fiscal Year: FY2001–FY2012 Request," in *The Cost of Iraq, Afghanistan, and Other Global War on Terror Operations since 9/11*, Congressional Research Service, March 29, 2011, http://www.fas.org/sgp/crs/natsec/RL33110.pdf (accessed July 20, 2012)

FIGURE 4.11

Department of Defense (DOD) funding and troop levels for Overseas Contingency Operations (OCO), fiscal years 2008–13

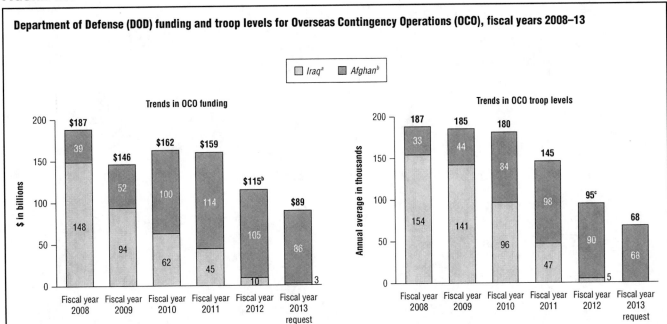

[Iraq[a]   Afghan[b]]

Trends in OCO funding

Trends in OCO troop levels

[a]Afghan data is for Operation Enduring Freedom. Iraq data is for Operation Iraqi Freedom and Operation New Dawn, and Iraq activities.
[b]Fiscal year 2012 number ($115B) includes $0.6B of rescissions that were applicable to fiscal year 2010 OCO appropriations.
[c]U.S. forces deployed in Iraq only for the first quarter of fiscal year 2012.

SOURCE: "Figure 6-2. OCO Funding and Troop Level Trends," in *Overview: United States Department of Defense Fiscal Year 2013 Budget Request*, U.S. Department of Defense, February 2012, http://comptroller.defense.gov/defbudget/fy2013/FY2013_Budget_Request_Overview_Book.pdf (accessed July 5, 2012)

CHAPTER 5
HOMELAND SECURITY

Protecting the U.S. homeland from terrorist attacks is a formidable and challenging task. The scope is enormous. U.S. borders span more than 100,000 miles (160,000 km) and are difficult to protect against illegal entry. There are hundreds of land border crossings, seaports, and international airports that must be secured. The United States has vast air and rail transportation systems and many highly concentrated metropolitan areas, all of which are attractive targets for terrorists. American society is relatively open with little restriction on movement or access to public places, and foreign visitors are welcomed.

To counter the vulnerabilities inherent to American society, the U.S. government has developed a homeland security infrastructure that coordinates the efforts of many agencies at the federal, state, and local levels. The overall goal is threefold: to prevent terrorists from striking in the United States, to fortify U.S. defenses against an attack, and to prepare the American people and emergency responders in case an attack does occur.

U.S. DEPARTMENT OF HOMELAND SECURITY

The U.S. Department of Homeland Security (DHS) was established by President George W. Bush (1946–) in 2002 and began operating in 2003. In *The Department of Homeland Security* (2002, http://www.dhs.gov/xlibrary/assets/book.pdf), Bush notes that homeland security responsibilities at that time were scattered among more than 100 different government agencies. He states, "America needs a single, unified homeland security structure that will improve protection against today's threats and be flexible enough to help meet the unknown threats of the future."

The DHS works in concert with other federal entities that are devoted to national security, particularly the intelligence community (IC), the U.S. military, and the Federal Bureau of Investigation (FBI). Besides this horizontal cooperation, the DHS is also charged with coordinating homeland security efforts in a vertical manner—across federal, state, and local government levels. State and local officials are particularly important to the task of emergency response, because they represent the first wave of government assistance in the event of a terrorist attack.

The DHS brought together dozens of agencies and offices that had previously operated as separate entities. Some had been independent; others had been part of larger organizations, such as the U.S. Departments of Justice, Treasury, Transportation, Energy, and Agriculture, the FBI, and the U.S. General Services Administration.

Figure 5.1 shows an organization chart for the DHS as of 2012. Major agencies under the DHS umbrella include the Transportation Security Administration, the U.S. Customs and Border Protection, the U.S. Citizenship and Immigration Services, the U.S. Immigration and Customs Enforcement, the U.S. Secret Service, the Federal Emergency Management Agency, and the U.S. Coast Guard.

The DHS's projected budget for fiscal year (FY) 2013 was $44.9 billion. (See Table 5.1.) Table 5.2 shows the number of full-time equivalent employees that were employed at each agency or in agency-wide functions as of February 2012. This table also lists the acronyms that are commonly used to indicate offices and agencies within the DHS. The following is a description of each appropriation and agency listed in Table 5.1 and Table 5.2 based on information contained in the DHS publication *FY 2013 Budget in Brief* (February 2012, http://www.dhs.gov/xlibrary/assets/mgmt/dhs-budget-in-brief-fy2013.pdf):

- Departmental Operations—this appropriation funds leadership, direction, and management elements of the DHS, including executive management, administrative support, financial management, and information technology.

- Analysis and Operations—this appropriation funds resources that support the Office of Intelligence and

FIGURE 5.1

Department of Homeland Security (DHS) organization chart, 2012

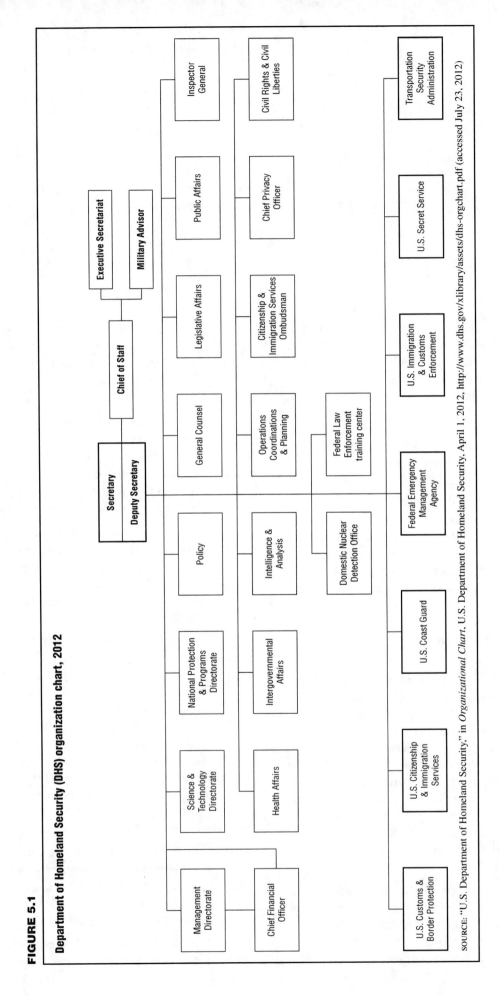

SOURCE: "U.S. Department of Homeland Security," in *Organizational Chart*, U.S. Department of Homeland Security, April 1, 2012, http://www.dhs.gov/xlibrary/assets/dhs-orgchart.pdf (accessed July 23, 2012)

TABLE 5.1

Department of Homeland Security (DHS) budget request for fiscal year 2013, by agency

	Fiscal year 2013 president's budget
	$000
Departmental Operations*	$812,978
Analysis and Operations (A&O)	$321,982
Office of the Inspector General (OIG)	$143,664
U.S. Customs & Border Protection (CBP)	$11,979,454
U.S. Immigration & Customs Enforcement (ICE)	$5,644,061
Transportation Security Administration (TSA)	$7,644,585
U.S. Coast Guard (USCG)	$9,966,651
U.S. Secret Service (USSS)	$1,850,863
National Protection and Programs Directorate (NPPD)	$2,518,778
Office of Health Affairs (OHA)	$166,458
Federal Emergency Management Agency (FEMA)	$10,659,504
FEMA: Grant Programs	$2,900,212
U.S. Citizenship & Immigration Services (USCIS)	$3,005,383
Federal Law Enforcement Training Center (FLETC)	$258,324
Science & Technology Directorate (S&T)	$831,472
Domestic Nuclear Detection Office (DNDO)	$327,977
Total budget authority:	**$59,032,346**
Mandatory, fee, and trust funds	**$(10,333,516)**
Discretionary offsetting fees	**$(3,756,720)**
Net disc. budget authority:	**$44,942,110**

*Departmental Operations is comprised of the Office of the Secretary & Executive Management, DHS Headquarters Consolidation, the Office of the Undersecretary for Management, the Office of the Chief Financial Officer, and the Office of the Chief Information Officer.

SOURCE: Adapted from "Total Budget Authority by Organization," in *FY 2013 Budget-in-Brief*, U.S. Department of Homeland Security, February 2012, http://www.dhs.gov/xlibrary/assets/mgmt/dhs-budget-in-brief-fy2013.pdf (accessed July 23, 2012)

TABLE 5.2

Acronyms and employee counts for Department of Homeland Security (DHS) appropriations and agencies, February 2012

DHS appropriation or agency	Agency acronym	Full time equivalent employees
Departmental Management and Operations		2,122
Analysis and Operations		849
Office of the Inspector General	OIG	683
U.S. Customs & Border Protection	CBP	61,160
U.S. Immigration and Customs Enforcement	ICE	20,265
Transportation Security Administration	TSA	57,188
U.S. Coast Guard	USCG	50,286*
U.S. Secret Service	USSS	7,061
National Protection and Programs Directorate	NPPD	2,787
Office of Health Affairs	OHA	101
Federal Emergency Management Agency	FEMA	10,056
U.S. Citizenship & Immigration Services	USCIS	10,700
Federal Law Enforcement Training Center	FLETC	1,103
Science & Technology Directorate	S&T	491
Domestic Nuclear Detection Office	DNDO	130

*Includes 42,069 military service members and 8,217 civilian employees. Additional personnel include 31,476 in the Coast Guard Auxiliary and 8,100 in the Military Selected Reserve.

SOURCE: Adapted from "Summary Information by DHS Organization," in *FY 2013 Budget-in-Brief*, U.S. Department of Homeland Security, February 2012, http://www.dhs.gov/xlibrary/assets/mgmt/dhs-budget-in-brief-fy2013.pdf (accessed July 23, 2012)

Analysis (I&A) and the Office of Operations Coordination and Planning (OPS). The I&A is the DHS's representative in the national IC. The OPS (2012, http://www.dhs.gov/about-office-operations-coordination-and-planning) monitors homeland security "on a daily basis" and coordinates homeland security activities within the DHS and with state and local partners.

- Office of the Inspector General—serves as an independent and objective audit, inspection, and investigative body to promote economy, effectiveness, and efficiency in DHS programs and operations and to prevent and detect fraud, waste, and abuse.

- U.S. Customs and Border Protection—protects the U.S. borders at and between official ports of entry. Also protects the nation's economic security by regulating and facilitating the lawful movement of goods and people across U.S. borders.

- U.S. Immigration and Customs Enforcement—investigates the illegal introduction of goods, terrorists, and other criminals seeking to cross U.S. borders.

- Transportation Security Administration—protects the transportation system and ensures the freedom of movement for people and commerce.

- U.S. Coast Guard—principal federal agency responsible for maritime safety, security, and stewardship. Besides its nonhomeland security responsibilities (e.g., search and rescue), the Coast Guard conducts law enforcement and national defense missions to protect homeland security.

- U.S. Secret Service—protects the president, vice president, and other dignitaries and designated individuals; enforces laws relating to obligations and securities of the United States (e.g., counterfeiting); investigates financial and electronic crimes; and protects the White House and other buildings in the Washington, D.C., area.

- National Protection and Programs Directorate—protects against "terrorist attacks, natural disasters, and other catastrophic incidents," protects U.S. physical infrastructure and cyber and communications infrastructure, performs risk management tasks, and coordinates partnerships within the DHS and between the DHS and outside partners.

- Office of Health Affairs—oversees medical and health preparedness for the DHS.

- Federal Emergency Management Agency—leading federal government agency that "manages and coordinates the Federal response to and recovery from major domestic disasters and emergencies of all types."

- U.S. Citizenship and Immigration Services—grants immigration and citizenship benefits and protects the integrity of the U.S. immigration system.

- Federal Law Enforcement Training Center—provides "world-class" training of federal law enforcement personnel from various agencies.

- Science and Technology Directorate—provides technological resources to federal, state, tribal, and local officials.

- Domestic Nuclear Detection Office—develops and deploys detection techniques and equipment for nuclear materials, including nuclear materials that might be smuggled into and used against the United States.

HOMELAND SECURITY STRATEGY AND GOALS

The terrorist attacks of September 11, 2001 (9/11), made U.S. leaders aware that the country lacked a coordinated strategy for protecting the U.S. homeland from terrorism. In July 2002 President Bush issued *National Strategy for Homeland Security* (http://www.ncs.gov/library/policy_docs/nat_strat_hls.pdf), which was updated in October 2007. The strategy lists three primary goals of homeland security:

- Prevent and disrupt terrorist attacks

- Protect the American people, critical infrastructure, and key resources

- Respond to and recover from incidents

The DHS has outlined its specific strategies for meeting these goals in various documents, including *Quadrennial Homeland Security Review Report* (February 2010, http://www.dhs.gov/xlibrary/assets/qhsr_report.pdf) and *Department of Homeland Security Strategic Plan Fiscal Years 2012–2016* (February 2012, http://www.dhs.gov/xlibrary/assets/dhs-strategic-plan-fy-2012-2016.pdf). The agency's detailed mission plan is shown in Table 5.3. The remainder of this chapter is devoted to detailing the DHS's actions and operations in the context of its three primary goals of homeland security.

PREVENT AND DISRUPT TERRORIST ATTACKS

The goal to prevent and disrupt terrorist attacks focuses primarily on gathering and sharing intelligence, securing the nation's borders and transportation systems, and conducting law enforcement counterterrorism activities.

Role of Intelligence

As described in Chapter 2, intelligence is information about one's enemies. The *National Strategy for Homeland Security* calls for a highly coordinated and integrated framework for intelligence gathering and analysis. One of the roles of the IC is tactical threat analysis. This is the collection and analysis of reliable information about terrorist plots and plans. This task is led by the director of national

TABLE 5.3

Missions and goals for homeland security

Mission 1: Preventing terrorism and enhancing security
- Goal 1.1: Prevent terrorist attacks
- Goal 1.2: Prevent the unauthorized acquisition or use of chemical, biological, radiological, and nuclear materials and capabilities
- Goal 1.3: Manage risks to critical infrastructure, key leadership, and events

Mission 2: Securing and managing our borders
- Goal 2.1: Effectively control U.S. air, land, and sea borders
- Goal 2.2: Safeguard lawful trade and travel
- Goal 2.3: Disrupt and dismantle transnational criminal organizations

Mission 3: Enforcing and administering our immigration laws
- Goal 3.1: Strengthen and effectively administer the immigration system
- Goal 3.2: Prevent unlawful immigration

Mission 4: Safeguarding and securing cyberspace
- Goal 4.1: Create a safe, secure, and resilient cyber environment
- Goal 4.2: Promote cybersecurity knowledge and innovation

Mission 5: Ensuring resilience to disasters
- Goal 5.1: Mitigate hazards
- Goal 5.2: Enhance preparedness
- Goal 5.3: Ensure effective emergency response
- Goal 5.4: Rapidly recover

SOURCE: "There are five homeland security missions. The missions and associated goals are as follows," in *Quadrennial Homeland Security Review Report*, U.S. Department of Homeland Security, February 2010, http://www.dhs.gov/xlibrary/assets/qhsr_report.pdf (accessed July 23, 2012)

intelligence (the head of the IC), the FBI, and the DHS. Intelligence achieved during this task allows the development of effective preventive action—that is, the disruption of planned terrorist plots and the capture of the terrorists. Preventive activities are spearheaded by the FBI through a collection of law enforcement entities called the joint terrorism task forces (JTTFs). The FBI describes in "Protecting America from Terrorist Attack" (2012, http://www.fbi.gov/about-us/investigate/terrorism/terrorism_jttfs) the JTTFs as "small cells of highly trained, locally based, passionately committed investigators, analysts, linguists, SWAT experts, and other specialists from dozens of U.S. law enforcement and intelligence agencies" and notes that there are more than 100 of them located throughout the country. The FBI also operates a national JTTF out of its headquarters in Washington, D.C.

A second important intelligence task is strategic analysis of the enemy. This is a deep and comprehensive delving into the history, motivations, workings, and structures of terrorist organizations to identify their members and means of financial support. The goal is to determine their vulnerabilities, intentions, and capabilities. This task is led by the director of national intelligence, the FBI, and the DHS.

Border Security

The U.S. Customs and Border Protection (CBP) is responsible for protecting U.S. borders from the illegal entry of people and goods. At the same time, it must ensure that legal visitors and cargo have relatively easy passage into and out of the United States. Since becoming a part of the DHS in 2003, the CBP has been given an important priority: detect terrorists and their weapons and prevent them from entering the United States. This is besides the CBP's many other responsibilities, including screening all traffic (people, vehicles, and cargo) into and out of the country for illegal activities or contraband. The task is enormous because U.S. borders are long, cross-border traffic is voluminous, and the country's economy is dependent on international trade. The CBP states in "On a Typical Day in Fiscal Year 2011" (2012, http://www.cbp.gov/linkhandler/cgov/about/accomplish/typical_day_fy11.ctt/typical_day_fy11.pdf) that in FY 2011 it managed 329 ports of entry, and on a typical day it processed 932,456 passengers and pedestrians and 64,483 truck, rail, and sea containers.

The security (or lack thereof) along the U.S. border with Mexico is a controversial political issue in terms of illegal immigration and Mexican-based criminal activities, particularly in illegal drugs and human trafficking. These problems are a prime concern to the U.S. states along the border, and their officials often accuse the federal government of failing to adequately secure the border. In 2006 President Bush deployed thousands of National Guard troops to the border to support CBP activities. In 2010 President Barack Obama (1961–) did likewise; however, both deployments were for limited durations and included tight restrictions on troop activities. The Posse Comitatus Act of 1878 forbids U.S. military forces from acting in a law enforcement role over civilians unless specifically authorized by the U.S. Constitution or Congress.

Aviation Security

The vulnerability of the nation's aviation system became painfully clear on 9/11. On that day 19 terrorists were able to board four commercial airliners as passengers, seize control of the cockpits during flight, and pilot the planes on missions of violent destruction. Three of the airliners were crashed into buildings: the twin towers of the World Trade Center in New York City and the U.S. Pentagon in Arlington, Virginia. The fourth plane crashed in a field in Pennsylvania after a revolt by the passengers. Its probable destination was the U.S. Capitol in Washington, D.C. The combined attacks left some 2,700 dead. Americans were stunned by the ease with which the terrorists were able to board and commandeer the planes. A variety of shortcomings and oversights in U.S. aviation security procedures had been exploited with disastrous results.

The events that transpired during the hijackings have been pieced together by investigators based largely on cell phone calls from crew members and passengers on the planes. A detailed chronology and description of these calls is included in *The 9/11 Commission Report* (July 2004, http://www.9-11commission.gov/report/911Report.pdf). The report was compiled by the National Commission on Terrorist Attacks upon the United States, an organization created by President Bush and Congress to investigate all the circumstances relating to the 9/11 terrorist attacks.

The commission believes the terrorists used small sharp items (e.g., box cutters) as weapons to attack and subdue crew members and passengers as the hijackings began. The terrorists were either allowed entry or forced their way into the cockpits, where they overcame and may have killed the cockpit crews. Before and during 9/11 it had been standard policy on commercial airliners for crew members to offer no resistance to armed hijackers. This policy evolved after a spate of hijackings in the United States during the late 1960s and early 1970s. In most of those events the hijackers demanded to be flown to a specific destination (often Cuba), and once there, they released the passengers and crew unharmed. The implementation of tougher security measures and x-ray screening at U.S. airports virtually eliminated hijacking aboard domestic U.S. flights. Thus, it had not been viewed as a serious threat to U.S. commercial aviation for some time. As a result, U.S. planes did not have fortified cockpit doors in 2001.

In 1988 Pan Am Flight 103 was en route from London to New York City when a bomb in the luggage compartment exploded, tearing apart the plane. It crashed near the small village of Lockerbie, Scotland, killing all 259 passengers and crew members and 11 people on the ground. It was later determined that terrorists had managed to hide a bomb inside a radio that was somehow tagged for placement aboard the plane, even though it did not belong to a passenger. Following this incident, the United States implemented stricter regulations and inspection of passenger baggage.

According to the *9/11 Commission Report*, it was standard procedure in 2001 to hold a high-risk passenger's luggage until that person had boarded the plane. This was to prevent a terrorist from checking baggage containing explosives and then not boarding the plane. It was assumed that if both passenger and luggage were aboard, then there was no danger posed by the luggage. Mohamed Atta (1968–2001) is believed to have been the ringleader of the 9/11 hijackers. He piloted American Airlines Flight 11 into the first tower at the World Trade Center. Before boarding his flight in Boston, Atta had been picked by a computerized prescreening system for heightened security measures. As a result, his checked baggage was not loaded onto the plane until it had been confirmed that he was aboard the aircraft.

The 9/11 terrorist attacks changed many assumptions and conventions that had guided aviation security for decades. It became obvious that terrorists were willing to die as part of their missions. Thus, it was not inconceivable that a terrorist could both check in luggage containing explosives and board the plane.

NEW AVIATION SECURITY MEASURES. In November 2001 Congress passed the Aviation and Transportation Security Act. It created the Transportation Security Administration (TSA) within the U.S. Department of Transportation. In 2003 the TSA was made a part of the newly created DHS. The TSA is responsible for protecting the United States' transportation systems. However, numerous other agencies and organizations, such as the IC, the CBP, and the FBI, work with the TSA to provide multiple levels of security for U.S. aviation. (See Figure 5.2.) The TSA explains in "Layers of Security" (September 26, 2012, http://www.tsa.gov/about-tsa/layers-security) that "a terrorist who has to overcome multiple security layers in order to carry out an attack is more likely to be pre-empted, deterred, or to fail during the attempt."

One security level is the so-called No-Fly List. This TSA-compiled list purportedly contains the names of people with ties to terrorism who are forbidden to fly on aircraft originating in or coming to the United States. A second list is called the Secondary Security Screening Selection List, or the selectee list, for short. People on the selectee list undergo secondary screening before being allowed to fly. The names on the lists and the criteria used to select them are secret. Various media sources report that thousands of names are on the lists.

Until 2007 the TSA was prohibited by the Privacy Act of 1974 from maintaining records of certain personal information for people not accused of or suspected of criminal activity. However, the TSA explains in "Secure Flight Program" (September 23, 2012, http://www.tsa.gov/stakeholders/secure-flight-program) that in November 2007 it issued a ruling exempting itself from certain provisions of the Privacy Act. The exemptions allowed the agency to begin implementing its Secure Flight Process for preflight passenger screening. The process requires airlines to obtain identifying information about potential passengers, including their full name, date of birth, and gender. (See Figure 5.3.) This information is relayed to the TSA and checked against the watch lists for possible matches. Cleared passengers can then be issued their boarding passes by the airlines.

The TSA also conducts preflight screening of passengers and baggage at airports and provides air marshals on selected flights. The Air Marshal Program began in 1970 in response to a rash of hijackings. At that time the program was overseen by the U.S. Customs Service (now the CBP). More than 1,000 agents were trained to thwart attempted hijackings. They flew undercover (dressed as passengers) on various flights and were armed. The program was discontinued in 1974. During the mid-1980s the program was restarted, but only for international flights of U.S. airlines. In "Brief History: Air Marshals" (Time.com, January 18, 2010), Laura Fitzpatrick notes that there were only a few dozen air marshals in the program when the 9/11 terrorist attacks occurred. President Bush greatly expanded the program and placed it

FIGURE 5.2

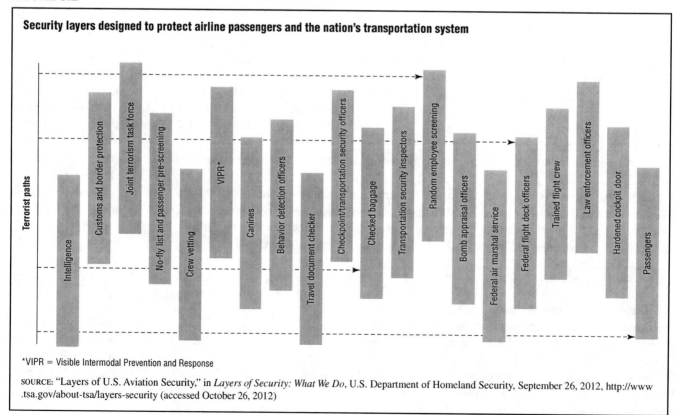

Security layers designed to protect airline passengers and the nation's transportation system

Terrorist paths

Intelligence · Customs and border protection · Joint terrorism task force · No-fly list and passenger pre-screening · Crew vetting · VIPR* · Canines · Behavior detection officers · Travel document checker · Checkpoint/transportation security officers · Checked baggage · Transportation security inspectors · Random employee screening · Bomb appraisal officers · Federal air marshal service · Federal flight deck officers · Trained flight crew · Law enforcement officers · Hardened cockpit door · Passengers

*VIPR = Visible Intermodal Prevention and Response

SOURCE: "Layers of U.S. Aviation Security," in *Layers of Security: What We Do*, U.S. Department of Homeland Security, September 26, 2012, http://www.tsa.gov/about-tsa/layers-security (accessed October 26, 2012)

FIGURE 5.3

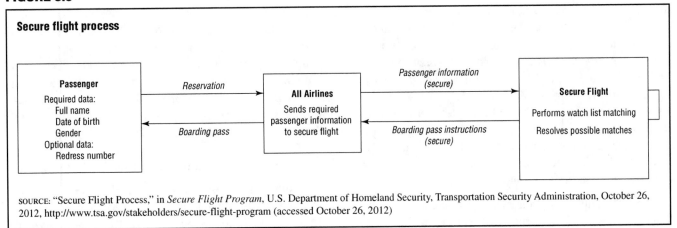

Secure flight process

SOURCE: "Secure Flight Process," in *Secure Flight Program*, U.S. Department of Homeland Security, Transportation Security Administration, October 26, 2012, http://www.tsa.gov/stakeholders/secure-flight-program (accessed October 26, 2012)

under the TSA. Several thousand new agents have been trained as air marshals. Besides flying undercover on domestic and international flights, these agents also staff positions in the National Counterterrorism Center and the JTTFs. Another program operated under the TSA allows certain airline crew members to fly armed. Federal flight deck officers are trained in firearm usage and taught other necessary skills to thwart a hijacker.

In December 2001 a man aboard a commercial airliner flying from Paris, France, to Miami, Florida, tried to detonate explosives hidden in his shoes. The so-called shoe bomber was overpowered by passengers aboard the plane and turned over to authorities. The incident prompted airport screeners to have passengers remove their footwear for closer inspection. Following the August 2006 discovery of a plot by British terrorists to use liquid explosives hidden in carry-on items, such as sports drinks and water bottles, the TSA temporarily banned the carrying on of all liquid and gel items. Eventually, a standard was adapted by the TSA (http://www.tsa.gov/traveler-information/make-your-trip-better-using-3-1-1) allowing each passenger to carry on only one quart-sized plastic bag holding containers of 3 ounces or less of liquids and gels.

In December 2009 a man flying from Amsterdam, Netherlands, to Detroit, Michigan, tried to set off explosives hidden in his underwear shortly before the plane landed. Even though he created a small fire, the explosives did not detonate. Passengers and crew members extinguished the fire and held the man for authorities. The incident prompted the TSA to greatly expand its use of whole-body imagers during airport screening. The imagers are more formally known as advanced imaging technology (AIT). The TSA reports in "Advanced Imaging Technology (AIT)" (September 28, 2012, http://www.tsa.gov/travelers-guide/advanced-imaging-technology-ait) that the imagers use either millimeter wave or backscatter technology. Millimeter wave imaging uses electromagnetic waves to create a three-dimensional image of the body. Backscatter imaging relies on x-rays to create a reflection of

the body. Both technologies reportedly reveal any metal and nonmetal objects, including explosives, that are hidden beneath a person's clothing. The TSA indicates that as of 2012 it had deployed approximately 700 of the units at more than 180 airports. In *Homeland Security: DHS and TSA Face Challenges Overseeing Acquisition of Screening Technologies* (May 9, 2012, http://www.gao.gov/assets/600/590729.pdf), the U.S. Government Accountability Office (GAO) indicates that the TSA plans to deploy a total of 1,250 AITs.

At first, whole-body imaging raised the concerns of privacy advocates because the images revealed detailed features of the human body. After a public outcry the TSA implemented new software that incorporates a generic outline of the human body, rather than person-specific bodily features. Regardless, the effectiveness of the AITs remains controversial. Jane Merrick reports in "Are Planned Airport Scanners Just a Scam?" (*Independent*, January 3, 2010) that private security experts do not believe that whole-body imagers would have revealed the explosives hidden in the underwear of the would-be Detroit bomber. Echoing this sentiment, the GAO acknowledges in *Aviation Security: TSA Is Increasing Procurement and Deployment of the Advanced Imaging Technology, but Challenges to This Effort and Other Areas of Aviation Security Remain* (March 17, 2010, http://www.gao.gov/new.items/d10484t.pdf) that after scrutinizing the capabilities of the AIT technology "it remains unclear whether the AIT would have detected the weapon used in the December 2009 incident."

The TSA notes in "Advanced Imaging Technology (AIT)" that whole-body imaging is an optional screening procedure. Passengers can choose a physical pat down instead.

Another area of concern in aviation security is air cargo, such as packages, crates, and other items that are shipped by air. The TSA explains in "Programs and Initiatives" (October 4, 2012, http://www.tsa.gov/stakeholders/programs-and-initiatives-1) that the Implementing the 9/11

Commission Recommendations Act of 2007 required that 100 percent of the cargo transported on commercial passenger aircraft be screened at a level of security equal to that used to screen passenger baggage by August 2010. However, in *Aviation Security: Actions Needed to Address Challenges and Potential Vulnerabilities Related to Securing Inbound Air Cargo* (May 2012, http://www.gao.gov/assets/600/590789.pdf), the GAO indicates that as of May 2012 the TSA was not yet screening all incoming air cargo and that the deadline had been extended to December 2012. However, the GAO remained uncertain if the 100% goal would be achieved by that date.

The TSA also performs electronic screening of passenger luggage at U.S. airports. According to the GAO, in *Checked Baggage Screening: TSA Has Deployed Optimal Systems at the Majority of TSA-Regulated Airports, but Could Strengthen Cost Estimates* (April 2012, http://www.gao.gov/assets/600/590513.pdf), the TSA uses two types of screening equipment: explosives detection systems (EDS) and explosives trace detection (ETD) machines. The GAO states that EDS "use X-rays with computer-aided imaging to automatically recognize the characteristic signatures of threat explosives." ETD machines are described as machines that allow baggage screeners to use "chemical analysis to manually detect traces of explosive materials' vapors and residue."

Surface Transportation Security

The 9/11 terrorist attacks resulted in the tightening of security measures for the nation's aviation system. However, deadly terrorist attacks on passenger trains and subways in Spain, England, and India have raised concerns about the security of the U.S. surface transportation system. In September 2009 authorities arrested an Afghan man in the United States for allegedly plotting to set off bombs in the New York City subway. By that time many subway systems across the country had implemented new security measures, such as surveillance cameras and random checks of passenger bags, briefcases, baggage, and so on. Amtrak, a national passenger rail service owned by the U.S. government, had also implemented similar measures. In addition, the TSA launched in 2005 the Surface Transportation Security Inspection Program to inspect rail shipments at terminals and rail stations.

Port Security

The TSA notes in "Port and Intermodal" (September 20, 2012, http://www.tsa.gov/stakeholders/port-and-intermodal) that 99% of the U.S. overseas trade volume enters or leaves U.S. ports. Port security is a combined effort of private and government entities. At the federal level, the U.S. Coast Guard and the CBP play the major roles. The TSA operates the Transportation Worker Identification Credential (TWIC) program, which runs security checks and grants special identification cards to workers who have access to certain areas of ports and to off-shore facilities, such as off-shore oil rigs. The TWIC program was established following passage of the Maritime Transportation Security Act of 2002. The TSA (http://www.twicinformation.com/twicinfo/) reports that as of September 2012 nearly 2.3 million workers had enrolled in the program and more than 2.1 million TWIC cards had been issued.

Identifying Terrorists and Thwarting Their Movement

Another major component of homeland security is the collection of information about suspected and known terrorists. The U.S. government is aware that terrorists may use fraudulent identification documents to prevent being identified. In fact, the *9/11 Commission Report* indicates that some of the terrorists involved in the 9/11 attacks had fraudulent travel documents (e.g., passports) and state-issued identification documents (e.g., driver's licenses). In response, the federal government has initiated several programs that are designed to better identify people and to thwart the movement of people with terrorist ties.

REAL ID. The *9/11 Commission Report* recommended that the federal government "set standards for the issuance of birth certificates and sources of identification, such as drivers licenses." In response, Congress passed the Intelligence Reform and Terrorism Prevention Act of 2004, which was later superseded by the REAL ID Act of 2005. It called for all state-issued driver's licenses and other state-issued identification documents to meet specific federal standards for security and integrity by May 2008. The act has been extremely controversial for a variety of reasons. Some analysts have expressed concerns about privacy issues, and state legislatures have complained about the costs and difficulties of implementing the act.

The DHS did not release final regulations for the REAL ID program until January 2008, which left states little time to meet the original deadline. As a result, the federal government delayed the final deadline to the end of 2009. However, several states remained steadfastly opposed to the act. In "Real ID Act Might Cause Real Hassles for Travelers" (NPR.org, December 7, 2009), Brian Naylor reports that as of December 2009, 13 states had passed legislation prohibiting themselves from fully complying with the REAL ID Act due to "cost or privacy issues." That same month the DHS postponed the deadline to May 2011. The states were emboldened, in part, by the Obama administration's distaste for the law. Democratic politicians began pushing an alternative program called PASS ID that kept only some security measures of the REAL ID program and incorporated more privacy controls. However, PASS ID legislation failed to pass during the 111th session of Congress (January 2009–January 2011). States that had waited to implement the REAL ID program in the hopes that PASS ID was going to pass found themselves with little time to meet the looming deadline.

In March 2011 the DHS extended the REAL ID deadline to January 15, 2013. In "Countdown to REAL ID" (March 4, 2011, http://www.ncsl.org/issues-research/transport/count-down-to-real-id.aspx), the National Conference of State Legislatures (NCSL) tracks the legislative measures that states have taken to implement or avoid implementing the REAL ID program. The NCSL notes in "State Legislative Activity in Opposition to the Real ID" (http://www.ncsl.org/documents/standcomm/sctran/REALIDComplianceReport.pdf) that as of June 2012, 17 states had in place statutory prohibitions against complying with the REAL ID program. Nonetheless, one of the states—Georgia—began implementing the program a month later. As of October 2012, it remained to be seen if all states would be in compliance with REAL ID requirements by January 2013.

TERRORIST DATABASES AND WATCH LISTS. The No-Fly List and the selectee list are actually subsets of the Consolidated Terrorist Screening Database, which is maintained by the FBI's Terrorist Screening Center (TSC). This database is often referred to as the Terrorist Screening Database or the Terrorist Watch List. Creation of the database was authorized by President Bush in September 2003 through issuance of Homeland Security Presidential Directive 6 (http://www.fas.org/irp/offdocs/nspd/hspd-6.html).

Figure 5.4 shows the process by which individuals are nominated and accepted or rejected for inclusion in the database. Nominations can originate from federal agencies, such as the CIA, the FBI, the Defense Intelligence Agency, or the U.S. Department of State. The names are submitted to the National Counterterrorism Center (NCTC), which maintains the Terrorist Identities Datamart Environment (TIDE) database. NCTC analysts collect information about the nominated individuals and

FIGURE 5.4

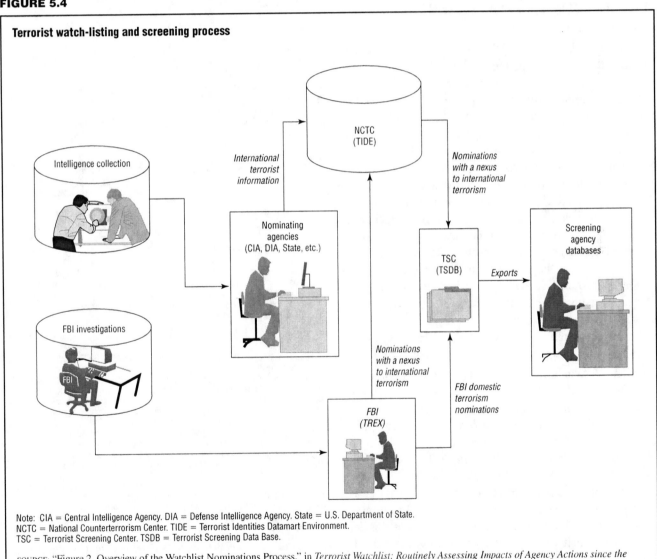

Terrorist watch-listing and screening process

Note: CIA = Central Intelligence Agency. DIA = Defense Intelligence Agency. State = U.S. Department of State.
NCTC = National Counterterrorism Center. TIDE = Terrorist Identities Datamart Environment.
TSC = Terrorist Screening Center. TSDB = Terrorist Screening Data Base.

SOURCE: "Figure 2. Overview of the Watchlist Nominations Process," in *Terrorist Watchlist: Routinely Assessing Impacts of Agency Actions since the December 25, 2009, Attempted Attack Could Help Inform Future Efforts*, U.S. Government Accountability Office, May 2012, http://www.gao.gov/assets/600/591312.pdf (accessed July 23, 2012)

distribute the names of those believed to have a connection to international terrorism to the TSC.

The TSC conducts its own screening process and accepted names are added to the Terrorist Screening Database (TSDB). The FBI (2012, http://www.fbi.gov/about-us/nsb/tsc/tsc_faqs/) reports that "only individuals who are known or reasonably suspected to be or have been engaged in conduct constituting, in preparation for, in aid of, or related to terrorism" are included in the database. As shown in Figure 5.4, information in the database is then made available to various federal, state, and local agencies and to selected foreign governments. As explained by the FBI, the consolidated database provides a single information source "so that every government screener is using the same terrorist watchlist—whether it is an airport screener, an embassy official issuing visas overseas, or a state or local law enforcement officer on the street."

PROTECT THE AMERICAN PEOPLE, CRITICAL INFRASTRUCTURE, AND KEY RESOURCES
Warning of Attacks

One of the tasks of the DHS is to operate a national warning system that keeps the public apprised about the nation's relative risk at any time to a terrorist attack. Prior to 2011, the Homeland Security Advisory System used a color-coded risk scheme to indicate risk. In April 2011 a new system called the National Terrorism Advisory System (NTAS) was implemented. According to the DHS, in "National Terrorism Advisory System" (2012, http://www.dhs.gov/files/programs/ntas.shtm), the new system relies on so-called alert bulletins that provide "timely, detailed information to the public, government agencies, first responders, airports and other transportation hubs, and the private sector." As of October 2012, no alerts had been issued under the new system; however, the DHS provides a sample NTAS alert at http://www.dhs.gov/xlibrary/assets/ntas/ntas-sample-alert.pdf.

Critical Infrastructure and Key Assets

The federal government's overall strategy for protecting the nation's critical infrastructure and key assets was laid out in February 2003 in *National Strategy for the Physical Protection of Critical Infrastructures and Key Assets* (http://www.dhs.gov/xlibrary/assets/Physical_Strategy.pdf). This document outlined policy directives that the DHS used to develop the *National Infrastructure Protection Plan* (2009, http://www.dhs.gov/xlibrary/assets/NIPP_Plan.pdf). The DHS defines critical infrastructure and key assets as including "systems and assets, whether physical or virtual, so vital to the United States that the incapacitation or destruction of such systems and assets would have a debilitating impact on national security, national economic security, public health or safety, or any combination of those matters."

Examples of critical infrastructure include sectors that are essential to survival (e.g., agriculture, food, and water) and those with economic, political, or social importance (e.g., the banking and chemical industries and the postal service). Infrastructure includes both distinct structures, such as buildings and dams, and the networks and components that make up the nation's telecommunications and cyber (Internet) systems. Key assets include "individual targets" that are not essential or vital, but have national importance. The Statue of Liberty is a prime example. The DHS also includes high-profile events, such as the Super Bowl.

Table 5.4 indicates how the responsibility for protecting critical infrastructure and key resources is divided among several federal agencies.

TABLE 5.4

Agencies responsible for critical infrastructure and key resources, 2012

Sector-specific agency	Critical infrastructure and key resources sector
Department of Agriculture[a] Department of Health and Human Services[b]	Food and agriculture
Department of Defense[c]	Defense industrial base
Department of Energy	Energy[d]
Department of Health and Human Services	Healthcare and public health
Department of the Interior	National monuments and icons
Department of the Treasury	Banking and finance
Environmental Protection Agency	Water[e]
Department of Homeland Security	
Office of Infrastructure Protection	Chemical
	Commercial facilities
	Critical manufacturing
	Dams
	Emergency services
	Nuclear reactors, materials, and waste
Office of Cybersecurity and Communications	Information technology Communications
Transportation Security Administration	Postal and shipping
Transportation Security Administration, United States Coast Guard[f]	Transportation systems[g]
Immigration and Customs Enforcement, Federal Protective Service	Government facilities[h]

[a]The Department of Agriculture is responsible for agriculture and food (meat, poultry, and egg products).
[b]The Department of Health and Human Services is responsible for food other than meat, poultry, and egg products.
[c]Nothing in the National Infrastructure Protection Plan (NIPP) impairs or otherwise affects the authority of the Secretary of Defense over the Department of Defense (DOD), including the chain of command for military forces from the president as commander in chief, to the Secretary of Defense, to the commander of military forces, or military command and control procedures.
[d]The energy sector includes the production, refining, storage, and distribution of oil, gas, and electric power, except for commercial nuclear power facilities.
[e]The water sector includes drinking water and wastewater systems.
[f]The U.S. Coast Guard is the sector-specific agency (SSA) for the maritime transportation mode.
[g]As stated in the Homeland Security Presidential Directive (HSPD)-7, the Department of Transportation and the Department of Homeland Security will collaborate on all matters relating to transportation security and transportation infrastructure protection.
[h]The Department of Education is the SSA for the education facilities subsector of the government facilities sector.

SOURCE: "Below is a List of SSAs and Sectors," in *Critical Infrastructure Resource Center*, U.S. Department of Homeland Security, undated, http://training.fema.gov/EMIWeb/IS/is860a/CIRC/sectorOverview.htm (accessed July 23, 2012)

CYBERSECURITY. Cybersecurity refers to safeguarding the nation's computer networks, data, and systems, including the Internet, from unauthorized access or hacking. The federal government's overall strategy for protecting these assets was described in February 2003 in *National Strategy to Secure Cyberspace* (http://www.dhs.gov/xlibrary/assets/ National_Cyberspace_Strategy.pdf). The GAO notes in *Cybersecurity: Threats Impacting the Nation* (April 24, 2012, http://www.gao.gov/assets/600/590367.pdf) that the sources of cyber threats include "criminal groups, hackers, terrorists, organization insiders, and foreign nations engaged in crime, political activism, or espionage and information warfare." According to the GAO, in a January 2012 hearing before the U.S. Senate's Select Committee on Intelligence the director of national intelligence identified China and Russia as countries of particular concern for posing cybersecurity threats to the United States.

Table 5.5 lists common types of cyber exploits. The GAO notes that these exploits include both intentional attacks and unintentional actions, for example, the accidental downloading of malicious software by an agency employee. Whatever the source, cyber threat incidents are a serious and growing concern to the federal government. The incidents are tracked by the U.S. Computer Emergency Readiness Team (US-CERT; http://www.us-cert.gov/), a division of the DHS. The GAO indicates that between 2006 and 2012 the number of cybersecurity incidents reported by federal agencies to US-CERT increased by nearly 680%; however, part of that growth is attributed to improved detection and reporting. US-CERT also operates the National Cyber Awareness System (http://www.us-cert.gov/alerts-and-tips/), which alerts the public about common cybersecurity threats.

Catastrophic Threats

Catastrophic threats are those posed by weapons of mass destruction (WMDs). WMDs are unconventional weapons that use nontraditional means to cause destruction and death. This primarily includes nuclear technology or the release of chemical or biological agents. The major goals under this mission are to develop more effective detection and data-sharing techniques, preventive agents (such as vaccines), and antidotes and treatments to counter the risks posed by WMD attacks.

The Centers for Disease Control and Prevention (CDC) is a federal agency within the U.S. Department of Health and Human Services. Since its founding in 1946, the CDC has been responsible for protecting national public health, including the prevention and control of infectious diseases and other hazards. The CDC was tasked with preparing the United States for the health threats posed by WMDs following the terrorist attacks of 9/11 and the incidents later that month, in which envelopes containing anthrax were mailed within the United States. The anthrax letter case is described in detail in Chapter 7.

TABLE 5.5

Types of cybersecurity threats

Type of exploit	Description
Cross-site scripting	An attack that uses third-party web resources to run script within the victim's web browser or scriptable application. This occurs when a browser visits a malicious website or clicks a malicious link. The most dangerous consequences occur when this method is used to exploit additional vulnerabilities that may permit an attacker to steal cookies (data exchanged between a web server and a browser), log key strokes, capture screen shots, discover and collect network information, and remotely access and control the victim's machine.
Denial-of-service	An attack that prevents or impairs the authorized use of networks, systems, or applications by exhausting resources.
Distributed denial-of-service	A variant of the denial-of-service attack that uses numerous hosts to perform the attack.
Logic bombs	A piece of programming code intentionally inserted into a software system that will cause a malicious function to occur when one or more specified conditions are met.
Phishing	A digital form of social engineering that uses authentic-looking, but fake, e-mails to request information from users or direct them to a fake website that requests information.
Passive wiretapping	The monitoring or recording of data, such as passwords transmitted in clear text, while they are being transmitted over a communications link. This is done without altering or affecting the data.
Structured Query Language (SQL) injection	An attack that involves the alteration of a database search in a web-based application, which can be used to obtain unauthorized access to sensitive information in a database.
Trojan horse	A computer program that appears to have a useful function, but also has a hidden and potentially malicious function that evades security mechanisms by, for example, masquerading as a useful program that a user would likely execute.
Virus	A computer program that can copy itself and infect a computer without the permission or knowledge of the user. A virus might corrupt or delete data on a computer, use e-mail programs to spread itself to other computers, or even erase everything on a hard disk. Unlike a computer worm, a virus requires human involvement (usually unwitting) to propagate.
War driving	The method of driving through cities and neighborhoods with a wireless-equipped computer—sometimes with a powerful antenna—searching for unsecured wireless networks.
Worm	A self-replicating, self-propagating, self-contained program that uses network mechanisms to spread itself. Unlike computer viruses, worms do not require human involvement to propagate.
Zero-day exploit	An exploit that takes advantage of a security vulnerability previously unknown to the general public. In many cases, the exploit code is written by the same person who discovered the vulnerability. By writing an exploit for the previously unknown vulnerability, the attacker creates a potent threat since the compressed timeframe between public discoveries of both makes it difficult to defend against.

SOURCE: "Table 2. Types of Cyber Exploits," in *Cybersecurity: Challenges in Securing the Electricity Grid*, U.S. Government Accountability Office, July 17, 2012, http://www.gao.gov/assets/600/592508.pdf (accessed July 23, 2012)

RESPOND TO AND RECOVER FROM INCIDENTS

Emergency Preparedness

The DHS office of National Protection and Programs has programs and activities that are designed for emergency response professionals and the general public. At the professional level, the DHS offers training programs and grants for emergency planning.

For the general public, the DHS (2012, http://www.ready.gov/) provides information on how Americans should prepare for emergencies, including natural disasters and terrorist attacks. The Ready Campaign calls on every American to do four activities:

- Put together an emergency supply kit (see Table 5.6 for the suggested list of items)

- Prepare a family emergency plan that includes detailed instructions about how family members will communicate their whereabouts to each other if they become separated

- Stay informed about local conditions, the potential for emergency situations to develop, and the appropriate responses to take for particular emergencies

- Get involved in local community preparedness activities

Emergency Response

In any emergency, including a terrorist attack, the initial response is by local and state officials. These so-called first responders include police officers, firefighters, emergency medical technicians, hazardous materials response teams, rescue squads, bomb squads, officials with local and state emergency management agencies, and similar personnel.

TABLE 5.6

Items recommended by the Department of Homeland Security for a basic emergency supply kit

A basic emergency supply kit could include the following recommended items:

- Water, one gallon of water per person per day for at least three days, for drinking and sanitation
- Food, at least a three-day supply of non-perishable food
- Battery-powered or hand crank radio and a NOAA weather radio with tone alert and extra batteries for both
- Flashlight and extra batteries
- First aid kit
- Whistle to signal for help
- Dust mask to help filter contaminated air and plastic sheeting and duct tape to shelter-in-place
- Moist towelettes, garbage bags and plastic ties for personal sanitation
- Wrench or pliers to turn off utilities
- Manual can opener for food
- Local maps
- Cell phone with chargers, inverter or solar charger

NOAA = National Oceanic and Atmospheric Administration.

SOURCE: Adapted from "Basic Disaster Supplies Kit," in *Ready: Build a Kit*, U.S. Department of Homeland Security, undated, http://www.ready.gov/basic-disaster-supplies-kit (accessed July 23, 2012)

FEDERAL ROLE. At the federal level the primary role of emergency preparedness and response is assumed by the Federal Emergency Management Agency (FEMA). FEMA became part of the DHS in 2003. FEMA personnel are dispatched following disasters (e.g., hurricanes and earthquakes) to provide large-scale services for displaced people. For example, after Hurricane Katrina hit the Gulf Coast in 2005, FEMA operated shelters and provided funds to victims who were left homeless by the devastation. The agency also offers training programs for first responders and helps local and state emergency management agencies prepare disaster and response plans.

Other DHS programs related to emergency preparedness and response are:

- National Disaster Medical System (http://www.phe.gov/Preparedness/responders/ndms/Pages/default.aspx)—this is a public/private system of hundreds of volunteer medical teams around the country. The system is overseen by FEMA and is designed to support local hospitals and emergency medical services in the event of a catastrophic disaster.

- Strategic National Stockpile—formerly called the National Pharmaceutical Stockpile, this is a national repository maintained by the CDC that includes large supplies of antibiotics, antidotes, and other medications, as well as medical and surgical supplies. According to the CDC, in "Strategic National Stockpile (SNS)" (March 8, 2012, http://www.cdc.gov/phpr/stockpile/stockpile.htm), one of the goals of the repository is to provide rapid delivery of Push Packages to disaster areas. Push Packages "are caches of pharmaceuticals, antidotes, and medical supplies designed to provide rapid delivery of a broad spectrum of assets for an ill defined threat in the early hours of an event."

- Citizen Corps—this is a national system of volunteers trained to respond at the local level to terrorism events. A National Citizen Corps Council is overseen by the DHS and includes members representing various emergency response organizations and groups from the public and private sectors. A listing of all Citizen Corps around the country is available at http://citizencorps.gov/citizencorps/councils/councilindex.shtm.

HOMELAND SECURITY GRANT PROGRAMS

Acting through the DHS, the federal government supports state and local homeland security programs by issuing grants (funds designated for specific tasks or functions). Table 5.7 lists the major programs around the country that received DHS security grants in FY 2012 and the amounts appropriated. In FY 2012 DHS security grants totaled over

TABLE 5.7

Department of Homeland Security grants, fiscal year 2012

Program	Award ($Millions)	Description
Homeland Security Grant Program		For states and urban areas to prevent, protect against, mitigate, respond to, and recover from acts of terrorism and other threats.
State Homeland Security Program	$294	Support the implementation of state homeland security strategies to build and strengthen preparedness capabilities at all levels.
Urban Areas Security Initiative	$490	Enhance regional preparedness and capabilities in 31 high-threat, high-density areas.
Operation Stonegarden	$46	Enhance cooperation and coordination among federal, state, territorial, tribal and local law enforcement agencies to jointly enhance security along the United States land and water borders.
Emergency Management Performance Grants Program	$339	Assist state and local governments in enhancing and sustaining all-hazards emergency management capabilities.
Tribal Homeland Security Grant Program	$6	For eligible tribal applicants to implement preparedness initiatives to help strengthen the nation against risk associated with potential terrorist attacks and other hazards.
Nonprofit Security Grant Program	$10	Support target hardening and other physical security enhancements for nonprofit organizations determined to be at high risk of a terrorist attack and located within one of the fiscal year 2012 UASI-eligible urban areas.
Intercity Passenger Rail (Amtrak) Program	$10	Protect critical surface transportation infrastructure and the traveling public from terrorism and increase the resilience of the Amtrak rail system.
Port Security Grant Program	$97	Help protect critical port infrastructure from terrorism, enhance maritime domain awareness, and strengthen risk management capabilities in order to protect against improvised explosive devices and other non-conventional weapons.
Transit Security Grant Program	$87	For owners and operators of transit systems to protect critical surface transportation and the traveling public from acts of terrorism and to increase the resilience of transit infrastructure.

SOURCE: Adapted from "Preparedness Grant Program Allocations for Fiscal Year 2012," in *DHS Announces More Than $1.3 Billion in Fiscal Year (FY) 2012 Preparedness Grant Awards*, U.S. Department of Homeland Security, June 29, 2012, http://www.dhs.gov/ynews/releases/20120629-dhs-announces-fy-2012-preparedness-grant-awards.shtm (accessed July 23, 2012)

$1.3 billion. The three largest recipients were the Urban Areas Security Initiative, with $490 million; the Emergency Management Performance Grants Program, with $339 million; and the State Homeland Security Program with $294 million. According to the DHS, in the press release "DHS Announces More Than $1.3 Billion in Fiscal Year (FY) 2012 Preparedness Grant Awards" (June 29, 2012, http://www.dhs.gov/ynews/releases/20120629-dhs-announces-fy-2012-preparedness-grant-awards.shtm), the Urban Areas Security Initiative concerns preparedness and response capabilities in 31 "high-threat, high-density areas." The Emergency Management Performance Grants Program assists state and local governments with their emergency management capabilities. The State Homeland Security Program supports state-based homeland security preparedness measures.

CHAPTER 6

COUNTRIES OF CONCERN

For much of its history, U.S. national security was focused primarily on other powerful nations. During the Cold War, the Soviet Union and China amassed huge military forces and thousands of nuclear weapons. For decades the United States fought the spread of communism with diplomatic and economic means and through military engagements in Korea and Vietnam. The United States, however, never engaged in direct military conflict with the Soviet Union or China for fear of starting a nuclear war. Since the end of the Cold War, the threats posed by other nations to the United States have greatly diminished, but they have not disappeared.

China has become strong politically, militarily, and economically, and it strives to wield more diplomatic power in the world. Even though the United States views this transformation uneasily, relatively good relations between the two countries have been maintained. The same is true for the U.S.-Russian relationship.

In *National Security Strategy* (May 2010, http://www .whitehouse.gov/sites/default/files/rss_viewer/national _security_strategy.pdf), the administration of President Barack Obama (1961–) states, "There is no greater threat to the American people than weapons of mass destruction, particularly the danger posed by the pursuit of nuclear weapons by violent extremists and their proliferation to additional states." Chapter 7 examines the general steps the United States has taken to limit the proliferation (growth or multiplication) of weapons of mass destruction (WMD) including nuclear weapons. Even though nearly all the nations of the world are party to international agreements regarding the development and spread of nuclear weapons, a handful of countries have refused to comply. India, Israel, Pakistan, and North Korea have all developed nuclear weapons outside of international agreements. The United States enjoys relatively good relations with these countries, with the exception of North Korea— an old enemy from the Korean War (1950–1953). North

Korea's nuclear weapons program is considered to be a major threat to U.S. national security.

The United States has also reacted strongly to efforts (or suspected efforts) by its non-allies to develop nuclear weapons. In 2003 the concern that Iraq was developing nuclear weapons was a major factor in the U.S. decision to invade that country and rout the Iraqi government from power. As explained in Chapter 3, U.S. officials ultimately learned their suspicions were incorrect: Iraq had not been actively developing nuclear weapons. With that threat out of the way, attention has turned to Iran, a country with a long history of poor relations with the United States. As shown in Table 6.1, a Gallup Organization poll conducted in February 2012 found that Iran was the most mentioned country when pollsters asked Americans to name "the United States' greatest enemy today." Nearly one-third (32%) of the respondents mentioned Iran. Concern about Iran has grown dramatically since 2001, when it received only 8% of mentions. (See Table 6.2.)

Iran and North Korea are a cause for concern because they are nuclear powers with historically hostile relations with the United States. Iran is also deemed a state sponsor of terrorism by the U.S. Department of State (DOS). (See Table 6.3.) According to the DOS, in "State Sponsors of Terrorism" (2012, http://www.state.gov/j/ct/list/ c14151.htm), the countries listed in Table 6.3 have been "determined by the Secretary of State to have repeatedly provided support for acts of international terrorism." Until 2008 North Korea was also on the list of state sponsors of terrorism. As of 2012, the only other countries on the list were Cuba, Sudan, and Syria. U.S. national security concerns about each of these five countries are described in the following sections.

IRAN

Iran lies in a section of Asia known as the Middle East. (See Figure 6.1.) The nation's capital is Tehran.

TABLE 6.1

Public opinion on the United States' greatest enemy, February 2012

WHAT ONE COUNTRY ANYWHERE IN THE WORLD DO YOU CONSIDER TO BE THE UNITED STATES' GREATEST ENEMY TODAY? [OPEN-ENDED]

	% mentioning
Iran	32
China	23
North Korea/Korea (nonspecific)	10
Afghanistan	7
Iraq	5
Russia	2
Pakistan	2
United States itself	1
Japan	1
Saudi Arabia	1
Other	3
None (vol.)	1
No opinion	11

[vol.] = Volunteered response.

Frank Newport, "What one country anywhere in the world do you consider to be the United States' greatest enemy today?" in *Americans Still Rate Iran Top U.S. Enemy*, The Gallup Organization, February 20, 2012, http://www.gallup.com/poll/152786/Americans-Rate-Iran-Top-Enemy.aspx (accessed July 3, 2012). Copyright © 2012 Gallup, Inc. All rights reserved. The content is used with permission; however, Gallup retains all rights of republication.

Iran's largest neighbors include Turkmenistan to the north, Afghanistan and Pakistan to the east, and Turkey and Iraq to the West. The Persian Gulf lies to the south of Iran and separates it from Kuwait, Saudi Arabia, Bahrain, and Qatar. The Strait of Hormuz, a narrow passage, separates Iran from the United Arab Emirates and Oman. The Strait of Hormuz is the only connection between the Persian Gulf and the open ocean.

For centuries Iran was part of a series of empires and was called Persia by the outside world. In 1935 its name was officially changed to Iran. Beginning in 1941 the country was led by Shah Mohammad Reza Pahlavi (1919–1980). In 1979 the shah was overthrown by his people and forced to leave the country during a revolution that swept the Islamic cleric Ruhollah Khomeini (1902?–1989) into power. The country then adopted a constitution. Khomeini initiated a cultural revolution that sought to remove influences of Western culture and instill conservative Islamic morals and customs. He served as Iran's supreme leader until his death in 1989, when he was replaced by Ali Khamenei (1939–).

Figure 6.2 shows the structure of the Iranian government. The supreme leader is considered to be Iran's spiritual leader and chief of state for life. Every four years or so the country elects government officials, including a

TABLE 6.2

Trends in public opinion on the United States' greatest enemy, selected dates, 2001–12

WHAT ONE COUNTRY ANYWHERE IN THE WORLD DO YOU CONSIDER TO BE THE UNITED STATES' GREATEST ENEMY TODAY? [OPEN-ENDED]

	2012 Feb 2–5	2011 Feb 2–5	2008 Feb 11–14	2007 Feb 1–4	2006 Feb 6–9	2005 Feb 7–10	2001 Feb 1–4
Iran	32	25	25	26	31	14	8
China	23	16	14	11	10	10	14
North Korea/Korea (non-specific)	10	16	9	18	15	22	2
Afghanistan	7	9	3	2	3	3	*
Iraq	5	7	22	21	22	22	38
Russia	2	3	2	2	1	2	6
Pakistan	2	2	2	*	*	*	—
United States itself	1	2	3	2	1	2	1
Japan	1	*	*	*	*	*	1
Saudi Arabia	1	1	1	3	1	2	4
Venezuela	*	—	1	*	*	—	—
Syria	*	—	*	*	1	2	—
Mexico	*	1	*	*	*	—	*
Yemen	*	1	—	—	—	—	*
Libya	*	—	—	—	—	*	4
Cuba	*	*	*	—	*	*	2
Egypt	—	1	—	—	—	—	—
France	—	*	*	*	1	2	—
The Palestinian Authority	—	*	—	—	*	*	1
Other	3	7	6	6	6	8	6
None (vol.)	1	1	2	1	1	2	2
No opinion	11	9	8	7	7	9	11

*Less than 0.5%.
—No mentions.

SOURCE: "What one country anywhere in the world do you consider to be the United States' greatest enemy today?" in *Gallup Poll Social Series: World Affairs—Final Topline*, The Gallup Organization, February 2012, http://www.gallup.com/file/poll/152795/Greatest_US_Enemy_120220.pdf (accessed October 30, 2012). Copyright © 2012 Gallup, Inc. All rights reserved. The content is used with permission; however, Gallup retains all rights of republication.

TABLE 6.3

Countries identified by U.S. government as state sponsors of terrorism, by date of designation

Country	Designation date
Cuba	March 1, 1982
Iran	January 19, 1984
Sudan	August 12, 1993
Syria	December 29, 1979

SOURCE: *State Sponsors of Terrorism*, U.S. Department of State, 2012, http://www.state.gov/j/ct/list/c14151.htm (accessed July 24, 2012)

FIGURE 6.1

Map of Iran, 2012

SOURCE: Adapted from "Map of Iran," in "Middle East: Iran," *The World Factbook*, Central Intelligence Agency, July 5, 2012, https://www.cia.gov/library/publications/the-world-factbook/geos/ir.html (accessed July 24, 2012)

president and members of the 290-seat Majles-e Khoebregan (the Iranian parliament). The most recent parliamentary elections were held in March 2012. In *Iran* (October 3, 2012, http://topics.nytimes.com/top/news/international/countriesandterritories/iran/index.html), the *New York Times* notes that a majority of the seats were won by Khamenei supporters. Presidential elections are held every four years. In 2005 the conservative Mahmoud Ahmadinejad (1956–) was elected president of Iran by a wide majority. He was reelected in 2009 with nearly 63% of the vote. However, the results prompted widespread protests in Iran amid claims of election fraud. According to the *New York Times*, Khamenei and Ahmadinejad have

been at odds with each other and are locked in a struggle for power. In "Elections in Iran Favor Ayatollah's Allies, Dealing Blow to President and His Office" (*New York Times*, March 4, 2012), Neil MacFarquhar notes that observers believe that Khamenei's strong showing in the parliamentary elections has greatly weakened Ahmadinejad's position in the government.

Table 6.4 provides vital statistics about Iran's geography, people, legal system, and economy. In July 2011 the population was estimated at nearly 79 million people. Approximately 98% of the population was Muslim. The Pew Forum on Religion and Public Life estimates in *The Future of the Global Muslim Population, Projections for 2010–2030* (January 2011, http://www.pewforum.org/uploadedFiles/Topics/Religious_Affiliation/Muslim/Future GlobalMuslimPopulation-WebPDF-Feb10.pdf) that in 2010 Iran's Muslim population was approximately 93% Shiite. That made the country the undisputed Shiite power in the world. Other countries with majority Shia populations in 2010 included Azerbaijan (70%), Bahrain (70%), and Iraq (67%).

In *World Factbook: Iran* (September 12, 2012, https://www.cia.gov/library/publications/the-world-factbook/geos/ir.html), the Central Intelligence Agency (CIA) indicates that Iran's gross domestic product (GDP; the total market value of final goods and services produced within an economy in a given year) was $1 trillion in 2011, the 18th-highest GDP in the world. Iran has substantial petroleum and natural gas resources. The U.S. Department of Energy (DOE) reports in *Country Analysis Briefs: Iran* (February 17, 2012, http://204.14.135.140/EMEU/cabs/Iran/pdf.pdf) that Iran contains the world's fourth-largest proven oil reserves (after Saudi Arabia, Venezuela, and Canada) and the world's second-largest proven natural gas reserves (after Russia). The DOE estimates that Iran exported 2.2 million barrels per day of crude oil in 2010, mostly to China, Japan, and India. However, the Iranian energy sector has since been hampered by international sanctions that will be described later in this chapter. In *Iran Sanctions* (July 16, 2012, http://fpc.state.gov/documents/organization/195396.pdf), Kenneth Katzman of the Congressional Research Service (CRS) notes that as of June 2012 Iran was exporting only about 1.2 million to 1.8 million barrels per day, as compared with 2011, when it exported an average of 2.5 million barrels per day.

The CIA indicates that as of 2011 Iran had two main military branches: the Artesh, which consists of regular forces (i.e., army, navy, and air force), and the Islamic Revolutionary Guard Corps, including the highly touted Qods Force, which conducts special operations. As explained in Chapter 4, during the 2003 war in Iraq U.S. authorities accused the Qods Force of training anti-American militias in Iraq.

FIGURE 6.2

Structure of the Iranian government, 2012

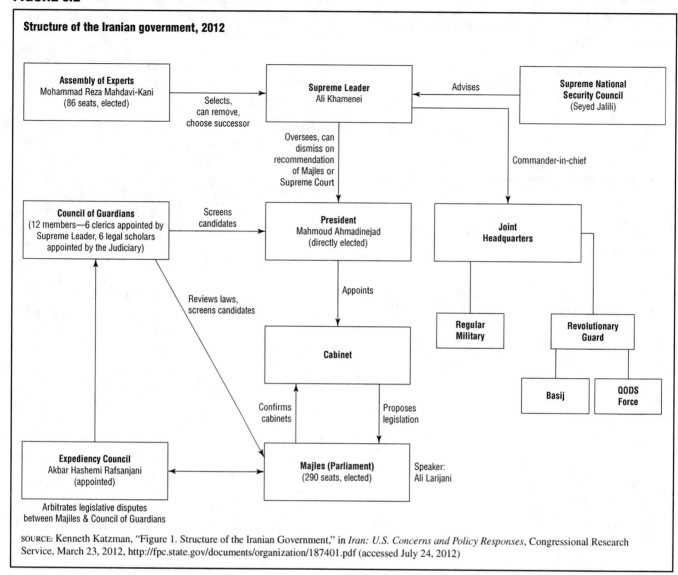

SOURCE: Kenneth Katzman, "Figure 1. Structure of the Iranian Government," in *Iran: U.S. Concerns and Policy Responses*, Congressional Research Service, March 23, 2012, http://fpc.state.gov/documents/organization/187401.pdf (accessed July 24, 2012)

TABLE 6.4

Statistics about Iran, 2012

Geographic area	1,648,195 square kilometers
Comparative size	Slightly smaller than Alaska
Population	78,868,711 (estimated July 2011)
Age structure	0–14 years: 24.1%; 15–64 years: 70.9%; 65 years and over: 5% (estimated July 2011)
Median age	26.8 years (estimated July 2011)
Ethnic groups	Persian 61%; Azeri 16%; Kurd 10%; Lur 6%; Baloch 2%; Arab 2%; Turkmen and Turkic tribes 2%; Other 1%
Religions	Muslim: 98% (Shia 89% and Sunni 9%); Other 2%
Languages	Persian (official) 53%; Azeri Turkic and Turkic dialects 18%; Kurdish 10%; Gilaki and Mazandarani 7%; Luri 6%; Balochi 2%; Arabic 2%; Other 2%
Number of provinces	31
Legal system	Religious legal system based on Sharia law
Gross domestic product	$1.003 trillion (estimated, in U.S. dollars), 18th highest in the world in 2011

SOURCE: Adapted from "Middle East: Iran," in *The World Factbook*, Central Intelligence Agency, July 5, 2012, https://www.cia.gov/library/publications/the-world-factbook/geos/ir.html (accessed July 24, 2012)

Foreign Relations

In 1979 President Jimmy Carter (1924–) allowed the ousted shah of Iran to enter the United States for medical treatment. The United States had supported the shah throughout his reign, even though his regime was considered to be brutal and corrupt by the Iranian people. The U.S. action incited radical elements within Iran who feared that the United States planned to reinstall the shah to power. Angry groups of students protested in the streets and then seized the U.S. embassy in Tehran. Dozens of Americans were held hostage at the embassy for 444 days until their release in 1981.

Despite repeated demands from the U.S. government, Khomeini refused to intervene in the hostage crisis. During and after the Iranian Revolution, Khomeini often criticized the United States, referring to it as "the great Satan." Carter tried a variety of diplomatic and military options to release the hostages during the long ordeal. Diplomatic relations with Iran were terminated and

Iranian assets in U.S. banks were frozen (made unavailable). A rescue attempt by U.S. troops in 1980 ended in disaster when some of the helicopters accidentally crashed after secretly entering Iran. Eight U.S. servicemen were killed. The hostage release was ultimately achieved via diplomatic means. The hostage crisis severely damaged U.S. relations with Iran, and as of October 2012 the two countries had not restored diplomatic relations with each other.

Saddam Hussein (1937–2006) launched an invasion of Iran by Iraqi forces in 1980. The resulting war lasted until 1988. In *Country Profile: Iraq* (August 2006, http://lcweb2.loc.gov/frd/cs/profiles/Iraq.pdf), the Library of Congress (LOC) explains that the war was motivated by a variety of political, religious, and ethnic factors. However, eight years of bloody fighting produced no clear winner, so a cease-fire was finally negotiated.

In 1984 the DOS designated Iran as a state sponsor of terrorism because of Iranian support for organizations such as Hamas, Hezbollah, and the Palestinian Islamic Jihad.

During the mid-1990s executive orders issued by President Bill Clinton (1946–) and passage of the Iran-Iraq Arms Nonproliferation Act of 1992 and the Iran-Libya Sanctions Act of 1996 put restrictions on U.S. and international investments in Iran. In 2006 the Iran-Libya Sanctions Act was renamed the Iran Sanctions Act because of improving relations between the United States and Libya. Other sanctions against Iran were implemented following passage of the Iran, North Korea, and Syria Nonproliferation Act of 2000.

During the late 1990s Iranian voters elected moderate reform-minded candidates to the presidency and the Majles-e Khoebregan, and many observers became optimistic about improved U.S.-Iranian relations. These expectations were dashed when conservatives reasserted their authority in the Iranian government, and Iran's nuclear ambitions were exposed.

Iran's Terrorist Connections

In *Country Reports on Terrorism 2011* (July 2012, http://www.state.gov/documents/organization/195768.pdf), the DOS indicates that Iran has long supported international terrorist organizations, particularly those targeting Israel and the United States. As noted in Chapter 3, Iran has strong ties with Hezbollah, which is based in Lebanon. According to the DOS, Iran has provided arms and "millions of dollars" to Hezbollah and has allowed "thousands" of Hezbollah fighters to come to Iran for paramilitary training. The DOS believes this training is provided by Iran's elite Qods Force, which is also accused of training, arming, and funding Shiite militant groups that targeted U.S. forces during the 2003 war in Iraq. Iraq and Iran were bitter enemies when Hussein

ruled Iraq. His ouster following the U.S.-led invasion allowed Shiite officials to assume positions of power in the new Iraqi government. As explained in Chapter 4, Iraq—with its large Shiite population—has grown ever closer with Iran, which is an unwelcome development in regards to U.S. interests in the region.

According to the DOS, Iran "increased its terrorist-related activity [in 2011], likely in an effort to exploit the uncertain political conditions resulting from the Arab Spring, as well as in response to perceived increasing external pressure on Tehran." As noted in Chapter 3, the so-called Arab Spring revolutions of 2010–11 ousted long-time rulers from power in Tunisia, Egypt, Libya, and Yemen. The upheaval in Egypt is particularly noteworthy to Iran, because Egypt's ousted regime was politically aligned with Iran's chief rival for power in the Middle East: Saudi Arabia, a key U.S. ally.

Overall, the DOS accuses Iran of using international terrorism "to further its foreign policy goals." Besides supporting terrorist groups, such as Hezbollah and Hamas, Iran is alleged to have committed the following "terrorist-related" activities during 2011:

- Plotting to assassinate Saudi Arabia's ambassador to the United States

- Providing "lethal support" to militant Iraqi Shiite groups

- Training and arming Taliban militants in Afghanistan

- Assisting the Syrian government in its "brutal crackdown" on pro-democracy demonstrators (this conflict is described in detail later in this chapter)

- Refusing to prosecute senior al Qaeda members believed to be detained in Iraq

- Allowing al Qaeda members to travel and transport goods through Iranian territory

- Failing to track and criminalize terrorist financing in accordance with international agreements

Iran's Nuclear Program

The Treaty on the Nonproliferation of Nuclear Weapons (NPT; 2000, http://www.un.org/en/conf/npt/2005/npttreaty.html) originally went into force in 1970 after being negotiated by the United Nations (UN). The United States and the Soviet Union were among the original signers of the treaty. It forbids countries with nuclear weapons from transferring nuclear weapons or related explosive devices "to any recipient whatsoever." No assistance can be offered to a nonnuclear weapon nation to manufacture or acquire the weapons. The parties to the treaty also agree to "preventing diversion of nuclear energy from peaceful uses to nuclear weapons" and to take measures leading toward nuclear disarmament. The International Atomic

Energy Agency (IAEA; http://www.iaea.org/) verifies that parties comply with the NPT.

According to Sharon Squassoni of the CRS, in *Iran's Nuclear Program: Recent Developments* (September 6, 2006, http://www.fas.org/sgp/crs/nuke/RS21592.pdf), the National Council of Resistance of Iran (NCR) alerted the world in 2002 about Iran's nuclear activities. The NCR is a coalition of Iranian dissident groups (groups that disagree with established political or religious systems or policies) based outside the country. The NCR reported that Iran had nuclear facilities at Natanz (which is approximately 100 miles [161 km] north of Esfahan) and near Arak (a small town southwest of Qom). (See Figure 6.1.)

IAEA investigators discovered that "significant" nuclear activities had been taking place that were not reported to the IAEA, which was a violation of the NPT that Iran ratified in 1970. Iranian officials admitted they had been conducting a number of undeclared activities and that during the late 1980s they received a so-called nuclear cookbook with instructions for producing nuclear weapon parts. The cookbook was allegedly created by the Pakistani scientist Abdul Qadeer Khan (1935–), who has been linked to many illicit transfers of nuclear technology to nonnuclear nations.

The World Nuclear Association explains in "Uranium Enrichment" (June 2012, http://world-nuclear.org/info/inf28.html) that natural uranium (U) consists mainly of two isotopes called U-235 and U-238. Isotopes are forms of a chemical element that contain the same number of protons, but different numbers of neutrons. It is the U-235 content that makes uranium useful in reactors and weapons. However, natural uranium contains less than 1% of U-235. Thus, uranium must be enriched to 3% to 5% of U-235 for use in common nuclear power reactors, to nearly 20% for use in certain nuclear research and development reactors, and to at least 90% for use in nuclear weapons.

Squassoni notes that IAEA inspectors found two uranium enrichment facilities at Natanz. In late 2003 Iran ceased some of its uranium enrichment activities and began negotiations with IAEA officials and diplomats from three European Union countries: Germany, France, and the United Kingdom. However, negotiations broke down in August 2005, and Iran resumed operations and construction at its nuclear facilities. The IAEA reported Iran to the UN Security Council for violating the NPT.

UN RESOLUTIONS. In the press release "Security Council Demands Iran Suspend Uranium Enrichment by 31 August, or Face Possible Economic, Diplomatic Sanctions" (July 31, 2006, http://www.un.org/News/Press/docs/2006/sc8792.doc.htm), the UN Security Council describes Resolution 1696, which called on Iran to "suspend all enrichment-related and reprocessing activities, including research and development" by the end of August 2006. Iran's failure to comply triggered four additional resolutions (1737, 1747, 1803, and 1835) that were passed through September 2008. According to Katzman, the resolutions call on Iran to suspend its nuclear activities and begin cooperating fully with IAEA investigators. Resolutions 1737, 1747, and 1803 basically demand that Iran suspend its uranium enrichment program and impose sanctions against the nation that are intended to pressure Iran to comply. In addition, the resolutions call on other nations to refuse to export arms to Iran or conduct new business with Iran and to monitor Iranian bank activities within their borders and air and sea shipments bound for Iran. Resolution 1835 simply reiterates previous demands without adding new sanctions.

In June 2010 the UN Security Council passed Resolution 1929. Katzman notes that this resolution prohibits countries from selling "most categories of heavy arms" to Iran, requires countries to prevent companies within their borders from engaging in business with Iran if such business could further Iran's WMD activities, and bans other countries from permitting Iran to invest in nuclear-related technologies within their borders.

The Status of U.S.-Iranian Relations

As noted earlier, the United States has had a contentious relationship with Iran since the 1979 hostage crisis. Numerous presidential executive orders and laws have been put into place in an effort to pressure Iran to change its behavior. The early measures focused only on Iran's involvement in international terrorism. However, once Iran's nuclear ambitions came to light, the U.S. government began an aggressive campaign of sanctions and urged its allies and the UN Security Council to do likewise. Israel, a strong American ally in the Middle East, has gone even further by publicly threatening to wage military strikes to prevent Iran from developing nuclear weapons. The two countries have an acrimonious relationship that has been aggravated by hostile anti-Israel statements made by Ahmadinejad and Khamenei. The *New York Times* notes in *Iran* that Ahmadinejad "has challenged the accuracy of the Holocaust [the mass killing of millions of Jews and other ethnic groups in Europe between 1933 and 1945] and predicted in a speech early in his tenure that Israel would one day be 'wiped off the map.'"

Israel and Iran have been engaged in a so-called shadow war, which Alan Cowell explains in "Iran Executes Man Accused as Israeli Spy and Assassin" (*New York Times*, May 15, 2012) is believed to have included bomb attacks on Israeli civilians and assassinations of prominent figures, including at least four Iranian nuclear scientists. As a close ally of Israel, the United States is considered to be guilty—either directly or by association—in the shadow war operations that have targeted Iran.

Another complication in the U.S.-Iranian relationship is the changing political makeup of the Middle East. As noted earlier, the ouster of Hosni Mubarak (1928–), the Egyptian ruler, during the Arab Spring revolutions seriously changed the balance of power in the Middle East. Mubarak's government was pro-American, had engaged in diplomatic relations with Israel, and had long shunned ties with Iran due to political and ideological differences. Mubarak's successor, Mohamed Mursi (1951–), is an Islamist (an adherent to the belief that governments should operate in strict accordance with Islamic law). In August 2012 Mursi made a state visit to Iran, the first such visit by an Egyptian leader since the 1970s. In *Iran*, the *New York Times* notes that "Iran has already benefited from the ouster or undermining of Arab leaders who were its strong adversaries and has begun to project its growing influence."

The United States has become increasingly concerned about Iran's intentions regarding nuclear weaponry and Israel's threats to take military action against Iran. The Obama administration has continued to try diplomatic solutions by imposing new sanctions and tightening existing sanctions against Iran. In January 2012 the European Union (EU) ratcheted up the pressure by imposing a ban—effective July 1, 2012—on all EU oil purchases from Iran. This move is significant, because according to Katzman, the EU buys approximately 20% of Iran's oil exports. According to the White House, in "Remarks by the President at AIPAC Policy Conference" (March 4, 2012, http://www.whitehouse.gov/the-press-office/2012/03/04/remarks-president-aipac-policy-conference-0), in March 2012 President Obama gave a speech during which he urged Israel to give the sanctions against Iran more time to work, noting that "now is not the time for bluster. Now is the time to let our increased pressure sink in, and to sustain the broad international coalition we have built." However, Obama did indicate there is a limit to U.S. patience, stating, "Iran's leaders should understand that I do not have a policy of containment; I have a policy to prevent Iran from obtaining a nuclear weapon. And as I have made clear time and again during the course of my presidency, I will not hesitate to use force when it is necessary to defend the United States and its interests."

In August 2012 the IAEA published an updated report on its Iranian inspection program that was not encouraging. In *Implementation of the NPT Safeguards Agreement and Relevant Provisions of Security Council Resolutions in the Islamic Republic of Iran* (August 30, 2012, http://www.iaea.org/Publications/Documents/Board/2012/gov2012-37.pdf), the IAEA complains that "Iran is not providing the necessary cooperation" and admits that "efforts to resolve all outstanding substantive issues have

achieved no concrete results." In particular, the agency notes that contrary to UN resolutions Iran has not suspended its enrichment-related activities or heavy water programs. (Heavy water is chemically modified water that can be used to facilitate nuclear reactions.) The IAEA also points out its continuing concerns "about the possible existence in Iran of undisclosed nuclear related activities involving military related organizations, including activities related to the development of a nuclear payload for a missile." The report greatly heightened fears about Iran's intentions, and as of October 2012, U.S.-Iranian relations remained strained.

NORTH KOREA

North Korea is a small country that sits on a peninsula jutting out of the coastline of East Asia. (See Figure 6.3.) The nation's capital is Pyongyang. North Korea is bordered on the north by China and Russia and to the south by South Korea. Japan lies a few hundred miles to the southeast, across the Sea of Japan. North and South Korea were once a single nation. Japan invaded Korea in 1905 and occupied it through World War II (1939–1945). Following the war the Allied powers split the Korea Peninsula into two countries, with the northern part falling under Soviet control and the southern part under U.S. control. In 1948 South

FIGURE 6.3

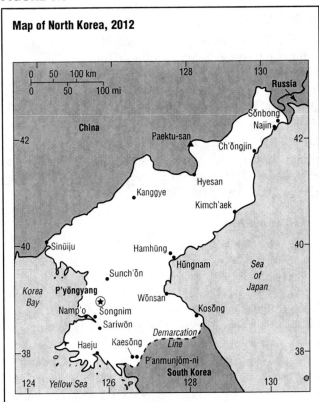

Map of North Korea, 2012

SOURCE: Adapted from "Map of North Korea," in "East and Southeast Asia: Korea, North," *The World Factbook*, Central Intelligence Agency, July 5, 2012, https://www.cia.gov/library/publications/the-world-factbook/geos/kn.html (accessed July 24, 2012)

Korea became an independent nation. North Korea was ruled by Kim Il Sung (1912–1994) from 1948 until his death in 1994. His son Kim Jong-Il (1942–2011) ruled until he died in December 2011, at which time his son, Kim Jong-Un (1983?–), assumed power.

In *World Factbook: North Korea* (October 2, 2012, https://www.cia.gov/library/publications/the-world-fact book/geos/kn.html), the CIA estimates that North Korea's population was 24.6 million in July 2012. The CIA describes North Korea as a "communist state one-man dictatorship." All of its political parties are controlled by the major party: the Korean Workers' Party. Even though elections were held in 2003, Kim Jong-Il was the only person nominated for chief of state and ran unopposed. The country has a 687-seat Supreme People's Assembly that has elections every five years (most recently in 2009); however, candidates are appointed by the nation's rulers and run unopposed in elections. The CIA reports that decades of poor governance and economic mismanagement have rendered North Korea unable to feed many of its people. The population is highly dependent on international food aid and is believed to suffer from widespread malnutrition and poor living conditions. Much of the country's resources are believed to be devoted to maintaining its military. The DOS states in "Background Note: North Korea" (April 4, 2012, http://www.state.gov/r/pa/ei/ bgn/2792.htm) that North Korea is estimated to have an active duty military force of 1.2 million—one of the largest armies in the world.

The CIA points out that "North Korea's history of regional military provocations, proliferation of military-related items, long-range missile development, WMD programs including tests of nuclear devices in 2006 and 2009, and massive conventional armed forces are of major concern to the international community." As shown in Table 6.2, 10% of Americans polled by the Gallup Organization in 2012 named North Korea as "the United States' greatest enemy." The percentage was up from only 2% in 2001.

Foreign Relations

As explained in Chapter 1, U.S. and allied forces under the UN went to war against North Korea during the early 1950s after North Korea invaded South Korea. North Korea was politically aligned with the Soviet Union and received help from the latter and from Chinese troops during the three-year long war. In 1953 a cease-fire agreement was reached that ended the armed conflict. Since that time an uneasy peace has been maintained along the 38th parallel (a line of latitude), which is the border separating North Korea from South Korea. North Korea has remained a communist nation and has established a massive military force. South Korea has become a democracy and is protected by UN troops (primarily U.S. forces).

During the war the United States imposed economic sanctions against North Korea that would last for decades. North Korea became highly dependent on its communist allies, particularly the Soviet Union and China, for foreign trade. The breakup of the Soviet Union during the early 1990s eliminated a major political ally and trading partner for North Korea; however, its close relationship with China has continued.

North Korea's Nuclear Program

Larry A. Niksch of the CRS notes in *North Korea's Nuclear Weapons Development and Diplomacy* (January 5, 2010, http://www.nkeconwatch.com/nk-uploads/nucle arweapons-1-5-10.pdf) that in 1985 North Korea signed the NPT. In 1987 it began operating an atomic reactor near Pyongyang, ostensibly to produce electrical power. U.S. intelligence agencies discovered in 1989 that the reactor had been shut down for more than two months. It was suspected that the used fuel rods in the reactor were removed and reprocessed for their plutonium content. (High-grade plutonium can be used to produce a nuclear weapon.) Similar reactor shutdowns occurred in successive years. During a May 1994 shutdown, approximately 8,000 used fuel rods were removed. Scientists estimated that the rods likely contained enough plutonium to produce four to six nuclear weapons.

AGREED FRAMEWORK. The U.S. government was disturbed by the removal of the used fuel rods and by IAEA reports that North Korea was withholding data, being uncooperative, and threatening to withdraw from the NPT. In response, the United States threatened to bring new economic sanctions against North Korea through the UN. The two countries eventually negotiated an agreement known as the Agreed Framework (November 2, 1994, http://www.iaea.org/Publications/Documents/Infcircs/ Others/infcirc457.pdf) that called for North Korea to remain a party to the NPT, to freeze its nuclear program, and to dismantle nuclear reactors under IAEA supervision in exchange for the following concessions from the United States:

- Easing of economic sanctions

- Full diplomatic relations

- Two light water nuclear reactors (i.e., reactors that use regular water rather than heavy water) and 3.7 million barrels of oil per year

- Formal assurance that the United States would not threaten to use or use nuclear weapons against North Korea

The United States began shipping oil to North Korea, made preliminary arrangements for the light water nuclear reactors, and started phasing out some economic sanctions. However, the United States and North Korea were unable to negotiate an arrangement in which the two countries have full diplomatic relations (i.e., have embassies or other diplomatic posts within each other's countries and exchange ambassadors).

In 2002 the Agreed Framework fell apart after the United States accused North Korea of operating since 1996 a secret program to develop nuclear weapons using highly enriched uranium instead of reprocessed plutonium. The United States immediately ceased oil shipments to North Korea; North Korea responded by expelling IAEA inspectors, withdrawing from the NPT, and restarting its plutonium reprocessing operations.

SIX-PARTY TALKS. In 2003 the United States and North Korea began a series of negotiations that included high-ranking officials from South Korea, China, Japan, and Russia. The so-called six-party talks were initiated after the United States refused to hold bilateral (two-party) meetings with North Korea. Many rounds were held in which virtually no progress was achieved in resolving the disputes at issue. Furthermore, the U.S. invasions of Afghanistan and Iraq in 2001 and 2003, respectively, made North Korea increasingly concerned about a military strike from U.S. forces. In 2003 North Korean officials publicly announced that the country had nuclear weapons. Subsequent announcements included hostile and threatening rhetoric toward the United States. After the November 2005 six-party talks, North Korea temporarily refused to meet again in protest of new accusations from the United States that North Korea was conducting illegal activities, including drug trafficking and the counterfeiting of U.S. currency.

In July 2006 the world was stunned when North Korea test-fired seven unarmed missiles toward the Sea of Japan to demonstrate their capabilities. One of the missiles was a Taepo Dong-2, which is thought to have a range of approximately 1,860 miles (2,993 km). That missile failed after approximately 40 seconds and fell into the sea. The other six missiles were short-range missiles.

Since 1999 North Korea had maintained a moratorium on the testing of long-range missiles following international outcry over such a test in 1998. Japan and South Korea, in particular, have expressed concern about North Korea's missile capabilities. Both nations host large U.S. military bases, which could be targets for the missiles in wartime. The timing of the July 2006 missile launches appears to have been politically motivated. Even though they were launched on July 5 in North Korea, it was still July 4 in the Western Hemisphere. The missile launches were protested strongly by U.S. officials. North Korea received further international condemnation in October 2006, when it conducted an underground test of a nuclear weapon. That same month the UN Security Council unanimously passed Resolution 1718, which urged North Korea to resume the six-party talks and prohibited member nations from transferring to North Korea luxury goods and either money or technology that could support the development of WMDs.

The DOS reports in "Background Note: North Korea" that the six-party talks resumed in December 2006 and that a bilateral meeting between North Korean and U.S. officials was held a month later. In February 2007 the six-party talks resulted in a plan for North Korea to freeze development of and begin disabling its nuclear facilities in exchange for foreign economic and energy aid. In June 2008 President George W. Bush (1946–) lifted most of the economic sanctions that had been in place against North Korea since 1950 under the Trading with the Enemy Act. He also notified Congress of his intention to remove North Korea from the state sponsor of terrorism list. According to the DOS, the removal took place in October 2008, after a verification program was established to confirm the declarations made by the North Korean government.

In April 2009 North Korea conducted another missile test. The DOS reports that a Taepo Dong-2 missile was fired toward the Sea of Japan. The UN promptly condemned the launch as a violation of Resolution 1718. North Korea responded by withdrawing from the six-party talks. It also expelled IAEA inspectors and U.S. technical experts who had been monitoring its nuclear activities and announced its intention to reactivate its nuclear facilities. In May 2009 North Korea disclosed that it had conducted another test of a "nuclear explosive device." In June 2009 the UN Security Council passed Resolution 1874, which further strengthened the arms embargo against North Korea. The country conducted additional missile tests throughout the remainder of the year. The DOS notes that in November 2009 North Korea announced that it had successfully conducted "experimental uranium enrichment."

In March 2010 the South Korean warship ROKS (Republic of Korea Ship) *Cheonan* exploded and sank in the Yellow Sea. Forty-six people out of the 100-person crew died. Suspicion immediately focused on North Korea. In May 2010 the Joint Civilian-Military Investigation Group, which included experts from South Korea, the United States, the United Kingdom, Australia, and Sweden, issued its findings in "Investigation Result on the Sinking of ROKS 'Cheonan'" (http://www.globalsecurity.org/military/library/report/2010/100520_jcmig-roks-cheonan/100520_jcmig-roks-cheonan.pdf). The group concludes: "Based on all such relevant facts and classified analysis, we have reached the clear conclusion that ROKS 'Cheonan' was sunk as the result of an external underwater explosion caused by a torpedo made in North Korea. The evidence points overwhelmingly to the conclusion that the torpedo was fired by a North Korean submarine. There is no other plausible explanation." North Korean officials strongly denied any involvement in the sinking.

In November 2010 South Korean forces were conducting military exercises near Yeonpyeong Island when they came under attack by North Korean artillery. South Korea responded with its own artillery fire for several hours until the hostilities ceased. According to John M. Glionna and Ethan Kim, in "Yeonpyeong Island a Korean Peninsula Hot Spot" (*Los Angeles Times*, November 26, 2010), ownership of the island has long been an issue of contention between the two sides. The North Korean artillery attack killed two South Korean marines and two civilians on the island and injured dozens of people. In addition, approximately 70% of the vegetation on the island was consumed by fire. It is not known if any North Korean forces were harmed during the skirmish. The CIA notes in *World Factbook: North Korea* that the *Cheonan* sinking and the Yeonpyeong attack spurred the South Korean government to "cut off most aid, trade, and bilateral cooperation activities" with North Korea.

According to the DOS, the United States held bilateral talks with North Korea beginning in 2011 that resulted in an agreement in February 2012 that North Korea would cease projects related to long-range missiles, nuclear tests, and uranium enrichment in exchange for food aid from the United States. In addition, North Korea consented to IAEA inspections to verify the moratorium on its uranium enrichment activities. However, the agreement was to be short-lived. In April 2012 North Korea launched what was purported to be a weather satellite; however, the rocket broke apart before reaching orbit. Alyssa Newcomb, Luis Martinez, and Martha Raddatz note in "North Korean Rocket Launch Fails: US Officials" (ABCNews.com, April 12, 2012) that "experts did not doubt the possibility of a satellite being attached to the rocket, but believed the satellite to be a cover in order to test a long-range missile." The launch was widely condemned as a violation of UN Security Council resolutions forbidding North Korea from engaging in ballistic missile activities. In addition, the launch was seen by the United States as a blatant violation of the agreement reached between the two nations less than two months before. As a result, the U.S. government refused to uphold its end of the agreement.

Meanwhile, as of October 2012, North Korea continued to periodically test-fire short-range missiles. The country's new leader, Kim Jong-Un, is a mysterious figure about whom little is known, even his age. Various media sources estimate him to be in his late 20s. It was widely reported during the summer of 2012 that he had married a woman named Ri Sol Ju. The article "State Media: North Korea's Kim Jong Un Has Married" (CNN.com, July 25, 2012) notes that Kim is believed to be the youngest head of state in the world and is the youngest son of Kim Jong-Il. According to the article, outside analysts are not certain how much power Kim

yields in North Korea and indicate there is a possibility that other family members may wield some control over the nation's military forces.

In "Progress Is Cited on New Reactor in North Korea" (*New York Times*, August 21, 2012), Choe Sang-hun reports that analysts believe that North Korea has made significant progress on a nuclear reactor project at Yongbyon. Sang-hun notes, "The experimental light-water reactor under construction—and North Korea's efforts to enrich uranium—could eventually provide the country with a means to increase its nuclear stockpile significantly, experts have warned." Table 6.5 lists the status of North Korea's nuclear power reactor projects as of 2012. According to Sang-hun, analysts believe the new reactor being constructed at Yongbyon will have a much higher rate of plutonium production than the older reactor at that location.

OTHER COUNTRIES OF CONCERN

Even though Iran and North Korea are considered to be the countries posing the most threat to U.S. national security, there are other countries of concern. (See Table 6.3.) These include three nations deemed state sponsors of terrorism: Cuba, Sudan, and Syria.

Cuba

Cuba is a small island lying between the Caribbean Sea to the south and the Gulf of Mexico and the North Atlantic Ocean to the north. (See Figure 6.4.) Cuba is only 90 miles (145 km) southeast of Key West, Florida. It is a communist state that was ruled for nearly five decades by one man: Fidel Castro (1926–). In February 2008 he stepped down as Cuba's president because of ill health. His brother, Raúl Castro (1931–), officially became Cuba's leader.

Historically, Cuba enjoyed close economic and military ties to the former Soviet Union. The demise of the Soviet Union during the early 1990s sent Cuba into a sharp economic recession from which it has never recovered. According to the CIA, in *World Factbook: Cuba* (September 5, 2012, https://www.cia.gov/library/publications/the-world-factbook/geos/cu.html), the standard of living for the average Cuban was less in 2012 than it was before the loss of Soviet aid.

Cuba and the United States have had a contentious relationship since Fidel Castro took power. In 1961 CIA-backed Cuban exiles attempted to invade Cuba and overthrow Castro. They were soundly defeated in a battle at the Bay of Pigs, a small bay located south of Matanzas along the southern coast of the island. Only a year later President John F. Kennedy (1917–1963) and the Soviet premier Nikita Khrushchev (1894–1971) faced off after U.S. intelligence agencies discovered that the Soviets had installed nuclear missile facilities in Cuba. After a

TABLE 6.5

North Korean nuclear power reactor projects, 2012

Location	Type/power capacity	Status	Purpose
Yongbyon	Graphite-moderated heavy water experimental reactor/5 MWe	Currently shut-down; cooling tower destroyed in June 2009 as part of Six-Party Talks; estimated restart time would be 6 months	Weapons-grade plutonium production
Yongbyon	Graphite-moderated heavy water power reactor/50 MWe	Never built; basic construction begun; project halted since 1994	Stated purpose was electricity production; could have been used for weapons-grade plutonium production
Yongbyon	Experimental light-water reactor/100 MWT (25–30 MWe)	U.S. observers saw basic construction begun in November 2010	Stated purpose is electricity production; could be used for weapons-grade plutonium production
Taechon	Graphite-moderated heavy water power reactor/200 MWe	Never built; basic construction begun; project halted since 1994	Stated purpose was electricity production; could have been used for weapons-grade plutonium production
Kumho district, Sinp'o	4 Light-water reactors/440 MW	Never built; part of 1985 deal with Soviet Union when North Korea signed the NPT; canceled by Russian Federation in 1992	Stated purpose is electricity production; could have been used for weapons-grade plutonium production
Kumho district, Sinp'o [KEDO project]	2 Light-water reactors (turn-key)/1,000 MWe	Never built; part of 1994 Agreed Framework, reactor agreement concluded in 1999; project terminated in 2006 after North Korea pulled out of Agreed Framework	Electricity production

MWe = megawatt electrical.
MWT = megawatt thermal.
MW = megawatt.

SOURCE: Mary Beth Nikitin, "Table 1. North Korean Nuclear Power Reactor Projects," in *North Korea's Nuclear Weapons: Technical Issues*, Congressional Research Service, February 29, 2012, http://fpc.state.gov/documents/organization/185913.pdf (accessed July 24, 2012)

FIGURE 6.4

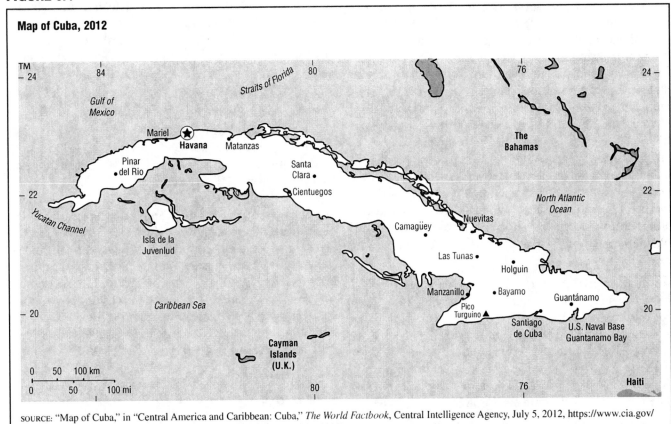

Map of Cuba, 2012

SOURCE: "Map of Cuba," in "Central America and Caribbean: Cuba," *The World Factbook*, Central Intelligence Agency, July 5, 2012, https://www.cia.gov/library/publications/the-world-factbook/geos/cu.html (accessed July 24, 2012)

suspenseful 12-day diplomatic standoff, the Soviets backed down and agreed to dismantle the facilities. The United States implemented the first of many economic sanctions against Cuba. With only a handful of exceptions, American citizens were forbidden to travel to Cuba. The United States issued an open invitation to Cuban citizens wanting to flee to the United States—they could become eligible for citizenship after only a year of residency. Over the next four decades a succession of U.S. presidents openly expressed support for Cuban exiles and dissidents seeking to overthrow Castro's government.

During the Carter administration the two countries decided to partially restore diplomatic relations. In 1977 the United States opened an Interests Section office in the Swiss embassy in Havana, the capital of Cuba. Then in 1996 the Cuban military shot down two U.S. civilian airplanes near Cuba, killing four people—all of whom were members of a Cuban-American group opposed to the Castro regime. In retaliation, President Clinton imposed new economic sanctions against Cuba that were passed by Congress in the Helms-Burton bill. In "Bill Clinton on Sanctions against Cuba: Amy Goodman Interviews Bill Clinton" (November 8, 2000, http://www.globalpolicy.org/security/sanction/cuba/00clintn.htm), an interview about Castro and the plane incident, Clinton said, "Sometimes I wonder if he shot them down just to make sure the embargo couldn't be lifted, because as long as he can blame the United States, then he doesn't have to answer to his own people for the failures of his economic policy."

In November 2001 Cuba was struck by Hurricane Michelle and suffered severe damage to its agricultural industry. In an unprecedented move, the United States sold shipments of food to Cuba as part of a humanitarian effort. There was talk in the United States of dropping the economic sanctions against Cuba. In the speech "Lift the United States Embargo on Cuba" (July 26, 2001, http://paul.house.gov/index.php?option=com_content&task=view&id=401&Itemid=60), Representative Ron Paul (1935–; R-TX) noted that "while sanctions may serve our patriotic fervor, they mostly harm innocent citizens and do nothing to displace the governments we claim as enemies." However, relaxing the sanctions was staunchly opposed by many conservatives in the U.S. government and by members of the politically powerful Cuban exile movement centered in Miami, Florida.

In 2002 former president Carter was invited by Castro to visit Cuba for a series of meetings. It was the first visit by a high-ranking U.S. official since Castro took power. However, the Bush administration decided to take a hard line against Cuba. Immediately before Carter's visit, the administration accused Castro of cooperating with terrorist organizations in the development of WMDs. Cuba has been on the DOS's list of state sponsors of terrorism since 1982.

In April 2009 President Obama announced the loosening of restrictions on travel, money transfers, and telecommunications between the United States and Cuba. In January 2011 additional restrictions related to travel and money transfers were relaxed. However, relations between the two nations cooled later that year when Cuba sentenced Alan Gross (1949–), an American subcontractor,

to 15 years in prison. Mark P. Sullivan of the CRS explains in *Cuba: Issues for the 112th Congress* (July 20, 2012, http://www.fas.org/sgp/crs/row/R41617.pdf) that Gross was a subcontractor working in Cuba on "democracy projects" funded by the U.S. Agency for International Development. He was charged with being a spy for the U.S. government, a claim the United States has denied. Despite repeated requests from U.S. officials and politicians for his release, Gross remained imprisoned in Cuba as of October 2012. Sullivan states, "While the United States and Cuba are cooperating on such issues as antidrug efforts and, through multilateral channels, on disaster preparedness and cooperation in the event of an oil spill, improvement of relations in other areas will likely be stymied until Alan Gross is released from prison."

Cuba's continued listing as a state sponsor of terrorism is increasingly under fire. According to Sullivan, critics believe the listing is due to "political considerations" in the United States rather than actual concerns about Cuba's support for terrorist organizations. In *Country Reports on Terrorism 2011*, the DOS plays down Cuba's ties to terrorism. The DOS notes that some former and current members of the Basque Fatherland Liberty terrorist organization were allowed to live in Cuba in 2011. However, the DOS acknowledges that it has evidence that the Cuban government has been "trying to distance itself" from the members by denying them certain state services.

Sudan

Sudan is an African country with a very troubled history. It became an independent state in 1956; however, it has suffered from decades of civil war, social unrest, and political instability. According to the CIA, in *World Factbook: Sudan* (September 21, 2012, https://www.cia.gov/library/publications/the-world-factbook/geos/su.html), the country's population was largely split between a northern region containing mostly Arabs and Muslims and a southern region containing mostly non-Arabs and non-Muslims. In 2005, after years of bloody civil war between the north and south, a peace agreement was reached that gave independence to the new nation of South Sudan in 2011. (See Figure 6.5.) Meanwhile, a separate violent conflict has wracked the Darfur region of Sudan since 2003. The CIA notes that an estimated 200,000 to 400,000 people have died in the conflict, which has also displaced nearly 2 million people.

Sudan is in the north-central part of the African continent and is bordered on the north by Egypt; on the west by Libya, Chad, and the Central African Republic; on the south by South Sudan and Ethiopia; and on the east by Eritrea. (See Figure 6.5.) The capital of Sudan is Khartoum. The northeastern portion of the country is bounded by the Red Sea. The Nile River flows across

FIGURE 6.5

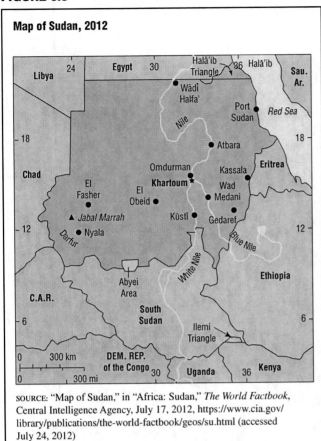

Map of Sudan, 2012

SOURCE: "Map of Sudan," in "Africa: Sudan," *The World Factbook*, Central Intelligence Agency, July 17, 2012, https://www.cia.gov/library/publications/the-world-factbook/geos/su.html (accessed July 24, 2012)

the eastern part of Sudan. According to the CIA, the ethnicity of the Sudanese population is mostly Sudanese Arab and the predominant religion is Sunni Islam.

The Sudanese government's crackdown on rebels has precipitated a humanitarian crisis in Darfur and has been criticized by the international community as attempted genocide. (Genocide is the eradication of an entire group of people based on their nationality, ethnicity, religion, or race.) In July 2007 the UN Security Council issued Resolution 1769, which authorized the deployment of a peacekeeping force in Darfur. The troops have been supplied by the African Union, a cooperative venture between several African nations.

In March 2009 the International Criminal Court (an international judicial body established in 2002) issued an arrest warrant for the Sudanese president Omar al-Bashir (1944–). He was wanted for the war crimes and crimes against humanity that he allegedly committed in Darfur. In April 2010 al-Bashir won a new five-year term as Sudan's president in an election that international observers indicated was tainted by fraud.

U.S.-Sudanese relations have been poor for decades. The rift was deepened by U.S. support for Israel during the Six-Day War in 1967 and by the murders of American diplomats in Sudan during the 1970s and 1980s. In

1989 al-Bashir overthrew the existing ruler and installed a government known as the National Islamic Front. Al-Bashir is believed to have supported many terrorist organizations during the 1990s and provided a safe haven for notorious terrorists, such as Osama bin Laden (1957?–2011) and Abu Nidal (1937–2002). In 1993 the United States designated Sudan as a state sponsor of terrorism. Throughout the remainder of the decade the United States imposed ever-stricter economic and trade sanctions against Sudan. In 1998 U.S. missile strikes were conducted against targets in Khartoum in retaliation for Sudanese involvement in the bombings of U.S. embassies in Kenya and Tanzania.

However, relations improved somewhat in the following years. The DOS states in *U.S. Relations with Sudan* (August 22, 2012, http://www.state.gov/r/pa/ei/bgn/5424.htm) that "Sudan has provided concrete cooperation against international terrorism since the September 11, 2001 terrorist strikes against the United States." The United States played a role in the 2005 peace agreement that helped South Sudan gain its independence, but has criticized Sudan for its crackdown on rebels in Darfur. In 2007 the U.S. government imposed new sanctions against Sudan for its actions in Darfur. According to the DOS, in *Country Reports on Terrorism 2011*, some terrorist groups, including al Qaeda, continued to operate in Sudan in 2011. However, the agency notes that the Sudanese government has taken steps against most terrorist operatives and admits the government lacks the information-gathering and military resources needed to wage a wholly successful counterterrorism effort. The DOS states, "With the exception of Hamas, whose members the Government of Sudan does not consider to be terrorists, the government does not openly support the presence of terrorist elements within its borders."

Syria

Syria is a small Middle Eastern nation bordered on the south by Iraq and Jordan and on the west by Israel and Lebanon. (See Figure 6.6.) To the north is Turkey, and the northwestern coast of Syria abuts the Mediterranean Sea. Syria's capital is Damascus, which is located in the southwestern part of the country near the Lebanese border. In 1946 Syria achieved independence after years of French rule. Decades of political instability and military coups culminated in 1970 with the assumption of power by Hafez Assad (1930–2000). According to the CIA, in *World Factbook: Syria* (September 21, 2012, https://www.cia.gov/library/publications/the-world-factbook/geos/sy.html), Assad was a member of the Alawi minority, which is a religion distantly related to the Shia form of Islam. After his death in 2000, the presidency was turned over to his son, Bashar al-Assad (1965–), also an Alawi. The CIA describes the Syrian government as a "republic under an authoritarian regime."

FIGURE 6.6

Map of Syria, 2012

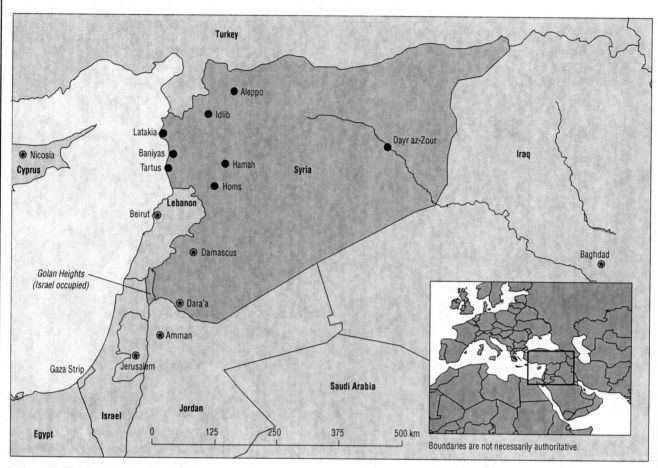

Land area: 185,180 sq km* (slightly larger than North Dakota)
*includes 1,295 sq km of Israeli-occupied territory
Population: 22,530,746 (July 2012 est.)
Religions: Sunni Muslim 74%, other Muslim (Alawite,
Druze, Shiite) 16%, Christian (various denominations) 10%
Jewish (tiny communities in Damascus, Al Qamishli, and Aleppo)
Ethnic groups: Arab 90.3%, Kurds, Armenians, and other 9.7%
GDP (PPP, growth rate): $107.6 billion (2011 est.), −2% (2011 est.)
GDP per capita: $5,100 (2011 est.)
Budget (spending): $18.31 billion (2011 est.)
Literacy (total, male/female): 79.6%, 86%/73.6% (2004 census)
Oil and natural gas reserves: 2.5 billion barrels; 6.19 billion cubic meters
Oil production: 401,000 barrels per day (2010 est.)

Notes: sq km = square kilometers. est. = estimated. GDP = gross domestic product.
PPP = purchasing power parity.

SOURCE: Jeremy M. Sharp and Christopher M. Blanchard, "Figure 2. Syria at a Glance," in *Armed Conflict in Syria: U.S. and International Response*, Congressional Research Service, July 12, 2012, http://fpc.state.gov/documents/organization/195385.pdf (accessed July 24, 2012)

FOREIGN RELATIONS. Syria and Israel have been enemies since the foundation of Israel in 1948 and have fought several wars. Most notable among them was the Six-Day War in 1967, during which Israel captured the Golan Heights. Israel has occupied this strategic piece of land along Syria's border with Israel ever since, deepening the divisions between the two countries. Syria has been on the U.S. list of state sponsors of terrorism since 1979, primarily for its support of groups that conduct terrorist activities against Israel. Alfred B. Prados of the

CRS explains in *Syria: U.S. Relations and Bilateral Issues* (March 13, 2006, http://fpc.state.gov/documents/organization/64491.pdf) that Syria openly admits supporting Palestinian, Hamas, and Hezbollah attacks against Israeli military forces that occupy disputed territories. Syria considers these attacks to be "legitimate resistance activity," rather than terrorism.

In 1976 Syria sent troops and intelligence personnel into neighboring Lebanon during the Lebanese civil war.

According to Prados, up to 40,000 Syrian troops were in Lebanon by the late 1970s, and Syria began wielding considerable influence over Lebanese politics. An agreement reached with the Arab League in 1989 was intended to sharply curtail Syrian involvement in Lebanon but was never fully implemented. In February 2005 Rafic Hariri (1944–2005), a former Lebanese prime minister, was assassinated. Hariri had been openly criticizing Syria's military presence in Lebanon, and Syrian agents were suspected in his assassination. Two months later Syria withdrew its troops from Lebanon following intense pressure from the Lebanese people and the international community.

According to Jeremy M. Sharp of the CRS, in *Syria: Issues for the 112th Congress and Background on U.S. Sanctions* (April 28, 2011, https://opencrs.com/document/RL33487/2011-04-28/download/1005/), the United States has maintained economic sanctions against Syria since the 1970s. U.S.-Syrian relations became particularly strained following the U.S.-led invasion of Iraq in 2003. U.S. officials accused Syria of allowing, and perhaps facilitating, the passage of militia fighters and arms across its border into Iraq to aid the insurgency against U.S. troops. Syria denied these claims. Other major issues have been Syria's continued "war of words" with Israel, its support for Hezbollah and Hamas (both of which are considered to be terrorist organizations by the United States), and its ties with Iran.

In 2007 the Israeli air force destroyed a complex that was believed to be a nuclear reactor under construction in northeastern Syria. Syria angrily denounced Israel and the United States for the raid and insisted that there were no nuclear activities at the complex. Syria is bound by the NPT, which it ratified in 1969. The IAEA reports in "Implementation of the NPT Safeguards Agreement in the Syrian Arab Republic" (February 18, 2010, http://www.isis-online.org/uploads/isis-reports/documents/IAEA_Report_Syria_18Feb2010.pdf) that the samples it collected at the bombed site in 2008 contained uranium particles "of a type not included in Syria's declared inventory of nuclear material." The IAEA notes that "Syria has stated that the origin of these particles was the missiles used to destroy the building. The Agency has assessed that there is a low probability that the source of these particles was the use of missiles. [However,] the presence of such particles points to the possibility of nuclear related activities at the site and adds to questions concerning the nature of the destroyed building."

In 2009 and 2010 Syria was implicated in several terrorist-related activities, including a series of bomb attacks in Iraq and transporting arms and missiles to Hezbollah. In February 2010 the Obama administration attempted to improve U.S.-Syrian relations by appointing Robert S. Ford (1958–) as the new U.S. ambassador to Syria. That position had been vacant since 2005. However,

Ford left the country for his own safety in late 2011. In "U.S. Ambassador to Syria Leaves Damascus amid Threats to Safety" (*New York Times*, October 24, 2011), Anthony Shadid indicates that Ford's outspoken criticism of the Syrian government prompted government supporters to attack his motorcade and to attempt to break into his residence. The Syrian government responded to Ford's departure by withdrawing its ambassador to the United States. In the press release "State Department on Suspending Embassy Operations in Syria" (http://iipdigital.usembassy.gov/), the DOS notes that in February 2012 it had suspended all operations at the U.S. embassy in Syria and all associated American personnel had left the country.

REVOLUTION. As noted earlier, the Arab Spring uprisings that began in 2010 swept dictators from power in four Middle Eastern countries. During the spring of 2011 simmering unrest in Syria also erupted into revolution. The events and their ramifications to U.S. interests are described in detail by Jeremy M. Sharp and Christopher M. Blanchard of the CRS in *Armed Conflict in Syria: U.S. and International Response* (July 12, 2012, http://fpc.state.gov/documents/organization/195385.pdf). According to Sharp and Blanchard, major antigovernment protests began in March 2011 after the government was accused of torturing children in Dara'a, a town in southern Syria. (See Figure 6.6.) The government responded to the protesters with violent force, which only fueled public anger. Violence was initially limited to scattered pockets of resistance; however, by 2012 the government and opposition forces were engaged in an "all-out armed conflict." As of July 2012, approximately 17,000 to 18,000 Syrians were believed to have been killed in the fighting. The rebel forces are led by Syria's majority Sunni population, which is supported by fellow Sunnis across the Middle East. Meanwhile, al-Assad's Alawite-dominated regime relies heavily on Iran, its closest ally, for political and military assistance.

The Syrian government crackdown has spurred widespread condemnation from the UN, the United States, and other Western countries, as well as from a majority of Sunni countries. For example, Saudi Arabia and Qatar have both publicly expressed their support for the rebels. However, Russia, a long-time trading and political partner with Syria, has defiantly defended al-Assad. Sharp and Blanchard note, "Russian leaders would likely view the downfall of the regime as a serious blow to their diplomatic prestige and Middle Eastern/Mediterranean influence and military access." As a result, Russia has resisted international efforts to pressure al-Assad to step down and has blamed the rebels for inciting violence. Iran has done likewise and gone even further. According to Sharp and Blanchard, Iran has reportedly provided al-Assad's regime with "weapons, cash, training, Internet surveillance equipment, and assistance in evading oil sanctions." Iraq, another country with a Shia-dominated government, is accused of purposely allowing Iranian shipments to Syria to cross Iraqi territory and air space.

The U.S. government has openly indicated support for the rebels' cause. Sharp and Blanchard note that in August 2011 President Obama stated, "We have consistently said that President Assad must lead a democratic transition or get out of the way. He has not led. For the sake of the Syrian people, the time has come for President Assad to step aside." In addition, since the uprising began the Obama administration has expanded sanctions against Syria; has provided "the Syrian opposition with non-lethal assistance, such as medical supplies, night-vision goggles, and communications equipment"; and has dispatched intelligence officers "to coordinate the delivery of lethal aid to elements of the armed Syrian opposition not affiliated with terrorist groups such as Al Qaeda and its affiliates."

Despite this support, the United States is concerned about the possible consequences of al-Assad's ouster. Even though Syria has a large stock of WMDs, the country is not a party to international agreements that ban the production of WMDs, such as the Chemical Weapons Convention. Syria is believed to have amassed large amounts of nerve gas and mustard gas at facilities near Aleppo, Damascus, Hamah, Latakia, and Homs. The greatest fear for the United States is that these WMDs fall into the hands of terrorist groups, the Iranian government, or other unfriendly parties.

As of October 2012, the revolution raged on in Syria with near-daily accounts by the media of bloodshed and suffering among the population. Sharp and Blanchard state that the Obama administration "has given no indication that it intends to pursue any form of military intervention." It remains to be seen what the outcome of the uprising will be and what consequences it may have on U.S. national security.

Syria's Terrorist Connections

In *Country Reports on Terrorism 2011*, the DOS indicates that in 2011 Syria supported "a variety of terrorist groups affecting the stability of the region and beyond." Syria, like Iran, has strong ties with Hezbollah. Besides providing political support and arms to Hezbollah, the Syrian government is also accused of allowing several terrorist groups to operate bases within its borders. These groups include Hamas, the Palestine Islamic Jihad, the Popular Front for the Liberation of Palestine, and the Popular Front for the Liberation of Palestine-General Command. The DOS notes that in 2011 al-Assad continued to make public statements supporting Palestinian terrorist groups as "elements of the resistance against Israel." He also allowed Iraqi militant groups to congregate in Damascus, Syria's capital. The DOS complains that Syria blatantly sanctions terrorist financing to take place and uses its counterterrorism laws mainly against political protesters and other opponents of al-Assad's regime.

CHAPTER 7
PROLIFERATION OF WEAPONS

Proliferation means growth or multiplication. The proliferation of powerful weapons around the world is a source of great concern to U.S. national security. These weapons include conventional armaments such as military-type guns, bombs, and missiles, and unconventional weapons. Unconventional weapons are those that use nontraditional means to reap destruction and death, primarily nuclear technology or the release of chemical or biological agents. Small numbers of these weapons are capable of killing vast numbers of people; hence, they are called weapons of mass destruction (WMD). The proliferation of WMDs is governed by many international agreements that have been brokered by the United Nations (UN). Therefore, the United States is most concerned about the acquisition and use of WMDs by terrorists and rogue nations (nations that ignore international restrictions on weapons proliferation).

U.S. goals for weapon nonproliferation (or counterproliferation) include stopping the development of new WMDs, reducing and safeguarding the stockpiles of existing conventional and unconventional weapons, and preventing the spread of WMD technology, particularly among enemies of the United States.

ARMS AROUND THE WORLD

Most nations of the world are heavily armed with conventional weapons. A handful of developed nations, including the United States, possess highly advanced conventional weapons that are enhanced by sophisticated technologies, such as laser guidance systems. The effectiveness of these weapons was demonstrated by the U.S. military in 1991 during the Persian Gulf War against Iraq.

The Congressional Research Service (CRS) provides an annual report to Congress on the proliferation of conventional arms. In *Conventional Arms Transfers to Developing Nations, 2003–2010* (September 22, 2011, http://fpc.state.gov/documents/organization/174196.pdf),

Richard F. Grimmett of the CRS notes that the value of worldwide conventional arms transfer agreements between governments in 2010 was $40.4 billion. (See Figure 7.1.) This value was down substantially from 2009. In 2010 U.S. arms sales agreements accounted for $21.3 billion, or 52.7% of the total. Russia was second with $7.8 billion, or 19.3% of the total. As shown in Figure 7.1, the vast majority of the agreements made between 2003 and 2010 were for sales to developing nations. The top-10 purchasing nations in the developing world between 2007 and 2010 are listed in Table 7.1. Saudi Arabia, India, and the United Arab Emirates were the top purchasers during this period.

Figure 7.2 shows the value of conventional arms delivered worldwide between 2003 and 2010. Arms deliveries were valued at $35 billion in 2010, down slightly from 2009. Nations in the developing world accounted for the majority of arms delivery recipients between 2003 and 2010. According to Grimmett, U.S. arms accounted for 39.2% of deliveries in 2010, totaling $8.6 billion in value. Russia ranked second with $4.8 billion in delivered arms, or 21.4% of the total.

The United States has become a major supplier of conventional arms to its allies around the world. In *U.S. Arms Sales: Agreements with and Deliveries to Major Clients, 2003–2010* (December 16, 2011, http://www.defencetalk.com/reports/179578.pdf), Grimmett lists the major clients for U.S. arms sales between 2003 and 2010. (See Table 7.2.) Between 2007 and 2010 the three top purchasers were Saudi Arabia, the United Arab Emirates, and Egypt.

MISSILES

Andrew Feickert of the CRS notes in *Missile Survey: Ballistic and Cruise Missiles of Foreign Countries* (March 5, 2004, http://fpc.state.gov/documents/organization/31999.pdf) that "while weapons of mass destruction

FIGURE 7.1

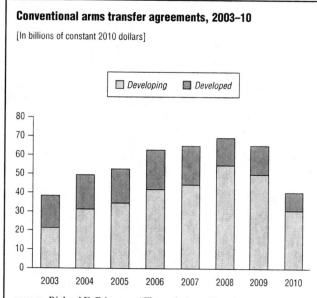

Conventional arms transfer agreements, 2003–10

[In billions of constant 2010 dollars]

SOURCE: Richard F. Grimmett, "Figure 1. Arms Transfer Agreements Worldwide, 2003–2010 Developed and Developing Worlds Compared," in *Conventional Arms Transfers to Developing Nations, 2003–2010*, Congressional Research Service, September 22, 2011, http://fpc.state.gov/documents/organization/174196.pdf (accessed July 24, 2012)

FIGURE 7.2

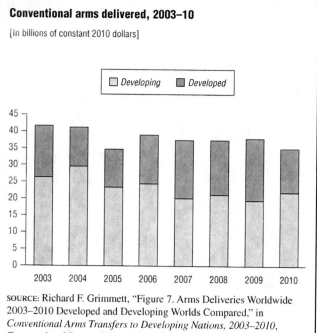

Conventional arms delivered, 2003–10

[In billions of constant 2010 dollars]

SOURCE: Richard F. Grimmett, "Figure 7. Arms Deliveries Worldwide 2003–2010 Developed and Developing Worlds Compared," in *Conventional Arms Transfers to Developing Nations, 2003–2010*, Congressional Research Service, September 22, 2011, http://fpc.state.gov/documents/organization/174196.pdf (accessed July 24, 2012)

TABLE 7.1

Top 10 purchasers in the developing world for conventional arms sales, 2007–10

Rank	Recipient	Agreements value 2007–2010
1	Saudi Arabia	28,900
2	India	17,400
3	U.A.E.	15,100
4	Egypt	8,600
5	Brazil	8,600
6	Venezuela	8,100
7	Pakistan	7,800
8	Iraq	7,400
9	South Korea	7,200
10	Taiwan	6,700

Notes: All data are rounded to the nearest $100 million. Where rounded data totals are the same, the rank order is maintained.

SOURCE: Adapted from Richard F. Grimmett, "Table 12. Arms Transfer Agreements with Developing Nations, 2003–2010: Agreements by the Leading Recipients," in *Conventional Arms Transfers to Developing Nations, 2003–2010*, Congressional Research Service, September 22, 2011, http://fpc.state.gov/documents/organization/174196.pdf (accessed July 24, 2012)

(WMD) can be delivered by a variety of means including aircraft, artillery, and asymmetric [other than typical] means, it is missile-delivered WMDs that garner the most domestic and international political attention."

Missiles fall into two broad categories: ballistic missiles and cruise missiles. Ballistic missiles are guided (steered) only during the initial portion of their flight. After that period the missiles go into free flight, during which they are totally under the influence of natural factors, such as gravity and wind. Cruise missiles are guided throughout their entire flight. In general, cruise missiles fly at low altitudes and with great precision. They may be guided by global positioning satellite data that are collected during flight.

Ballistic Missiles

The Arms Control Association (ACA) is a U.S.-based nonprofit organization that supports arms control. According to the ACA, in the fact sheet "Worldwide Ballistic Missile Inventories" (January 2012, http://www.armscontrol.org/factsheets/missiles), the ranges of ballistic missiles are:

- Short-range ballistic missile (SRBM)—less than 621 miles (1,000 km)

- Medium-range ballistic missile (MRBM)—621 to 1,864 miles (1,000 to 3,000 km)

- Intermediate-range ballistic missile (IRBM)—1,864 to 3,418 miles (3,000 to 5,500 km)

- Intercontinental ballistic missile (ICBM)—greater than 3,418 miles (5,500 km)

The ACA states that ICBMs are also known as long-range or strategic ballistic missiles. Ballistic missiles can be further categorized by their fuel type (liquid or solid propellant), payload or warhead type (conventional or nuclear arms or chemical or biological agents), launch method (e.g., submarine-launched), and delivery path (e.g., surface to surface).

TABLE 7.2

Top 10 purchasers of U.S. conventional arms and services, 2003–10

[In current U.S. dollars, rounded to nearest 10 million or 10th of a billion]

	Worldwide agreements 2003–2006			Worldwide agreements 2007–2010			Worldwide agreements 2010	
1	Egypt	$4.5 billion	1	Saudi Arabia	$13.8 billion	1	Taiwan	$2.7 billion
2	Saudi Arabia	$4.2 billion	2	U.A.E.	$10.4 billion	2	Egypt	$1.8 billion
3	Poland	$4.1 billion	3	Egypt	$7.8 billion	3	Saudi Arabia	$1.5 billion
4	Australia	$2.9 billion	4	Taiwan	$6.6 billion	4	Australia	$1.3 billion
5	Japan	$2.9 billion	5	Australia	$6.4 billion	5	U.K.	$1.2 billion
6	Greece	$2.6 billion	6	Iraq	$5.6 billion	6	Israel	$1.1 billion
7	South Korea	$2.4 billion	7	Pakistan	$4.1 billion	7	Iraq	$840 million
8	Kuwait	$2.1 billion	8	U.K.	$4.0 billion	8	Jordan	$650 billion
9	Turkey	$2.1 billion	9	Turkey	$3.8 billion	9	South Korea	$640 million
10	Israel	$1.6 billion	10	South Korea	$3.8 billion	10	Singapore	$530 million

SOURCE: Richard F. Grimmett, "Table 6. Leading Purchasers of U.S. Defense Articles and Services, Total Values of Worldwide Agreements Concluded," in *U.S. Arms Sales: Agreements with and Deliveries to Major Clients, 2003–2010*, Congressional Research Service, December 16, 2011, http://www.defencetalk.com/reports/179578.pdf (accessed July 24, 2012)

According to the U.S. Department of Defense (DOD), in *Missile Defense Agency Program Update 2011* (August 10, 2011, http://www.mda.mil/global/documents/pdf/The_Missile_Defense_Program.pdf), only nine countries had ballistic missiles in 1972. By 2011 that number grew to more than 20. However, many of these countries were allied with the United States through the North Atlantic Treaty Organization (NATO). The DOD estimates that in 2011 more than 6,000 ballistic missiles were held by countries other than the United States, fellow NATO members, China, or Russia.

Figure 7.3 shows the locations of the countries posing the greatest ballistic missile threat to U.S. national security interests as of August 2011. All these countries are clustered in and around the Middle East and South Asia.

BALLISTIC MISSILE DEFENSE. As described in Chapter 1, since 1958 the United States and Canada have operated the North American Aerospace Defense Command (NORAD). NORAD's (2012, http://www.norad.mil/about/index.html) primary mission is to provide aerospace warning and control for North America against hostile aircraft, missiles, and space vehicles. It utilizes a network of satellites and ground-based and airborne radar systems to detect these threats. During the Cold War NORAD's ability to detect incoming Soviet missiles would have given the United States time to warn the American public and to launch its own missiles in retaliation. This scenario never occurred. As military technology has advanced, the United States has progressed beyond depending only on warning systems and has developed weapons that are designed to intercept and destroy incoming ballistic missiles.

In February 2010 the DOD published the results of its first-ever *Ballistic Missile Defense Review Report* (http://www.defense.gov/bmdr/docs/BMDR%20as%20of%2026

JAN10%200630_for%20web.pdf). The review examines U.S. policies, strategies, programs, and plans regarding ballistic missile defense (BMD). The DOD notes that "today, only Russia and China have the capability to conduct a large-scale ballistic missile attack on the territory of the United States, but this is very unlikely and not the focus of U.S. BMD." Of greater concern are so-called regional threats, primarily North Korea, Iran, and Syria, all of which have SRBMs, MRBMs, and IRBMs that "threaten U.S. forces, allies and partners in regions where the United States deploys forces and maintains security relationships." U.S. relations with these countries of concern are described in detail in Chapter 6.

The United States has operated a BMD program since the 1980s. At that time the major threat to U.S. national security was the Soviet Union. In 1983 President Ronald Reagan (1911–2004) announced a new military venture called the Space Defense Initiative (SDI). The SDI planned to put a satellite shield in space to protect the United States from incoming Soviet nuclear missiles. Such a feat was well beyond the technical capabilities of the era (and was still in its earliest stages as of October 2012). The media nicknamed the SDI the "Star Wars" project after the hit 1977 movie, which featured elaborate space weapons. The DOD began developing and testing interceptor missiles that were designed to intercept and destroy incoming ballistic missiles. By the early 1990s the Soviet Union had disintegrated into separate countries, including Russia, that were no longer directly hostile to the United States. However, the United States' BMD program continued to operate. A new concern became the proliferation of missiles around the world and their possession by terrorists and unfriendly nations. In 2002 the United States withdrew from the Antiballistic Missile Treaty of 1972. Forged with the Soviet Union (and later Russia), this treaty had strictly limited each nation's deployment of antiballistic missiles.

FIGURE 7.3

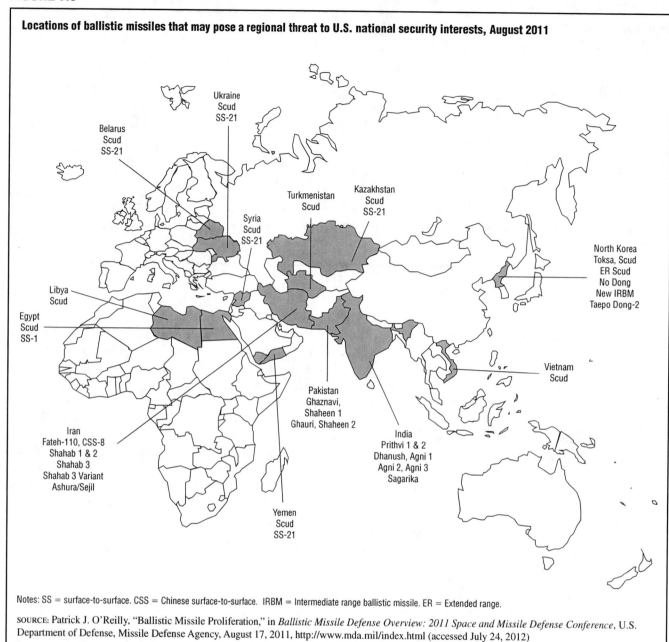

Locations of ballistic missiles that may pose a regional threat to U.S. national security interests, August 2011

Notes: SS = surface-to-surface. CSS = Chinese surface-to-surface. IRBM = Intermediate range ballistic missile. ER = Extended range.

SOURCE: Patrick J. O'Reilly, "Ballistic Missile Proliferation," in *Ballistic Missile Defense Overview: 2011 Space and Missile Defense Conference*, U.S. Department of Defense, Missile Defense Agency, August 17, 2011, http://www.mda.mil/index.html (accessed July 24, 2012)

As of October 2012, the United States' BMD program was under the direction of the DOD's Missile Defense Agency (MDA). The MDA is developing and testing ground- and sea-based interceptor missiles and space-based tracking systems. As shown in Figure 7.4, funding for the MDA increased from $1.4 billion in fiscal year (FY) 1985 to $9 billion in FY 2009. Slightly lower amounts were appropriated to the agency in FY 2010 ($7.9 billion), FY 2011 ($8.5 billion), and FY 2012 ($8.4 billion). By the end of FY 2012, the United States will have invested $149.5 billion in missile defense. According to the MDA, in "Missile Defense Agency Fiscal Year (FY) 2013 Budget Outline" (February 2012, http://www.mda.mil/global/documents/pdf/budget fy13.pdf), President Barack Obama (1961–) requested nearly $7.8 billion for the MDA in his proposed FY 2013 budget.

Figure 7.5 shows the capabilities of the four main components of the BMD system:

- Ground-based Midcourse Defense (GMD)—ground-based missiles in silos at Fort Greely, Alaska, and at Vandenberg Air Force Base in California. They are designed to intercept ICBMs.

- Aegis BMD—a sea-based missile system that is installed on U.S. Navy ships. Ships fire standard missile (SM) interceptors that are designed to intercept all four types of missiles.

FIGURE 7.4

Historical funding for the Missile Defense Agency (MDA), 1985–2012*

[Fiscal year $ in billions]

Fiscal years	1985	1986	1987	1988	1989	1990	1991	1992	1993	1994	1995	1996	1997	1998	1999	2000	2001	2002	2003	2004	2005	2006	2007	2008	2009	2010	2011	2012
Appropriation passed	1.4	2.8	3.2	3.6	3.7	4.0	2.9	4.1	3.8	2.8	2.8	3.4	3.7	3.8	3.5	3.6	4.8	7.8	7.4	7.7	9.0	7.8	9.4	8.7	9.0	7.9	8.5	8.4

Total to date—$149.5B

*Historical funding levels are for Strategic Defense Initiative Organization (SDIO), Ballistic Missile Defense Organization (BMDO), and MDA (Missile Defense Agency).

SOURCE: Adapted from "Historical Funding for MDA FY85-12," in *Funding Missile Defense*, U.S. Department of Defense, Missile Defense Agency, June 27, 2012, http://www.mda.mil/global/documents/pdf/histfunds.pdf (accessed July 24, 2012)

FIGURE 7.5

Major components and capabilities of the U.S. ballistic missile defense system

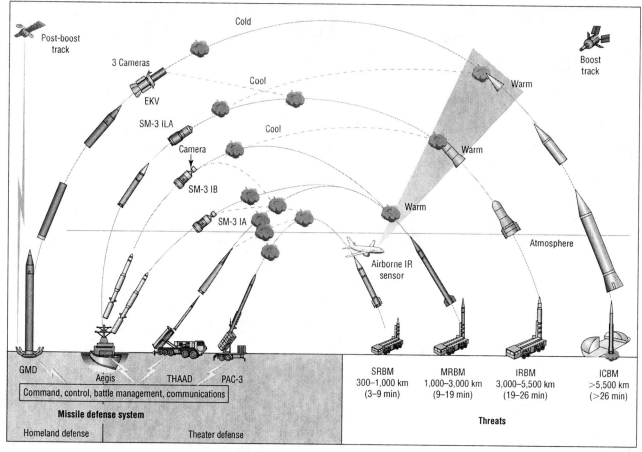

GMD = Ground-based Midcourse Defense. THAAD = Terminal High Altitude Area Defense. PAC-3 = Patriot Advanced Capability-3. SRBM = Short Range Ballistic Missile. MRBM = Medium Range Ballistic Missile. IRBM = Intermediate Range Ballistic Missile. ICBM = Intercontinental Ballistic Missile. IR = Infrared. SM = Standard Missile. EKV = Exoatmospheric Kill Vehicle.

SOURCE: "Interceptor Fundamentals," in *The Missile Defense Program 2009–2010*, U.S. Department of Defense, August 3, 2009, http://www.a-2-562.org/The_Missile_Defense_Program.pdf (accessed July 27, 2012)

- Terminal High Altitude Area Defense (THAAD)—transportable missiles that are designed to intercept MRBMs and SRBMs during their termination phase (i.e., their downward path after leaving and reentering the earth's atmosphere)

- Patriot Advanced Capability-3 (PAC-3)—transportable missiles that are designed to intercept SRBMs.

In the fact sheet "Ballistic Missile Defense Intercept Flight Test Record" (June 26, 2012, http://www.mda.mil/global/documents/pdf/testrecord.pdf), the MDA reports that 54 of 68 hit-to-kill intercept attempts conducted since 2001 have been successful. A hit-to-kill intercept occurs when an interceptor missile collides with and destroys an airborne target.

According to the DOD, in *Missile Defense Agency Program Update 2011*, the BMD system at the end of FY 2011 included 30 GMD missiles, 23 Aegis-equipped ships, 159 sea-based SMs, 18 THAAD interceptors, 2 THAAD fire units, 903 PAC-3 missiles, and 56 PAC-3 fire units.

Cruise Missiles

Christopher Bolkcom of the CRS states in *Cruise Missile Defense* (March 15, 2007, http://assets.opencrs.com/rpts/RS21921_20070315.pdf) that cruise missiles are basically "unmanned attack aircraft" that can strike their targets with great accuracy. They are often equipped with sophisticated guidance and targeting systems and can fly "low terrain-hugging" paths. Cruise missiles are generally categorized by their launch method (e.g., air-launched or submarine-launched) or by their intended use (e.g., antiship or land attack). Feickert notes that during the early months of Operation Iraqi Freedom (the U.S. invasion of Iraq in 2003) the United States launched approximately 700 Tomahawk cruise missiles at Iraqi targets. U.S. defense officials claim that less than 10 of these missiles failed to hit their intended targets. The Iraqi military reportedly fired five cruise missiles at U.S. forces. According to Feickert, this was the first time in history that U.S. ground forces had been attacked by enemy cruise missiles.

CRUISE MISSILE DEFENSE. Before 2006 the United States did not have a coordinated cruise missile defense (CMD) program, because CMD efforts were conducted by the various military services. In 2006 CMD responsibility was given to the U.S. Strategic Command, which is headquartered at Offutt Air Force Base in Nebraska. Bolkcom explains that defending against cruise missile attack is challenging. Cruise missiles fly at low altitudes and can be mistaken for "friendly or neutral" aircraft. The missiles can also be programmed to take "elusive" flight paths, making them difficult to track. Bolkcom notes that incoming cruise missiles can be destroyed with gunfire or interceptor missiles. The MDA (June 27, 2012, http://www.mda.mil/faqs.html) reports that the PAC-3 system, which is designed to defend against relatively low-flying SRBMs, can also intercept and destroy incoming cruise missiles.

Man-Portable Air Defense Systems

Man-portable air defense systems (MANPADS) are more commonly called shoulder-fired antiaircraft missile systems (SAMS). They fire short-range surface-to-air missiles that are typically 4 to 6.5 feet (1.2 to 2 m) in length and only a few inches in diameter. Combined, a missile and its launcher can weigh less than 60 pounds (27 kg). Thus, a MANPADS can be carried and fired by a single individual and is easily transported and concealed. These qualities make them attractive weapons for terrorists and guerrilla fighters. However, MANPADS are difficult to aim with precision and shoot relatively slow-moving missiles. As such, they have limited effectiveness against most military aircraft.

In the fact sheet "MANPADS: Combating the Threat to Global Aviation from Man-Portable Air Defense Systems" (July 27, 2011, http://www.state.gov/t/pm/rls/fs/169139.htm), the U.S. Department of State (DOS) describes the U.S. government's concerns about the threat posed by MANPADS to civil and commercial aircraft. According to the DOS, in 2002 rebels in Kenya fired two MANPADS at a civilian airliner. During the late 1990s three airliners were shot down by rebels in Africa using MANPADS, killing 64 people. In 2007 a cargo aircraft over Somalia was shot down with a MANPADS, killing the crew of 11 people.

The DOS notes that as of July 2011, the United States had facilitated the destruction of 32,500 MANPADS in dozens of countries around the world. In addition, the Transportation Security Administration has visited and advised dozens of foreign airports about defense against MANPADS attacks.

CONVENTIONAL WEAPONS CONTROLS

The Convention on Prohibitions or Restrictions on the Use of Certain Conventional Weapons Which May Be Deemed to Be Excessively Injurious or to Have Indiscriminate Effects (2012, http://www.un-documents.net/cpruccw.htm) took effect in 1983. It restricts certain conventional weapons that are considered to have particularly horrific effects. The Convention on Conventional Weapons (as it is commonly called) originally had three protocols that covered weapons producing fragments not detectable in the human body by x-rays; land mines, booby traps, and related devices; and incendiary weapons (weapons purposely designed to start fires or cause burns). In 1995 a fourth protocol was added to control the proliferation of laser weapons designed to permanently blind their victims. In 2003 a fifth protocol was added that requires bound parties to clear and destroy unexploded ordnances left over after a conflict has ended. As of October 2012, the United States was a party to all protocols of the convention, having agreed to abide by the first and second protocols during the 1990s and the remaining protocols in 2009.

The Wassenaar Arrangement on Export Controls for Conventional Arms and Dual-Use Goods and Technologies (2012, http://www.wassenaar.org/) is a multilateral agreement established in 1996 that concerns the export of conventional weapons and dual-use (military and civilian) technologies that could pose a threat to a country's national security if they are acquired by that country's enemies. The arrangement replaces the older Coordinating Committee for Multilateral Export Controls (CoCom), which had been in place since the 1940s. The sole purpose of CoCom was to prevent the export of weapons from Western nations to the Soviet Union and its allies. The end of the Cold War during the early 1990s precipitated the new agreement for which the stated purpose is to promote "transparency and greater responsibility in transfers of conventional arms and dual-use goods and technologies, thus preventing destabilising accumulations. Participating States seek, through their national policies, to ensure that transfers of these items do not contribute to the development or enhancement of military capabilities which undermine these goals, and are not diverted to support such capabilities." The United States is a party to the Wassenaar Arrangement.

NUCLEAR WEAPONS

One legacy of the Cold War was the development and stockpiling of thousands of nuclear weapons by the United States and the Soviet Union. In 1961 the Soviets conducted nuclear tests in the atmosphere. The United States responded with its own atmospheric tests. The rest of the world watched uneasily as the two great superpowers seemed to edge closer and closer to a nuclear showdown.

A crucial event in the nuclear arms race occurred in 1962: the Cuban missile crisis. U.S. intelligence agencies discovered the Soviets had installed nuclear missile facilities in Cuba, only 90 miles (145 km) from the U.S. coast. President John F. Kennedy (1917–1963) confronted the Soviets. He imposed a naval blockade around Cuba and demanded that the nuclear facilities be removed. After a suspenseful 12-day standoff the Soviets complied. It proved to be a turning point in the Cold War, as the two nations began negotiating treaties on limiting the testing and proliferation of nuclear weapons.

Nuclear Club

By 1964 there were five nations in the so-called nuclear club: the United States, the Soviet Union, the United Kingdom, France, and China. Before the end of the decade an important multilateral nuclear treaty had been signed by dozens of nations. The Treaty on the Nonproliferation of Nuclear Weapons (NPT; 2012, http://www.un.org/events/npt2005/npttreaty.html) acknowledged "the devastation that would be visited upon all mankind by a nuclear war" and included the following provisions:

- No transfer of nuclear weapons or nuclear-related technical assistance from a nuclear state to a non-nuclear state

- No manufacture of nuclear weapons by nonnuclear states or acquisition of the weapons or associated technologies from nuclear states

- Acceptance by nuclear states of safeguards overseen and verified by the International Atomic Energy Agency to prevent conversion of peaceful nuclear energy projects to nuclear weapons development; these safeguards also apply to transfers of peaceful-purpose nuclear materials from nuclear states to nonnuclear states

NPT Outsiders

In the decades since the NPT was developed, several other nations have tested (or are believed to have tested) nuclear weapons and refused to join or comply with international agreements governing safeguards and verification procedures. These "rebel" members of the nuclear club are India, Israel, Pakistan, and North Korea. In regards to the NPT, these countries are not officially considered to be nuclear states. The United States enjoys relatively good relations with all of these countries, except North Korea. North Korea's nuclear program is described in detail in Chapter 6.

Nuclear Weapon Treaties

In *Arms Control and Nonproliferation: A Catalog of Treaties and Agreements* (September 20, 2011, http://fpc.state.gov/documents/organization/174239.pdf), Amy F. Woolf, Mary Beth Nikitin, and Paul K. Kerr of the CRS

provide a list of arms control and nonproliferation treaties and agreements to which the United States is a party.

As of October 2012, the most recent treaty to enter into force, the so-called New START Treaty, became effective on February 5, 2011, between the United States and Russia. In the fact sheet "New START Treaty Entry into Force" (February 5, 2011, http://www.state.gov/r/pa/prs/ps/2011/02/156037.htm), the DOS notes that the treaty places specific limits on each country's number of warheads, launchers, and heavy bombers, as follows:

- Deployed strategic nuclear warheads—1,550

- Deployed and nondeployed strategic launchers and heavy bombers—800

- Deployed strategic launchers and heavy bombers—700

Even though scaled deadlines are built into the treaty, all of the limits must be reached by February 5, 2018.

U.S. Nuclear Weapons Stockpile

In May 2010 the DOD published "Fact Sheet: Increasing Transparency in the U.S. Nuclear Weapons Stockpile" (http://www.defense.gov/news/d20100503stockpile.pdf), which provided newly declassified information about the U.S. nuclear weapons stockpile. The release was directed by President Obama as part of his administration's focus on the nonproliferation of nuclear weapons. Figure 7.6 shows the U.S. nuclear weapons stockpile for FYs 1945 to 2009. (The federal government's fiscal year runs from October through September.) As of September 30, 2009, the total U.S. stockpile contained 5,113 warheads. This included both active and inactive warheads. The DOD notes that the United States dismantled 8,748 nuclear warheads between FYs 1994 and 2009. Thousands more "retired" nuclear warheads were scheduled to be dismantled.

Table 7.3 shows the types of nuclear weapons in the U.S. stockpile as of September 2011. There are eight total systems used either by the U.S. Air Force, the U.S. Navy, or both military branches. Table 7.3 also lists the national laboratory with design responsibility for each system and the date(s) the system entered the U.S. stockpile.

RADIOLOGICAL WEAPONS

Radiological weapons are different from nuclear weapons. The latter use nuclear reactions to create a destructive force. Radiological weapons rely on conventional explosives to disperse radioactive materials into the air. Radiological dispersal devices are commonly known as dirty bombs. Even though a dirty bomb does not have the destructive power of a nuclear bomb, it is an effective tool for creating terror. The detonation of a dirty bomb and the subsequent release of radiation could temporarily fool people into believing that a nuclear bomb has been detonated, leading to widespread panic.

FIGURE 7.6

U.S. stockpile of nuclear weapons, fiscal years 1945–2009

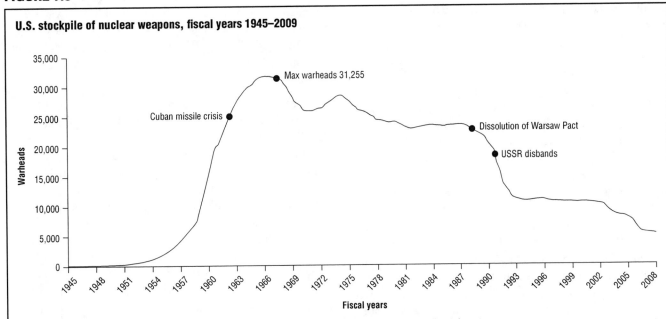

Note: Includes active and inactive warheads. Several thousand additional nuclear warheads are retired and awaiting dismantlement.

SOURCE: "U.S. Nuclear Weapons Stockpile, 1945–2009," in *Fact Sheet: Increasing Transparency in the U.S. Nuclear Weapons Stockpile*, U.S. Department of Defense, May 3, 2010, http://www.defense.gov/news/d20100503stockpile.pdf (accessed July 27, 2012)

TABLE 7.3

Types of nuclear weapons in the U.S. stockpile as of September 2011

Warhead or bomb	Description	Military service	Laboratory	Date of entry into stock pile
B61-3/4/10	Tactical bomb	Air Force	LANL, SNL	1979/1979/1990
B61-7/11	Strategic bomb	Air Force	LANL, SNL	1985/1996
W76-0/1	SLBM warhead[a]	Navy	LANL, SNL	1978/2008
W78	ICBM warhead[b]	Air Force	LANL, SNL	1979
W80-0/1[c]	Cruise missile warhead	Navy/Air Force	LLNL, SNL	1984/1982
B83-1	Strategic bomb	Air Force	LLNL, SNL	1993
W87	ICBM warhead	Air Force	LLNL, SNL	1986
W88	SLBM warhead	Navy	LANL, SNL	1989

[a]Submarine-launched ballistic missile.
[b]Intercontinental ballistic missile.
[c]The Department of Defense concluded in 2010 that the Navy's W80-0 serves a redundant purpose and should be retired.

Note: LANL = Los Alamos National Laboratory. SNL = Sandia National Laboratories. LLNL = Lawrence Livermore National Laboratory.
SLBM = Submarine/sea-launched ballistic missile. ICBM = Intercontinental ballistic missile.

SOURCE: "Table 1. Nuclear Weapons in the U.S. Stockpile, as of September 2011," in *Nuclear Weapons: NNSA Needs to Improve Guidance on Weapon Limitations and Planning for Its Stockpile Surveillance Program*, U.S. Government Accountability Office, February 2012, http://www.gao.gov/assets/590/588307.pdf (accessed July 25, 2012)

The radioactive materials that can be used to manufacture a dirty bomb are widely used in industrial and medical equipment. Examples include low-level radioactive waste, such as protective clothing and shoe covers, tools and equipment, discarded reactor parts and filters, rags, mops, reactor water treatment residues, luminous dials, and laboratory and medical supplies. Sealed radiological sources are small sealed containers containing a radionuclide in solid or powder form. U.S. law requires that all sealed radiological sources be safeguarded by the licensees that use them. The U.S. Department of Energy is responsible for providing disposal for sources that are not needed any more. According to the U.S. Government Accountability Office (GAO), in *Nuclear Security: DOE Needs Better Information to Guide Its Expanded Recovery of Sealed Radiological Sources* (September 2005, http://www.gao.gov/new.items/d05967.pdf), the sealed radiological sources that are considered to be most attractive to terrorists contain the radionuclides americium-241, cesium-137, plutonium-238, and strontium-90. A dirty bomb containing sufficient concentrations of one or several of these substances could cause radiation sickness in some victims exposed to the bomb.

CHEMICAL AND BIOLOGICAL WEAPONS

Chemical and biological weapons are considered to be WMDs because relatively small amounts of the substances can expose large numbers of people to potentially lethal effects. The use of chemical weapons during warfare is not new. Jonathan Tucker describes in *War of Nerves: Chemical Warfare from World War I to al-Qaeda* (2006) their use by German forces during World War I (1914–1918). In the spring of 1915 German forces reached a stalemate in Belgium against the Allied forces of France, Britain, and Canada. Both sides were huddled in trenches that crisscrossed the countryside. On April 22, German troops simultaneously opened more than 5,000 cylinders containing chlorine gas. The wind blew the yellowish-green cloud across no-man's-land to the Allied trenches, where hundreds of soldiers were incapacitated almost immediately. The remainder of the troops fled in terror, many suffering from seared eyes and bronchial passages. At the time, Germany was a party to international treaties that prohibited the use of munitions to deliver chemical agents.

The horrors unleashed in the German attack led British forces to retaliate with chemical attacks of their own. Throughout the remainder of the war both sides employed toxic gases against one another with varying levels of success. The article "Gas Warfare" (January 15, 2000, http://www.worldwar1.com/arm006.htm) lists the chemical agents that were used during World War I. Public revulsion prevented the use of similar agents on the battlefield during World War II (1939–1945). They were employed by both sides during the Iran-Iraq War (1980–1988). In addition, the former Iraqi leader Saddam Hussein (1937–2006) was accused of using chemical weapons in 1988 against the minority Kurdish population in his own country.

In 1997 the Chemical Weapons Convention (CWC) went into effect. It prohibits the development, production, stockpiling, and use of chemical weapons and includes a verification regime to ensure that certain chemicals are produced or traded only for peaceful purposes. According to the Organization for the Prohibition of Chemical Weapons (http://www.opcw.org/about-opcw/member-states/), as of October 2012, there were 188 parties to the CWC, including the United States.

Chemical Agents as Weapons

Table 7.4 categorizes various hazardous chemicals by chemical type toxicity. The chemical agents that are considered to be of greatest interest to terrorists are cyanide compounds (blood agents), mustard (a blister agent), and nerve agents, such as sarin, tabun, and VX. Videos recovered from terrorist training facilities in Afghanistan show

dogs being killed in cyanide gas chambers. Cyanide compounds are easily available because they have a variety of commercial uses. Mustard gas is not commercially available, but it is relatively easy to synthesize (produce) in the laboratory. Nerve agents are military-grade chemicals and thus extremely difficult for terrorists to obtain.

Even though these chemical agents are highly toxic, effective dissemination techniques have not yet been developed to make them strategically useful to terrorists. Airborne chemicals dissipate quickly unless they are in a confined space. Also, they may be detectable by human senses before reaching a lethal concentration. For example, hydrogen cyanide and cyanogen chloride have distinctive odors. It is likely that potential victims would flee the area before being overcome by such gases.

Chemical Weapons Destruction

Several countries around the world are known to have developed chemical weapons at one time or another, including the United States. According to the GAO, in *Chemical Demilitarization: Additional Management Actions Needed to Meet Key Performance Goals of DOD's Chemical Demilitarization Program* (December 2007, http://www.gao.gov/new.items/d08134.pdf), the U.S. stockpile includes mustard gas and two nerve agents called GB (also known as sarin gas) and VX. The U.S. Army Chemical Material Agency (CMA) is responsible for destroying the U.S. stockpile of chemical weapons. The CMA (http://www.cma.army.mil/aboutcma.aspx) indicates that as of January 2012 it had completed the destruction of chemical weapons at the following facilities by the year shown in parentheses:

- Johnston Island, South Pacific (2000)—6% of the original U.S. stockpile
- Aberdeen Proving Ground, Maryland (2006)—4% of the original U.S. stockpile
- Newport Chemical Depot, Indiana (2008)—4% of original U.S. stockpile
- Pine Bluff Arsenal, Arkansas (2010)—12% of the original U.S. stockpile
- Anniston Army Depot, Alabama (2011)—7% of the original U.S. stockpile
- Umatilla Chemical Depot, Oregon (2011)—12% of the original U.S. stockpile
- Deseret Chemical Depot, Utah (2012)—44% of the original U.S. stockpile

As of September 2012, destruction activities continued at the Blue Grass Army Depot near Richmond, Kentucky, and the Pueblo Chemical Depot near Pueblo, Colorado. As an original signatory to the CWC, the United States has committed to destroy 100% of its chemical weapons stockpile. In "Fact Sheet: Chemical Weapons Convention"

TABLE 7.4

Chemical agents, by category

Category	Description	Examples	
Biotoxins	Poisons that come from plants or animals	Abrin Brevetoxin Colchicine Digitalis Nicotine	Ricin Saxitoxin Strychnine Tetrodotoxin Trichothecene
Blister agents/vesicants	Chemicals that severely blister the eyes, respiratory tract, and skin on contact	Mustards Lewisites	Chlorarsine Agents Phosgene oxime
Blood agents	Poisons that affect the body by being absorbed into the blood	Arsine Carbon Monoxide Cyanide	Sodium monofluoroacetate (compound 1080)
Caustics (acids)	Chemicals that burn or corrode people's skin, eyes, and mucus membranes (lining of the nose, mouth, throat, and lungs) on contact	Hydrofluoric acid (hydrogen fluoride)	
Choking/lung/pulmonary agents	Chemicals that cause severe irritation or swelling of the respiratory tract (lining of the nose, throat, and lungs)	Ammonia Bromine Chlorine Hydrogen chloride Methyl bromide Methyl isocyanate Osmium tetroxide	Phosgene Phosphine Phosphorus, elemental, white or yellow Sulfuryl fluoride
Incapacitating agents	Drugs that make people unable to think clearly or that cause an altered state of consciousness (possibly unconsciousness)	BZ Fentanyls & other opioids	
Long-acting anticoagulants	Poisons that prevent blood from clotting properly, which can lead to uncontrolled bleeding	Super warfarin	
Metals	Agents that consist of metallic poisons	Arsenic Barium	Mercury Thallium
Nerve agents	Highly poisonous chemicals that work by preventing the nervous system from working properly	G agents (e.g., Sarin, Soman, Tabun)	V agents (e.g., VX)
Organic solvents	Agents that damage the tissues of living things by dissolving fats and oils	Benzene	
Riot control agents/tear gas	Highly irritating agents normally used by law enforcement for crowd control or by individuals for protection (for example, mace)	Bromobenzylcyanide Chloroacetophenone Chlorobenzylidenemalononitrile	Chloropicrin Dibenzoxazepine
Toxic alcohols	Poisonous alcohols that can damage the heart, kidneys, and nervous system	Ethylene glycol	
Vomiting agents	Chemicals that cause nausea and vomiting	Adamsite	

SOURCE: Adapted from "Chemical Agents, A to Z," in *Emergency Preparedness and Response: Chemical Emergencies*, Centers for Disease Control and Prevention, 2012, http://www.bt.cdc.gov/agent/agentlistchem-category.asp (accessed July 25, 2012)

(November 22, 2011, http://www.cma.army.mil/fndocumentviewer.aspx?DocID=003672525), the CMA notes that the original deadline was April 2007. In 2006 the United States was granted a five-year extension until April 2012; however, the CMA indicates that when the United States received the extension it notified the Organization for the Prohibition of Chemical Weapons that it did not expect to fully meet the April 2012 deadline, but that it would continue to work to reach 100% destruction.

In May 2006 the GAO reported in *Cooperative Threat Reduction: DOD Needs More Reliable Data to Better Estimate the Cost and Schedule of the Shchuch'ye Facility* (http://www.gao.gov/new.items/d06692.pdf) that Russia had the world's largest-known stockpile of chemical weapons. In 1992 Congress first authorized the DOD to assist the Russians in destroying their stockpile under the Cooperative Threat Reduction (CTR) program. The Nuclear Threat Initiative (NTI), a private nonprofit organization devoted to WMD nonproliferation, indicates in "Country Profile: Russia" (July 2012, http://www.nti.org/country-profiles/russia/chemical/) that Russian authorities reported in March 2012 that Russia had destroyed more than 60% of its stockpile and was expected to achieve 100% destruction by 2015.

The CTR program is managed by the DOD's Defense Threat Reduction Agency. Completion of the project is a high priority for the U.S. government because of the possibility of diversion and theft at the Russian storage facilities.

Biological Agents as Weapons

In *National Strategy for Countering Biological Threats* (November 2009, http://www.whitehouse.gov/sites/default/files/National_Strategy_for_Countering_Bio Threats.pdf), the National Security Council (NSC) notes that in the last two decades bioterrorism has become a "serious threat" to U.S. national security. In particular, the NSC reports that in 2001 coalition forces in Afghanistan uncovered a "significant body of evidence" that the terrorist group al Qaeda has been working to develop biological weapons.

Table 7.5 lists the biological agents and diseases that could be used in a terrorist attack. The agents are divided

TABLE 7.5

Biological warfare agents

Agent	Possible means of delivery
Bacterium	
Anthrax	Aerosol
Brucellosis	Aerosol, expected to mimic a natural disease
Cholera	Sabotaged food and water supply; aerosol
Plague	Contaminated fleas, causing bubonic type, or aerosol, causing pneumonic type
Q fever	Dust cloud from a line or point source
Tularemia	Aerosol
Typhoid	Sabotaged food and water
Typhus	Contaminated lice or fleas
Toxin	
Botulinum	Sabotaged food and water supply; aerosol
Ricin	Aerosol
Virus	
Ebola	Aerosol; direct contact
Marburg	Aerosol; direct contact
Smallpox	Airborne
Venezuelan equine encephalitis	Airborne
Yellow fever	Aerosol

SOURCE: Adapted from "Table 7. Biological Warfare Agents," in *Homeland Security: First Responders' Ability to Detect and Model Hazardous Releases in Urban Areas Is Significantly Limited*, U.S. Government Accountability Office, June 2008, http://www.gao.gov/new.items/d08180.pdf (accessed July 25, 2012). Non-government data from Analytic Services, Inc. and Edgewood Chemical Biological Center.

into three categories: bacterium, toxin, and virus. The Central Intelligence Agency explains in *Terrorist CBRN: Materials and Effects (U)* (May 2003, https://www.cia.gov/library/reports/general-reports-1/CBRN_threat.pdf) that anthrax and botulism are the diseases likely of most interest to terrorists. Anthrax is a bacterial disease caused by the *Bacillus anthracis* bacteria, with onset one to six days after exposure. There are two common routes of exposure: inhalation and cutaneous (through the skin). Inhaled anthrax is generally fatal unless antibiotics are given within the first few hours after exposure. Cutaneous anthrax is easily treated and rarely fatal.

Shortly after the terrorist attacks of September 11, 2001, several envelopes containing high-grade anthrax spores were discovered at various locations in the eastern United States. Five people died of inhalation exposure and more than a dozen other people became sick but survived. The Federal Bureau of Investigation (FBI) suspected that the anthrax had originated at the U.S. Army Medical Research Institute in Fort Detrick, Maryland. The agency vigorously pursued one scientist from that facility, only to admit later that he was not the culprit. In July 2008 the FBI cleared the first suspect and paid him nearly $6 million to settle a lawsuit in which he claimed that the agency had violated his civil rights. A second scientist from the same facility, Bruce Ivins (1946–2008), was named the prime suspect in the case, but he committed suicide before being charged. In February 2010 the U.S. Department of Justice (DOJ) released *Amerithrax*

Investigative Summary (http:www.justice.gov/amerithrax/docs/amx-investigative-summary.pdf), which is a 96-page report that summarizes the FBI's case against Ivins and announces the case closed. The DOJ continues to maintain that Ivins was responsible for the 2001 anthrax attack.

Botulism is caused by the ingestion or inhalation of the *Clostridium botulinum* bacteria. The CIA reports that recovered terrorist training manuals have included procedures for producing small quantities of botulinum toxin. The onset of symptoms from botulism usually occurs two to three days after exposure and includes severe gastrointestinal illnesses. Another biological agent of interest to terrorists is ricin. It is an extremely toxic agent that can be extracted from castor beans.

U.S. NONPROLIFERATION PROGRAMS

As noted earlier, the United States is party to several treaties that bind countries to limit and/or destroy WMDs, including nuclear and chemical weapons. In addition, the U.S. government operates several programs that are devoted to the nonproliferation of WMDs. These programs are primarily operated by the DOD, the DOS, and the Department of Energy's National Nuclear Security Administration (NNSA).

In the fact sheet "DTRA, SCC-WMD and SJFHQ-E" (May 2012, http://www.dtra.mil/docs/system-documents/DTRA_Fact_Sheet_-_23_May_2012.pdf?sfvrsn=0), the DOD describes its Defense Threat Reduction Agency (DTRA), which was established in 1998. The DTRA operates programs that are devoted to the following goals:

- Cooperative reduction and elimination of WMDs and related systems, materials, and infrastructure at their source

- Detecting, tracking, and intercepting WMDs and defeating WMD threats

- Responding to WMD usage and mitigating the effects

- Supporting DOD policy-making and strategy setting regarding WMDs

- Supporting U.S. nuclear weapons programs in the areas of accountability, safety, security, and inspections

The DOS includes the Office of Cooperative Threat Reduction (http://www.state.gov/t/isn/58381.htm), which operates Global Threat Reduction (GTR) programs that are intended to reduce the WMD threats posed by terrorist groups and "states of concern." GTR programs target biorisks (e.g., infectious diseases) and chemical and nuclear security. One fear is that scientists engaged in these fields, particularly in countries that are struggling financially, will be tempted to sell their expertise to terrorist groups or nations that are hostile to the United States. As a result, DOS programs engage scientists in Russia, Libya,

Iraq, and other countries in productive work, for example, by furthering the peaceful use of nuclear energy.

As noted in Chapter 2, the NNSA has various responsibilities within the United States, including managing and ensuring the security of the U.S. nuclear weapons stockpile. In addition, the agency furthers nuclear nonproliferation around the world. This work took on extra significance in 2009, after President Obama made a pledge regarding WMDs. On April 5, 2009, in Prague, the Czech Republic, Obama (http://www.whitehouse.gov/the_press_office/Remarks-By-President-Barack-Obama-In-Prague-As-Delivered/) stated: "So today I am announcing a new international effort to secure all vulnerable nuclear material around the world within four years. We will set new standards, expand our cooperation with Russia, pursue new partnerships to lock down these sensitive materials."

In *Securing Nuclear Materials: The 2012 Summit and Issues for Congress* (March 7, 2012, http://fpc.state.gov/documents/organization/187391.pdf), Mary Beth Nikitin of the CRS notes that in April 2010 Obama hosted the first Nuclear Security Summit, which was attended by the leaders of 47 countries. Nikitin presents statistics from various sources indicating that as of March 2012 Belarus, the Czech Republic, Kazakhstan, Mexico, Serbia, South Africa, Ukraine, and Vietnam had removed or were in the process of removing all of their highly enriched uranium supplies. Highly enriched uranium is the key component for the simplest type of nuclear explosive device. Also in March 2012 a second Nuclear Security Summit was held in South Korea.

Focus on the Former Soviet Republics

The breakup of the Soviet Union during the early 1990s into individual republics ended the Cold War but produced new security concerns for the United States. In particular, the United States is concerned about the safety of the enormous stockpile of WMDs that the Soviets had accumulated. The new republics have struggled economically, producing fears that WMDs or related technologies might be sold on the black market and wind up in the hands of terrorists or rogue nations. Therefore, the security of the old Soviet stockpile is a major concern to U.S. national security.

In 1991 two senators of rival parties collaborated on an act intended to prevent the spread of WMDs from the former Soviet Union. The Nunn-Lugar Act was spearheaded by Senators Sam Nunn (1938–; D-GA) and Richard G. Lugar (1932–; R-IN). It provides funding for the destruction of missiles and chemical weapons and employment opportunities for former weapons scientists. The act also resulted in the creation of the CTR program office within the Office of the Assistant to the Secretary of Defense for Nuclear, Chemical, and Biological Defense Programs. The CTR office's mission is to implement the Nunn-Lugar program to reduce WMDs subject to international arms control treaties.

As of May 2012, over 19,000 weapons-related items had been destroyed, deactivated, or dismantled. (See Table 7.6.) This represents a significant decrease in the CTR baseline inventory of these items.

TABLE 7.6

Goals and progress of Nunn-Lugar program, as of May 2012

Weapons/materials	Soviet declared amounts	Reductions to date	Percent of 2012 targets	2012 targets
Warheads deactivated	13,300	7,619	82%	9,265
Intercontinental ballistic missiles (ICBM) destroyed	1,473	902	87%	1,041
ICBM silos eliminated	831	498	76%	652
ICBM mobile launchers destroyed	442	191	53%	359
Nuclear weapons carrying submarines destroyed	48	33	85%	39
Submarine launched ballistic missiles (SLBM) eliminated	936	680	93%	729
SLBM launchers eliminated	728	492	80%	612
Nuclear air-to-surface missiles destroyed	906	906	100%	906
Bombers eliminated	233	155	100%	155
Nuclear test tunnels/holes sealed	194	194	100%	194
Nuclear weapons transport train shipments	—	565	68%	929
Nuclear weapons storage site security upgrades	—	24	100%	24
Biological monitoring stations built and equipped	—	38	61%	62

Notes: Ukraine, Kazakhstan and Belarus are nuclear weapons free.
ICBM = Intercontinental Ballistic Missile.
SLBM = Submarine/sea-launched Ballistic Missile.

SOURCE: Adapted from "The Nunn-Lugar Scorecard," in *Richard G. Lugar, United States Senator for Indiana*, Richard G. Lugar, 2012, http://lugar.senate.gov/nunnlugar/scorecard.html (accessed July 25, 2012)

CHAPTER 8
AMERICAN CIVIL LIBERTIES

Civil liberties (or civil rights) are individual rights that are designated by law. They are legal shields that protect citizens from abuses by their own government. Historically, times of war in the United States have produced situations in which the U.S. government has given national security concerns a higher priority than protection of the public's civil liberties. Most often, these transgressions have been instigated by the executive branch—the president and the departments and offices under his direct control. However, the framers of the U.S. Constitution included a system of checks and balances that allow individuals to challenge such transgressions in the courts. In addition, the Constitution's guarantee of freedom of speech allows the American press to publicize conflicts between the interests of national security and the protection of civil liberties. A debate over how best to balance these two important priorities has raged since the nation began and takes on new importance as the United States wages war once again.

HISTORICAL CONTEXT

In the United States the U.S. Constitution is considered to be the ultimate definer of Americans' civil rights. The original document, written in 1787, included seven articles that outlined the structure and workings of the federal government. Over the next two years 10 amendments known as the Bill of Rights were added to the Constitution. They were specifically designed to limit the power of the new government and ensure that certain individual rights are protected by law. An additional 17 amendments have been enacted since that time.

Times of war in the United States have often produced contentious debates over the proper balance between protecting national security and protecting civil liberties. History shows that some civil rights have not been honored by the U.S. government when the nation was threatened, a condition known by the Latin term *Inter*

arma enim silent leges, popularly translated as "In times of war, the laws fall silent." These civil liberty conflicts most often involve individual rights that are protected by the First, Fourth, and Fifth Amendments of the Constitution, which read as follows:

- First Amendment—"Congress shall make no law respecting an establishment of religion, or prohibiting the free exercise thereof; or abridging the freedom of speech, or of the press; or the right of the people peaceably to assemble, and to petition the government for a redress of grievances."

- Fourth Amendment—"The right of the people to be secure in their persons, houses, papers, and effects, against unreasonable searches and seizures, shall not be violated, and no warrants shall issue, but upon probable cause, supported by oath or affirmation, and particularly describing the place to be searched, and the persons or things to be seized."

- Fifth Amendment—"No person shall be held to answer for a capital, or otherwise infamous crime, unless on a presentment or indictment of a grand jury, except in cases arising in the land or naval forces, or in the militia, when in actual service in time of war or public danger; nor shall any person be subject for the same offense to be twice put in jeopardy of life or limb; nor shall be compelled in any criminal case to be a witness against himself, nor be deprived of life, liberty, or property, without due process of law; nor shall private property be taken for public use, without just compensation."

The rights to free speech and peaceable assembly guaranteed by the First Amendment receive exceptional attention when they are exercised during wartime by people who are opposed to the government's actions. The protections afforded under the Fourth and Fifth Amendments relate to judicial procedures, legal due process, and privacy issues. A right to privacy is not specifically spelled out in the Constitution but is believed to result inherently if the government operates in accordance with the articles of the Constitution and respects the Bill of Rights.

Civil War: Suspension of Habeas Corpus

During the Civil War (1861–1865) President Abraham Lincoln (1809–1865) suspended the writ of habeas corpus (a legal procedure in which a court can order that a prisoner held by the government be presented to the court for determination if the imprisonment is legal or not). Article One of the Constitution allows such a suspension "when in cases of rebellion or invasion the public safety may require it." Lincoln's action allowed Union troops to detain Southern sympathizers and anyone else deemed to be a threat to public safety and hold them indefinitely. In addition, military commissions tried and convicted civilian detainees who were accused of crimes. Thus, martial law went into effect, meaning that the military took over powers normally held by the civilian law enforcement system.

The consequences of the suspension were highly controversial and led to a legal battle in the U.S. Supreme Court after the war ended. In the 1866 case *Ex parte Milligan* (71 U.S. 2), the court ruled that martial law cannot be imposed so long as civilian courts and governments are still in operation. In addition, any imposition of martial law must be confined to a limited area in which war is actually occurring. The Posse Comitatus Act of 1878 made it unlawful for the U.S. military to execute legal authority over civilians unless specifically authorized by the Constitution or an act of Congress. It should be noted that this prohibition does not apply to National Guard troops under state government command.

World War I: Free Speech?

The World War I era is associated with many serious conflicts between national security and civil liberties. Around the turn of the 20th century a number of movements associated with labor rights, anarchy, and socialism became active in the United States. Some elements of these groups incited violence and were considered subversive (advocating the overthrow of the government). As such, the nation was in a wary mood when World War I erupted in Europe in 1914.

The United States' entry into the war in 1917 was accompanied by the passage of several federal laws that were aimed at squelching what the government considered to be anti-American activities. The Espionage Act of 1917 and the related Sedition Act of 1918 included a variety of provisions that were designed to prevent the passage of national security information to the enemy. The acts also made it illegal for anyone to obstruct military recruiting or enlistment. Most troubling to civil libertarians were provisions in the Sedition Act that made it illegal to say or write anything "disloyal" about the

U.S. government, Constitution, flag, or military forces. The act also prohibited any expression of resistance to the United States or support for its enemies. In other words, acts of dissent (disagreement with the government) were forbidden during the course of the war.

The acts were used by the government against many socialists, anarchists, and other activists who had begun a vocal antiwar campaign. In 1919 the Supreme Court heard a case involving a socialist who had mailed circulars to recent military draftees urging them to defy the government and oppose the draft system. In *Schenck v. United States* (249 U.S. 47), the court ruled in favor of the government and noted, "When a nation is at war many things that might be said in time of peace are such a hindrance to its effort that their utterance will not be endured so long as men fight and that no Court could regard them as protected by any constitutional right." Most of the provisions of the wartime acts were repealed during the 1920s.

World War II: Internment of Japanese-Americans

One of the most often referenced violations of American civil rights in wartime took place during World War II (1939–1945), when the U.S. government detained U.S. citizens of Japanese descent. In 1942 President Franklin D. Roosevelt (1882–1945) signed Executive Order 9066, which authorized the removal and internment of all people of Japanese descent living in California and in the western portions of Oregon and Washington. The military and civilian government decisions leading up to issuance of the executive order are described by Stetson Conn in "The Decision to Evacuate the Japanese from the Pacific Coast" (August 27, 1996, http://www.army.mil/cmh-pg/books/70-7_05.htm).

Conn notes that the military originally planned to forcibly evacuate only aliens (non-U.S. citizens) who were Japanese, German, or Italian and lived near strategic areas along the Pacific coast. Ultimately, the plan evolved into forced internment of both aliens and U.S. citizens of Japanese descent. This change was precipitated by a variety of factors, primarily widespread and persistent paranoia among the U.S. population that Japanese-American citizens had not been and would not be loyal to the United States. This feeling was aggravated by widely circulated, but false, rumors that traitors within the Japanese-American community had helped facilitate the surprise attack on the U.S. naval base at Pearl Harbor in December 1941 and were engaging in acts of espionage to support a Japanese invasion of the U.S. mainland.

The National Archives and Records Administration explains in "Executive Order 9066: Resulting in the Relocation of Japanese (1942)" (2012, http://www.ourdocuments.gov/doc.php?flash=true&doc=74) that approximately 122,000 people of Japanese descent, including children and elderly people, were detained under Executive Order 9066. Nearly 70,000 of them were U.S. citizens. The detainees were forced to leave their homes quickly and allowed to take only a minimum of possessions with them. They spent the duration of the war in internment camps throughout the Midwest and West (excluding the coastal states). These camps were surrounded by barbed wire and patrolled by armed guards. Following the war, the internees were released; however, many found it difficult to return to their previous homes and jobs.

In 1988 the Civil Liberties Act acknowledged that a "grave injustice" had been perpetrated on Japanese-Americans during World War II by the U.S. government and offered a payment of $20,000 to each internee as restitution.

Cold War: McCarthyism

McCarthyism describes a phenomenon that occurred in the United States when intense paranoia about communism created a social and political environment in which civil liberties were trampled in the interest of national security. The term is named after Senator Joseph R. McCarthy (1908–1957; R-WI), who served in the U.S. Senate from 1947 until his death in 1957. Even though the Soviet Union had been a U.S. ally during World War II, deep philosophical differences fostered a period of mutual distrust and animosity between the two nations after the war ended in 1945. In the United States many people believed the Soviets wanted to overthrow (subvert) the U.S. government and were being aided by American members of the Communist Party and sympathizers called fellow travelers.

Committees were formed within the U.S. House of Representatives and the Senate to investigate alleged communist activities by Americans. People who refused to cooperate were sent to prison or, at the very least, lost their job and reputation. Their names were put on a so-called blacklist, which meant that other companies and businesses were afraid to hire them. McCarthy also began holding hearings and accusing fellow politicians of having communist sympathies. In "Censure of Senator Joseph McCarthy (1954)" (April 30, 2007, http://eca.state.gov/education/engteaching/pubs/AmLnC/br60.htm), the U.S. Department of State (DOS) notes that McCarthy and his aides "made wild accusations, browbeat witnesses, destroyed reputations and threw mud at men."

In January 1954 McCarthy's hearings were televised for the first time. The DOS notes that "day after day the public watched McCarthy in action—bullying, harassing, never producing any hard evidence, and his support among people who thought he was 'right' on communism began to evaporate." The political tide turned against McCarthy, and in December 1954 the Senate passed a censure (official condemnation) of him for abusing his

powers. The U.S. Supreme Court and state courts began ruling against the tactics that had been used on committee witnesses and government employees. Many rulings found that civil liberties had been violated during the anticommunist fervor.

Vietnam War: Domestic Surveillance

The 1960s and early 1970s were a time of domestic strife in the United States. Many groups and movements became active in protesting against the government for a host of reasons, including opposing the Vietnam War (1954–1975) and advocating the enforcement of civil rights for minorities and women. Political and social activism became a common means of expressing discontent in public. Even though some groups were openly subversive, many sought change through legal methods or civil disobedience (breaking civil laws in a nonviolent fashion, such as by trespassing or blocking traffic and refusing police orders to cease).

As described in Chapter 2, the nation's intelligence agencies conducted massive campaigns of domestic surveillance in the name of national security during this period. Many abuses of power and violations of civil liberties were later uncovered and publicly disclosed through federal investigations, such as those of the Subcommittee on Constitutional Rights (chaired by Senator Sam J. Ervin [1896–1985; D-NC]) and the Senate Select Committee to Study Governmental Operations with Respect to Intelligence Activities (chaired by Senator Frank Forrester Church III [1924–1984; D-ID]). Public distaste with domestic surveillance drove massive reforms within the intelligence community, including the Central Intelligence Agency, the Defense Intelligence Agency, and the Federal Bureau of Investigation (FBI).

THE WAR ON TERROR: NEW CONFLICTS ARISE

The United States enjoyed more than two decades of relative peace following the end of the Vietnam War in 1975. The disintegration of the Soviet Union during the early 1990s effectively ended the Cold War. As a result, issues related to conflicts between civil liberties and national security became less prominent. This condition changed dramatically following the terrorist attacks of September 11, 2001 (9/11). The United States began a new and completely different kind of war—a war against terrorism—that has brought back many of the historic concerns about the protection of civil liberties during wartime. Once again, national security issues are weighed against constitutional rights and societal fears.

PATRIOT ACT

As described in Chapter 2, the Uniting and Strengthening America by Providing Appropriate Tools Required to Intercept and Obstruct Terrorism (USA PATRIOT)

Act of 2001—known simply as the Patriot Act—was passed by Congress in response to the 9/11 terrorist attacks. Many of the provisions of the act deal with surveillance procedures and financial security enhancements that have implications for civil liberty issues.

The Patriot Act allows federal agents to obtain business records relevant to national security investigations without going through the grand jury process to obtain a subpoena. Instead, the request is made through the Foreign Intelligence Surveillance Court (a federal court), which can grant permission if the government meets certain criteria. Other components of the act facilitate information sharing and cooperation between different government agencies, increase the penalties for terrorist-related crimes, and designate new criminal offenses, such as harboring people who have committed or plan to commit terrorist acts.

Controversy Erupts

The Patriot Act was not considered to be highly controversial when it was initially passed in October 2001. The act received overwhelming support in the House (passing 357 to 66) and in the Senate, where only one senator out of 100 voted against it. (See Figure 8.1 and Figure 8.2.) The lone "nay" vote was cast by then Senator Russell D. Feingold (1953–; D-WI).

Since its passing, however, the Patriot Act has received harsh criticism from groups, such as the American Civil Liberties Union (ACLU) and the Electronic Privacy Information Center (EPIC). Headquartered in New York City, the ACLU is a private nonprofit organization that is devoted to defending American civil liberties. In "National Security" (2012, http://www.aclu.org/national-security), the ACLU complains, "Over the last few years, the federal government has returned to the bad old days of unchecked spying on ordinary Americans, as part of a broad pattern of executive abuses that use 'national security' as an excuse for encroaching on our privacy and free speech rights without adequate—or any—judicial oversight."

EPIC is also a private nonprofit organization. It calls itself a public interest research center and is based in Washington, D.C. EPIC is most concerned with emerging civil liberty and privacy issues that have arisen since the advent of electronic media. It also maintains the website "USA Patriot Act" (http://epic.org/privacy/terrorism/usapatriot/). EPIC claims that the 2001 act was passed so quickly in the aftermath of 9/11 that few traditional safeguards afforded by the Constitution were included to protect American civil liberties. Both organizations work to publicize what they consider to be civil liberty abuses committed by federal government agencies under the Patriot Act.

Some cities and municipalities and even states have passed nonbinding resolutions expressing their opposition

FIGURE 8.1

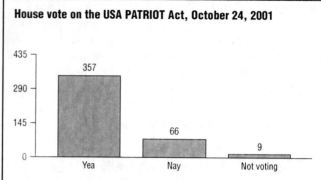

House vote on the USA PATRIOT Act, October 24, 2001

SOURCE: "House Vote on the USA PATRIOT Act, Vote #398—10/24/01," in *Passed by Congress*, U.S. Department of Justice, undated, http://www.justice.gov/archive/ll/subs/p_congress.htm (accessed July 27, 2012)

FIGURE 8.2

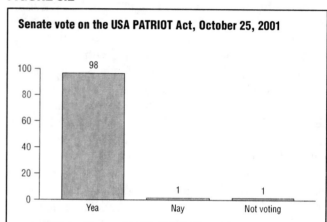

Senate vote on the USA PATRIOT Act, October 25, 2001

SOURCE: "Senate Vote on the USA PATRIOT Act, Vote #313—10/25/01," in *Passed by Congress*, U.S. Department of Justice, undated, http://www.justice.gov/archive/ll/subs/p_congress.htm (accessed July 27, 2012)

to certain provisions of the Patriot Act. The organization Bill of Rights Defense Committee claims in "Resolutions Passed and Efforts Underway, by State" (http://www.bordc.org/list.php) that as of October 2012, 414 resolutions had been passed.

Reauthorizations

The 2001 Patriot Act included a provision that 16 sections of the act would sunset (automatically expire) after four years unless Congress chose to renew them. In late 2005 intense debate began in Congress over whether those provisions should be renewed. In December 2005 the House voted 251 to 174 to renew the provisions with some modifications. (See Figure 8.3.) In March 2006 the USA PATRIOT Improvement and Reauthorization Act of 2005 also passed the Senate by a vote of 89 to 10. (See Figure 8.4.) The refurbished act made permanent 14 of the original 16 sunset provisions and placed new four-year sunset periods on the two remaining provisions

FIGURE 8.3

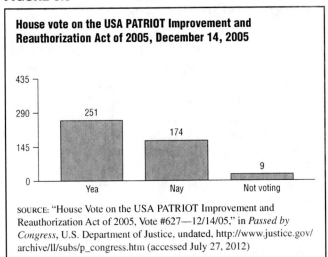

House vote on the USA PATRIOT Improvement and Reauthorization Act of 2005, December 14, 2005

SOURCE: "House Vote on the USA PATRIOT Improvement and Reauthorization Act of 2005, Vote #627—12/14/05," in *Passed by Congress*, U.S. Department of Justice, undated, http://www.justice.gov/archive/ll/subs/p_congress.htm (accessed July 27, 2012)

FIGURE 8.4

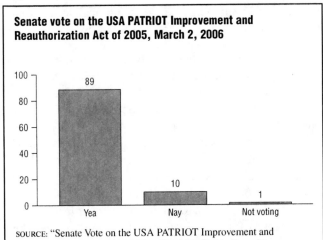

Senate vote on the USA PATRIOT Improvement and Reauthorization Act of 2005, March 2, 2006

SOURCE: "Senate Vote on the USA PATRIOT Improvement and Reauthorization Act of 2005, Vote #29—3/2/06," in *Passed by Congress*, U.S. Department of Justice, undated, http://www.justice.gov/archive/ll/subs/p_congress.htm (accessed July 27, 2012)

(which concern surveillance techniques and the acquisition of business records). According to the U.S. Department of Justice (DOJ), in the fact sheet "USA Patriot Act Improvement and Reauthorization Act of 2005" (March 2, 2006, http://www.usdoj.gov/opa/pr/2006/March/06_opa_113.html), Congress added "dozens of additional safeguards to protect Americans' privacy and civil liberties" as part of the reauthorization. The reauthorized act also extended a provision of the Intelligence Reform and Terrorism Prevention Act of 2004 (IRTPA) that was scheduled to expire at the end of 2005. The so-called lone wolf provision concerns individual terrorists who are not linked to a foreign government or foreign terrorist organization.

The four-year sunsets authorized in 2005 were scheduled to expire in December 2009. However, as the sunset date neared, Congress decided to delay the reauthorization decision for two months. In February 2010 the House voted 315 to 97 to renew (without change) the two expiring provisions of the Patriot Act and the expiring provision of the IRTPA through February 2011. The extensions were officially titled "An Act to Extend Expiring Provisions of the USA PATRIOT Improvement and Reauthorization Act of 2005 and Intelligence Reform and Terrorism Prevention Act of 2004 until February 28, 2011" and were passed as part of the Medicare Physician Payment Reform Act of 2009. As shown in Table 8.1, the extensions were widely supported by both Democrats and Republicans. The Senate approved the measure by a voice vote, meaning that it was not debated on the Senate floor. The three renewed provisions and their controversial features are as follows:

- Patriot Act Section 206—modifies the Foreign Intelligence Surveillance Act (FISA) to allow roving wiretaps. Roving wiretaps are authorized under U.S. criminal law, but require authorities to identify the targeted individual and the device, such as a cell phone, to be wiretapped. These requirements are not included in the FISA. In "Reform the Patriot Act" (2012, http://www.aclu.org/reform-patriot-act), the ACLU complains, "This provision is contrary to traditional notions of search and seizure, which require government to state with particularity what it seeks to search or seize."

- Patriot Act Section 215—modifies the FISA to allow the FBI to "make an application for an order requiring the production of any tangible things (including books, records, papers, documents, and other items) for an investigation to protect against international terrorism or clandestine intelligence activities, provided that such investigation of a United States person is not conducted solely upon the basis of activities protected by the first amendment to the Constitution." Critics complain that the phrases "any tangible things" and "investigation to protect" are too broad and allow the government sweeping powers. The ACLU notes that in criminal law the government must "show reasonable suspicion or probable cause before undertaking an investigation that infringes upon a person's privacy." Such a showing is not part of the provision.

- IRTPA Section 6001—power to conduct surveillance of suspects who are not affiliated with a country or organization, provided the suspects are not U.S. citizens. Critics worry that the government might abuse this power to spy on people, such as protesters, who are not specifically linked to terrorism.

The three renewed provisions were authorized through February 2011.

In February 2011 Congress approved a 90-day extension to the three expiring provisions. As the May 2011 deadline approached, there was a push by some

TABLE 8.1

House vote on extending specific provisions of the USA Patriot Act, February 25, 2010

	Yeas	Nays	Not voting
Democratic	162	87	5
Republican	153	10	15
Independent	—	—	—
Totals	**315**	**97**	**20**

SOURCE: Adapted from "Final Vote Results for Roll Call 67," in *U.S. House of Representatives Roll Call Votes 111th Congress—2nd Session (2010)*, U.S. House of Representatives, February 25, 2010, http://clerk.house.gov/evs/2010/roll067.xml (accessed July 27, 2012)

FIGURE 8.5

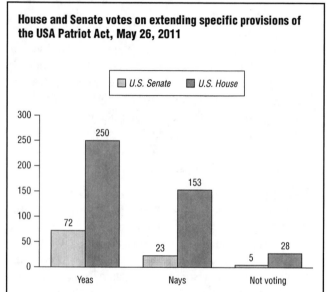

House and Senate votes on extending specific provisions of the USA Patriot Act, May 26, 2011

SOURCE: Adapted from "Final Vote Results for Roll Call 376," in *U.S. House of Representatives Roll Call Votes 112th Congress—1st Session (2011)*, U.S. House of Representatives, May 26, 2011, http://clerk.house.gov/evs/2011/roll376.xml (accessed July 25, 2012), and "Vote Counts," in *U.S. Senate Roll Call Votes 112th Congress—1st Session*, U.S. Senate, May 26, 2011, http://www.senate.gov/legislative/LIS/roll_call_lists/roll_call_vote_cfm.cfm?congress=112&session=1&vote=00084#top (accessed July 25, 2012)

congressional members to amend the Patriot Act to include greater protections of civil rights. The fight was led by Democrats who found an ally in Senator Rand Paul (1963–; R-KY). David Welna indicates in "Patriot Act Extension Came down to the Wire" (May 27, 2011, http://www.npr.org/2011/05/27/136704247/renewing-the-patriot-act-came-down-to-the-wire) that Paul had "grave misgivings" about the extension and upset his party's top leaders by delaying its passage and proposing amendments to the act. The amendments were defeated, and the Patriot Sunsets Extension Act of 2011 passed readily. (See Figure 8.5.) The vote in the House was 250 to 153, while the vote in the Senate was 72 to 23. The three disputed provisions of the Patriot Act/IRTPA were extended for four years to May 2015.

CONTROVERSY SURROUNDING ELECTRONIC SURVEILLANCE

The advent of the telephone and recording devices during the late 1800s introduced a new question to the debate over civil liberties: Does the use of equipment to intercept and record a private conversation constitute a "seizure" under the Fourth Amendment? In 1928 the Supreme Court ruled in *Olmstead v. United States* (277 U.S. 438) that the Fourth Amendment does not require a warrant for a wiretap placed on phone lines outside a suspect's residence. The case was decided on a narrow 5–4 vote, and the decision was highly controversial. Over the following decades Congress and the federal courts gradually chipped away at the legal precedent set in the 1928 case. In 1967 the decision was reversed by the Supreme Court in *Berger v. New York* (388 U.S. 41) and in *Katz v. United States* (389 U.S. 347). Thus, judicial warrants became necessary to conduct electronic surveillance in criminal investigations. However, the gathering of intelligence related to national security has been treated differently by legal authorities.

In 1968 Congress passed the Omnibus Crime Control and Safe Streets Act, which authorized the use of electronic surveillance for certain classes of crimes so long as a judicial warrant is obtained. Section 2511 (3) of the act notes that the act does not limit "the constitutional power of the President to take such measures as he deems necessary" to obtain foreign intelligence information that is considered essential to national security, to protect national security information from falling into foreign hands, and to protect against hostile acts of a foreign power, overthrow of the government by force or other unlawful means, or any other "clear and present danger to the structure or existence of the Government." This section stipulates that information obtained via electronic surveillance conducted under the authority of the president pursuant to these powers can be used as evidence in a trial so long as the conduct is "reasonable." In general, this section was interpreted as meaning that the U.S. attorney general (operating under the authority of the president) could conduct warrantless electronic surveillance for national security purposes.

This interpretation was challenged in the 1972 Supreme Court case of *United States v. United States District Court* (407 U.S. 297). In this case the government had used taped phone conversations to indict three American defendants in the bombing of a Central Intelligence Agency office in Ann Arbor, Michigan. The electronic surveillance had been conducted at the direction of the U.S. attorney general and without a warrant. The U.S. District Court for the Eastern District of Michigan ruled that the warrantless surveillance violated the Fourth Amendment. The Supreme Court agreed, noting that "the freedoms of the Fourth Amendment cannot properly be guaranteed if domestic security surveillances are conducted solely within the discretion of the Executive Branch without the detached judgment of a neutral magistrate."

FOREIGN INTELLIGENCE SURVEILLANCE COURT

In 1978 Congress passed the FISA, creating the Foreign Intelligence Surveillance Court (FISC). The FISA stipulates that the government must obtain a special warrant from the FISC before conducting specific intelligence-gathering activities that are related to national security within the United States. The original act related primarily to electronic surveillance. Subsequent amendments have allowed covert "physical searches," access to "tangible things" (e.g., business records), and the use of National Security Letters (NSLs). NSLs are letters used by intelligence agencies to request information (e.g., to request a suspect's credit card records from a financial institution). The recipient of an NSL does not have to comply with the request but must keep secret certain information about the request.

The creation of the FISC was driven by *United States v. United States District Court* and by a host of allegations that emerged during the early 1970s regarding spying by government intelligence agencies on U.S. citizens. These allegations were investigated by various government bodies, most notably the Senate Select Committee to Study Governmental Operations with Respect to Intelligence Activities. This committee found evidence that the executive branch of the federal government had abused its power by conducting domestic electronic surveillance that it claimed was in the interest of national security.

The FISC originally consisted of seven federal district court judges who were designated by the chief justice (the head of the judicial branch of the federal government who presides over the U.S. Supreme Court) for seven-year terms. However, the Patriot Act of 2001 changed the number to 11 judges on the FISC. At least one of the judges must be a member of the U.S. District Court for the District of Columbia. The chief justice appoints one member of the FISC to be the presiding (or head) judge. The FISC is not in session regularly but convenes in Washington, D.C., when needed. Because the judges live at various locations around the country, they attend hearings on a rotating basis. It should be noted that the federal code governing FISC operations (http://www.law.cornell.edu/uscode/50/1803.html) calls for the entire FISC panel to meet as needed, for example, to consider matters of "exceptional importance." In "Surveillance Court Quietly Moving" (*Washington Post*, March 2, 2009), Del Quentin Wilber reports that only one judge sits on the court at a time, each for a one-week shift in Washington, D.C. In 2009 the FISC courtroom moved from a location within DOJ facilities to the federal courthouse for the District of Columbia.

The workings of the FISC are described by the Federal Judicial Center (2012, http://www.fjc.gov/history/home.nsf/page/courts_special_fisc.html), an education and research agency for the federal courts. The process is as follows:

- A federal intelligence agency requests a warrant application

- The warrant application is drafted by attorneys at the National Security Agency (NSA)

- The application has to include certification from the U.S. attorney general that the target of the surveillance or search is a U.S. citizen or resident alien who "may be involved in the commission of a crime" or a foreign power or the agent of a foreign power

- The application is presented before the judges of the FISC

- If an application is denied, the government can appeal the decision to the Foreign Intelligence Surveillance Court of Review, which is presided over by three district or appeals court judges who are designated by the chief justice

According to the Federal Judicial Center, the Court of Review was first convened in 2002.

The FISC is often called a "secret" court, because much of its work is conducted in secrecy. The sensitive nature of national security matters means that the decisions of the court are based on classified information. However, the FISA does require the U.S. attorney general to submit an annual report to Congress noting the number of applications filed with the FISC and the number of orders issued by the court. The Federation of American Scientists, a nonprofit organization that is headquartered in Washington, D.C., maintains the website "Foreign Intelligence Surveillance Act" (2012, http://www.fasorg/irp/agency/doj/fisa/), which provides copies of the annual reports. The first annual report covers 1979 and states that the FISC issued 207 orders that gave the government authority to use electronic surveillance as part of national security investigations.

As of October 2012, the most recent report (April 30, 2012, http://www.fas.org/irp/agency/doj/fisa/2011rept.pdf) indicated that the FISC reviewed 1,745 applications in 2011 for authority to conduct electronic surveillance and/or physical searches. Of this total, 1,676 of the applications included requests to conduct electronic surveillance. None of the applications were denied in full or in part. Two of the applications were withdrawn by the federal government, and the FISC modified the proposed orders in 30 of the applications. As a result, the FISC approved 1,674 applications in 2011 that contained requests to conduct electronic surveillance. In addition, 205 applications were reviewed and approved by the FISC for access to certain business records for "foreign intelligence purposes." The FISC modified the proposed orders in 176 of the applications.

WIRETAPPING WITHOUT FISC APPROVAL

In 2005 the *New York Times* published an article that accused the administration of George W. Bush (1946–) of conducting wiretap operations without FISC approval. The media eventually began calling this practice warrantless wiretapping.

In "Bush Lets U.S. Spy on Callers without Courts" (*New York Times*, December 16, 2005), James Risen and Eric Lichtblau allege that in early 2002 President Bush issued a secret executive order authorizing the NSA to bypass the FISC process for conducting domestic surveillance. Headquartered at Fort Meade, Maryland, the NSA oversees signals intelligence operations for the U.S. intelligence community. (Signals intelligence is the interception of signals, such as radio, for the purpose of intelligence gathering.)

Risen and Lichtblau estimate that the international phone calls and e-mails of "hundreds, perhaps thousands" of Americans had been monitored to search for links to international terrorism. They claim unnamed government officials told the *New York Times* about the program in 2004 out of concern regarding its constitutionality. The newspaper said it delayed publishing the story for a year at the request of the White House because "it could jeopardize continuing investigations and alert would-be terrorists that they might be under scrutiny." Risen and Lichtblau report that the surveillance program had been credited by the government with uncovering several terrorist plots against targets in the United States and the United Kingdom.

President Bush allegedly based the program on his belief that a September 2001 congressional resolution granted him "broad powers" in the War on Terror to protect U.S. interests. Risen and Lichtblau claim that several members of Congress had been briefed about the monitoring program and at least one, Senator John D. Rockefeller IV (1937–; D-WV), had expressed concerns about it to the White House. Risen and Lichtblau note that it was puzzling why top officials decided to bypass the FISC process, considering that the FISC is believed to have granted nearly every request it has ever considered. Sources for the article note that it takes the FISC several hours to issue emergency approval for wiretaps and that the Bush administration considered this delay to be unacceptable. In addition, each FISC authorization requires information about specific surveillance targets, whereas the intelligence community is interested in monitoring many communications from a variety of sources at once.

According to Risen and Lichtblau, the program was suspended temporarily in mid-2004 because of concerns about its legality. Reportedly, the suspension was spurred by a complaint from the federal judge overseeing the FISC. The program was "revamped" and continued to operate. Declan McCullagh indicates in "Attorney General: NSA Spy Program to Be Reformed" (CNET News, January 17, 2007) that the U.S. attorney general Alberto Gonzales (1955–) announced in January 2007 that future electronic surveillance would be "subject to the approval of the Foreign Intelligence Surveillance Court." Thus, it is presumed that the practice of warrantless wiretapping ceased at that time.

Repercussions

Publicity about the warrantless surveillance program led to several repercussions for the Bush administration. One of the FISC judges resigned, supposedly to show his displeasure with the White House over the controversy. In 2006 the ACLU filed a lawsuit against the NSA, claiming that the surveillance program violated the First and Fourth Amendments of the Constitution and that President Bush had exceeded his authority under the separation of powers principles of the Constitution. The lawsuit sought a court order to dismantle the program. A federal judge granted that court order on the grounds that the surveillance program violated the FISA and the Fourth Amendment. The judge also ruled that President Bush had exceeded his authority under the Constitution. The DOJ immediately filed an appeal, and top government officials defended the program as legal and necessary to combat terrorist attacks. In 2007 an appeals court ruled in favor of the government. The ACLU asked the U.S. Supreme Court to reconsider the ruling, but in 2008 the court declined to hear the case.

Numerous other lawsuits were filed against the federal government on behalf of clients alleging to have been the targets of warrantless wiretapping. DOJ officials with the administration of President Bush and President Barack Obama (1961–) have had nearly all the cases dropped, arguing that the allegations cannot be proven without the release of top secret documents, which would harm national security. This is known in legal terms as the State Secrets Privilege.

However, one case did proceed to trial: *Al Haramain Islamic Foundation v. Obama* (Case No. 09-15266; originally filed in 2006 as *Al-Haramain Islamic Foundation v. Bush* [Case No. 3:2007cv00109]). In "Saudi Group Alleges Wiretapping by U.S." (*Washington Post*, March 2, 2006), Carol D. Leonnig and Mary Beth Sheridan note that the suit alleges that in 2004 the NSA conducted warrantless eavesdropping of conversations between the foundation's director in Saudi Arabia and two of its U.S.-based attorneys. The foundation, which Leonnig and Sheridan describe as a nonprofit Saudi charity operating in Oregon, subsequently ceased to operate after it was deemed a foreign terrorist organization and had its assets frozen by the U.S. government. The federal government filed numerous motions to have the case dropped based on the State Secrets Privilege, but the motions were denied. In 2010 a federal judge in San Francisco ruled in favor of the plaintiffs and ordered the government to pay them approximately $20,000 each in damages and $2.5 million in legal fees. However, in August 2012 a federal appeals court panel reversed the lower court's decision to award damages and legal fees to the plaintiffs after finding that the government enjoyed "sovereign immunity" in the case. David Kravets indicates in "Appeals Court OKs Warrantless Wiretapping" (*Wired*, August 7, 2012) that the plaintiffs' attorney was considering appealing the decision to the U.S. Supreme Court.

COLLECTING PHONE CALL DATA

In "NSA Has Massive Database of Americans' Phone Calls" (*USA Today*, May 11, 2006), Leslie Cauley reports that shortly after 9/11 the NSA began secretly collecting phone call data on "tens of millions of Americans." Cauley alleges that the agency was compiling a database of phone records to search for links to international terrorism. The database included information such as the calling and receiving phone numbers and the duration of calls. Cauley claims that the telecommunications companies AT&T, Verizon, and Bell South turned over phone call data to the NSA but that other companies—including Qwest—refused to do so because of legal concerns. The NSA did not obtain warrants for the information but simply asked (and may have paid) the companies to cooperate. According to Cauley, Qwest's lawyers asked the agency to process the request through the FISC, but the agency refused to do so.

Cauley's article led to media criticism of the phone companies for complying with the NSA request. Bell South and Verizon subsequently denied that they turned over records to the NSA. AT&T executives refused to confirm or deny the allegations but insisted that they had not endangered customer privacy. Leslie Cauley et al. retract in "Lawmakers: NSA Database Incomplete" (*USA Today*, June 30, 2006) part of Cauley's original story, noting that her sources could not confirm that Bell South and Verizon had cooperated with the NSA. Cauley et al. report that dozens of class-action lawsuits had been filed against the telecommunications companies linked to the story. However, these lawsuits were eventually stymied by provisions that were included in the FISA Amendments Act of 2008.

THE FISA AMENDMENTS ACT OF 2008

Throughout 2007 and early 2008 lawmakers considered ways to amend the FISA. Elizabeth B. Bazan of the Congressional Research Service describes this process in detail in *The Foreign Intelligence Surveillance Act: A Sketch of Selected Issues* (July 7, 2008, http://www.fas.org/sgp/crs/intel/RL34566.pdf). Bazan notes that in early

August 2007 the director of national intelligence released a statement asking congressional leaders to amend the FISA to include two critical changes: release the government from the requirement for a court order to gather intelligence on foreign people located overseas and provide liability protection for companies that had furnished assistance to the government in foreign intelligence collection activities in the past.

In August 2007 the Protect America Act (PAA) was enacted into law. This short-term law was in effect only through February 2008. Its purpose was to allow the federal government to continue certain types of electronic surveillance while long-term changes to the FISA were debated. The PAA specifically allowed surveillance that targeted foreign people located overseas. Bazan explains this meant that warrantless surveillance of people "reasonably believed to be located outside the United States" was allowed. Civil libertarians complained that American phone calls and e-mails could be unintentionally intercepted as part of the surveillance effort.

In July 2008 President Bush signed the FISA Amendments Act of 2008, which incorporated the provisions of the PAA. Critics complain that the law allows government surveillance without judicial oversight and gives immunity to the telecommunications companies that aided the government in its warrantless wiretapping program. The FISA Amendments Act of 2008 was scheduled to expire on December 31, 2012, unless it was extended by Congress. In June 2012 House and Senate committees approved bills (H.R. 5949 and S. 3276, respectively) that would extend the FISA Amendments Act of 2008 as enacted for five more years. The House committee (August 2, 2012, http://www.fas.org/irp/congress/2012_rpt/hrpt112-645pt2.html) notes that the extension was requested by the Obama administration and indicates that the director of national intelligence and the U.S. attorney general have called it "the top legislative priority of the Intelligence Community." In September 2012 H.R. 5949 was passed by the House. As of October 2012, an extension had not been passed by the Senate.

NSL CONTROVERSY

As noted earlier, NSLs are letters sent by intelligence agencies to third parties to request information about a suspect. In the 2011 annual FISA report to Congress (April 30, 2012, http://www.fas.org/irp/agency/doj/fisa/2011rept.pdf), the U.S. attorney general notes that "in 2011, the FBI made 16,511 NSL requests (excluding requests for subscriber information only) for information concerning United States persons. These sought information pertaining to 7,201 different United States persons."

NSLs are not a new national security tool. Their use dates back several decades. However, critics complain that the Patriot Act greatly expanded the scope and conditions under which the government can issue the letters. First, NSLs do not require prior judicial approval. Second, until 2007 the FBI was able to impose a nondisclosure requirement (or "gag order") forbidding NSL recipients from discussing indefinitely the NSLs they received.

A Critical Report on the NSL Program

The DOJ's Office of the Inspector General (OIG) criticizes some aspects of the NSL program in *A Review of the FBI's Use of National Security Letters: Assessment of Corrective Actions and Examination of NSL Usage in 2006* (March 2008, http://www.usdoj.gov/oig/special/s0803b/final.pdf). This report is unclassified, but redacted, meaning that parts of it are blacked out or omitted to protect national security interests. In particular, the OIG finds that some of the requests violated agency rules. The FBI's tracking and reporting program for NSLs is sharply criticized as well.

The OIG lists the number of NSLs requested by the FBI between 2003 and 2006. During this period the FBI made a total of 192,499 NSL requests. In 2006 a majority (11,517, or 57%) of the NSL requests were for U.S. citizens. The numbers of NSL requests made between 2007 and 2010 are disclosed in the FISA annual reports mentioned earlier. In 2007 the FBI made 16,804 NSL requests for information concerning 4,327 different U.S. citizens. In 2008 the agency made 24,744 NSL requests regarding 7,225 different U.S. citizens. In 2009 the FBI made 14,788 NSL requests for information related to 6,114 different U.S. citizens. In 2010 the FBI submitted 24,287 requests regarding 14,212 different U.S. citizens.

In "Statement before the Senate Committee on the Judiciary Washington, DC" (March 27, 2007, http://www.fbi.gov/news/testimony/the-fbis-use-of-national-security-letters-2), Robert S. Mueller III (1944–), the director of the FBI, promised to reform the agency's NSL procedures, noting, "The OIG report made 10 recommendations designed to provide both the necessary controls over the issuance of NSLs and the creation and maintenance of accurate records. I fully support each recommendation and concur with the inspector general that, when implemented, these reforms will ensure full compliance with both the letter and the spirit of the authorities entrusted to the Bureau by the Congress and the American people."

ACLU Lawsuit

The NSL nondisclosure requirement was challenged in federal court in 2004 by the ACLU on behalf of an anonymous client. In 2006, when Congress reauthorized the Patriot Act, it added a provision allowing NSL recipients to petition a federal judge to modify or overturn the gag order. The ACLU continued its court battle arguing that this change did not go far enough to protect the First Amendment rights (i.e., the right to free speech)

of NSL recipients. In 2007 a federal court ruled that the gag order provision was unconstitutional. This ruling was upheld in 2008 by a federal appeals court. In particular, the court ruled unconstitutional the provision that an NSL recipient opposed to the gag order has to initiate court action. Instead, the court put the burden of proof that a gag order is needed onto the NSL issuer. In other words, the issuer of the NSL letter has to obtain judicial review and show why a gag order is justified. In the press release "Obama Administration Will Not Ask Supreme Court to Take up National Security Letter 'Gag Order' Decision" (May 18, 2009, http://www.aclu.org/national-security/obama-administration-will-not-ask-supreme-court-take-national-security-letter-gag-), the ACLU reports that the Obama administration decided not to appeal the decision to the U.S. Supreme Court.

DETENTION CONTROVERSY

Chapter 9 discusses in detail the complex debate over the human and legal rights of the detainees who have been captured and detained by the United States since 2001, when the so-called War on Terror began. The issue becomes even more complicated when detainees are U.S. citizens who have rights granted by the U.S. Constitution. In December 2011 President Obama signed into law the National Defense Authorization Act for Fiscal Year 2012. National Defense Authorization Acts (NDAAs) are passed yearly and provide funding for U.S. national defense operations. The NDAA for Fiscal Year 2012 contains some special provisions that were inserted by congressional members to further U.S. counterterrorism activities. Section 1021 of the law is titled "Affirmation of Authority of the Armed Forces of the United States to Detain Covered Persons Pursuant to the Authorization for Use of Military Force." The provision refers to the Authorization for Use of Military Force (AUMF) that was quickly passed by Congress following the 9/11 attacks. As will be explained in Chapter 9, the AUMF has been upheld by the courts as giving the president the authority to order the U.S. military to detain people captured in connection with the War on Terror. That authority was granted to both President Bush and President Obama.

The NDAA for Fiscal Year 2012 provides the first legal definition for the term *covered persons* (i.e., people who are subject to the AUMF). There are two categories of covered people:

1. A person who planned, authorized, committed, or aided the terrorist attacks that occurred on September 11, 2001, or harbored those responsible for those attacks.

2. A person who was a part of or substantially supported al-Qaeda, the Taliban, or associated forces that are engaged in hostilities against the United States or its coalition partners, including any person

who has committed a belligerent act or has directly supported such hostilities in aid of such enemy forces.

Civil libertarians are mostly concerned with the second category, because it does not clearly define what types of actions might be considered supportive. In addition, the law includes four possible "dispositions" for detainees, including trials and transfer of custody of foreign citizens to foreign governments. However, the first listed disposition allows for "Detention under the law of war without trial until the end of the hostilities authorized by the Authorization for Use of Military Force." This provision raises the specter that U.S. citizens can be seized by the U.S. military and held without trial indefinitely. As noted earlier, the Posse Comitatus Act of 1878 made it unlawful for the U.S. military to execute legal authority over civilians unless specifically authorized by the Constitution or an act of Congress.

Section 1021 of the NDAA for Fiscal Year 2012 has proven to be extremely controversial. After signing the law, President Obama issued "Statement by the President on H.R. 1540" (December 31, 2011, http://www.whitehouse.gov/the-press-office/2011/12/31/statement-president-hr-1540), in which he stated that he had "serious reservations with certain provisions that regulate the detention, interrogation, and prosecution of suspected terrorists." In addition, he said, "I want to clarify that my Administration will not authorize the indefinite military detention without trial of American citizens." Regardless, the president's assurances did not squash debate on the issue.

In "Indefinite Detention, Endless Worldwide War and the 2012 National Defense Authorization Act" (February 22, 2012, http://www.aclu.org/indefinite-detention-endless-worldwide-war-and-2012-national-defense-authorization-act), the ACLU complains that Obama's statement about the troubling provisions "only applies to how his administration would use them, and would not affect how the law is interpreted by subsequent administrations."

Uncertainty about the law's scope prompted an immediate legal challenge. Bob Van Voris notes in "Military Detention Law Blocked by New York Judge" (Bloomberg.com, September 12, 2012) that in January 2012 a group of writers and activists filed a lawsuit against the Obama administration regarding the new law. In May 2012 a federal judge issued a preliminary injunction blocking the government from carrying out the detention provision for the second category of covered people under the act (i.e., those who are accused of supportive activities). According to Van Voris, the plaintiffs feared they could be subject to detention simply for their "speech and associations." In *Hedges v. Obama* (12 Civ. 331), Judge Katherine Forrest (1964–) of the U.S. district court agreed, noting, "The vagueness of § 1021 does not allow the average citizen, or even the government itself, to understand with the type of definiteness to which our citizens are entitled, or what conduct comes within its scope." The article "U.S. Appeals Ruling against Military Detention Law" (Reuter, August 6, 2012) indicates that the federal government had filed a notice of appeal in the case. As of October 2012, the appeal had not been heard.

FIGURE 8.6

Public opinion on civil liberties and government steps to prevent terrorism in the United States, 2002–11

WHICH COMES CLOSER TO YOUR VIEW—(THE GOVERNMENT SHOULD TAKE ALL STEPS NECESSARY TO PREVENT ADDITIONAL ACTS OF TERRORISM IN THE U.S. EVEN IF IT MEANS YOUR BASIC CIVIL LIBERTIES WOULD BE VIOLATED, (OR) THE GOVERNMENT SHOULD TAKE STEPS TO PREVENT ADDITIONAL ACTS OF TERRORISM BUT NOT IF THOSE STEPS WOULD VIOLATE YOUR BASIC CIVIL LIBERTIES)?

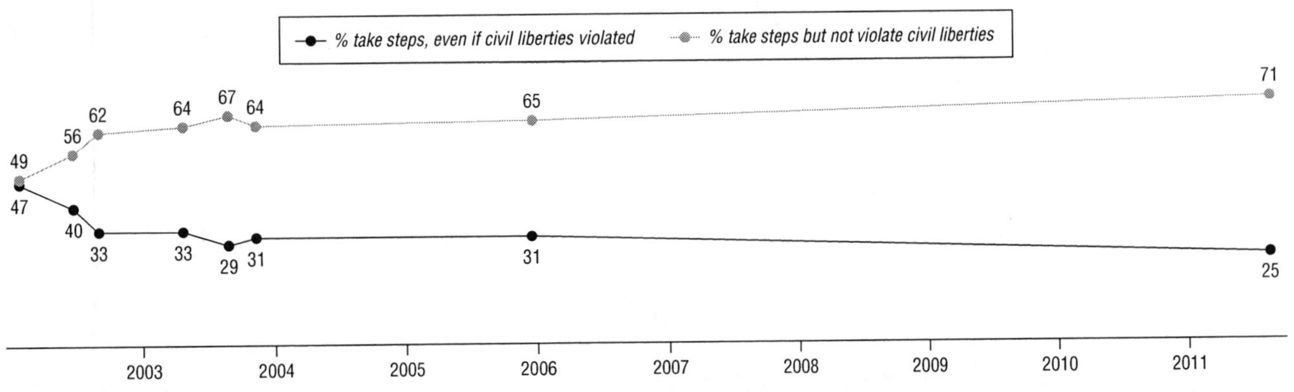

SOURCE: "Which comes closer to your view—(the government should take all steps necessary to prevent additional acts of terrorism in the U.S. even if it means your basic civil liberties would be violated, (or) the government should take steps to prevent additional acts of terrorism but not if those steps would violate your basic civil liberties)?" in *Civil Liberties*, The Gallup Organization, 2012, http://www.gallup.com/poll/5263/Civil-Liberties.aspx (accessed July 25, 2012). Copyright © 2012 Gallup, Inc. All rights reserved. The content is used with permission; however, Gallup retains all rights of republication.

PUBLIC OPINION

The Gallup Organization notes in *Civil Liberties* (2012, http://www.gallup.com/poll/5263/Civil-Liberties .aspx) that at various times between 2002 and 2011 it conducted polls to gauge American attitudes about balancing civil liberties against national security. In January 2002 the respondents were evenly split, with 47% expressing the view the government should "take steps, even if civil liberties [are] violated," to prevent terrorist attacks in the United States. (See Figure 8.6.) Only slightly more (49%) respondents said government steps against terrorism should not violate civil liberties. This poll was conducted only four months after 9/11. Over time, public opinion drifted toward greater protection of civil liberties. By August 2003 just over two-thirds (67%) of those asked were opposed to civil liberty violations as an acceptable measure in the fight against terrorism. By August 2011 this percentage of Americans had grown to 71%. Only 25% of those asked in August 2011 said the government should take all steps necessary to prevent additional acts of terrorism, even if it means that civil liberties will be violated.

(194... ...n ...ist ...fort Bush
included tt... ...ntually October
2012, the war in ... ...while the
war in Afghanistan conti... ... has been
nontraditional in that the Unite... not fought
against uniformed military forces of th.... representing
a national government. This has confused the legal status
of people who are captured and detained by U.S. military
forces during the hostilities. Detainees are not considered
soldiers, but civilians from various countries fighting for
a common agenda or ideological purpose that the U.S.
government defines as terrorism. As a result, a legal and
political battle has raged within the United States over
what kinds of human and legal rights should be afforded
to detainees.

ENEMY COMBATANTS

Historically, the United States has treated enemy soldiers in accordance with specific humanitarian standards
and international agreements, such as the Geneva Conventions. (See Table 9.1.) The Geneva Conventions pre-
scribe minimum humanitarian standards for captured
civilians and soldiers. Among other things, they prohibit
torture and cruel, humiliating, and degrading treatment.
Similar restrictions are proscribed in the United Nations
(UN) Convention against Torture and Other Cruel, Inhuman,
or Degrading Treatment or Punishment (http://www2
.ohchr.org/english/law/cat.htm) to which the United States
is a party. Likewise, U.S. behavior during wartime is
governed by the War Crimes Act, which was signed into
law in 1996 and amended in 1997. Basically, this act
defines war crimes as violations of specific provisions
of various international agreements, including the Geneva
Conventions.

When the War on Terror began in late 2001, the Bush
administration decided that most combatants fighting
against the United States were not soldiers in the
traditional sense but were war criminals. (Note that this
distinction did not apply to the uniformed military forces
of Iraq.) Captured nonsoldiers were not granted the
protections afforded prisoners of war (POWs) under
international law. In fact, captured combatants were
called detainees, rather than POWs. President Bush made
the decision that captured enemy civilians who were considered terrorists were officially considered enemy combatants. In "Guantanamo Detainee Processes" (October 2,
2007, http://www.defenselink.mil/news/Sep2005/d2005
0908process.pdf), the U.S. Department of Defense (DOD)
defines an enemy combatant as "an individual who was
part of or supporting Taliban or al Qaeda forces, or associated forces that are engaged in hostilities against the
United States or its coalition partners. This includes any
person who has committed a belligerent act or has directly
supported hostilities in aid of enemy armed forces."

Once terrorists were declared enemy combatants,
they left the realm of law enforcement and became legitimate targets of military action. In other words, terrorists
could be killed outright by U.S. soldiers during the course
of hostilities. Likewise, captured terrorists fell under
military jurisdiction rather than law enforcement jurisdiction and could be detained in military detention facilities.

An important distinction in U.S. law is the difference
between a lawful and unlawful enemy combatant. When
the Bush administration began its War on Terror, the U.S.
position was that lawful enemy combatants were uniformed members of an enemy nation's armed forces that
adhered to a military hierarchy, bore their weapons
openly, and conducted their operations in accordance
with the laws and customs of warfare. Terrorists do not
meet these criteria and as a result were deemed unlawful
enemy combatants.

TABLE 9.1

The Geneva Conventions

Part	Title	Treaty date	Ratified by U.S.	Scope
First Geneva Convention	Amelioration of the condition of the wounded in armies in the field	1949	1955	Concerns treatment of sick and wounded military forces and the neutrality of medical personnel assisting them
Second Geneva Convention	Amelioration of the condition of wounded, sick and shipwrecked members of armed forces at sea	1949	1955	Extends First Geneva Convention to naval warfare
Third Geneva Convention	Treatment of prisoners of war (POW)	1949	1955	Calls for humane treatment of POWs and all other combatants no longer active in hostilities
Fourth Geneva Convention	Protection of civilian persons in time of war	1949	1955	Governs the status and protection of civilian populations during wartime
Protocol I	Protection of victims of international armed conflicts	1977	No*	Protects people involved in battles for self-determination of their nations
Protocol II	Protection of victims of non-international armed conflicts	1977	No*	Protects people involved in internal national conflicts
Protocol III	Adoption of an additional distinctive emblem	2005	2007	Adds a new distinctive emblem called the red crystal

*The United States signed the protocol, but as of July 2010 had not ratified it. Other signatories that have not ratified the protocol are Iran and Pakistan.

SOURCE: Created by Kim Masters Evans for Gale, 2012

The Bush administration also maintained that the Geneva Conventions are international treaties signed and ratified by nation-states. Because terrorist groups such as al Qaeda are private organizations, they cannot be party to the conventions. Foreign individuals fighting against the United States without official sanction from their governments also cannot be party to the conventions.

DETAINEES AND DETENTION FACILITIES

Since 2001 the United States has captured and detained thousands of enemy combatants, both lawful and unlawful, at several detention facilities. The major detention facilities have included U.S. military prisons in Bagram, Afghanistan; Abu Ghraib, Iraq; and Guantá-namo Bay, Cuba. The Guantánamo Bay detention facility is located within a U.S. naval base in the southeast corner of Cuba on land that has been leased by the United States from the Cuban government since 1903. (For a map of Cuba, see Figure 6.4 in Chapter 6.) Every detention facility has been plagued by accusations that its detainees have suffered mistreatment and even torture.

Abu Ghraib

Following the invasion of Iraq in March 2003, the U.S. military began using an existing prison in Abu Ghraib to detain prisoners. These included both enemy combatants and common criminals. In 2004 the media began reporting on several digital photos taken by soldiers at Abu Ghraib that showed prisoners posing in sexually explicit positions and enduring humiliating and abusive treatment. Many of the photos included smiling U.S. soldiers posing with the prisoners.

The photos caused an uproar around the world and inflamed anti-American sentiment, particularly among Muslim populations. A series of investigations was launched by U.S. officials. Eventually, the *Final Report of the Independent Panel to Review DoD Detention*

Operations (http://www.defenselink.mil/news/Aug2004/d20040824finalreport.pdf) was issued in August 2004 by the Independent Panel to Review DOD Detention Operations, a group created by the U.S. secretary of defense Donald H. Rumsfeld (1932–). The panel concluded that "acts of brutality and purposeless sadism" had been committed at the detention facility by both military police and military intelligence personnel. This "deviant behavior" on the part of U.S. personnel was blamed on "a failure of military leadership and discipline." Aggravating factors included severe overcrowding and understaffing (approximately 90 U.S. personnel were responsible for guarding up to 7,000 prisoners) and frequent attacks on the facility by local insurgents.

The panel found that the abuses depicted in the photographs were conducted primarily for the entertainment of the U.S. personnel involved and were not part of interrogation procedures. In fact, the victims in the photographs were not intelligence targets but civilian or criminal detainees. However, the panel noted that additional "egregious abuses" that were not photographed occurred during interrogation sessions. Eventually, 11 U.S. soldiers were convicted of crimes related to the abuse of detainees at Abu Ghraib.

Interrogation Techniques

Confusion about appropriate interrogation techniques among U.S. military personnel in Afghanistan and Iraq was well documented in the panel's final report. Table 9.2 lists interrogation techniques that were approved by DOD officials at one point or another between 2002 and 2004 for use on unlawful enemy combatants at the Guantánamo Bay detention facility.

The techniques in use during much of 2002 came from the *U.S. Army Field Manual* dating from 1992. In December 2002 Rumsfeld approved additional, more intense, techniques for use under certain conditions and with his express approval on specific detainees at

TABLE 9.2

Department of Defense-approved interrogation techniques for Guantánamo Bay detainees, 2004

Interrogation techniques	FM 34–52 (1992) Jan 02–01 Dec 02	Secretary of Defense approved tiered system 02 Dec 02–15 Jan 03	FM 34–52 (1992) with some Cat I 16 Jan 03–15 Apr 03	Secretary of Defense memo 16 Apr 03–present
Direct questioning	X	X	X	X
Incentive/removal of incentive	X	X	X	X
Emotional love	X	X	X	X
Emotional hate	X	X	X	X
Fear up harsh	X	X	X	X
Fear up mild	X	X	X	X
Reduced fear	X	X	X	X
Pride and ego up	X	X	X	X
Pride and ego down	X	X	X	X
Futility	X	X	X	X
We know all	X	X	X	X
Establish your identity	X	X	X	X
Repetition approach	X	X	X	X
File and dossier	X	X		X*
Mutt and Jeff				X
Rapid fire	X	X	X	X
Silence	X	X	X	X
Change of scene	X	X	X	X
Yelling		X (Cat I)	X	
Deception		X (Cat I)		
Multiple interrogators		X (Cat I)	X	
Interrogator identity		X (Cat I)	X	
Stress positions, like standing		X (Cat II)		
False documents/reports		X (Cat II)		
Isolation for up to 30 days		X (Cat II)		X*
Deprivation of light/auditory stimuli		X (Cat II)		
Hooding (transportation & questioning)		X (Cat II)		
20-interrogations		X (Cat II)		
Removal of ALL comfort items, including religious items		X (Cat II)		
MRE-only diet		X (Cat II)		X*
Removal of clothing		X (Cat II)		
Forced grooming		X (Cat II)		
Exploiting individual phobias, e.g. dogs		X (Cat II)		
Mild, non-injurious physical contact, e.g. grabbing, poking or light pushing		X (Cat III)		
Environmental manipulation				X
Sleep adjustment				X
False flag				X

*Techniques require SOUTHCOM approval and SECDEF notification.
Notes: MRE=meal, ready to eat. FM=field manual. Cat=category.

SOURCE: "Evolution of Interrogation Techniques—GTMO," in *Final Report of the Independent Panel to Review DoD Detention Operations*, U.S. Department of Defense, August 2004, http://www.defenselink.mil/news/Aug2004/d20040824finalreport.pdf (accessed July 25, 2012).

Guantánamo Bay. Many of these techniques lost their approval only a few weeks later in January 2003 after concerns were raised about their legality by military legal experts. U.S. officials later learned that the December 2002 list of interrogation techniques was widely circulated in Afghanistan and Iraq and that some commanders mistakenly assumed it applied to detainees under all circumstances.

In April 2003 the list was revised again, reauthorizing two of the more intense techniques and authorizing three new techniques known as environmental manipulation (such as exposure to loud music), sleep adjustment (changing the regular sleeping hours of a detainee; this technique does not include sleep deprivation), and the false-flag technique (fooling a detainee into believing that he is being questioned by a representative from another country, typically a Muslim country).

James Risen, David Johnston, and Neil A. Lewis report in "Harsh C.I.A. Methods Cited in Top Qaeda Interrogations" (*New York Times*, May 13, 2004) that after 9/11 the Central Intelligence Agency (CIA) began using "harsh" interrogation methods against detainees considered to be "high-level leaders and operatives of Al Qaeda." Risen, Johnston, and Lewis describe an interrogation technique called "waterboarding," in which detainees are strapped to a board and lowered under water to make them believe they might drown.

Office of the Inspector General Report on Interrogation Techniques

In *A Review of the FBI's Involvement in and Observations of Detainee Interrogations in Guantanamo Bay, Afghanistan, and Iraq* (October 2009, http://www.justice.gov/oig/special/s0910.pdf), the U.S. Department of

Justice's (DOJ) Office of the Inspector General (OIG) summarizes its findings regarding the observations and participation of Federal Bureau of Investigation (FBI) agents in detainee interrogations conducted at military facilities in Guantánamo Bay, Afghanistan, and Iraq between 2001 and 2004. The OIG reviewed relevant documents, interviewed over 200 witnesses, and surveyed more than 1,000 FBI agents as part of the investigation. The report is unclassified, but redacted, meaning that parts of it are blacked out or omitted to protect national security interests.

The OIG acknowledges that FBI agents witnessed interrogation techniques "that caused them concern." Questions and protests made by FBI agents in the field to the interrogators "sometimes resulted in friction between the FBI and the military." This was particularly true at Guantánamo Bay, where FBI agents reported serious concern about military interrogation techniques that were used against certain "high-value" detainees, including Muhammad al-Qahtani (1979–). Al-Qahtani is believed to have been involved in the planning of the 9/11 terrorist attacks. FBI agents complained that in late 2002 and early 2003 al-Qahtani was subjected to many "aggressive techniques" including being put on a leash and forced to do dog tricks, held in "stress positions," having women's underwear put on his head, and ordered to pray to an idol shrine. The OIG finds that FBI complaints to the DOD about the legality and effectiveness of these techniques were never officially addressed.

In total, more than 200 FBI agents who served at Guantánamo Bay reported witnessing or hearing about "harsh" interrogation techniques used by the military. Some of these techniques were in violation of DOD regulations effective at the time. A smaller unnamed number of FBI agents reported similar problems in Afghanistan. Over 300 FBI agents reported observing or hearing about "harsh" interrogation techniques used by the military on detainees in Iraq. (See Table 9.3.) One hundred and twelve of the agents personally observed these techniques. However, the OIG notes that the "vast majority" of FBI agents stationed at Guantánamo Bay, Afghanistan, and Iraq reported neither observing nor hearing about harsh interrogation techniques.

New Detainee Rules

By 2005 continued allegations and reports about the mistreatment of detainees had become a major problem for the U.S. government. In December 2005 Congress approved the Department of Defense, Emergency Supplemental Appropriations to Address Hurricanes in the Gulf of Mexico, and Pandemic Influenza Act of 2006, an appropriations bill for the DOD. Title X of the act is called the Detainee Treatment Act of 2005. In it Congress outlaws the use of torture or cruel and inhuman treatment

of detainees by military and civilian federal agencies. It requires that military interrogators use only interrogation techniques that are listed in the *U.S. Army Field Manual*, which adheres to the requirements of the Third Geneva Convention for the treatment of POWs.

On September 5, 2006, the DOD issued Directive 2310.01E (http://www.dtic.mil/whs/directives/corres/pdf/231001p.pdf), which calls for all detainees to be treated in accordance with humanitarian standards, including the Geneva Conventions. That same month the U.S. Army released a new version of the *U.S. Army Field Manual*, known as *FM 2-22.3 (FM 34-52) Human Intelligence Collector Operations* (http://www.fas.org/irp/doddir/army/fm2-22-3.pdf). The new manual prohibits cruel, inhuman, and degrading treatment of detainees. Specific prohibitions on the treatment of detainees are listed in Table 9.4.

Secret CIA Prisons Acknowledged

Risen, Johnston, and Lewis report that after 9/11 the CIA began operating a secret detention system that housed up to 20 high-level detainees. Furthermore, the CIA refused to allow independent observers or human rights groups access to the prisoners. Dana Priest provides more detail about this program in "CIA Holds Terror Suspects in Secret Prisons" (*Washington Post*, November 5, 2005). The prison system allegedly included facilities in several countries in eastern Europe and Thailand and was conducted with the cooperation of those governments. Priest claims that CIA interrogators were allowed to use "enhanced interrogation techniques," such as waterboarding, that are prohibited by international law and the U.S. military.

According to Adam Liptak, in "Interrogation Methods Rejected by Military Win Bush's Support" (*New York Times*, September 8, 2006), President Bush admitted in a September 6, 2006, speech that the CIA had been operating secret overseas prisons. However, he denied that the detainees had been tortured, claiming they had been subjected to techniques that "were tough, and they were safe and lawful and necessary." All the detainees were believed to have been transferred to military control.

In July 2007 President Bush issued Executive Order 13340, which required CIA interrogators to use interrogation techniques on terror suspects in accordance with the Geneva Conventions. Later that year the director of the CIA admitted that videotapes of some detainee interrogations had been destroyed by the agency.

Redefining War Crimes

In October 2006 Bush signed the Military Commissions Act of 2006 (MCA of 2006). Michael John Garcia of the Congressional Research Service describes the effect of the new law on the War Crimes Act and the

TABLE 9.3

Survey of FBI agents who observed interrogation techniques in Iraq between March 2003 and December 2004

	Interrogation technique	Personally observed	Observations led me to believe	Detainee told me	Others described to me	None of the above
1	Depriving a detainee of food or water	—	—	1	2	284
2	Depriving a detainee of clothing	5	3	3	5	273
3	Depriving a detainee of sleep, or interrupting sleep by frequent cell relocations or other methods	10	6	7	28	234
4	Beating a detainee	—	3	7	4	274
5	Using water to prevent breathing by a detainee or to create the sensation of drowning	1	—	—	—	287
6	Using hands, rope, or anything else to choke or strangle a detainee	—	—	—	—	287
7	Threatening other action to cause physical pain, injury, disfigurement, or death	1	—	2	—	281
8	Other treatment or action causing significant physical pain or injury, or causing disfigurement or death	—	1	2	—	287
9	Placing a detainee on a hot surface or burning a detainee	—	3	4	—	281
10	Using shackles or other restraints in a prolonged manner	6	—	1	5	277
11	Requiring a detainee to maintain, or restraining a detainee in, a stressful or painful position	6	1	2	5	274
12	Forcing a detainee to perform demanding physical exercise	1	—	1	4	277
13	Using electrical shock on a detainee	—	—	1	2	283
14	Threatening to use electrical shock on a detainee	—	—	—	—	289
15	Intentionally delaying or denying detainee medical care	—	—	—	—	289
16	Hooding or blindfolding a detainee other than during transportation	22	3	—	1	260
17	Subjecting a detainee to extremely cold or hot room temperatures for extended periods	1	1	1	1	285
18	Subjecting a detainee to loud music	11	1	3	19	252
19	Subjecting a detainee to bright flashing lights or darkness	6	1	2	7	268
20	Isolating a detainee for an extended period	20	1	1	6	257
21	Using duct tape to restrain, gag, or punish a detainee	1	—	—	1	286
22	Using rapid response teams and/or forced cell extractions	2	3	1	9	275
23	Using a military working dog on or near a detainee other than during detainee transportation	1	—	—	3	285
24	Threatening to use military working dogs on or near a detainee	2	—	—	1	284
25	Using spiders, scorpions, snakes, or other animals on or near a detainee	—	—	—	—	288
26	Threatening to use spiders, scorpions, snakes, or other animals on a detainee	—	—	—	—	287
27	Disrespectful statements, handling, or actions involving the Koran	—	—	2	—	287
28	Shaving a detainee's facial or other hair to embarrass or humiliate a detainee	2	—	1	1	285
29	Placing a woman's clothing on a detainee	—	—	—	—	286
30	Touching a detainee or acting toward a detainee in a sexual manner	—	—	—	—	290
31	Holding detainee(s) who were not officially acknowledged or registered as such by the agency detaining the person.	1	2	—	4	280
32	Sending a detainee to another country for more aggressive interrogation	2	—	2	5	279
33	Threatening to send a detainee to another country for detention or more aggressive interrogation	6	—	—	2	278
34	Threatening to take action against a detainee's family	3	—	2	1	283
35	Other treatment or action causing severe emotional or psychological trauma to a detainee	—	—	—	—	290
36	Other religious or sexual harassment or humiliation of a detainee	1	—	—	—	287
37	Other treatment of a detainee that in your opinion was unprofessional, unduly harsh or aggressive, coercive, abusive, or unlawful	1	1	—	1	284
	Observation totals	**112**	**30**	**46**	**117**	**10,333**

SOURCE: "Table 10.1. Survey Results Concerning Interrogation Techniques Observed in Iraq," in *A Review of the FBI's Involvement in and Observations of Detainee Interrogations in Guantanamo Bay, Afghanistan, and Iraq*, U.S. Department of Justice, Office of the Inspector General, October 2009, http://www.justice.gov/oig/special/s0910.pdf (accessed July 25, 2012)

Detainee Treatment Act of 2005 in *The War Crimes Act: Current Issues* (October 2, 2006, http://fpc.state.gov/documents/organization/75257.pdf). According to Garcia, the MCA of 2006 criminalized only certain "grave breaches" of the Geneva Conventions regarding the treatment of captured individuals. He notes that "previously, *any* violation … constituted a criminal offense under the War Crimes Act." The MCA of 2006 also specifically provided a statutory defense for U.S. personnel accused of crimes against detainees under the War Crimes Act. The defense was that the personnel were operating with the authorization of the administration and under the reasonable belief that their actions were lawful. Garcia notes that U.S. personnel are not immune from prosecution for alleged violations of the War Crimes Act for their treatment of detainees, but the MCA of 2006 did give them a defense against criminal liability.

Analysts believe that passage of the MCA of 2006 was driven by fears within the Bush administration that officials could be held legally culpable for the alleged mistreatment of detainees. Calls for such prosecutions were being made publicly, such as by Amnesty International (AI), a London-based private independent group

TABLE 9.4

List of detainee treatments specifically prohibited by U.S. Army Field Manual, 2006

<u>Section 5-74</u>
Specifically prohibited treatments under all circumstances:

Forcing an individual to perform or simulate sexual acts or to pose in a sexual manner.
Exposing an individual to outrageously lewd and sexually provocative behavior.
Intentionally damaging or destroying an individual's religious articles.

<u>Section 5-75</u>
Specifically prohibited treatments during interrogations:

Forcing the detainee to be naked, perform sexual acts, or pose in a sexual manner.
Placing hoods or sacks over the head of a detainee; using duct tape over the eyes.
Applying beatings, electric shock, burns, or other forms of physical pain.
"Waterboarding."
Using military working dogs.
Inducing hypothermia or heat injury.
Conducting mock executions.
Depriving the detainee of necessary food, water, or medical care.

SOURCE: Adapted from "Cruel, Inhuman or Degrading Treatment Prohibited," in *FM 2-22.3 (FM 34-52) Human Intelligence Collector Operations*, U.S. Army, September 2006, https://rdl.train.army.mil/catalog/view/100.ATSC/10492372-71C5-4DA5-8E6E-649C85E1A280-1300688170771/2-22.3/toc.htm (accessed July 25, 2012)

concerned with human rights. In *Amnesty International Report 2006: The State of the World's Human Rights* (2006, http://www.amnestyusa.org/state-of-the-world-report/2006/page.do?id=1041003&n1=2&n2=18&n3=782), AI claims that in 2005 the United States was holding thousands of detainees without charge and operating secret detention facilities called "black sites" in various countries. The AI report also claims that U.S. officials practiced rendition (exporting U.S.-held detainees to countries known to practice torture) and were subjecting detainees to cruel, inhuman, or degrading treatment.

Likewise, the UN was highly critical of U.S. government actions regarding detainees. In *Consideration of Reports Submitted by States Parties under Article 19 of the Convention* (July 25, 2006, http://www.unhcr.org/), the UN Committee against Torture presented more than a dozen "concerns" about U.S. treatment of detainees, including failure to follow the Geneva Conventions, "enforced disappearances" of suspects, detainees being deprived of "fundamental legal safeguards," and detainee renditions (transfers) to countries believed to practice torture. The committee also recommended that the Guantánamo Bay detention facility be closed as soon as possible.

Public Opinion on Detainee Treatment

Darren K. Carlson of the Gallup Organization reports in *Public Believes U.S. Government Has Tortured Prisoners* (November 29, 2005, http://www.gallup.com/poll/20170/Public-Believes-US-Government-Has-Tortured-Prisoners.aspx) that in November 2005, 74% of Americans believed U.S. troops and government officials had tortured prisoners in Iraq and in other countries, whereas 20% believed torture had not taken place. Carlson notes that this poll was conducted only weeks after President Bush and Porter J. Goss (1938–), the director of the CIA, had assured the American public that prisoners in the War on Terror were not being tortured.

During the same poll respondents were asked about their willingness to have the government torture known terrorists with details about future terrorist attacks. Carlson notes in *Would Americans Fight Terrorism by Any Means Necessary?* (March 1, 2005, http://www.gallup.com/poll/15073/Would-Americans-Fight-Terrorism-Any-Means-Necessary.aspx) that this same question was asked by Gallup pollsters in October 2001 (only weeks after the 9/11 terrorist attacks) and in January 2005. In all three polls a majority of the respondents opposed the use of torture to obtain vital information about future attacks. In November 2005, 56% of those asked had this viewpoint, compared with 38% who were willing to use torture.

U.S. Senate Report on Detainee Treatment

In December 2008 the U.S. Senate Committee on Armed Services published its findings after conducting a lengthy investigation of detainee treatment. In *Senate Armed Services Committee Inquiry into the Treatment of Detainees in U.S. Custody* (http://www.gwu.edu/~nsarchiv/torturingdemocracy/documents/20081211.pdf), the committee outlines the Bush administration's decisions and policies that ultimately influenced the treatment of detainees.

In particular, the committee focuses on interrogations that employ Survival Evasion Resistance and Escape (SERE) techniques. The DOD's Joint Personnel Recovery Agency (JPRA) conducts training classes known as SERE schools, in which U.S. military personnel are trained to withstand interrogation techniques that are forbidden by the Geneva Conventions. The students (who volunteer for the training) are subjected to interrogation methods that include "stripping students of their clothing, placing them in stress positions, putting hoods over their heads, disrupting their sleep, treating them like animals, subjecting them to loud music and flashing lights, and exposing them to extreme temperatures." The committee notes that some SERE schools in the past also included waterboarding. All the forbidden techniques are based, in part, on the techniques that were used by Chinese interrogators on U.S. POWs during the Korean War (1950–1953). The purpose of the SERE schools is to expose students to interrogation techniques to which they might be subjected if captured by an enemy that does not adhere to the Geneva Conventions and to help them to withstand the techniques.

The committee finds that after the War on Terror began, "senior government officials" began asking the

JPRA for training not on how to withstand the illegal techniques, but on how to administer them to detainees. The committee points out, however, that the JPRA personnel who teach these techniques in SERE schools are not trained interrogators—that is, they have not been trained in how best to obtain reliable and useful information from prisoners. Nevertheless, the JPRA was actively involved in detainee interrogations for at least two years at the request of senior U.S. officials. At the same time, senior lawyers within the Bush administration and the DOD were writing legal opinions "justifying the legality of the techniques."

The committee notes that in September 2002 officials at Guantánamo Bay specifically asked for permission from Rumsfeld to use SERE interrogation techniques on detainees. In December 2002 Rumsfeld authorized the use of most, but not all, of the requested SERE techniques on Guantánamo Bay detainees based on recommendations from William J. Haynes II (1958–), the general counsel for the DOD. The committee finds that other senior legal officials within the DOD, particularly the chief counsels for the U.S. Army, the U.S. Air Force, the U.S. Navy, and the U.S. Marine Corps, had expressed serious reservations about the effectiveness and legality of the techniques. In addition, the committee claims that "Rumsfeld authorized the techniques without apparently providing any written guidance as to how they should be administered." Nevertheless, SERE trainers were dispatched to Guantánamo Bay, and interrogators there began using the techniques. The committee notes that allegations of detainee mistreatment were soon raised by some DOD personnel and FBI agents at the facility.

In January 2003 Rumsfeld reversed his earlier decision and withdrew his approval for use of the SERE techniques at Guantánamo Bay. However, his December 2002 memorandum had already been widely distributed to military officers in Afghanistan and Iraq, who believed that the SERE techniques had Rumsfeld's express support. SERE trainers were summoned to those countries, and SERE techniques were subsequently used on detainees, including those at the Abu Ghraib detention facility in Iraq. In 2004 public allegations about detainee mistreatment led senior DOD officials to cancel all future plans for SERE training for the purpose of detainee interrogation.

The committee concludes that "the abuse of detainees in U.S. custody cannot simply be attributed to the actions of 'a few bad apples' acting on their own. The fact is that senior officials in the United States government solicited information on how to use aggressive techniques, redefined the law to create the appearance of their legality, and authorized their use against detainees. Those efforts damaged our ability to collect accurate intelligence that could save lives, strengthened the hand of our enemies, and compromised our moral authority."

The Obama Administration

During his 2008 presidential campaign, Senator Barack Obama (1961–) pledged to end interrogation techniques that were considered to be torture and to close the Guantánamo Bay detention facility. On January 22, 2009—two days after his inauguration as president—Obama issued three executive orders that were related to detainees. Executive Order 13491, titled "Ensuring Lawful Interrogations" (http://edocket.access.gpo.gov/2009/pdf/E9-1885.pdf), includes the following major directives:

- Revokes Bush's Executive Order 13340 and all previous executive directives and regulations concerning detainee interrogations that are inconsistent with Executive Order 13491

- Establishes the standards of the Geneva Conventions as the minimum standards for detainee treatment

- Forbids the use by DOD personnel of any interrogation techniques or methods not authorized by and listed in *FM 2-22.3*

- Requires non-DOD personnel (such as FBI agents) to use interrogation processes "substantially equivalent" to those in *FM 2-22.3* or to use other "non-coercive techniques"

- Requires the CIA to close as quickly as possible any detention facilities under its operation and forbids the agency from operating any such detention facilities in the future

- Requires all departments and agencies of the federal government to allow the International Committee of the Red Cross "timely" access to any detainee

PROSECUTION OF BUSH ADMINISTRATION OFFICIALS? In April 2009 the Obama administration released to the public Bush administration legal memorandums that justified the harsh interrogation techniques that some consider to be torture. Mark Thompson describes in "Obama's Growing Dilemma on Torture Prosecution" (*Time*, April 22, 2009) the intense pressure on Obama from fellow Democrats and from human rights groups to prosecute Bush administration officials for sanctioning the interrogation techniques. Thompson notes that Obama had already declined to pursue prosecution of the interrogators themselves, because they were following "government-approved guidelines." In an April 19, 2009, interview on the television show *This Week* (http://abcnews.go.com/ThisWeek/story?id=7373578&page=1), Chief of Staff Rahm Emanuel (1959–) said Obama also believed that the officials who devised the interrogation policies should not be prosecuted.

LEGAL RIGHTS OF DETAINEES

Besides the controversy over detainees' human rights, there is also debate concerning their legal rights.

These two types of rights are intertwined. For example, the Geneva Conventions prohibit countries at war from subjecting captured individuals to criminal punishments, including executions, that are conducted without due legal process. This provision (http://www.un-documents .net/gc-1.htm) specifically requires that defendants receive "all the judicial guarantees which are recognized as indispensable by civilized peoples." The U.S. Constitution sets forth many judicial guarantees and legal rights for U.S. citizens. As explained in Chapter 8, conflicts between legal rights and national security concerns often arise during wartime. This has certainly been the case for U.S. citizens who have been detained during the War on Terror. The issue is even more complicated for alien (i.e., noncitizen) detainees. Controversy rages over what, if any, legal rights that are protected by the U.S. justice system should be afforded to alien detainees. As a result, many court battles have taken place regarding detainee legal rights and the power of the executive branch (i.e., the president and the agencies under his control) over detainees.

Another consideration has been the admittedly "harsh" (some say tortuous) interrogation techniques that were used on detainees during the Bush administration. Under U.S. law information that is obtained via torture from a criminal suspect is not admissible in court. In fact, torture is forbidden under the U.S. Constitution's prohibition against "cruel and unusual punishment." However, U.S. officials have certainly extracted information, perhaps confessions, from detainees using measures that could be considered "cruel and unusual." This is particularly true for the so-called high-value detainees, such as

Khalid Sheikh Mohammed (1964–), who has been in U.S. custody since 2003 and is believed to have been the primary planner behind the 9/11 terrorist attacks. The article "Khalid Sheikh Mohammed Guantanamo Hearing Gets Chaotic Start" (BBC News, May 6, 2012) notes that "CIA documents confirm that he was subjected to simulated drowning, known as waterboarding, 183 times."

The Obama administration has instituted legal maneuvers that it claims will help ensure "fair trials" for the detainees. However, critics complain that the measures fall far short of what is acceptable under U.S. and international law.

A chronological listing of the major milestones in the battle over detainee legal rights is provided in Table 9.5.

The Bush-Era Military Commissions

As noted in Chapter 8, in September 2001 Congress passed the Authorization for Use of Military Force (AUMF; http://frwebgate.access.gpo.gov/cgi-bin/getdoc .cgi?dbname=107_cong_public_laws&docid=f:publ040 .107.pdf), which states: "The President is authorized to use all necessary and appropriate force against those nations, organizations, or persons he determines planned, authorized, committed, or aided the terrorist attacks that occurred on September 11, 2001, or harbored such organizations or persons, in order to prevent any future acts of international terrorism against the United States by such nations, organizations or persons."

Two months later, in November 2001, President Bush signed the military order Detention, Treatment, and Trial of Certain Non-citizens in the War against

TABLE 9.5

Important milestones in U.S. policies regarding detainee treatment, 2001–11

Milestone	Date	Description
Authorization for Use of Military Force	September 18, 2001	Public Law 107-40
Detention, Treatment, and Trial of Certain Non-Citizens in the War Against Terrorism	November 13, 2001	President George W. Bush–Military Order
Hamdi v. Rumsfeld	June 28, 2004	Supreme Court case
Rasul v. Bush	June 28, 2004	Supreme Court case
Combatant Status Review Tribunal Process	July 7, 2004	Process established by U.S. Department of Defense
Detainee Treatment Act of 2005	December 30, 2005	Public Law 109-148
Hamdan v. Rumsfeld	June 29, 2006	Supreme Court case
Memorandum regarding application of Common Article 3 of the Geneva Conventions to the treatment of detainees in the Department of Defense	July 7, 2006	Department of Defense order that detainees be treated in accordance with Common Article 3 of the Geneva Conventions
Military Commissions Act of 2006	October 17, 2006	Public Law 109-366, Title X
Interpretation of the Geneva Conventions Common Article 3 as Applied to a Program of Detention and Interrogation Operated by the Central Intelligence Agency	July 20, 2007	President George W. Bush–Executive Order 13340
Boumediene v. Bush	June 12, 2008	Supreme Court case
Ensuring Lawful Interrogations, Review and Disposition of Individuals Detained at the Guantanamo Bay Naval Base and Close of Detention Facilities, and Review of Detention Policy Options	January 22, 2009	President Barack Obama–Executive Orders 13491, 13492, and 13493
Military Commissions Act of 2009	October 28, 2009	Public Law 111-84, Title XVIII
al-Bahani v. Obama	January 5, 2010	U.S. District Court of Appeals case
National Defense Authorization Act	December 31, 2011	Public Law 112-81, Title X, Subtitle D

SOURCE: Created by Kim Masters Evans for Gale, 2012

Terrorism (http://www.law.cornell.edu/background/war power/fr1665.pdf), which granted him power to determine whether a captured person was a member of al Qaeda and had committed terrorist acts. It also stated that military commissions would be used to try unlawful enemy combatants who were captured during the War on Terror.

The use of military commissions (tribunals) in such situations has historical precedent. In *Ex Parte Quirin* (317 U.S. 1 [1942]), the U.S. Supreme Court decided that President Franklin D. Roosevelt (1882–1945) had the authority to convene a military tribunal to try eight civilian Germans who had entered the United States to commit sabotage during World War II. Six of the men were ultimately executed by electric chair. The court noted that "unlawful combatants" could be subjected to trial and punishment by military tribunals, rather than by civilian courts.

Hamdi v. Rumsfeld and *Rasul v. Bush*

In June 2004 the U.S. Supreme Court issued two rulings regarding detainee legal rights. The first ruling, *Hamdi v. Rumsfeld* (542 U.S. 507), involved Yaser Esam Hamdi (1980–), a U.S. citizen. Hamdi was captured in Afghanistan in 2001 and was accused of being part of a Taliban military unit. He was turned over to U.S. authorities, who labeled him as an "enemy combatant." Initially imprisoned at the Guantánamo Bay detention facility, Hamdi was transferred to a U.S. brig in 2002 after authorities learned that he was a U.S. citizen. His father filed a petition for a writ of habeas corpus (a legal procedure in which a court can order that a prisoner held by the government be presented to the court for determination if the imprisonment is legal or not). The petition alleged that Hamdi was being held illegally without access to legal counsel and without being formally charged with a crime, both of which violate the U.S. Constitution. The Supreme Court ruled in favor of Hamdi, finding that even though the military had the authority to detain him, he had the right as a U.S. citizen to contest his detention before a "neutral decision-maker." Several months after the ruling, Hamdi was released without being charged. The court did recognize, however, the authority of the executive branch to hold detainees for the duration of the War on Terror.

The second ruling, *Rasul v. Bush* (542 U.S. 466), involved two Australians and 12 Kuwaitis who were being held as enemy combatants at the Guantánamo Bay detention facility. The detainees filed a petition in U.S. district court challenging the legality of their detention. They claimed they had never been charged with a crime, permitted to have legal counsel, or provided access to the courts. The district court considered the petition a request for habeas corpus and dismissed it

because this right has previously been deemed not to extend to aliens detained outside "United States sovereign territory." However, the U.S. Supreme Court overruled the district court, ruling that Naval Base Guantánamo Bay is under the "complete jurisdiction and control" of the United States. This ruling precipitated the filing of dozens of habeas corpus petitions on behalf of Guantánamo Bay detainees.

In July 2004 the DOD announced in the press release "Combatant Status Review Tribunal Order Issued" (http://www.defenselink.mil/releases/release.aspx?releaseid=7530) the creation of a Combatant Status Review Tribunal (CSRT) process for detainees held at the Guantánamo Bay detention facility. The DOD described the CSRT "as a forum for detainees to contest their status as enemy combatants."

The Detainee Treatment Act

The Detainee Treatment Act of 2005 is described by Garcia in *Boumediene v. Bush: Guantanamo Detainees' Right to Habeas Corpus* (September 8, 2008, http://fas.org/sgp/crs/natsec/RL34536.pdf). According to Garcia, the act eliminated the jurisdiction of federal courts to consider habeas corpus petitions by aliens who challenged their detention at the Guantánamo Bay detention facility. The U.S. Court of Appeals for the District of Columbia Circuit (the D.C. Appeals Court) was granted sole jurisdiction over the review of determinations made by CSRTs and military commissions. In other words, the act made clear that alien combatants who are detained outside the United States do not have constitutional rights. It also stripped the courts of jurisdiction to hear habeas corpus petitions from detainees.

Hamdan v. Rumsfeld

In June 2006 the Supreme Court ruled in *Hamdan v. Rumsfeld* (548 U.S. 557) that U.S. law does not allow military commissions such as those created by President Bush's military order. The case centered on a Yemeni citizen named Salim Ahmed Hamdan (1979–), who was allegedly a chauffeur for Osama bin Laden (1957?–2011) in Afghanistan. In 2001 Hamdan was captured and sent to the Guantánamo Bay detention facility. In 2004 he was officially charged with conspiracy to commit war crimes, murder, and terrorism. Hamdan's lawyers successfully argued that the president did not have the power under the Constitution to establish military commissions to try enemy combatants. Following the ruling, President Bush announced his intentions to work with Congress to set up a suitable legal process for detained enemy combatants.

In July 2006 the DOD issued the memorandum "Application of Common Article 3 of the Geneva Conventions to the Treatment of Detainees in the Department of Defense" (http://www.washingtonpost.com/wp-srv/

nation/nationalsecurity/genevaconvdoc.pdf). The DOD ordered all of its personnel to treat detainees in accordance with Common Article 3 of the Geneva Conventions. Common Article 3 prohibits "the passing of sentences and the carrying out of executions without previous judgment pronounced by a regularly constituted court, affording all the judicial guarantees which are recognized as indispensable by civilized peoples." This was interpreted to mean that detainees have a legal right to challenge their detention. That same month congressional hearings began on developing a constitutional process for trying detainees. One of the key issues was the handling of classified information during trial. DOD officials testified that the court-martial process under the Uniform Code of Military Justice is not suitable for detainees, because it could require the release of intelligence information that could harm national security.

Military Commissions Act of 2006

Congress responded to *Hamdan v. Rumsfeld* by passing the MCA of 2006. The act established procedures for the use of military commissions to try alien enemy combatants who engage in hostilities against the United States. Jennifer K. Elsea of the Congressional Research Service describes the act in *The Military Commissions Act of 2006: Analysis of Procedural Rules and Comparison with Previous DOD Rules and the Uniform Code of Military Justice* (September 27, 2007, http://www.fas .org/sgp/crs/natsec/RL33688.pdf). Elsea explains that the act authorizes the president to establish military commissions and allows the DOD to create rules for the commissions that differ from the rules of the Uniform Code of Military Justice.

In March 2007 the Australian David Hicks (1975–) was the first Guantánamo Bay detainee sentenced under the MCA of 2006. Detained since 2002, Hicks was charged with many serious crimes, including attempted murder and conducting terrorist acts for the Taliban in Afghanistan. He ultimately pleaded guilty to only one charge (providing material support for terrorism) and was turned over to Australia to serve the remaining nine months of his sentence.

Boumediene v. Bush

In June 2008 the U.S. Supreme Court ruled in *Boumediene v. Bush* (553 U.S. ___; combined with *Al Odah v. United States*) that alien enemy combatants detained at the Guantánamo Bay detention facility do have the constitutional privilege of habeas corpus. Garcia describes this ruling in detail in *Boumediene v. Bush: Guantanamo Detainees' Right to Habeas Corpus*. According to Garcia, the court found unconstitutional the section of the MCA of 2006 that stripped the courts of jurisdiction to hear habeas corpus petitions.

Hamdan Is Sentenced

In August 2008 Hamdan was found guilty of providing material support to terrorism; however, he was acquitted of a more serious conspiracy charge. Even though Hamdan faced a sentence of life in prison, he was given a sentence of only 66 months. Because he had already been detained for five years and one month, the judge ruled that Hamdan would serve only five additional months in prison. In November 2008 Hamdan was transferred to his native country of Yemen to serve the remainder of his sentence. He was released from prison in January 2009. The article "Yemen Releases Former bin Laden Driver from Jail" (Reuters, January 11, 2009) reports that Hamdan "signed a pledge not to commit violent acts" after his release.

Obama's Executive Orders

As noted earlier, in January 2009 President Obama issued three executive orders (13491, 13492, and 13493) dealing with detainees. Executive Order 13491 has already been discussed. Executive Order 13492, titled "Review and Disposition of Individuals Detained at the Guantánamo Bay Naval Base and Closure of Detention Facilities" (http://edocket.access.gpo.gov/2009/pdf/E9-1893.pdf), states that between 2002 and 2009 approximately 800 detainees deemed by the DOD as enemy combatants had been detained at the Guantánamo Bay detention facility. More than 500 of those detainees had subsequently been moved to their home countries or other countries. The executive order notes that most of the remaining 200 detainees had been detained at Guantánamo Bay for at least four years. It calls for a "prompt and thorough review" of each individual's circumstances and legal status and the closure of the Guantánamo Bay detention facility within one year or upon finalization of the dispositions of all the detainees.

The executive order resulted in the formation of the Guantanamo Detainee Review Task Force that in January 2010 issued a report specifying on a case-by-case basis which Guantánamo Bay detainees should be prosecuted, which should be released, and which should be detained without trial. Peter Finn reports in "Justice Task Force Recommends about 50 Guantanamo Detainees Be Held Indefinitely" (*Washington Post*, January 22, 2010) that the task force assessed the cases of 196 detainees at the Guantánamo Bay detention facility. Finn explains that of the 196 detainees, the task force recommended that approximately 35 should be prosecuted in federal or military courts; about 110 should be released, either immediately or eventually; and about 50 should be detained without trial. Finn notes that human rights groups are opposed to detainees being held indefinitely without trial. However, the Obama administration reportedly believes that such detainees are "dangerous to release but unprosecutable because officials fear trials could compromise intelligence-gathering and because detainees could challenge evidence obtained through coercion."

Executive Order 13493, titled "Review of Detention Policy Options" (http://edocket.access.gpo.gov/2009/pdf/E9-1895.pdf), orders the creation of a Special Interagency Task Force on Detainee Disposition to review "lawful options available to the Federal government with respect to the apprehension, detention, trial, transfer, release, or other disposition of individuals captured or apprehended" during U.S. military and counterterrorism operations. In July 2009 the task force issued the preliminary report "Memorandum for the Attorney General" (http://www.fas.org/irp/agency/doj/detention072009.pdf), in which it recommended changes to the MCA of 2006 to ensure that military commissions are "fair, effective, and lawful" and outlined the criteria for determining whether a detainee should be tried in a federal court or by a military commission.

Military Commissions Act of 2009

In late 2009 Congress passed the National Defense Authorization Act for Fiscal Year 2010, which included the Military Commissions Act of 2009 (MCA of 2009). The MCA of 2009 provides the authority for military tribunals or commissions to try "alien unprivileged enemy belligerents." As noted earlier, aliens are noncitizens of the United States. The act broadly defines "unprivileged enemy belligerents" as individuals who have been members of the al Qaeda terrorist organization and individuals who have "engaged in" or "purposefully and materially supported" hostilities against the United States or its coalition partners. The act details the makeup and activities of the military commissions and specifies particular legal rights for the detainees. One notable provision forbids the use against the accused of statements obtained "by the use of torture or by cruel, inhuman, or degrading treatment," as defined by the Detainee Treatment Act of 2005.

Detainee Trials within the United States?

The Obama administration had hoped to move some Guantánamo Bay detainees to a detention facility within the United States. However, the plan encountered stiff opposition from members of Congress who either oppose transfers to the United States on principle or only want temporary transfers for the purpose of conducting military commissions or trials.

As noted earlier, Khalid Sheikh Mohammed has been in U.S. custody since 2003 and is believed to be the primary planner behind the 9/11 terrorist attacks. In November 2009 the Obama administration announced that Mohammed and four other detainees with ties to the 9/11 attacks would be tried in federal court in New York City. Some critics are opposed to the idea of granting civilian (nonmilitary) trials to high-profile terrorists for fear that the accused terrorists will have access to constitutional rights that they should not be given.

In January 2010 the Obama administration abandoned its plan to hold Mohammed's trial in New York City after the city's mayor and other officials raised concerns about the tight security measures that would be required. In addition, since 2009 Congress has passed several laws that prohibit the use of DOD funds to transfer Guantánamo Bay detainees to the United States.

The Obama-Era Military Commissions

In March 2011 President Obama announced that the U.S. government will use military commissions to try Guantánamo Bay detainees. Even though he also called for detainees to be prosecuted in U.S. criminal courts, when appropriate, analysts indicate that this is not likely to happen.

That same month President Obama issued Executive Order 13567, titled "Periodic Review of Individuals Detained at Guantanamo Bay Naval Station Pursuant to the Authorization for Use of Military Force" (http://www.whitehouse.gov/the-press-office/2011/03/07/executive-order-periodic-review-individuals-detained-guant-namo-bay-nava). It requires detainees to undergo periodic status reviews before a periodic review board (PRB). The PRB will determine whether each detainee should be further detained or released. After an initial review each detainee who is kept in captivity will undergo a subsequent PRB review every three years. Critics immediately complained that the new process permits indefinite detention without trial and essentially ensures that the Guantánamo Bay detention facility will not be closed as President Obama had originally promised.

THE 9/11 CHARGES. In June 2011 murder and terrorism charges were refiled against Khalid Sheikh Mohammed and four other men accused of participating in the 9/11 attacks. The five men were originally charged in 2008, but those charges were dropped in 2009 when the Obama administration attempted unsuccessfully to switch the men to criminal court jurisdiction in New York City.

In May 2012 the five men had their arraignment hearing at the Guantánamo Bay detention facility, during which the formal charges against them were presented. The article "Khalid Sheikh Mohammed Guantanamo Hearing Gets Chaotic Start" indicates that the defendants used a variety of delaying tactics and refused to answer questions or enter pleas during their long and "chaotic" hearing. Their trials by military commissions are tentatively expected to begin in mid-2013.

Detainee Dispositions

The U.S. Supreme Court's decision in *Boumediene v. Bush* unleashed a stream of habeas petitions from Guantánamo Bay detainees to the D.C. Appeals Court.

In 2009 Ghaleb Nassar al-Bihani (1981?–), a Yemeni citizen and detainee, contested his denied petition in an appeal to the D.C. Appeals Court. Al-Bihani is alleged to have been a cook associated with the Taliban. He was captured in Afghanistan and had been held without charge or trial at the Guantánamo Bay detention facility since 2001. In *al-Bahani v. Obama* (590 F. 3d 866 [2010]), the appeals court upheld the lower court's decision. Al-Bihani's lawyers argued that his indefinite detention violated international laws of war. However, the appeals court rejected this notion, noting that the AUMF and subsequent U.S. laws permit indefinite detention. The U.S. Supreme Court declined to review the case.

Likewise, in June 2012 the U.S. Supreme Court rejected appeals by seven other Guantánamo Bay detainees. In "Guantanamo Prisoner Appeals Rejected by U.S. High Court" (Bloomberg.com, June 11, 2012), Laurie Asseo notes that the appeals cases hinged on the procedures that were used by the district court in considering the detainees' habeas petitions. For example, one appeal argued that the district court had improperly allowed hearsay evidence against the accused. Hearsay evidence is not generally admissible in U.S. criminal court cases. However, the appeals court ruled that strict interpretations of U.S. law do not apply to the detainees. According to Asseo, another appeal complained that "lower courts 'have erected insurmountable barriers'" for the detainees to overcome in their defense.

As of the summer of 2012, various news media outlets estimated that 160 to 170 detainees remained at the Guantánamo Bay detention facility. James Vicini indicates in "U.S. Top Court Rejects Appeals by Guantanamo Prisoners" (Reuters, June 11, 2012) that as of June 2012 more than 30 detainees had been ordered released and 27 detainees had their petitions denied upon appeal. At that time, approximately 90 detainees seeking release had "unresolved cases."

In July 2012 a Sudanese detainee at the Guantánamo Bay detention facility was released under a plea deal and returned to his native country. In "Guantánamo Prisoner Is Repatriated to Sudan" (*New York Times*, July 11, 2012), Charlie Savage notes that Ibrahim al-Qosi (1960–) was convicted of being a member of the al Qaeda terrorist group and pleaded guilty before a military commission to conspiracy and supporting terrorism. According to Savage, al-Qosi is the first detainee to be returned to his native country after being convicted under the new military commission system that was established by the Obama administration.

National Defense Authorization Act for Fiscal Year 2012

As of October 2012, the most recently passed federal law covering detainees was the National Defense Authorization Act for Fiscal Year 2012. As explained in Chapter 8, the law funds the DOD for fiscal year 2012 and includes special provisions devoted to U.S. counterterrorism activities. (See Table 9.6.) Among other things, the law prohibits the use of DOD funds for the transfer or release of detainees from the Guantánamo Bay detention facility to the United States. It also prohibits the use of DOD funds to construct or modify detention facilities within the United States that might be intended to house Guantánamo Bay detainees. Overall, the act effectively ensures that the Guantánamo Bay detention facility will remain in operation indefinitely.

TABLE 9.6

Counterterrorism sections of the National Defense Authorization Act for Fiscal Year 2012

Title X—General Provisions, Subtitle D—Counterterrorism	
Sec. 1021.	Affirmation of authority of the armed forces of the United States to detain covered persons pursuant to the Authorization for Use of Military Force.
Sec. 1022.	Military custody for foreign al-Qaeda terrorists.
Sec. 1023.	Procedures for periodic detention review of individuals detained at United States Naval Station, Guantanamo Bay, Cuba.
Sec. 1024.	Procedures for status determinations.
Sec. 1025.	Requirement for national security protocols governing detainee communications.
Sec. 1026.	Prohibition on use of funds to construct or modify facilities in the United States to house detainees transferred from United States Naval Station, Guantanamo Bay, Cuba.
Sec. 1027.	Prohibition on the use of funds for the transfer or release of individuals detained at United States Naval Station, Guantanamo Bay, Cuba.
Sec. 1028.	Requirements for certifications relating to the transfer of detainees at United States Naval Station, Guantanamo Bay, Cuba, to foreign countries and other foreign entities.
Sec. 1029.	Requirement for consultation regarding prosecution of terrorists.
Sec. 1030.	Clarification of right to plead guilty in trial of capital offense by military commission.
Sec. 1031.	Counterterrorism operational briefing requirement.
Sec. 1032.	National security planning guidance to deny safe havens to al-Qaeda and its violent extremist affiliates.
Sec. 1033.	Extension of authority to make rewards for combating terrorism.
Sec. 1034.	Amendments relating to the Military Commissions Act of 2009.

SOURCE: Adapted from *National Defense Authorization Act for Fiscal Year 2012*, U.S. Government Printing Office, December 2011, http://www.gpo.gov/fdsys/pkg/BILLS-112hr1540enr/pdf/BILLS-112hr1540enr.pdf (accessed July 25, 2012)

CHAPTER 10

U.S. RELATIONS WITH THE ISLAMIC WORLD

Terrorism became a serious threat to U.S. national security after World War II (1939–1945). The vast majority of terrorist acts committed against Americans during this period were perpetrated by Muslims, or at least by people who claim to be acting in accordance with Islamic principles. This raises troubling issues about the nature and future of relations between the United States and Muslims around the world. Do terrorists who claim to be Muslims represent the true spirit of Islam, or are they rebels and rogues who have hijacked the religion for their own violent purposes? How deep are the ideological and political divides between the Islamic and non-Islamic world? Can they be bridged?

WHAT IS ISLAM?

Islam translates into English as "submission" and advocates submission to God by its followers. As described in Chapter 1, Muslims believe that during the seventh century the angel Gabriel revealed God's messages to the prophet Muhammad (c. 570–632). Those messages were eventually written down to form the Koran, Islam's holy book.

Sharia is the body of Islamic law and is based on the Koran. It covers all aspects of life, rather than just matters of a legal nature. The hadith are also important to Muslims. They are a collection of Muhammad's sayings and actions that help Muslims follow a way of life (called Sunna) modeled after Muhammad and based on the Koran.

The Council on American Islamic Relations (CAIR) notes in "About Islam and American Muslims" (2012, http://www.cair.com/AboutIslam/IslamBasics.aspx) that there are five pillars of Islam:

- Declaration of faith—a person becomes a Muslim by declaring the following: "There is no deity but God, and Muhammad is the messenger of God"

- Obligatory prayers—Muslims are required to pray five times per day at set times

- Zakat—this is charitable giving to those in need

- Fasting—Muslims fast from sunrise to sunset during the Islamic lunar month called Ramadan if they are physically able to do so

- Hajj—this is a pilgrimage to Mecca, a sacred site in Saudi Arabia, that all Muslims are supposed to make at least once during their lifetime if they are physically and financially able to do so

Islam recognizes many prophets from the Judeo-Christian tradition, including Abraham (c. 1996–c. 1821 BC), Jacob (1838?–1689 BC), Moses (1392?–1272? BC), David (1000–c. 960 BC), and Solomon (985?–925? BC). Unlike Christians, Muslims believe that Jesus (4? BC–AD 29?) was a prophet rather than a divine messiah. Islam lacks a centralized leadership. There is no single religious leader (such as the pope in Roman Catholicism) who speaks on behalf of all Muslims. In fact, there is not even a structured hierarchy. Islam esteems many respected elders, learned men, and Islamic scholars, some of whom have titles such as mufti (judge) or sheikh (sheik). Prayer, worship, and other religious activities often take place at mosques, which are meeting places for Muslims.

The Diversity of Islam

Different people practice Islam in different ways around the world. While they agree on certain core tenets, they may diverge over many other aspects of their faith. In some cases they may disagree so strongly that one group will not recognize another as being Muslim at all. In this, Islam is no different than any other active and widespread faith or ideology. For example, there are many differences among those who call themselves Christians.

There are two main sects within Islam: Sunni and Shia. Their followers have historical disagreements about issues related to governance and theological interpretations. However, there are also differences among

Muslims that center around social, moral, and political issues. These will be explored in more detail in this chapter.

THE ISLAMIC WORLD

There are various estimates of the number of Muslims in the world. The Pew Forum on Religion and Public Life estimates in *The Future Global Muslim Population Projections for 2010–2030* (January 2011, http://www.pewforum.org/uploadedFiles/Topics/Religious_Affiliation/Muslim/FutureGlobalMuslimPopulation-WebPDF-Feb10.pdf) that in 2010 there were 1.6 billion Muslims, which accounted for 23.4% of the total world population of 6.9 billion. Table 10.1 lists the 10 countries with the largest Muslim populations in 2010. Indonesia, Pakistan, India, and Bangladesh were the top-four countries, with each containing more than 148 million Muslims. It is a common misconception among Americans that all Muslims are Arabs from the Middle East. However, as noted in Chapter 1, Arabs are an ethnic group, not a religious sect. In fact, none of the top-four Muslim countries listed in Table 10.1 contained Arab-majority populations.

According to the Pew Forum on Religion and Public Life, the Muslim population is forecast to increase at approximately twice the rate of the non-Muslim population between 2010 and 2030. By 2030 the Muslim population is projected to be 2.2 billion, or 26.4% of the world's total population. Table 10.2 lists the 10 countries that are expected to have the largest Muslim populations by 2030. Pakistan leads the list with more than 256 million, followed by Indonesia (238.8 million), India (236.2 million), and Bangladesh (187.5 million). By 2030, 79 countries are projected to have at least 1 million Muslim inhabitants, compared with 72 countries in 2010. The vast majority of the Muslims in 2030 will inhabit Asia-Pacific (approximately 60% of the total) and the Middle East and North Africa (approximately 20% of the total).

Many countries in the Islamic world have experienced an explosive population growth over the past two decades. As a result, Islamic countries tend to have younger populations, in general, than the rest of the world. The Central Intelligence Agency (CIA) lists in *The World Factbook* (2012, https://www.cia.gov/library/publications/the-world-factbook/) the median age for countries around the world. The median age is the midline age of the population. In other words, half the population is younger than that age, and half the population is older than that age. According to the CIA, in 2012 the median age in the United States was 37.1 years. By contrast, many Muslim-majority countries had much younger median ages, including Indonesia (28.5 years), Iran (27.4 years), Saudi Arabia (25.7 years), Pakistan (21.9 years), and Yemen (18.3 years).

The Pew Forum on Religion and Public Life estimates that the sectarian breakdown of Muslims in 2010 was 87% to 90% Sunni and 10% to 13% Shia. This breakdown is expected to continue through 2030. As of 2010, the countries with the largest Sunni-majority populations were Egypt, Indonesia, Bangladesh, and Pakistan. In all these nations Sunnis accounted for more than 87% of the Muslim population. The countries with the largest Shia-majority populations in 2010 were Iran, Azerbaijan, Bahrain, and Iraq. At least two-thirds of the Muslims in these nations were Shiites.

TABLE 10.1

Ten countries with the largest Muslim populations, 2010

Country	Estimated Muslim population
Indonesia	204,847,000
Pakistan	178,097,000
India	177,286,000
Bangladesh	148,607,000
Egypt	80,024,000
Nigeria	75,728,000
Iran	74,819,000
Turkey	74,660,000
Algeria	34,780,000
Morocco	32,381,000

Population estimates are rounded to thousands.

SOURCE: "10 Countries with the Largest Number of Muslims in 2010," in *The Future Global Muslim Population Projections for 2010–2030*, Pew Research Center's Forum on Religion & Public Life, January 2011, http://www.pewforum.org/The-Future-of-the-Global-Muslim-Population.aspx (accessed July 25, 2012). From the Pew Research Center's Forum on Religion & Public Life, "The Future of the Global Muslim Population," © 2011, Pew Research Center. http://pewforum.org/.

TABLE 10.2

Ten countries projected to have the largest Muslim populations, 2030

Country	Projected Muslim population
Pakistan	256,117,000
Indonesia	238,833,000
India	236,182,000
Bangladesh	187,506,000
Nigeria	116,832,000
Egypt	105,065,000
Iran	89,626,000
Turkey	89,127,000
Afghanistan	50,527,000
Iraq	48,350,000

Population estimates are rounded to thousands.

SOURCE: "10 Countries with the Largest Projected Number of Muslims in 2030," in *The Future Global Muslim Population Projections for 2010–2030*, Pew Research Center's Forum on Religion & Public Life, January 2011, http://www.pewforum.org/The-Future-of-the-Global-Muslim-Population.aspx (accessed July 25, 2012). From the Pew Research Center's Forum on Religion & Public Life, "The Future of the Global Muslim Population," © 2011, Pew Research Center. http://pewforum.org/.

HISTORICAL CONTEXT FOR U.S. RELATIONS

The roots of U.S.-Muslim relations can be traced back to medieval clashes between the Islamic world and the European kingdoms. The Middle Ages encompassed a period in history that began with the fall of the Roman Empire during the fifth century. At one time the Roman Empire covered a great swath of land from western Asia, across the Middle East, and west to Spain and Britain. A remnant—now known as the Byzantine Empire— survived from the fourth century to the 15th century along the eastern Mediterranean Sea and had its capital at Constantinople (modern-day Istanbul, Turkey).

The early centuries of the Middle Ages are called the Dark Ages because few known scientific and cultural achievements were made by Western societies during the period. This was not the case in the Islamic world (which began with the seventh-century establishment of Islam by the prophet Muhammad). Arab and Persian scholars made many important advancements in science and math, particularly in algebra, geometry, chemistry, and astronomy. Some historians refer to the period between 750 and 1200 as the Islamic Golden Age.

Crusades

During the Middle Ages Catholic Church authorities wielded great power over the peoples of Europe. This was especially true of the popes—the supreme leaders of the Roman Catholic Church. Catholicism was the dominant religion of Europe throughout the Middle Ages. Medieval Europeans were politically divided among many competing kingdoms and tribal groups. However, they were often united by their shared religion. Such was the case in 1095, when the Byzantine emperor Alexius I Comnenus (c. 1048–1118) asked Pope Urban II (1042?–1099) for military assistance against the Islamic tribes that had recently captured Jerusalem—a city considered sacred by Christians, Jews, and Muslims. In 1096 armies of European knights and soldiers began the first of what would later be called the Crusades. In 1099 the European armies captured Jerusalem, only to lose it in 1187 to Muslim forces led by Saladin (1138–1193)—a renowned figure in Islamic history. In 1192 Saladin and King Richard I (1157–1199) of England signed a treaty agreeing that Jerusalem would remain under Muslim control but Christian pilgrims would be allowed to visit the city. Crusaders captured the city again in 1229 only to lose it to the Muslims for the last time in 1244. Thus, for nearly two centuries European armies followed papal orders to fight for control of Muslim-held territory in the Middle East.

Within Western history and literature, the Crusades have become highly romanticized adventures that focus on the feats of King Richard I and the European knights. By contrast, the Islamic world regards the Crusades as a brutal invasion by European nations that foreshadows later colonial rule. Peter Ford reports in "Europe Cringes at Bush 'Crusade' against Terrorists" (*Christian Science Monitor*, September 19, 2001) that President George W. Bush (1946–) was chastised by Muslims after the September 11, 2001 (9/11), terrorist attacks for referring to U.S. retaliation as a "crusade" against terrorism. For Americans, it was a clue that events centuries old still resonate with many Muslim people.

Colonial Resentment

By the 13th century the Crusades were ending, and the Islamic world entered a new political age under the rule of the Ottoman Empire (named after Osman I [c. 1259–1326], its first leader). The Ottomans eventually conquered the Byzantine Empire and controlled much of Eurasia. During the 1500s the Ottoman Empire reached the height of its geopolitical importance with territories around the Red, Black, and Mediterranean Seas. It included much of modern-day Turkey and the Middle East and extended to the outskirts of modern-day Vienna, Austria, in Europe. A series of wars with European powers and the growth of nationalism within regions controlled by the Ottoman Empire gradually reduced its strength and influence.

The death blow for the Ottoman Empire came during World War I (1914–1918), when it was defeated and dissolved by the Allies. The League of Nations placed Iraq and Palestine under the administration of Great Britain, and Syria and Lebanon under the administration of France. All nations but Palestine eventually achieved their independence. The lack of an official homeland for the Palestinians became a major point of contention in the Middle East.

Even before the demise of the Ottoman Empire, most Muslim nations fell under European control at one time or another. Great Britain, France, and Italy all had colonies in the Middle East and/or North Africa during the 1800s and early 1900s. Even nations that were not colonized experienced some level of protection or influence by European powers, particularly Great Britain. The major exception is Saudi Arabia, which has been under continuous Muslim control for centuries.

By the 1950s most Muslim countries had achieved their independence. However, resentment about colonial rule and interference still plays a major factor in Middle Eastern politics. Even though the United States did not exist at the time of the Crusades and was not a colonial power in the Middle East like its European allies, it must still contend with old grievances in the region. In "Roots of Rage" (*Time*, September 23, 2001), Lisa Beyer notes "the U.S. inherits the weight of centuries of Muslim bitterness over the Crusades and other military campaigns, plus decades of indignation over colonialism."

IDEOLOGICAL DIFFERENCES

In many cases, there are deep differences between the Islamic and non-Islamic world regarding political, social, and moral ideologies. These typically relate to one key point: the role of religion in a nation's government and legal system. Most Islamic nations strongly intertwine their religious beliefs into their mode of governance and rule of law. This is not true in much of the non-Islamic world, particularly Western nations that champion the separation of church and state.

Political and Legal Systems

Many followers of Islam feel that it should influence all aspects of society. They see it as a method for living life, governing nations, and maintaining law and order. For example, Saudi Arabia uses the Koran and Sunna as its Constitution. According to the Saudi Network, in "Saudi Arabia—Constitution" (2012, http://www.the-saudi.net/saudi-arabia/saudi-constitution.htm), the nation's rulers are believed to derive their power from the Koran. The government is a political system called a theocracy (a government that is ruled by or subject to religious authority). Iran also has a strongly theocratic government. Since the 1979 Iranian Revolution an Islamic cleric has been the supreme leader and chief of state. Some governments in the Middle East are more secular (not controlled by religion) than others, with Turkey being considered the most secular nation in the region.

Many Muslim countries are ruled by autocrats (rulers with vast or unlimited power). These include kings in monarchies in which rule remains in the royal family. Examples include Saudi Arabia, Jordan, Morocco, and Kuwait. Several Islamic countries have less autocratic forms of government, including Indonesia and Egypt.

Muslim nations allow various degrees of democratic representation. In 2005 and 2011 Saudi Arabia conducted limited municipal elections; however, only men were allowed to vote and run for office. The Saudi government has promised that women will be allowed to vote and run for office in the planned 2015 elections. Iran has elections that determine the nation's president and legislative members. Turkey is often heralded as the most democratic nation in the Muslim world. Formerly part of the Ottoman Empire, it evolved into a strong democracy after achieving independence.

Toni Johnson and Lauren Vriens of the Council on Foreign Relations explain in "Islam: Governing under Sharia" (October 24, 2011, http://www.cfr.org/religion/islam-governing-under-sharia/p8034) that sharia means "path" in Arabic. It is based on the Koran, the Sunna, interpretations by legal scholars, and "the consensus of the Muslim community." Sharia basically provides a legal code for dealing with both criminal and civil matters, such as marriage, divorce, and inheritance. Sharia is applied in varying degrees in Muslim countries. Johnson and Vriens note that Saudi Arabia's legal system strictly adheres to sharia, but that other Muslim-majority nations have a two-part system that includes both secular and sharia courts. The secular courts deal with criminal matters, whereas the sharia courts oversee civil matters (e.g., family law). Criminal punishments under sharia can be notoriously brutal, including amputations, flogging, and death by stoning; however, Johnson and Vriens point out that these measures are seldom used and serve more as a deterrent to criminal behavior.

Tolerance for Other Religions

Religious tolerance (the tolerance of a government and its people toward religions other than any official or majority religion) is a controversial topic in U.S. relations with Islamic nations. In the Western world religious tolerance is generally favored as a means to further social harmony. This is not the case in much of the Muslim world, where strict adherence to religious traditions and teachings requires complete devotion to the Islamic faith.

The U.S. Department of State (DOS) issues an annual report that assesses the state of religious freedom around the world. In *Annual Report on International Religious Freedom: 2011* (2011, http://www.state.gov/j/drl/rls/irf/religiousfreedom/index.htm#wrapper), the DOS states, "Everyone has the right to freedom of thought, conscience, and religion; this right includes freedom to change his religion or belief, and freedom either alone or in community with others and in public or private, to manifest his religion or belief in teaching, practice, worship and observance."

Many Muslim-majority nations have declared Islam their official religion in their constitutions. The constitutions of some Islamic countries also allow, in theory, for freedom of other religious beliefs and expressions. This is true for Egypt and Iran. However, the DOS explains that the Egyptian government "places restrictions on these rights in policy and practice" by failing to investigate or prosecute citizens who are accused of violent acts against peoples of minority religions. The DOS cites significant problems in Iran of government-sanctioned (allowed or even encouraged) discrimination, harassment, and intimidation of people who are members of non-Islam or non-Shia religious groups. Shia is the major form of Islam practiced in Iran. Extremely conservative Muslim nations, such as Saudi Arabia, do not provide any legal rights for people to practice a religion other than Islam. In fact, the public practice of a non-Islamic religion is forbidden by law. Likewise, converting from Islam to another religion is considered to be a crime in some predominantly Muslim countries.

Freedom of Speech

Freedom of speech is another highly regarded principle in Western democracies. As such, Western speakers and writers feel free to openly discuss matters of religion, including matters that relate to Islam. This has led to clashes with Muslims who hold many subjects within Islam to be so sacred or sensitive that they cannot be discussed in a manner deemed disrespectful. In addition, most Muslims consider it blasphemous to visually depict God or the prophet Muhammad in any media, including artwork.

In 1988 the Indian-born writer Salman Rushdie (1947–) published in Great Britain *The Satanic Verses*, which included dreamlike sequences involving Muhammad and the Koran. The book sparked outrage among many Muslims who felt it was blasphemous. Ruhollah Khomeini (1902?–1989), the supreme leader of Iran, issued a fatwa (religious edict) calling on Muslims around the world to kill Rushdie. The author was forced to go into hiding. The incident severely strained Iran's relations with other nations, particularly Great Britain, which severed diplomatic ties with Iran. During the late 1990s moderates within the Iranian government played down the fatwa. However, Iran took a conservative turn in 2005. The article "Iran Adamant over Rushdie Fatwa" (BBC News, February 12, 2005) states that the fatwa against Rushdie was reaffirmed that same year by Iran's religious leaders.

The provocative 10-minute film *Submission: Part 1* was released in 2004 in the Netherlands. It included several naked women with verses from the Koran written on their bodies. The film was a commentary on the alleged mistreatment of women in Islamic society. Its release led to the murder of its director, Theo van Gogh (1957–2004; a descendant of the painter Vincent van Gogh [1853–1890]), by Mohammed Bouyeri (1978–), a man of Moroccan-Dutch descent who was affiliated with Islamic extremists. Toby Sterling reports in "Prosecutors: Van Gogh's Alleged Killer Cites Holy War" (*Seattle Times*, January 27, 2005) that the police arrested a dozen conspirators, all members of a terrorist group called the Hofstad network. The prosecutor called the crime "terrorism, inspired by an extreme interpretation of Islam."

Another freedom of speech furor erupted in 2005 after *Jyllands-Posten*, a newspaper in Denmark, published a series of comic strips that featured Muhammad as a character. One of the drawings depicted Muhammad wearing a turban with a bomb underneath it. Muslims reacted with anger. Dozens of people were killed in riots across the Middle East, and Scandinavian embassies and diplomatic offices in the region were attacked and set on fire. The newspaper received many bomb threats, and the comic strip artists had to go into hiding for fear of their lives. Several Muslim countries initiated an economic boycott of Danish goods.

The publication of the comics (or cartoons as they were called in Europe) and the resulting fury sparked a debate across Europe about the freedom of expression. Within a few months the newspaper issued a formal apology. However, in "Why I Published Those Cartoons" (*Washington Post*, February 19, 2006), Flemming Rose, the editor who had published the comics, defends his decision. He argues that the newspaper had a tradition of using satirical drawings to lampoon public figures, even religious ones. He rejected calls for self-censorship by the media to prevent insulting Muslims, noting "if a believer demands that I, as a nonbeliever, observe his taboos in the public domain, he is not asking for my respect, but for my submission. And that is incompatible with a secular democracy."

The furor over the comics did not subside. According to Souad Mekhennet and Alan Cowell, in "Qaeda Group Says It Bombed Embassy" (*New York Times*, June 6, 2008), 17 Danish newspapers republished the comics in February 2008 "as a statement of solidarity and press freedom." The republication reportedly followed the arrest of three Muslims for plotting to kill one of the cartoonists. Several months later, in June 2008, a suicide car bomber attacked the Danish embassy in Islamabad, Pakistan, leaving six people dead. The terrorist group al Qaeda claimed responsibility for the attack as an act of revenge for the Danish comics.

Frank Jordans reports in "Muslim Countries Seek Blasphemy Ban" (Associated Press, November 23, 2009) that in 2009 Islamic nations began campaigning the United Nations (UN) for an international treaty to "protect religious symbols and beliefs from mockery." The Organisation of Islamic Cooperation (OIC; formerly the Organisation of the Islamic Conference) was behind the initiative. As of 2012, the OIC (http://www.oic-oci.org/page_detail.asp?p_id=52) included 57 nations and called itself "the collective voice of the Muslim world" with the purpose of ensuring, safeguarding, and protecting the interests of the Muslim people. The OIC proposal faced stiff opposition from Western democracies, such as the United States, that value freedom of speech. However, Jordans notes that the OIC and its member states believed the ban would further human rights, the way that laws against racism protect the human rights of minority races. In *Annual Report on International Religious Freedom: 2011*, the DOS indicates the United States "strongly opposed" the OIC initiative, seeing it as an assault on free speech. In 2011 an alternative measure was agreed on. The DOS notes that UN Resolution 16/18, titled "Combating Intolerance, Negative Stereotyping, and Stigmatization of, and Discrimination, Incitement to Violence, and Violence against Persons Based on Religion or Belief," received the backing of both Western and Muslim nations in the UN. The resolution (http://www.unhcr.org/refworld/type, RESOLUTION,,,4db960f92,0.html) contains no bans on speech or actions by member nations. Instead, it expresses "deep concern" about intolerance, discrimination, violence, "derogatory stereotyping," and related problems that may be associated with religious beliefs. The resolution also calls on governments to promote religious freedom and to "foster a global dialogue for the promotion of a culture of tolerance and peace at all levels."

In September 2012 another furor erupted over the free speech issue after an anti-Islamic video made in the United States was posted on the Internet. *Innocence of Muslims* was described by various media sources as an amateurish or crudely made video lasting about 13 minutes. In "Man Tied to Anti-Islam Video Held on Probation Charge" (*New York Times*, September 27, 2012), Brooks Barnes states that the video "depicts the Prophet Muhammad as a buffoon, a womanizer and a child molester." It first appeared in English in June 2012 on YouTube (a video sharing website) and was then translated into Arabic and "uploaded several more times."

Many people in the United States first became aware of the video on September 11, 2012, when it triggered violent protests at U.S. embassies in Egypt and Yemen. That same day the U.S. ambassador to Libya and three of his staffers were killed in Libya. The killings were at first blamed on video protesters; however, blame soon shifted to Libyan militias with ties to terrorism. (See Chapter 3 for details on the Libyan attack.) U.S. officials, including President Barack Obama (1961–) and the U.S. secretary of state Hilary Rodham Clinton (1947–), strongly condemned the video, but that did little to quell outrage in the Muslim world. Again, there were calls from Muslim nations for an international ban on blasphemy. Google, Inc., the owner of YouTube, refused to remove the video; however, it did block access to the video in certain countries. According to Barnes, in late September 2012 Nakoula Basseley Nakoula (1957–), the purported maker of the video, was arrested in Los Angeles, California, for violating the terms of his probation on a 2010 bank fraud charge. Barnes also notes that a Pakistani cabinet minister had offered a $100,000 reward "for the death of the person behind the video." In his first court appearance on October 10, 2012, Nakoula denied the charges against him. An evidentiary hearing was scheduled to take place in November 2012. As of October 2012, Nakoula had not spoken publicly about his alleged involvement in the making of the video.

Public Relations

Despite the ideological differences between Islamic and non-Islamic nations, fairly good relations exist between the two at the government-to-government level. For example, the United States has good relations with Saudi Arabia, which is an extremely conservative Muslim country that allows virtually no democracy, religious

tolerance, or freedom of speech. Likewise, the United States enjoys good foreign relations with the governments of most other Muslim-majority countries. However, as noted earlier the governments of many of these countries are autocratic and suppressive, rather than democratic in nature. Thus, the actions of the government may not represent the general will of the people.

The Israeli-Palestinian conflict is described in detail in Chapter 1. Both sides believe they hold historical rights to the land now known as Israel. The United States has been a close ally of Israel since the latter's creation in 1948. U.S. political and financial support for Israel over the decades is a source of deep resentment among the predominantly Muslim peoples of the Middle East. The 2001 invasion of Afghanistan and the 2003 invasion of Iraq (both Muslim-majority countries) significantly degraded opinions of the United States in Islamic countries. President Bush became very unpopular in the Muslim world because his administration's War on Terror was seen as an attack on Islam. However, Muslim public opinion about the United States improved slightly with the advent of the Obama administration. President Obama has ties to the Islamic world: his father was born into a Muslim and Christian family, and when Obama was a boy he lived in Indonesia, a Muslim-majority country.

Since 2002 the Pew Global Attitudes Project has conducted public opinion polls in dozens of countries around the world. Many of the polls conducted in Muslim-majority countries have revealed deep disfavor toward the United States, even in the more secular and democratic nations. As of October 2012, the most recent results (http://www.pewglobal.org/database/?indicator=1) reflect polling done in 21 countries during the spring of 2012. They show that favorability ratings for the United States were below 50% in all six of the Muslim-majority countries included: Lebanon (48%), Tunisia (45%), Egypt (19%), Turkey (15%), Jordan (12%), and Pakistan (12%). In fact, favorability toward the United States was below 30% in most of these countries dating back to 2002.

As far as U.S. foreign policy issues are concerned, the Pew Global Attitudes Project (http://www.pewglobal.org/database/?indicator=8&mode=chart) indicates that in 2012 there was little support (i.e., less than 35% support) in Lebanon, Tunisia, Turkey, Pakistan, Egypt, and Jordan for U.S. "anti-terrorism efforts."

In November 2010 the Gallup Organization published the results of polls that were conducted by the Abu Dhabi Gallup Center between 2006 and 2010 in 55 countries, including many Muslim-majority countries. In *Measuring the State of Muslim-West Relations: Assessing the "New Beginning"* (November 28, 2010, http://www.gallup.com/poll/File/144959/MWRelations_2010_report.pdf), Gallup notes, "When Gallup asked Muslims around the world what they resent about the West, the most

FIGURE 10.1

International public opinion about respect by the West for the Muslim world, 2010

DO YOU BELIEVE THE WESTERN WORLD RESPECTS THE MUSLIM WORLD?

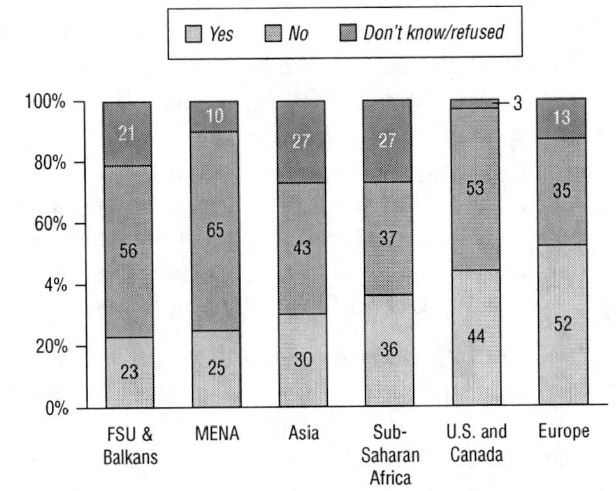

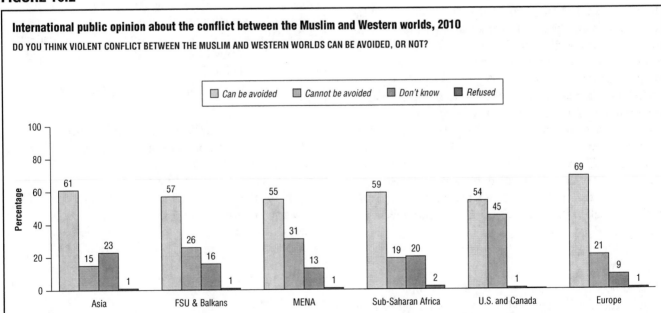

Note: FSU = Former Soviet Union. MENA = Middle East and North Africa.

frequent answer was 'disrespect for Islam.'" Figure 10.1 shows the results of polling on this subject on a regional basis. Nearly two-thirds (65%) of those asked in the Middle East and North Africa said the Western world does not respect the Muslim world. Even respondents in the Western world strongly agreed that lack of respect exists. For example, more than half (53%) of those asked in the United States and Canada said the Western world does not respect the Muslim world.

Despite the general negativity about mutual relations, a majority of those asked in the Muslim and Western worlds felt that "violent conflict" between the two worlds is avoidable. Between 54% and 69% of respondents in each region said that violent conflict can be avoided. (See Figure 10.2.) Regardless, people in the United States and Canada were the most pessimistic about the inevitability of violent conflict—45% of those asked said that violent conflict between the two worlds cannot be avoided.

There is no doubt that influencing international opinion in favor of the United States is a very difficult task. Thomas L. Friedman observes in *Longitudes and Attitudes: Exploring the World after September 11* (2002), "Since the end of the cold war anti-Americanism has overtaken soccer as the world's favorite sport." U.S. politicians and reporters often refer to the effort to make Muslim opinions more favorable toward the United States as "winning hearts and minds." Since the 9/11 terrorist attacks the United States has made the spread of

FIGURE 10.2

International public opinion about the conflict between the Muslim and Western worlds, 2010

DO YOU THINK VIOLENT CONFLICT BETWEEN THE MUSLIM AND WESTERN WORLDS CAN BE AVOIDED, OR NOT?

Note: FSU = Former Soviet Union. MENA = Middle East and North Africa.

democracy among Muslims, and especially in the Middle East, an important priority. After invading Afghanistan in 2001 and Iraq in 2003 the United States helped devise new, democratic constitutions for those nations. It has also pushed for democratic-style governments in other autocratic countries in the Middle East.

As described in Chapter 2, the DOS conducts programs of public diplomacy in an attempt to influence the attitudes and behaviors of people around the world. As part of this effort the U.S. government finances radio and television networks to counter what it considers to be misinformation disseminated about the United States by the state-run media in many Middle Eastern countries. Radio Sawa, an Arabic-language radio station that plays pop music, news, sports, and other programs, was launched in 2002. Alhurra Television provides commercial-free Arabic-language news and feature stories throughout the Middle East. Radio Farda is a Persian-language station that broadcasts specifically for the Iranian audience and features music, news, and information programs. In 2003 the DOS provided millions of dollars for the new magazine *Hi* that was designed to reach the teenage populations of Arabic countries. Its sales were dismal, and the program was suspended in late 2005.

Middle Eastern youth, particularly boys, are the primary target of U.S. information campaigns. It is hoped that the information will help counteract the radical version of Islam that is associated with many Islamic religious schools called madrassas. These boarding schools are financed by wealthy Muslims and provide room and board for poor boys throughout the Islamic world. The educational studies are devoted almost exclusively to the Koran and sharia. There are believed to be thousands of madrassas throughout the Middle East. The National Commission on Terrorist Attacks upon the United States notes in *The 9/11 Commission Report* (July 2004, http://www.9-11commission.gov/report/911Report.pdf) that as of 2004 there were 859 madrassas in Karachi, Pakistan, educating over 200,000 students and that some of these schools "have been used as incubators for violent extremism." The commission emphasizes the importance of an effective U.S. information campaign with this warning: "If the United States does not act aggressively to define itself in the Islamic world, the extremists will gladly do the job for us."

Foreign Aid

Another key element of U.S. public diplomacy is foreign aid. Providing food, money, and other aid to struggling countries has been a hallmark of U.S. foreign policy since the end of World War II. Under the Marshall Plan billions of dollars went to European countries to help them rebuild infrastructure and industries that were devastated during the war. The money helped ensure political stability, stave off communist interference, and create trading partners for the United States.

Muslim-majority countries have been the beneficiaries of U.S. foreign aid in the past. These countries received new emphasis when the War on Terror (later the Overseas Contingency Operations) began in September 2001. In "Foreign Assistance Fast Facts: FY2010" (2012, http://gbk.eads.usaidallnet.gov/data/fast-facts.html), the U.S. Agency for International Development reports the top-five recipients by region of U.S. economic and military assistance during fiscal year 2010. The Muslim-majority countries that were among the top recipients included Afghanistan ($4.6 billion), Pakistan ($1.9 billion), Iraq ($1.1 billion), Senegal ($698 million), and the West Bank/Gaza Strip ($693 million).

THE MIDDLE EAST PARTNERSHIP INITIATIVE. In 2002 the DOS created a new foreign aid program called the Middle East Partnership Initiative (MEPI). The MEPI's goals are to expand political participation, strengthen civil society and the rule of law, empower women and youth, create educational opportunities, and foster economic reform. The DOS (2012, http://mepi.state.gov/about-us.html) notes that between 2002 and 2012 the MEPI contributed more than $600 million to over 1,000 projects in the program. The MEPI provides funds to government agencies and to nongovernmental organizations, such as private firms and academic institutions.

CONDEMNING OR EXCUSING TERRORISM?

Many Muslims have publicly stated that terrorists are extremists who have misunderstood the true nature of Islam. At the same time, however, the reaction to terrorism by Islamic religious figures and political leaders is not always as strong as some Americans feel it should be. In "America Has to Face Reality" (*Newsweek*, October 13, 2001), Christopher Dickey calls it the "this is horrible, but..." syndrome.

In *Holy War, Inc.: Inside the Secret World of Osama bin Laden* (2001), Peter L. Bergen describes at length the terrorist exploits of Osama bin Laden (1957?–2011) and the al Qaeda network. According to Bergen, the 2000 bombing of the USS *Cole* in Yemen elicited the following comments from Abdul Wahab al-Anesi, the country's former deputy prime minister: "There was no justification for the *Cole* bombing. I was shocked and surprised. But the U.S. bears a great degree of responsibility for the incident for the way the U.S. deals with issues in the Middle East."

The article "Giuliani Rejects $10 Million from Saudi Prince" (CNN.com, October 12, 2001) explains that following the 9/11 terrorist attacks the Saudi prince Al-Walid bin Talal bin Abd al-Aziz Al Saud (1955–) presented the New York City mayor Rudy Giuliani (1944–)

with a $10 million donation for relief efforts and expressed his condolences for the victims. However, later that day the prince made public statements in which he said the United States should "address some of the issues that led to such a criminal attack" and "re-examine its policies in the Middle East and adopt a more balanced stand toward the Palestinian cause." Giuliani angrily returned the prince's check and denounced the attempted linkage between the terrorist attacks and U.S. foreign policy.

In "Where's the Outrage?" (*USA Today*, September 12, 2006), Karen Hughes (1957–), a former undersecretary of public diplomacy and public affairs for the DOS, laments the lack of worldwide "moral outrage" regarding terrorism and notes, "As I have traveled the world, I have met those who try to justify the violence based on policy differences, long-held grievances or a perceived threat from the West."

CAIR disputes the notion that prominent Muslims excuse terrorist attacks against the United States. In *Response to September 11, 2001 Attacks* (March 28, 2007, http://www.cair.com/Portals/0/pdf/September_11_state ments.pdf), CAIR includes statements from dozens of Islamic scholars from around the world who have condemned terrorist attacks that kill innocent people. CAIR also published *Islamic Statements against Terrorism* (2005, http://www.cair.com/Portals/0/pdf/Condemnation _of_London_Bombings.pdf) after the July 7, 2005, bombings in London.

AMERICAN PUBLIC OPINION ABOUT ISLAM AND MUSLIMS

Public opinion polls conducted in the United States by the Gallup Organization reveal negative feelings among Americans about Islam relative to other religions. In *In U.S., Religious Prejudice Stronger against Muslims* (January 21, 2010, http://www.gallup.com/poll/125312/ Religious-Prejudice-Stronger-Against-Muslims.aspx), Gallup reports that more than half (53%) of the respondents in a poll that was conducted between October and November 2009 expressed unfavorable views about Islam. In contrast, Buddhism, Judaism, and Christianity were viewed much more favorably. In addition, 43% of those asked admitted having "feelings of prejudice" toward Muslims. Only 14% to 18% expressed prejudiced feelings toward Christians, Jew, or Buddhists.

In other Gallup polls Americans were asked to assess the opinion of people in Muslim countries regarding the United States. Frank Newport of the Gallup Organization indicates in *Americans Still Say Muslims Have Negative View of U.S.* (June 3, 2009, http://www.gallup.com/poll/ 118991/Americans-Still-Say-Muslims-Have-Negative-View-of-US.aspx) that in 2009 a large majority (80%) said people in Muslim countries have an unfavorable view of the United States. This percentage changed little from 2002, when the question was first asked. Most Americans believed Muslims' unfavorable views of the United States are due to "misinformation" that is spread by their media and governments. Far lower percentages believed the negative views of Muslims are based on previous or current U.S. actions.

However, Americans admit they have limited knowledge about the opinions and beliefs of people living in Muslim countries. According to Newport, in 2009 only 10% of respondents said they have a "great deal" of knowledge on the subject. Far higher percentages said they have a "moderate amount" of knowledge (43%) or "not much" knowledge (36%) on the subject. Eleven percent said they have no knowledge whatsoever about the opinions and beliefs of people living in Muslim countries.

MUSLIM RELATIONS WITHIN THE UNITED STATES

The United States has a relatively small population of Muslims. Because the U.S. Census does not ask people about religious affiliation, there is no official count by the U.S. government. However, various private groups have published estimates. For example, the Pew Forum on Religion and Public Life estimates in *The Future Global Muslim Population Projections for 2010–2030* that the Muslim-American population was around 2.6 million in 2010, or approximately 0.8% of the total U.S. population. By contrast, CAIR states in "About Islam and American Muslims" that the Muslim-American population was around 7 million in 2012.

Islamophobia?

Since the 9/11 attacks Muslim-Americans have faced heightened scrutiny (and hostility) from fellow Americans who are concerned about the terrorist threat posed by some individuals and groups that claim to represent Islamic interests. The fear and general ill will directed toward Muslims, or people perceived to be Muslims, has been dubbed Islamophobia by the media.

The U.S. government considers hate crimes to be crimes motivated by an offender's personal prejudice or bias against a victim. As shown in Figure 10.3, there was a sharp uptick in anti-Muslim hate crimes in 2001. In *Confronting Discrimination in the Post-9/11 Era: Challenges and Opportunities Ten Years Later* (October 19, 2011, http://www.justice.gov/crt/publications/post911/post 911summit_report_2012-04.pdf), the U.S. Department of Justice (DOJ) notes "the first threats of violence and acts of violence against people perceived to be Arab, Muslim, Sikh, and South Asian occurred within hours of the 9/11 attacks. The violence intensified for the next three weeks, eventually tapering off but never falling below the levels documented before 9/11."

The U.S. Equal Employment Opportunity Commission (EEOC) enforces federal laws that prohibit discrimination against job applicants or employees based on their race, color, religion, sex, national origin, disability, or genetic information. According to the DOJ, the number of discrimination charges filed with the EEOC "based on Muslim religion" surged following the 9/11 attacks. (See Figure 10.4.) After declining through the middle of the decade, the number of charges began a gradual climb again, reaching around 800 per year in 2009 and 2010.

In August 2011 the Abu Dhabi Gallup Center released the results of polls it conducted in 2010 regarding relations between Muslims and other religious groups within the United States. The center notes in *Muslim Americans: Faith, Freedom, and the Future, Examining U.S. Muslims' Political, Social, and Spiritual Engagement 10 Years after September 11* (http://www.gallup.com/strategicconsulting/153611/REPORT-Muslim-Americans-Faith-Freedom-Future.aspx) that Muslims reported more experiences of racial or religious discrimination than did members of other religious groups. (See Figure 10.5.) Nearly half (48%) of Muslims said they had personally experienced such discrimination, compared with 18% to 31% among the other groups.

Muslim-Americans have also encountered stiff resistance to their efforts to build or expand mosques

FIGURE 10.3

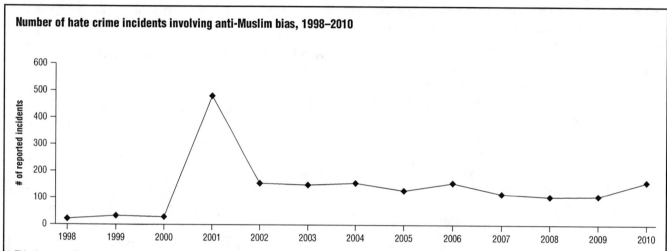

Number of hate crime incidents involving anti-Muslim bias, 1998–2010

This chart maps Federal Bureau of Investigation (FBI) data collected from 1998 to 2010, pursuant to the Hate Crimes Statistics Act, on crimes motivated by anti-Muslim bias.

SOURCE: "Anti-Muslim Hate Crimes per Year," in *Confronting Discrimination in the Post-9/11 Era: Challenges and Opportunities Ten Years Later*, U.S. Department of Justice, Civil Rights Division, October 19, 2011, http://www.justice.gov/crt/publications/post911/post911summit_report_2012-04.pdf (accessed July 26, 2012)

FIGURE 10.4

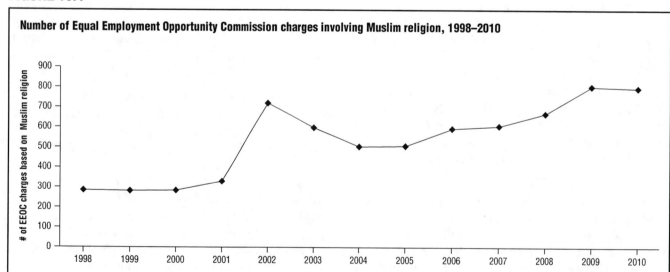

Number of Equal Employment Opportunity Commission charges involving Muslim religion, 1998–2010

SOURCE: "EEOC Charges Based on Muslim Religion, 1998–2010," in *Confronting Discrimination in the Post-9/11 Era: Challenges and Opportunities Ten Years Later*, U.S. Department of Justice, Civil Rights Division, October 19, 2011, http://www.justice.gov/crt/publications/post911/post911summit_report_2012-04.pdf (accessed July 26, 2012)

FIGURE 10.5

FIGURE 10.6

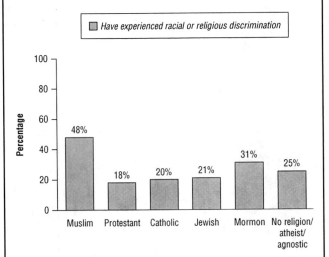

Poll respondents' reported experiences of racial or religious discrimination, 2010

HAVE YOU PERSONALLY EXPERIENCED RACIAL OR RELIGIOUS DISCRIMINATION IN THE PAST YEAR?

Surveys conducted via Muslim American polls from February 10–March 11, 2010, and October 1–21, 2010.

SOURCE: "Muslims Most Likely to Have Experienced Racial or Religious Discrimination," in *Muslim Americans: Faith, Freedom, and the Future, Examining U.S. Muslims' Political, Social, and Spiritual Engagement 10 Years after September 11*, The Gallup Organization, Abu Dhabi Gallup Center, August 2011, http://www.gallup.com/strategicconsulting/153611/REPORT-Muslim-Americans-Faith-Freedom-Future.aspx (accessed November 1, 2012). Copyright © 2011 Gallup, Inc. All rights reserved. The content is used with permission; however, Gallup retains all rights of republication.

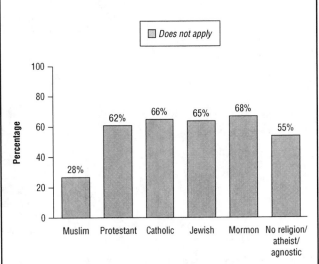

Public opinion on Muslims speaking out against terrorism, October 2010

NOW THINKING SPECIFICALLY ABOUT MUSLIMS, DO YOU THINK EACH OF THE FOLLOWING APPLIES, OR DOES NOT APPLY, TO MUSLIMS LIVING IN THIS COUNTRY? SPEAKING OUT ENOUGH AGAINST TERRORISM

Surveys conducted via Muslim American polls from October 1–21, 2010.

SOURCE: "Most Religious Groups Say Muslims Not Speaking out Enough against Terrorism," in *Muslim Americans: Faith, Freedom, and the Future, Examining U.S. Muslims' Political, Social, and Spiritual Engagement 10 Years after September 11*, The Gallup Organization, Abu Dhabi Gallup Center, August 2011, http://www.gallup.com/strategicconsulting/153611/REPORT-Muslim-Americans-Faith-Freedom-Future.aspx (accessed November 1, 2012). Copyright © 2011 Gallup, Inc. All rights reserved. The content is used with permission; however, Gallup retains all rights of republication.

within the United States. One case in particular made national headlines. A Muslim group aroused great controversy in New York City when it announced plans to build a mosque and Islamic community center within two blocks of "ground zero," the former site of the World Trade Center buildings that were destroyed in the 9/11 attacks. Critics protested that the project was disrespectful to the thousands of people who died in the attacks, whereas supporters touted the project as a forum for moderate Muslims to practice their faith and build relationships in the community. Despite fierce opposition, the center quietly opened in late 2011. It is operated by the Cordoba Initiative (http://www.cordobainitiative.org/about), which calls itself a "multi-national, multi-faith organization dedicated to improving understanding and building trust among people of all cultures and religions."

Loyalty and Terrorism

In *Muslim Americans: Faith, Freedom, and the Future, Examining U.S. Muslims' Political, Social, and Spiritual Engagement 10 Years after September 11*, the Abu Dhabi Gallup Center reports that majorities of respondents within various U.S. religious groups said they believe that "Muslims living in this country are loyal to this country." Nearly all (93%) of the Muslim respondents agreed with this viewpoint. There was less assurance among Jews (80%); atheists, agnostics, and people with no religion (69%); Catholics (59%); Mormons (56%); and Protestants (56%). The center also found strong belief among non-Muslims that Muslims do not speak out enough against terrorism. (See Figure 10.6.) Between 55% and 68% of non-Muslims said that Muslims fall short in this regard. Only 28% of Muslims agreed. The Abu Dhabi Gallup Center notes that Muslim-American organizations have spoken out publicly against terrorism, but that they tend to do so via their websites and email lists. The center states "the websites where condemnations are posted are generally of most interest to U.S. Muslims and may not be seen by a wider audience."

Interestingly, the Abu Dhabi Gallup Center finds that Muslims, more than the members of any other religious groups, tend to believe that unfavorable views of the United States in Muslim countries are based on U.S. actions rather than on misinformation. As shown in

FIGURE 10.7

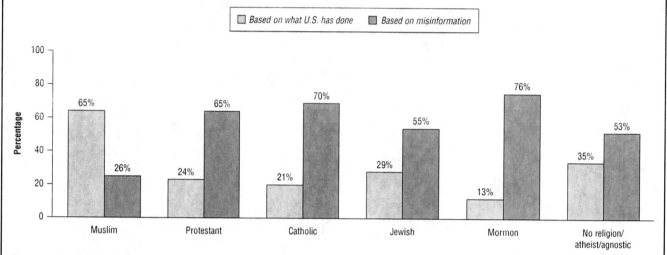

Public opinion regarding U.S. actions in Muslim countries, 2010

DO YOU THINK THE UNFAVORABLE VIEWS PEOPLE IN MUSLIM COUNTRIES HAVE OF THE UNITED STATES ARE BASED MOSTLY ON WHAT THE U.S. HAS DONE OR BASED MOSTLY ON MISINFORMATION PROVIDED BY THE MEDIA AND GOVERNMENT ABOUT WHAT THE U.S. HAS DONE? (ASKED OF THOSE WHO SAID PEOPLE IN MUSLIM COUNTRIES HAVE VERY UNFAVORABLE, OR SOMEWHAT UNFAVORABLE VIEWS OF THE UNITED STATES.)

Surveys conducted via Muslim American polls from February 10–March 11, 2010, and October 1–21, 2010. This question was asked of a subset of the population.

SOURCE: "Muslim Americans Are the Most Likely to See U.S. Actions As Causing Unfavorable Views of U.S. in Muslim Countries," in *Muslim Americans: Faith, Freedom, and the Future, Examining U.S. Muslims' Political, Social, and Spiritual Engagement 10 Years after September 11*, The Gallup Organization, Abu Dhabi Gallup Center, August 2011, http://www.gallup.com/strategicconsulting/153611/REPORT-Muslim-Americans-Faith-Freedom-Future.aspx (accessed November 1, 2012). Copyright © 2011 Gallup, Inc. All rights reserved. The content is used with permission; however, Gallup retains all rights of republication.

Figure 10.7, nearly two-thirds (65%) of Muslims blamed U.S. actions for the United States' poor reputation in the Muslim world. Only 13% to 35% of respondents within non-Muslim groups thought similarly. Members of non-Muslim groups were much more likely to blame the United States' poor reputation on misinformation provided by media sources and governments in foreign countries.

Radicalization of U.S. Muslims

As noted in Chapter 3, since 2009 the United States has seen a dramatic increase in terrorism charges against people who were either born in the United States (i.e., "homegrown" suspects) or had become U.S. citizens. Many of these suspects converted to Islam from other religions and/or became radicalized—meaning that they embraced a very radical Islamic view that condones violence. In "Attorney General's Blunt Warning on Terror Attacks" (ABC News, December 21, 2010), Jack Cloherty quotes the U.S. attorney general Eric Holder (1951–) as saying: "The threat has changed from simply worrying about foreigners coming here, to worrying about people in the United States, American citizens—raised here, born here, and who for whatever reason, have decided that they are going to become radicalized and take up arms against the nation in which they were born."

According to Cloherty, 50 U.S. citizens were indicted on terrorism charges between 2008 and 2010. Holder tells Cloherty that many of the suspects were linked to Anwar al-Awlaki (1971–2011), a U.S. citizen and Muslim cleric who operated out of Yemen to recruit Americans for the al Qaeda terrorist group. Al-Awlaki was killed by a U.S. missile attack in 2011.

In 2011 Representative Peter T. King (1944–; R; NY) chaired the U.S. House of Representatives Committee on Homeland Security. He decided to hold a series of hearings around the country regarding the extent and threat of radicalization of U.S. Muslims. The results were reported in *The American Muslim Response to Hearings on Radicalization within their Community* (June 20, 2012, http://homeland.house.gov/sites/homeland.house.gov/files/06-20-12-Report.pdf). Table 10.3 summarizes the committee's major findings. The committee concludes that "the increasing frequency of Muslim-Americans becoming radicalized is an alarming trend and a great concern for U.S. national security." The committee offered no potential solutions or recommendations to counter the problem of radicalization and stoked fierce criticism for holding the hearings in the first place. The *New York Times* reports in *Pete King* (March 11, 2011, http://topics.nytimes.com/topics/reference/timestopics/people/k/peter_t_king/index.html) that King's hearings "provoked uproar from both

TABLE 10.3

Findings of U.S. House hearings on the radicalization of Muslim Americans, June 2012

Hearing #1: "The extent of radicalization in the American Muslim community and that community's response."

Finding #1: The radicalization of Muslim-Americans constitutes a real and serious homeland security threat.
Finding #2: There is not enough Muslim-American community cooperation with law enforcement.
Finding #3: There is a need to confront the Islamist ideology driving radicalization.

Hearing #2: "The threat of Muslim-American radicalization in U.S. prisons."

Finding #4: The radicalization of prison inmates to an extremist form of Islam is a significant problem, which can often manifest once radicalized prisoners are released.
Finding #5: The radicalization of prison inmates is often precipitated by the presence of radical clergy or extremist materials within the prison.

Hearing #3: "Al-Shabaab: recruitment and radicalization within the Muslim-American community and the threat to the homeland."

Finding #6: There are direct ties between Al-Shabaab and Al Qaeda and its affiliates, and Al-Shabaab recruits are often indoctrinated into Al Qaeda's ideology and network.
Finding #7: More than 40 Muslim-Americans radicalized and recruited by Al-Shabaab may pose a direct threat to the national security of the United States and its allies.
Finding #8: The committee's hearings on the radicalization of Muslim-Americans have empowered Muslims to effectively address this issue.

Hearing #4: "Homegrown Terrorism: The threat to military communities inside the United States."

Finding #9: The terrorist threat to military communities is severe and on the rise.
Finding #10: The "insider" threat to military communities is a significant and potentially devastating development.
Finding #11: Political correctness continues to stifle the military's ability to effectively understand and counter the threat.
Finding #12: The administration chose political correctness over accurately labeling and identifying certain terrorist attacks appropriately, thereby denying Purple Hearts medals to killed and wounded troops in domestic terror attacks.

SOURCE: "Committee Findings," in *Committee on Homeland Security: "The American Muslim Response to Hearings on Radicalization within Their Community"*, U.S. House of Representatives, Committee on Homeland Security, June 20, 2012, http://homeland.house.gov/sites/homeland.house.gov/files/06-20-12-Report.pdf (accessed July 26, 2012)

the left and the right. The left has accused Mr. King of embarking on a witch hunt. The right has accused him of capitulation for calling Muslims like Representative Keith Ellison, Democrat of Minnesota, to testify while denying a platform to popular critics of Islamic extremism." Criticism was particularly acute from some elements within the Muslim-American community who feared that the hearings encouraged Islamophobia.

IMPORTANT NAMES
AND ADDRESSES

American Civil Liberties Union
125 Broad St., 18th Floor
New York, NY 10004
(212) 549-2500
URL: http://www.aclu.org/

Amnesty International USA
Five Penn Plaza
New York, NY 10001
(212) 807-8400
FAX: (212) 627-1451
E-mail: aimember@aiusa.org
URL: http://www.amnestyusa.org/

**Centers for Disease Control and
Prevention**
1600 Clifton Rd.
Atlanta, GA 30333
1-800-232-4636
URL: http://www.cdc.gov/

Central Intelligence Agency
Office of Public Affairs
Washington, DC 20505
(703) 482-0623
FAX: (703) 482-1739
URL: http://www.cia.gov/

**Congressional Research Service
Library of Congress**
101 Independence Ave. SE
Washington, DC 20540
URL: http://www.loc.gov/crsinfo/

Council on American Islamic Relations
453 New Jersey Ave. SE
Washington, DC 20003
(202) 488-8787
FAX: (202) 488-0833
URL: http://www.cair.com/

Defense Threat Reduction Agency
8725 John J. Kingman Rd., Stop 6201
Fort Belvoir, VA 22060-6201
(703) 767-5870
1-800-701-5096
FAX: (703) 767-4450

E-mail: dtra.publicaffairs@dtra.mil
URL: http://www.dtra.mil/

Electronic Privacy Information Center
1718 Connecticut Ave. NW, Ste. 200
Washington, DC 20009
(202) 483-1140
FAX: (202) 483-1248
URL: http://www.epic.org/

Federal Bureau of Investigation
J. Edgar Hoover Bldg.
935 Pennsylvania Ave. NW
Washington, DC 20535-0001
(202) 324-3000
URL: http://www.fbi.gov/

Federal Emergency Management Agency
500 C St. SW
Washington, DC 20472
(202) 646-2500
URL: http://www.fema.gov/

International Atomic Energy Agency
Vienna International Centre
PO Box 100A-1400
Vienna, Austria
(011-431) 2600-0
FAX: (011-431) 2600-7
E-mail: Official.Mail@iaea.org
URL: http://www.iaea.org/

International Committee of the Red Cross
19 avenue de la Paix CH 1202
Geneva, Switzerland
(011-41-22) 734-60-01
FAX: (011-41-22) 733-20-57
URL: http://www.icrc.org/eng

Joint Chiefs of Staff
9999 Joint Staff Pentagon
Washington, DC 20318-9999
URL: http://www.dtic.mil/jcs

National Guard
111 S. George Mason Dr.
Arlington, VA 22204

(703) 607-2584
URL: http://www.nationalguard.mil/

National Security Agency
(301) 688-6524
FAX: (301) 688-6198
E-mail: nsapao@nsa.gov
URL: http://www.nsa.gov/

North Atlantic Treaty Organization
Blvd. Leopold III
1110 Brussels, Belgium
URL: http://www.nato.int/cps/en/natolive/
index.htm

Office of the Director of National Intelligence
Washington, DC 20511
(703) 733-8600
URL: http://www.dni.gov/

Transportation Security Administration
601 S. 12th St.
Arlington, VA 22202
(571) 227-2829
1-866-289-9673
E-mail: TSA-ContactCenter@dhs.gov
URL: http://www.tsa.gov/

United Nations
First Avenue at 46th St.
New York, NY 10017
URL: http://www.un.org/

U.S. Agency for International Development
Ronald Reagan Bldg.
Washington, DC 20523-0016
(202) 712-4320
FAX: (202) 216-3524
URL: http://www.usaid.gov/

U.S. Air Force
Office of the Secretary of the Air Force
Public Affairs Resource Library
1690 Air Force Pentagon
Washington, DC 20330-1690
(703) 571-2784
URL: http://www.af.mil/

U.S. Army
Media Relations Division
Office of the Chief of Public Affairs
1500 Army Pentagon
Washington, DC 20310-1500
URL: http://www.army.mil/

U.S. Citizenship and Immigration Services
425 I St. NW
Washington, DC 20536
1-800-375-5283
URL: http://www.uscis.gov/portal/site/uscis

U.S. Coast Guard
2100 Second St. SW
Washington, DC 20593
URL: http://www.uscg.mil/

U.S. Customs and Border Protection
1300 Pennsylvania Ave. NW
Washington, DC 20229
(202) 344-1780
1-877-227-5511
URL: http://www.cbp.gov/

U.S. Department of Defense
1400 Defense Pentagon
Washington, DC 20301-1400
(703) 571-3343
URL: http://www.defense.gov/

U.S. Department of Energy
1000 Independence Ave. SW
Washington, DC 20585
(202) 586-5000
URL: http://energy.gov/

U.S. Department of Homeland Security
Washington, DC 20528
(202) 282-8000
URL: http://www.dhs.gov/

U.S. Department of Justice
950 Pennsylvania Ave. NW
Washington, DC 20530-0001
(202) 514-2000
E-mail: AskDOJ@usdoj.gov
URL: http://www.justice.gov/

U.S. Department of State
2201 C St. NW
Washington, DC 20520
(202) 647-4000
URL: http://www.state.gov/

U.S. Department of the Treasury
1500 Pennsylvania Ave. NW
Washington, DC 20220
(202) 622-2000
FAX: (202) 622-6415

URL: http://www.treasury.gov/Pages/default.aspx

U.S. Government Accountability Office
441 G St. NW
Washington, DC 20548
(202) 512-3000
E-mail: contact@gao.gov
URL: http://www.gao.gov/

U.S. Marine Corps
Director of Public Affairs
2 Navy Annex
Washington, DC 20380-1775
(703) 614-1034
FAX: (703) 614-2358
URL: http://www.marines.mil/Pages/Default.aspx/

U.S. Navy
Chief of Information
1200 Navy Pentagon
Washington, DC 20350-1200
URL: http://www.navy.mil/

White House
1600 Pennsylvania Ave. NW
Washington, DC 20500
(202) 456-1414
URL: http://www.whitehouse.gov/

RESOURCES

Several government agencies and organizations provided resources for this book. The U.S. Government Accountability Office (GAO) is the investigative arm of Congress and posts its many publications online. GAO reports on national security, weapons of mass destruction, and federal government agencies and spending were invaluable. The Congressional Research Service (CRS) is a division of the Library of Congress and publishes regularly updated reports on U.S. policies and laws and other issues of interest to members of Congress. CRS reports on foreign policy and civil and human rights were a major source of information for this book.

Other government agencies and offices consulted during the compilation of this book include the Broadcasting Board of Governors, the Central Intelligence Agency, the Federal Bureau of Investigation, the Library of Congress, the Nunn-Lugar Cooperative Threat Reduction Program, the Office of the Coordinator for Counterterrorism, the U.S. Agency for International Development, the U.S. Department of Defense, the U.S. Department of Energy, the U.S. Department of Homeland Security, the U.S. Department of Justice, the U.S. Department of State, the U.S. Department of the Treasury, the U.S. House of Representatives' Committee on Homeland Security, the U.S. National Counterterrorism Center, and the White House. The latter provided national strategy and planning documents, budgetary information, and the text of presidential speeches and executive orders.

Commissions appointed by U.S. presidents, Congress, or agency heads have produced reports on topics related to national security. The Central Intelligence Agency's *World Factbook* provides a wealth of information about countries around the world and is updated frequently. Other valuable resources in the intelligence community are the National Counterintelligence Executive and the Office of the Director of National Intelligence.

The following news organizations and outlets were useful for providing timely features about national security: ABC News, Associated Press, BBC News, CNN.com, National Geographic, *Newsweek*, *New York Times*, Reuters, *Seattle Times*, *Time*, *USA Today*, *Wall Street Journal*, and *Washington Post*.

Private domestic and international organizations that provided information for this book include the American Civil Liberties Union, Amnesty International, the Arms Control Association, the Council on American Islamic Relations, the Council on Foreign Relations, the Electronic Frontier Foundation, the Electronic Privacy Information Center, the Federal Judicial Center, the Federation of American Scientists, the International Committee of the Red Cross, the Nuclear Threat Initiative, the Organisation of Islamic Cooperation, the Pew Research Center, the United Nations, and the World Nuclear Association. As always, much thanks to the Gallup Organization for its insightful articles and poll results.

INDEX

Asaib Ahl al-Haq, 77
Asia, 34
Asiri, Ibrahim al-, 45
Assad, Bashar al-, 109, 111–112
Assad, Hafez, 109
Assembly, freedom of, 127
AT&T, 135
Atta, Mohamed, 87
Authorization for Use of Military Force, 136, 146
Autocracy
    Arab Spring, 42
    Western *vs.* Muslim ideology, 154
Aviation
    airline hijackings and attacks, 49–52
    security, 87–90, 88*f*, 89*f*
    shoulder-fired antiaircraft missiles, 119
Aviation and Transportation Security Act, 88
Awlaki, Anwar al-, 45, 53, 162

B

Baggage screening, 88
Balfour, James, 8
Balfour Declaration, 8
Bali, Indonesia, 50
Ballistic missiles and ballistic missile defense, 114–116, 116*f*, 118, 118*f*
Bashir, Omar al-, 109
Basque Fatherland Liberty, 108
Bay of Pigs, 106
Bell South, 135
Ben Ali, Zine el Abidine, 42
Benghazi attack, 44, 50
Berger v. New York, 132
Bhutan, 31, 33
bin Laden, Osama
    Afghanistan, 60–61
    al Qaeda, 43
    death of, 68, 70
    embassy bombings, 49
    killing of, 47
    Sudan, 109
Biological weapons, 93, 123–124, 124*t*
Bioterrorism. *See* Biological weapons
Black market, 125
Bombings. *See* Terrorism
Border security, 85, 86–87
Botulism, 124
Boumediene v. Bush, 148, 150
Bouyeri, Mohammed, 155
Britain. *See* United Kingdom
Broadcasting
    open-source intelligence, 31
    public diplomacy, 34, 158
Broadcasting Board of Governors, 34, 36(*f*2.7)
Budget. *See* Spending
Budget Control Act of 2011, 22

Bulgaria, 48
Bureau of Counterterrorism, Department of State, 40
Bush, Boumediene v., 148, 150
Bush, George H. W., 73
Bush, George W.
    aviation security, 88–89
    border security, 87
    "crusade" term, 153
    Cuba, relations with, 108
    detainees, 139–140
    Iraq War, 73–75
    military commissions, 146–147
    National Security Branch, FBI, 29
    North Korea, 105
    Operation Enduring Freedom, 61–62
    secret CIA prisons, 142
    Terrorist Screening Database, 91–92
    warrantless surveillance, 134
Bush, Rasul v., 147
Byzantine Empire, 153

C

CAIR (Council on American Islamic Relations), 151, 159
Caliphates, 41–42, 44
Canada, 4, 115
Cargo screening, 89–90
Carter, Jimmy
    Cuba, relations with, 108
    Iran, 100–101
    Pakistan aid, 5
    post–Vietnam War military spending, 6
    Soviet invasion of Afghanistan, 5
Castro, Fidel, 106–107
Castro, Raúl, 106
Casualties
    Afghanistan, 67–68, 67*f*, 68*t*
    Iraq War, 74, 75, 75*t*, 76–77, 76*t*
    military deaths worldwide in selected military operations, 6*t*
    military personnel and casualties in major wars, 3*t*
    Vietnam War, 6
CDC (Centers for Disease Control and Prevention), 93
Censorship, 155
Centers for Disease Control and Prevention (CDC), 93
Central Intelligence Agency (CIA)
    detention facilities, 145
    interrogation techniques, 141
    organization chart, 26*f*
    organization and role, 25, 27
    reform, 27–28
    secret prisons, 142
Central Intelligence Agency Act, 25, 27
Central Intelligence Group, 25

Chemical weapons, 73, 93, 112, 122–123, 123*t*
Chemical Weapons Convention, 122–123
Cheonan (ship), 105
China
    cybersecurity threat, 93
    Korean War, 5
    North Korea, relations with, 104
    United States relations with, 97
Church, Frank Forrester, III, 129
"Church and state," 41, 154
CIA. *See* Central Intelligence Agency (CIA)
Citizen Corps, 94
Citizenship and Immigration Services, U.S., 86
Civil liberties
    Civil War, U.S., 128
    Cold War, 129
    Constitutional provisions, 127–128
    detainees, 136–137
    National Security Letters, 135–136
    Patriot Act, 129–132
    phone call data collection, 135
    public opinion on civil liberties and counterterrorism, 137*f*, 138
    surveillance, 132–135
    Vietnam War, 129
    World War I, 128
    World War II, 128–129
    See also Legal rights and status of detainees
Civil Liberties Act of 1988, 129
Civil War, U.S., 128
Civilian casualties
    Afghanistan, 68, 69(*f*4.6)
    Pakistan, 70
Clinton, Bill, 101, 108
Clinton, Hillary Rodham, 70, 156
Coast Guard, U.S., 29, 85
Cold War
    ballistic missile defense, 115
    civil liberties, 129
    Committee for Multilateral Export Controls, 119
    Cuba, 106–107
    former Soviet Union weapons, 125
    history, 1, 3–6
    Korea, 103–104
    National Security Branch, FBI, 29
Colonial America, 1–2
Colonialism, 153
Combatant commands, 19
Combatant Status Review Tribunal (CSRT), 147
Comic strips, 155
Commission on the Intelligence Capabilities of the United States, 74–75
Committee against Torture, UN, 144
Committee for Multilateral Export Controls, 119

O

CPSIA information can be obtained
at www.ICGtesting.com
Printed in the USA
FFOW032149310513
1243FF